ACHIEVING THE
# ASEAN ECONOMIC COMMUNITY 2015

# ACHIEVING THE ASEAN ECONOMIC COMMUNITY 2015

Challenges for Member Countries & Businesses

EDITED BY

## SANCHITA BASU DAS

ISEAS

**INSTITUTE OF SOUTHEAST ASIAN STUDIES**

*Singapore*

First published in Singapore in 2012 by ISEAS Publishing
Institute of Southeast Asian Studies
30 Heng Mui Keng Terrace
Pasir Panjang
Singapore 119614

E-mail: publish@iseas.edu.sg
Website: <http://bookshop.iseas.edu.sg>

*The responsibility for facts and opinions in this publication rests exclusively with the authors and their interpretations do not necessarily reflect the views or the policy of the publisher or its supporters.*

**ISEAS Library Cataloguing-in-Publication Data**

Achieving the ASEAN economic community 2015 : Challenges for member
   countries and businesses / edited by Sanchita Basu Das.
   Based on papers presented to an ASEAN Roundtable on 29 April 2010 and
   experts' discussions at the "Brainstorming Session on Achieving the ASEAN
   Economic Community 2015 : Challenges for Member Countries
   and Businesses" on 23 September 2010, in Singapore
   1.   Southeast Asia—Economic integration—Congresses.
   2.   Business enterprises—Southeast Asia—Congresses.
   3.   Regionalism—Southeast Asia—Congresses.
   4.   ASEAN—Congresses.
   I.   Basu Das, Sanchita.
   II.  ASEAN Roundtable (2010 : Singapore)
   III. Brainstorming Session on Achieving the ASEAN Economic
        Community 2015 : Challenges for Member Countries and Businesses
        (2010 : Singapore)
HC441 A17                    2012

ISBN 978-981-4379-64-9 (soft cover)
ISBN 978-981-4379-65-6 (e-book, PDF)

Typeset by International Typesetters Pte Ltd
Printed in Singapore by Photoplates Pte Ltd

# CONTENTS

## PART II: CHALLENGES FOR THE PRIVATE SECTOR

### PART III: CONCLUSION AND RECOMMENDATIONS

# FOREWORD

The papers compiled in this volume were presented during the ASEAN Roundtable on 29 April 2010 and during a brainstorming session on 23 September 2010 by the ASEAN Studies Centre of the Institute of Southeast Asian Studies.

They examine, from the point of view of each of the member countries of the Association of Southeast Asian Nations (ASEAN), the prospects for achieving an ASEAN Economic community (AEC) by 2015, the target date set by ASEAN itself, and the obstacles in the way of its achievement.

No doubt, when 2015 comes around, whether at its beginning in January or its end in December or sometime in between, ASEAN will proclaim the AEC to have been achieved. In certain ways, it will be right. The AEC, like the two other pillars of the ASEAN Community — the Political-Security and the Socio-Cultural Communities — is a work in progress, and 2015, the year of its supposed achievement, is a mere aspirational goal rather than a hard-and-fast target.

However, the AEC Blueprint, which ASEAN adopted in 2007, contains specific quantifiable measures with clear timelines as milestones in the realization of a "single market and production base". The question in our minds today, and one that will surely be asked as 2015 approaches and in 2015 itself, is: have these milestones been attained? From the state's perspective, this question can be translated into: Has the required infrastructure been constructed? Have enough human resources been developed? Have the necessary institutions been built and are they operating effectively?

Perhaps more telling and pertinent are the questions pertaining to the business community, whether state-owned enterprises or the private sector. After all, it is business firms and individuals that trade and invest. Does the prospect of an AEC or its progress thus far figure in a firm's trading and investment decisions? Does the firm expect the AEC to lower transaction costs, attract investment, create jobs, increase incomes, increase competition, reduce prices, raise productivity?

Half of the chapters in this volume, which is edited by Sanchita Basu Das, lead economics researcher at the ASEAN Studies Centre, address these questions, albeit tentatively in some respects.

Apart from the chapters by ASEAN's Deputy Secretary-General S. Pushpanathan and by Sanchita Basu Das, the pieces in this volume are addressed to the situation in each individual ASEAN country. This is by design. It is also indicative of the fact that we do not yet consider Southeast Asia as one integrated economy, rather fragmented ones with their different regimes and rules.

Will we do so by 2015?

Rodolfo C. Severino<br>
Head, ASEAN Studies Centre, ISEAS<br>
Former Secretary-General, ASEAN

# MESSAGE

For several years now the ASEAN Studies Centre of the Institute of Southeast Asian Studies has been working across the ASEAN community to urge and to support initiatives that are designed to move all of the ASEAN communities into a more common foundation. The work to date has produced many successes and has helped to open markets and to encourage continuing work by many people across the entire ASEAN community. As you read through the pages presented in this book you will see many of these successes.

I have been asked to comment briefly on the interest and attention this work has captured among the business sectors in ASEAN and across the region. Unfortunately, I fear that the business community, in many cases, is moving on without the value and the advantages that so many people have worked hard to try and create.

While the ASEAN community has worked to create a common platform for business, businesses themselves are essentially looking for the features and characteristics in a market that will best suit their individual business preferences. And many things have changed in the regional markets over the last years. When the ASEAN Vision 2020 was adopted in 1997, the markets in Asia looked very different to the business community. Most companies were then producing goods to be shipped back to home markets in the West, and only a few regional markets attracted serious sales interest from the global companies.

But Asian markets have now become the hottest markets in the world. Companies from all over the world clamour to capture a strong sales position in key Asian markets. The question of whether the market is in ASEAN or in another part of Asia is important primarily to the degree it provides sales or production opportunities for the businesses. And each business sector will find a different value to a different market. For example, while Indonesia is starting to produce coveted raw materials, China is developing high value customer markets in some of its major cities. Few people expected to see such trends emerge so quickly in Asia.

What does this mean for ASEAN? It means the nations must move even faster to enhance their markets, to develop them to the maximum extent, and to be prepared to keep up with new market demands. Businesses have to be more focused, must reach out further than they have before, and must move quickly to meet customer demands. And nations must recognize their potential and develop it to the maximum.

Nations in ASEAN need to work to understand the kinds of products they can produce at a competitive price. The skill levels of their workers are key to this, as is the infrastructure necessary to package, ship, and deliver the completed work product to its destination. As a region, ASEAN countries can work together across country borders to develop production chains, whereby one area with emerging skill levels produces a core part of a product, while a more-developed region produces the more sophisticated components of the product. With this breadth of skills, manufacturers from around the world could find new homes in ASEAN for their production operations.

The ASEAN community is important. These nations know how to work together and can enhance the entire region by recognizing each other's capabilities and by pulling together to enhance the collective business value of the critical companies and markets in each region.

Phillip Overmyer
Chief Executive
Singapore International Chamber of Commerce

# PREFACE

The Association of Southeast Asian Nations (ASEAN) Vision 2020, adopted in December 1997, envisaged "a stable, prosperous and highly competitive ASEAN economic region in which there is a free flow of goods, services, investment and freer flow of capital, equitable economic development and reduced poverty and socioeconomic disparities" by the year 2020. To realize this, at the Ninth ASEAN Summit in October 2003, the ASEAN leaders signed the Declaration of ASEAN Concord II (Bali Concord II) aiming at an ASEAN Economic Community (AEC) as an end goal of its economic integration. Later, that deadline was brought forward to 2015.

ASEAN achieved a major milestone at the November 2007 ASEAN Summit in Singapore when its leaders adopted the AEC Blueprint, which laid out a road map to accelerate economic integration, and included action plans, targets, and timelines to facilitate the process. It became a binding declaration of commitments by all Member Countries. The blueprint is organized along the AEC's four main characteristics, namely:

1. a single market and production base;
2. a highly competitive economic region;
3. a region of equitable economic development; and
4. a region that is fully integrated into the global economy.

The highlights of the blueprint are shown in Box 1. The blueprint envisions ASEAN as internationally competitive and integrated in the global economy, with benefits for all ten ASEAN member countries.

### BOX 1: Main Highlights from the AEC Blueprint

I. **Single Market and Production Base**
   5 core elements:

|  | Liberalization | Facilitation |
|---|---|---|
| Free flow of goods | Tariff and NTB elimination Synchronized external tariff alignment | Customs integration Standards and technical barriers to trade |
| Free flow of services | Full market access and national treatment Remove substantially all restrictions on trade in services | Mutual Recognition Arrangements (MRAs) on professional services; professional exchange |
| Free flow of investment | All industries and services incidental to these industries to ASEAN investors | Transparency; streamlined procedures, avoidance of double taxation; joint promotion |
| Freer flow of capital | Relax capital control measures on intra-ASEAN portfolio investments | Harmonize capital market-standards; facilitate market driven efforts to establish exchange and debt market linkages |
| Free flow of skilled labour | Remove discrimination on employment | Harmonization of standards in education and training; MRA on vocational training |

**Priority Integration Sectors (PIS)**
- Conduct a biannual review to monitor the status, progress, and effectiveness of the PIS road maps to ensure timely implementation
- Identify sector-specific projects or initiatives through regular dialogues or consultation with stakeholders, particularly the private sector.

**Food, Agriculture and Forestry**
- Enhance trade and long-term competitiveness of ASEAN food, agriculture, and forestry products
- Promote cooperation with international and regional organizations and private sector

---

**II. Competitive Economic Region**
- Develop a competition policy
- Strengthen consumer protection
- Regional cooperation in intellectual property rights (IPRs)
- Regional cooperation in infrastructure development
- Complete network of bilateral agreements on avoidance of double taxation
- Promote electronic commerce (e-commerce)

**III. Equitable Economic Development**
- Accelerate the development of small and medium-sized enterprises (SMEs)
- Enhance the Initiative for ASEAN Integration (IAI) to narrow the development gap

**IV. Integration into the Global Economy**
- Achieve a coherent approach towards external economic relations, including its negotiations for free trade area (FTAs) and comprehensive economic partnerships (CEP) agreements
- Enhance participation in global supply networks

---

In view of the advanced target date, the AEC and its blueprint look ambitious and there is much to be done to achieve this goal. First, a single market and production base means a larger production and market place. This entails the removal of all kinds of trade barriers. While tariffs on intra-ASEAN trade have been lowered on paper, there still exist many non-tariff barriers to that trade. Secondly, to achieve a competitive economic region, the member countries have to develop their infrastructure. Thirdly, ASEAN is still grappling with the issue of the development divide, especially since the admission of Cambodia, Lao PDR, Myanmar, and Vietnam (CLMV). The CLMV countries need to narrow the gap dividing them from the ASEAN-6, that is, the earlier members, Brunei Darussalam, Indonesia, Malaysia, the Philippines, Singapore, and Thailand, so that they can participate more effectively in the AEC.

However, all this requires cooperation and coordination among different sectors of the economy. Each member country has to ensure that it should not lag far behind the others. The governments of ten countries need to take steps to continue domestic reform so as to comply with ASEAN commitments on time.

In order to discuss the above, the ASEAN Studies Centre (ASC) at the Institute of Southeast Asian Studies (ISEAS) in Singapore along with the Konrad Adenauer Stiftung (KAS) convened the ASEAN Round Table 2010 on 29 April 2010 at the Shangri-La Hotel, Singapore. The objectives of the round table were to examine the state of readiness (or lack thereof) of the member countries for regional integration, and to determine the progress of each of them with regard to the four characteristics of the AEC. The round table also sought to define the national-level challenges that need to be addressed if ASEAN is to achieve an efficient economic community by 2015.

Private firms, both regional and multinational, are also important players in the process of regional integration. Until now ASEAN businesses have shown little or no interest in ASEAN developments. This may pose the greatest threat to realizing an AEC by 2015. To address this issue and more, the ASC conducted a brainstorming session on 23 September 2010 at ISEAS. The discussion looked at the challenges to ASEAN businesses and identified possible solutions. The session also recommended practical measures for facilitating trade and investment, and implementing ASEAN integration initiatives on the ground effectively.

Both the ASEAN Round Table 2010 and the brainstorming session gathered Southeast Asian experts from the region to discuss the current state of the member countries and businesses with respect to the goals of AEC by 2015. The round table had Dr S. Pushpanathan, Deputy Secretary-General of ASEAN for the AEC at the ASEAN Secretariat in Jakarta, as the keynote speaker, and he gave an account of ASEAN's readiness in achieving AEC by the target year, 2015. Thereafter, the sessions examined the progress in, or the challenges faced by, each member country in order to meet the objectives of the AEC. The later discussion looked at the ASEAN private sector to determine the extent of its involvement in the economic integration process. This includes both participation at the policymaking level and the utilization of various ASEAN economic agreements.

The vigorous discussions during both events constitute this volume's chapters. It begins with a brief introduction and summarizes the important observations made during the sessions. This is followed by country chapters by experts both on the economy and the private sector. The book concludes with the recommendations made in the discussions.

I hope this book will help ASEAN stakeholders and other interested public members in understanding the current state of readiness of member countries and the private sector for regional integration. I hope that the policymakers benefit from the recommendations.

Sanchita Basu Das
ASEAN Studies Centre, ISEAS, Singapore

# ACKNOWLEDGEMENTS

Acknowledgements for a project with two conferences are the most essential part of the job for an editor. First of all we would like to thank the Konrad Adenauer Stiftung for its financial support of the ASEAN Round Table 2010. Many contributed substantially to the round table and brainstorming session and to the subsequent publication of this book. These include Ambassador K. Kesavapany, former ISEAS director, who extended his kind support to see the project through to completion. I am also grateful to Dr Wilhelm Hofmeister, director, Regional Program "Political Dialogue with Asia", of Konrad Adenauer Stiftung, Singapore, for his interest in and support of the ASEAN Round Table 2010. To Ambassador Rodolfo C. Severino, head of the ASEAN Studies Centre, ISEAS, I owe an immense debt as he oversaw the whole project and gave his insightful comments and time for idea-refining discussions throughout the process. I was assisted by Mark Tallara and Lily Koh at critical junctures of the conferences and thank them for that. My sincere thanks to the staff of the ISEAS Publications Unit, especially its head, Triena Ong, for their professionalism in getting this book published. Finally, I wish to thank the contributors of the volume who made the conferences a success and the publication possible.

# CONTRIBUTORS

Sanchita Basu Das is Lead Researcher for Economic Affairs at the ASEAN Studies Centre, Institute of Southeast Asian Studies, Singapore.

Pushpanathan Sundram is Deputy Secretary-General of ASEAN, the ASEAN Secretariat, Jakarta.

Ong Keng Yong is Director of the Institute of Policy Studies, Singapore.

Juliana Giam, at the time of writing, was Deputy Director, International Business Advisory, Global Business Division, Singapore Business Federation.

Rajah Rasiah is Holder of the Khazanah Nasional Chair of Regulatory Studies and Professor of Technology and Innovation Policy, University of Malaya.

Mahani Zainal Abidin is Chief Executive of the Institute of Strategic and International Studies, Malaysia.

Loh Geok Mooi is Senior Fellow at the Institute of Strategic and International Studies, Malaysia.

Nor Izzatina Abdul Aziz is Researcher at the Institute of Strategic and International Studies, Malaysia.

Raymond Atje is Head, Department of Economics, Centre for Strategic and International Studies, Jakarta.

The late Hadi Soesastro was Senior Economist, Centre for Strategic and International Studies, Jakarta.

Widdi Mugijayani is Researcher at the Centre for Strategic and International Studies, Jakarta.

Pratiwi Kartika is Researcher at the Centre for Strategic and International Studies, Jakarta.

Nipon Poapongsakorn is President, Thailand Development Research Institute, Thailand.

Eggaluck Suwannakarn is Senior Researcher at the Fiscal Policy Research Institute, Bangkok, and a guest lecturer at the University of the Thai Chamber of Commerce, Bangkok, Thailand.

Pisesporn Wasawong is Researcher at the Fiscal Policy Research Institute, Thailand.

Jenny D. Balboa is Supervising Research Specialist at the Philippine Institute for Development Studies, the Philippines.

Fatima Lourdes E. Del Prado is Research Specialist at the Philippine Institute for Development Studies, the Philippines.

Josef T. Yap is President, Philippine Institute for Development Studies, the Philippines.

Maureen Ane D. Rosellon is Senior Research Specialist at the Philippine Institute for Development Studies, the Philippines.

Lim Jock Hoi is Permanent Secretary, Ministry of Foreign Affairs and Trade, Brunei Darussalam.

Pushpa Thambipillai is Senior Lecturer, Department of Public Policy, Faculty of Business, Economics and Policy Studies, University of Brunei Darussalam.

Vo Tri Thanh is Vice-President, Central Institute for Economic Management, Hanoi, Vietnam.

Nguyen Anh Duong is Researcher at the Central Institute for Economic Management, Hanoi, Vietnam.

Chan Sophal is President of the Cambodian Economic Association, Phnom Penh, Cambodia.

Larry Strange is Executive Director of the Cambodia Development Resource Institute, Phnom Penh, Cambodia.

Pradeep Srivastava is Senior Regional Cooperation Specialist, Southeast Asia Department, Asian Development Bank, Manila, the Philippines.

# Abbreviations

| | |
|---|---|
| ABAC | APEC Business Advisory Council |
| ACD | ASEAN Cosmetic Directive |
| ACFTA | ASEAN-China Free Trade Agreement |
| ACIA | ASEAN Comprehensive Investment Agreement |
| ADB | Asian Development Bank |
| AEC | ASEAN Economic Community |
| AEGC | ASEAN Experts Group on Competition |
| AFAS | ASEAN Framework Agreement on Services |
| AFTA | ASEAN Free Trade Area |
| AIA | ASEAN Investment Area |
| AICO | ASEAN Industrial Cooperation |
| AJCEP | ASEAN-Japan Comprehensive Economic Partnership |
| AKFTA | ASEAN-Korea Free Trade Agreement |
| APPS | ASEAN Pioneer Project Scheme |
| APSC | ASEAN Political-Security Community |
| ARI | agriculture resource intensive |
| ASC | ASEAN Studies Centre |
| ASCC | ASEAN Socio-Cultural Community |
| ASEAN | Association of Southeast Asian Nations |
| ASEAN-BAC | ASEAN Business Advisory Council |
| ASEAN-BIS | ASEAN Business and Investment Summit |
| ASEAN-CCI | ASEAN Chambers of Commerce and Industry |
| ASW | ASEAN Single Window |
| ASYCUDA | Automated System for Customs Data |
| ATIGA | ASEAN Trade in Goods Agreement |

| | |
|---|---|
| BIMP-EAGA | Brunei-Indonesia-Malaysia-Philippines–East ASEAN Growth Area |
| BMSMED | Bureau of Micro, Small and Medium Enterprise Development (Philippines) |
| BRIC | Brazil, Russia, India, China |
| CAB | Civil Aeronautics Board (Philippines) |
| CAFTA | China-ASEAN Free Trade Agreement |
| CBM | coordinated border management |
| CBTA | Cross-Border Transport Agreement |
| CECP | common external commercial policy |
| CEP | comprehensive economic partnerships |
| CEPT | common effective preferential tariffs |
| CGIF | Credit Guarantee and Investment Facility |
| CLM | Cambodia, Laos, Myanmar |
| CLMV | Cambodia, Laos, Myanmar, and Vietnam |
| CMIM | Chiang Mai Initiative Multilateralization |
| CTAS | Custom Transit System |
| DEPD | Department of Economic Planning and Development (Brunei) |
| EMU | European Monetary Union |
| EPIRA | Electric Power Industry Reform Act (Philippines) |
| ERIA | Economic Research Institute for ASEAN and East Asia |
| FDI | foreign direct investment |
| FINL | Foreign Investment Negative List |
| FTA | Initiative for ASEAN Integration |
| GATS | General Agreement on Trade in Services |
| GDCE | General Department of Customs and Excise |
| GEL | general exclusion list |
| GMS | Greater Mekong Subregion |
| GSP | Generalized System of Preferences |
| HCI | human capital intensive |
| HDI | human development index |
| IAI | Initiative for ASEAN Integration |
| ICT | information and communication technology |
| IFC | World Bank's International Finance Corporation |
| IJEPA | Indonesia-Japan Economic Partnership Agreement |

| | |
|---|---|
| IPR | intellectual property rights |
| ISEAS | Institute of Southeast Asian Studies |
| JETRO | Japan External Trade Organization |
| JICA | Japan International Cooperation Agency |
| JMC | Japan Machinery Center for Trade and Investment |
| KAS | Konrad Adenauer Stiftung |
| KLBI | Klasifikasi Baku Lapangan Usaha Indonesia – Standard classification of business fields |
| KPPU | Komisi Pengawas Persaingan Usaha – Commission for the Supervision of Business Competition (Indonesia) |
| LDC | least developed countries |
| LPP | Laos Pilot Project |
| MAFF | Ministry of Agriculture, Forestry and Fisheries (Cambodia) |
| MEF | Ministry of Economy and Finance (Cambodia) |
| MFN | most favoured nation |
| MIME | Ministry of Industry, Mines and Energy (Cambodia) |
| MITI | Ministry of Trade and Industry (Malaysia) |
| MNC | multinational corporation |
| MRAs | mutual recognition arrangements |
| MRI | mineral resource intensive |
| NCTFC | National Cross-Border Transport Facilitation Committee |
| NEM | New Economic Model (Malaysia) |
| NEP | New Economic Policy (Malaysia) |
| NSW | National Single Window |
| NTBs | non-tariff barriers |
| NTMs | non-tariff measures |
| PAL | Philippines Airlines |
| PIC/S | Pharmaceutical Inspection co-operation Scheme |
| PIS | priority integration sectors |
| PLDT | Philippine Long Distance Company |
| PMP | Privatization Master Plan |
| R&D | research and development |
| RGC | Royal Government of Cambodia |
| ROO | rules of origin |
| SBF | Singapore Business Federation |
| SEZ | special economic zones |

| | |
|---|---|
| SMEs | small and medium enterprises |
| SOE | state-owned enterprise |
| SPS | sanitary and phytosanitary |
| TAFTA | Thailand-Australia Free Trade Agreement |
| TBT | technical barriers to trade |
| TI | technology intensive |
| TTF | transport and trade facilitation |
| ULI | unskilled-labour intensive |
| WTO | World Trade Organization |

# 1

# Introduction: State of Readiness of ASEAN Economies and Businesses

Sanchita Basu Das

ASEAN leaders have repeatedly conveyed their political will and commitment to building an ASEAN Economic Community (AEC) by 2015. They signed the ASEAN Charter in 2007, which puts in place the institutions and mechanism to build up an ASEAN Community. The AEC Blueprint adopted the same year gave a master plan for building an economic community characterized by a single market and production base; a competitive economic region with equitable development and a region that is engaged with the global economy. During the ASEAN ministers' meetings in 2010, the leaders agreed that ASEAN would focus efforts on ensuring financial stability, fostering regional infrastructure development and connectivity, promoting sustainable development, and narrowing the development gap. They adopted the Master Plan on ASEAN Connectivity at the 17th ASEAN Summit, which is expected to be implemented in the next four years.

These progressive developments show the leaders' increased confidence in the process of economic integration. It also shows their greater willingness to move faster, especially after the financial crisis, and to enhance the competitiveness of the region to face increased competition from China and India.

## ASEAN Economies

But what is the state of readiness (or lack thereof) of member countries? With regard to the first feature of the AEC Blueprint — a single market and production base — ASEAN secured a major landmark when, on 1 January 2010, the ASEAN-6 countries applied zero tariffs on 99 per cent of goods. The CLMV (Cambodia, Lao PDR, Myanmar and Vietnam) countries are also not far behind as they traded 98.6 per cent of goods at 0–5 per cent of tariff rate. However, there exist many non-tariff barriers (NTBs), which lower the potential benefits under the ASEAN Free Trade Area (AFTA). For example, in Malaysia and Indonesia, there exist protectionist measures in the form of subsidies and import restrictions to sensitive industries. In the past decade, the Philippines observed higher technical barriers to trade, as businesses believed that with the reduction in tariff, NTBs could provide some protection to local industries and manage the competition from imports. Trade in Laos and Cambodia is also challenged by effective coordination on the borders (customs, different agencies, various standards and procedures).

In addition to tariffs and NTBs, there are other aspects of government policy that hinder economic integration. Within ASEAN, there are several sectors and state-owned enterprises (such as the Malaysian automotive industry, the Thai telecom industry, the agriculture sector in Thailand and Indonesia) that continue to thrive under, and demand continued, government protection from external competition. This leads to government intervention through subsidies, tax incentives, special loans, and market entry barriers to create a form of special protection for some businesses. The links between government and business distort the "single market" objective of ASEAN. In order to remove economic restrictions, the task challenging ASEAN is the removal of political barriers from government and business relations.

Regulation on free movement of labour is another issue holding back full integration. For example, in Thailand, the Alien Employment

Act prohibits foreigners from employment in certain professions (civil engineering, legal services) and other professions are regulated by professional associations. In Malaysia, the shortage of skilled labour became a prime reason for the hollowing out of the electronics sector. This shortage of skilled labour impedes countries not only from attracting new investments, but also discourages the manufacturing sector from moving up the value chain in the regional production network.

Liberalizing the services sector is a major challenge among ASEAN countries such as Indonesia and Thailand. The commitment for these countries under the ASEAN Framework Agreement on Services (AFAS) is not significantly deeper and, in many cases, is not beyond status quo. Their governments also offer limited foreign equity participation. Some of the health care sub-sectors in Indonesia are closed to foreign investors (e.g., general medical clinic, ambulance services) or require special permission from the Ministry of Health (e.g., pharmaceutical sellers). Thailand is yet to raise the foreign equity share cap in four priority sectors to at least 51 per cent. The commitment in services liberalization is poor mainly because the sector accounts for a significant proportion in most of the economies (52 per cent in Indonesia, 49 per cent in Thailand, 54 per cent in the Philippines) and member countries are doubtful about the benefits of such liberalization. Services sector liberalization also requires coordination across many government agencies and, unlike the manufacturing sector with its clear industrial policy, there is no clear services-sector policy in place.

The second AEC characteristic on "competitive economic region" has two interrelated aspects: one is an effective, standardized competition policy, which would presumably render firms and, by extension, the region, more strongly competitive with firms in other areas; the other is the region's competitiveness with other parts of the world for markets and investments, which would require infrastructure, human resources, and policies that foster an attractive investment climate. Most countries, such as Malaysia, the Philippines, and Brunei, are lagging in this area and are yet to enact anti-monopoly laws. On the other hand, Indonesia, Singapore, Thailand, and Vietnam have propagated a competition law and have established independent competition authorities.

Member countries also have to ensure the effectiveness of their infrastructure for integrating the regional economy. The Philippines,

Lao PDR, and Vietnam are lagging in this area and need to catch up with more advanced ASEAN members. At the 17th ASEAN Summit in October 2010, ASEAN leaders adopted the Master Plan on ASEAN Connectivity submitted by the High Level Task Force. The Master Plan will be implemented from 2011 to 2015 and is expected to link ASEAN by enhancing the development of physical infrastructure, institutional connectivity, and people connectivity.

In the case of "equitable economic development", ASEAN developed the Initiative for ASEAN Integration (IAI) Work Plan 2 (2009–15), which identified the needs of the CLMV countries in terms of human capital and institutional strengthening. In the next few years, it is necessary to strengthen the implementation and supervision process of the projects, expand the participation of other partners, including the private sector, and increase promotional activities. The promotion of small and medium enterprises (SMEs) in the region is still in the "planning" phase. ASEAN SMEs in their regionalization drive face several challenges, such as credit constraints, labour mobility, market demand, and political risk. ASEAN leaders must take note that SMEs are a critical sector for growth and development and therefore need full support in terms of access to financing and research and development (R&D) to enable them to compete with domestic and international players.

As for the last attribute of the AEC — engaging with its trading partners — the ASEAN grouping saw the realization of the ASEAN-China and ASEAN-Korea FTAs (free trade agreements), and the commencement of the implementation of the ASEAN-Australia-New Zealand FTA and the ASEAN-India Trade in Goods agreement. However, an FTA can also bring with it some hiccups. The ASEAN-China FTA created a lot of anxieties among Indonesians, Thais, and Filipinos. This is because many believe that the Chinese authorities artificially create the higher efficiency of the Chinese production process by intervening in factor markets. This may have some repercussions on the ability of the governments to implement their AEC commitments in the future.

From the above, it is evident that although ASEAN leaders have consistently shown their political will and commitment to integrate ASEAN economies, the process of implementation at the national and provincial levels remains slow. This is mainly because ASEAN members show significant diversity in terms of their level of economic development and capacity (Salazar and Basu Das 2007). Given the members' uneven capabilities, the process of creating the AEC is complicated and difficult.

The premise of the AFTA and AEC is based on the creation of a single market and production base. But since the AFTA was launched in 1992, there have been constant changes in the global economy. There were two economic and financial crises that led to major setbacks in ASEAN member economies. There is an ongoing change in the regional context with the emergence of China, the changing behaviour of multinational companies, and developments in technology. In the last few years, besides creating the AFTA, ASEAN has also been involved in many FTAs. The region has been keen to solidify its economic relationship with its major trading partners — China, Japan, Korea, India, Australia, and New Zealand (Hew 2007). Although it is believed that ASEAN stands to gain by these trading agreements and by creating an FTA hub that would strengthen ASEAN's efforts to establish an AEC, they still add to the challenges of facing scarce resources.

Finally, integration takes time (Hew 2005). For instance, it took about forty years before the European Union was able to establish a common market. While it is considered a success, the process faced a lot of opposition and problems — even till today. For ASEAN, while the vision of an ASEAN Economic Community was stated in 2003, the AEC Blueprint, which identified the end goal and the process to reach the end goal, was adopted only in 2007. The blueprint stated that the economic integration has to go much broader and deeper than the removal of barriers to trade and investment through the AFTA and the ASEAN Investment Area (AIA) projects. Clear rules and institutions, in the form of the ASEAN Charter, were also adopted in 2007.

Therefore, in the next three years, what is needed is the strong commitment by member countries to progress ASEAN's goals of regional economic integration. It should be realized that at present, time is a big constraint. The core elements of the AEC must be in place by the target year of 2015. Failure to do so will add to more competitive pressures from China and India and will send the wrong signal to the international community. In addition, ASEAN is engaged in a number of bilateral FTAs, both as a region and through its individual members, most of which will be completed by 2015.

Given the imperative of time and the necessity to deliver on a bold action plan, each member state must believe convincingly in the AEC as a tool for increasing economic prosperity within the region as it can potentially increase intraregional trade and investment within ASEAN, and link ASEAN as a common market to the global economy.

## ASEAN Businesses

As ASEAN governments are busy providing the policy framework for regional integration by 2015, integration can only be achieved through the decisions and actions of ASEAN's businessmen. Trade and investment facilitation reforms must therefore benefit the private sector. But what is the current state and opinion of the ASEAN private sector on the prospects of achieving the AEC by 2015? The following observations came out during discussions in a brainstorming session organized by the ASEAN Studies Centre (ASC) at ISEAS:

- While in some cases there is hope that the AEC 2015 may bring advantages, this is often overshadowed by caution and scepticism. The private sector is disappointed by the slow pace of implementation measures to create an AEC. Although, according to the ASEAN official Scorecard I (2008–9), ASEAN has achieved around 75 per cent of its targets, it defies the understanding of the private sector. The scorecard deals only with official measures and agreements. It does not assess their benefits in terms of lower transaction costs, reduced prices, attractiveness to investments, and expanded consumer choices.
- Lack of awareness of ASEAN agreements seems to be uniform across all countries, although there is some understanding of the ASEAN Free Trade Area (AFTA), a process that was initiated in 1992. In most ASEAN countries, awareness of ASEAN agreements amongst the small and medium enterprises (SMEs) is quite low.
- The utilization rate of the AFTA tariff preference is about 15–17 per cent for the Philippines and 20 per cent for Vietnam. Across ASEAN, the AFTA utilization rate in 2008 was 23 per cent. The high administrative cost, low margin of preference (the Philippines, Vietnam), and complicated rules of origin (Thailand, Vietnam) are cited as the most common reasons for the low

utilization rate. The private sectors of some countries feel that the product structures of ASEAN member countries are relatively similar. Consequently, ASEAN member countries find little interest in importing products from one another. The AFTA utilization rate varies according to the sector. For example, in Thailand, basketwork has a high AFTA usage rate, whereas traders of pearls and precious stones have very low usage of AFTA tariff preferences.

- For trade in goods, business people have identified the "elimination of non-tariff barriers" as the most important area for implementation. In the opinion of Singapore and Thai private firms, the elimination of non-tariff barriers (NTBs) would help businesses to reduce cost and enhance competitiveness in the region. For trade in services, some companies consider government domestic policy as the leading obstacle to their efforts to expand overseas. For example, Malaysia has restrictions on student intake in tertiary education, as government officials seek to prevent overproduction of health-related professionals. With regard to the investment agreement, the private sector gets discouraged from investing in ASEAN countries by factors such as strikes in Vietnam, limited local knowledge, and lack of capital. Nevertheless, the private sector views the increasing number of professions covered by ASEAN Mutual Recognition Arrangements (MRAs) as a positive development.

- The size of a company affects how it views ASEAN regionalism. For example, SMEs of Singapore tend to be more optimistic as they are attracted to ASEAN neighbours by their market size, geographical proximity, and lower costs due to production networks. However, they are yet to take the AEC as part of their business strategy. The larger players in Malaysia, Thailand, and the Philippines are relatively better informed and are more positive about the ASEAN economic integration.

- For the private sectors of some countries — both home-grown and multinationals (MNCs) — ASEAN agreements have gained importance because of other factors: The private sector may not want to put all its eggs in one basket, that is, in China. They would prefer to diversify their investments to ASEAN. Private firms also prioritize their investment decisions according to the market for final demand. Thus, China or India become important. Indeed, there are firms that consider increased market access a major benefit of using ASEAN free trade agreements.

- In less-developed ASEAN countries such as Cambodia, slowness in translating ASEAN legal documents for ratification by the government is also preventing them from complying with AEC measures. These countries also suffer from language limitations and difficulty in understanding ASEAN materials. For both the policymakers and private sector in Cambodia and Vietnam, domestic issues take priority over regional concerns. In these countries, private sector engagement with and preparedness for the AEC get further complicated by their membership in the Greater Mekong Subregion (GMS) and similar subregional programmes.

Thus, at the moment, there is very little awareness about ASEAN economic integration in the ASEAN private sector. There is a lack of an outreach programme to promote better appreciation and understanding of ASEAN economic issues with the business community and public sector agencies.

This is because in the past, under the "ASEAN way", an agreement was reached first and the details were negotiated afterwards, earning the region the nickname, "Agree First Talk After" (Soesastro 2005). The private sector was mostly not discussed before an agreement was signed. Moreover, in some ASEAN countries, the private sector is not strong enough to undergo the process of economic transformation and gain from opportunities provided by regional economic integration. This could be due to domestic structural constraints or institutional weaknesses. However, it should be borne in mind that it is the businesses — MNCs, domestic enterprises, and the SMEs — which have to play the most important role in creating a single market and production base in ASEAN. Without them, the realization of an effective AEC by 2015 remains questionable.

## REFERENCES

Hadi Soesastro. "Accelerating ASEAN Economic Integration: Moving Beyond AFTA". CSIS Working Paper Series, WPE 091, March 2005

Hew, Denis, ed. *Roadmap to an ASEAN Economic Community*. Singapore: Institute of Southeast Asian Studies, 2005.

————, ed. *Brick by Brick: The Building of an ASEAN Economic Community*. Singapore: Institute of Southeast Asian Studies, 2007.

Salazar, L. and S. Basu Das. "Bridging the ASEAN Development Divide: Challenges and Prospects". *ASEAN Economic Bulletin* 24, no. 1 (2007).

# 2

# ASEAN's Readiness in Achieving the AEC 2015: Prospects and Challenges

S. Pushpanathan

## ASEAN in Today's Context

In today's rapidly evolving economic and financial landscape spurred by globalization, ASEAN lies in the midst of the strategic and dynamic region of East Asia. To maintain its centrality in the region and as an increasingly important player on the global stage, ASEAN needs to be more integrated as a grouping; more engaged with the global economy; and more proactive and nimble to respond to changing circumstances in a rapidly shifting, but increasingly interdependent world. New issues and challenges are confronting ASEAN and therefore pushing ahead with integration and strengthening ASEAN institutions, mechanisms, and processes will be crucial for the region to address these developments.

As a region, ASEAN member states have worked together to ensure peace, stability, prosperity, and development for all of them and the region as a whole. The regional resilience that ASEAN has brought about has contributed to national resilience and vice versa. ASEAN has enjoyed rapid growth and development in the last four decades. The development has helped ASEAN to be a pillar of strength and a catalyst for regionalism in Asia. The regional role of ASEAN has been further enhanced by its community building efforts, particularly the ASEAN Economic Community (AEC).

## ASEAN Charter and ASEAN's Readiness for Community Building

The readiness of ASEAN for community building was clearly reflected by the signing of the ASEAN Charter in 2007 and its later ratification in 2008. After four decades, ASEAN has a constitution to base its work on and to pursue with determination the establishment of an ASEAN Community with three interlocking pillars, of which the AEC is one. The other two are the ASEAN Political-Security Community and the ASEAN Socio-Cultural Community.

The Charter also puts in place the institutions and mechanisms that will support the building of the ASEAN Community. For the economic pillar, an AEC Council was established and given the mandate to oversee the implementation of the AEC. The Committee of Permanent Representatives to ASEAN was also set up to handle the day-to-day work of ASEAN covering all three pillars. This body coordinates closely with the ASEAN Secretariat in moving the agenda of the ASEAN Community forward.

The Secretary-General of ASEAN has also been given more mandates to coordinate the work of ASEAN as its chief administrative officer. The secretariat itself has undergone a complete transformation in 2009, from just providing basic services to that of initiating, coordinating, and facilitating the community building agenda of ASEAN. Indeed, the mechanisms under the Charter had provided the much needed coordination between the national and regional levels to see through the implementation of the AEC Blueprint.

Apart from setting the mechanisms under the Charter in motion, ASEAN also adopted the blueprints for the three communities. The AEC Blueprint was adopted in 2007 and serves as a comprehensive and coherent master plan for building the economic community characterized by a single market and production base; a competitive economic region with equitable development, and a region that is fully plugged into the global economy.

In order to ensure a more rules-based ASEAN Community, the ASEAN Secretariat was also given the mandate to undertake a compliance review for the three pillars to ensure member states are implementing their commitments under the three blueprints in a timely manner. For the AEC, a scorecard mechanism was adopted to track the implementation of measures in the AEC Blueprint, which is reported to the AEC Council and the ASEAN Summit. The public version of the first AEC Scorecard has been issued and the secretariat hopes to receive the comments and inputs of the business community, scholars, and other stakeholders to improve the scorecard further.

Efforts are also ongoing to beef up the procedures to put into operation the dispute settlement mechanism under the AEC for economic agreements that are covered so that festering economic disputes can be resolved in a more rules-based manner and quickly, thereby promoting greater confidence and transparency for the business community in the region. A protocol to the ASEAN Charter on Dispute Settlement Mechanisms has been adopted recently that aims to put in place a mechanism to help member states resolve disputes concerning the interpretation or application of the ASEAN Charter. The mechanism also applies to other ASEAN instruments that do not specifically provide for dispute settlement mechanisms.

## Milestone Achievements in 2010

Apart from the institutional mechanisms and processes, ASEAN's readiness for the AEC 2015 is reflected by its achievements in the last two years since the signing of the Charter and the adoption of the AEC Blueprint. In this regard, ASEAN has secured a few landmark achievements in 2010. Beginning 1 January 2010, the ASEAN-6 countries achieved zero tariffs covering 99.65 per cent and for the CLMV 98.6 per cent at 0–5 per cent tariff rates of the total tariff lines traded under the Common Effective Preferential Tariff Scheme for the ASEAN Free Trade Area (CEPT-AFTA). This is the most tangible high-impact outcome for ASEAN.

1 January 2010 also saw the realization of the ASEAN-China and ASEAN-Korea Free Trade Agreements (FTAs) and the commencement of the implementation of the ASEAN-Australia-New Zealand FTA and the ASEAN-India Trade in Goods Agreement. ASEAN's success in engaging proactively with its major trading partners in free trade agreements is bearing fruit. Two-way trade has been enhanced and cements ASEAN's

central role within the region. ASEAN's trade with China, Korea, and Japan remains strong and is growing, while ASEAN is also expected to reap benefits from its newly signed FTAs with Australia, New Zealand, and India.

Another important achievement of ASEAN is that despite the 2008 financial crisis, it has been able to achieve full economic recovery supported by the fiscal and monetary stimulus packages of the individual member states and the improving economic situation. Overall, ASEAN achieved a growth rate of 7.3 per cent, after a feeble 1.5 per cent in 2009 due to the global economic crisis. This will provide further incentive for ASEAN to push ahead with its economic integration.

## Progress in Implementing the AEC Blueprint

Some of the key areas of progress achieved in economic integration, which is another indication of the commitment and readiness of ASEAN to achieve the AEC by 2015, are discussed below.

The ASEAN Trade in Goods Agreement (ATIGA) entered into force on 17 May 2010. The ATIGA is a single legal enactment to implement effectively the stipulated tariff reduction up to 2015, as well as to promote trade facilitation.

To further ensure tariff reductions are not nullified by non-tariff measures (NTMs), ASEAN is working on trade facilitation issues to ensure NTMs do not impede trade. ASEAN has adopted a Trade Facilitation Framework to address systematically issues such as the removal of non-tariff barriers, simplification and harmonization of customs, standards, and conformance, and sanitary and phytosanitary measures. It is planning to establish an ASEAN Trade Repository by 2015 that would serve as a gateway of regulatory information at the regional and national levels.

With a view to achieving more expeditious customs clearance, member states are developing the ASEAN Single Window, which would provide an integrated platform of partnership among government agencies and end users in the movement of goods across the region by connecting their National Single Windows. The ASEAN Secretariat is also working on a self-certification scheme for the declaration of origin. This will permit certified economic operators to self-certify the originating status of goods in place of the existing system of presenting certificates of origin issued by government authorities.

On improving standards and conformity assessment, ASEAN has concluded two Mutual Recognition Arrangements (MRAs) in the electrical and electronic sector and the cosmetic sector. MRAs for agro-based products and automotives are being developed. The ASEAN Secretariat is also working on a conformity marking scheme to support the expeditious clearance through customs of products that have conformed to ASEAN harmonised technical regulations/requirements.

In the area of services, ASEAN member states are close to the completion of the seventh package of services commitments under the ASEAN Framework Agreement on Services (AFAS). The services sector of ASEAN received the highest amount of foreign direct investment (FDI), which accounted for 50.6 per cent of total ASEAN FDI in 2009. ASEAN's exports of commercial services to the world is also showing an encouraging trend, more than doubling from US$68 billion in 2000, to US$162.8 billion in 2009.

In investment, ASEAN has witnessed a steady increase in intra-ASEAN FDI flows, accounting for 18.2 per cent (US$10.8 billion) of total ASEAN FDI (US$59.7 billion) inflows in 2008, compared with a share of 13.8 per cent in 2006. For the same period, total FDI inflows increased by 8.6 per cent. The ASEAN Comprehensive Investment Agreement (ACIA), will help to market ASEAN as a single investment destination and buttress the single market and production base of ASEAN. It will liberalize, facilitate, promote, and protect investments in the region by ASEAN investors and ASEAN-based foreign investors.

MRAs in the services sector are being actively pursued to facilitate the flow of professional services providers in the region, in accordance to domestic rules and regulations. The MRAs include surveyors, engineering services, nursing services, architectural services, tourism professionals, accountancy, professionals, medical practitioners, and dental practitioners. More is expected to be negotiated and concluded in the near future to support the development of the services sector in ASEAN.

In the finance sector, the enlarged US$120 billion swap arrangement under the Chiang Mai Initiative Multilateralization (CMIM) was operationalized on 24 March 2010. This multilateral swap facility will assist ASEAN and the Plus Three countries of China, Japan, and the Republic of Korea with short-term liquidity difficulties. An independent surveillance office for the CMIM was established in Singapore in 2011.

The establishment of the US$700-million Credit Guarantee and Investment Facility (CGIF) was also launched in 2010 by the ASEAN

Plus Three Finance Ministers. This will help in the development of deep and liquid local currency and regional bond markets. An ASEAN infrastructure fund is also being considered to finance regional infrastructure building crucial for the establishment of a well-connected and integrated single market and production base in ASEAN.

In the transport sector, three framework agreements on facilitation of goods in transit, multimodal transport, and facilitation of interstate transport have been concluded. These agreements will simplify and harmonize trade and transport procedures and documentation, formulate uniform guidelines and requirements for registration of transit transport and multimodal transport operators, and promote ICT applications for seamless cargo transportation.

Additionally, the ASEAN Multilateral Agreement on Full Liberalization of Passenger Air Services, extending unlimited air traffic rights to all cities in ASEAN, has been finalized. In terms of air connectivity, negotiations with China have entered into the final stages. Meanwhile the ASEAN Strategic Transport Plan for 2011–15 is being developed to cover all modes and aspects of transport connectivity.

As connectivity is crucial to building a vibrant internal market and linking it to the global economy, ASEAN has endorsed a Master Plan on Connectivity. The Master Plan focuses, among other things, on transport, information and communication technology (ICT), energy and cross-border linkages, and the facilitation of the smooth movement of people, goods, and services.

## Challenges to Address

However, there are several challenges facing ASEAN in achieving AEC 2015. Firstly, ASEAN has to manage the integration process and achieve the targets within the time frames that have already been agreed. The 16th ASEAN Summit in Vietnam has called for the speeding up of the implementation of ASEAN agreements through timely ratification of agreements and protocols, as well as concrete actions. ASEAN leaders have emphasized the need to set up a monitoring mechanism to ensure effective implementation, identification of priorities for each period and implementing bodies, and improve the coordination among the pillars, as well as resource mobilization. These are very important issues to be addressed if ASEAN is to see the successful implementation of the ASEAN Community as a whole by 2015.

According to the first AEC Scorecard, ASEAN has a 75.5 per cent achievement rate for the period 2008 to 2009. This is primarily due to the non-implemented measures involving the ratification of important economic agreements related to trade in goods, investment, transport and the cosmetics directive. Indeed, of the 124 economic agreements under AEC, only 73 per cent of them have been ratified by all ASEAN member states. ASEAN member states will have to look at ratifying them in a timely manner so that integration can be speeded up.

More importantly, ASEAN member states will have to transpose these regional commitments into national obligations through their respective domestic processes and at a quicker pace. The domestic legal enactments relating to ASEAN commitments could be monitored as part of the scorecard process.

Secondly, ASEAN countries should actively address the non-implementation of regional commitments, which should include capacity building to tackle any inadequacies in implementing commitments; peer reviews for sharing and learning of best practices, as well as transparency and confidence building; and utilizing the dispute settlement mechanisms already in place to resolve issues in a rules-based manner. There could also be specific target setting to encourage ASEAN to achieve more. For example, there could be specific targets for bringing down the costs of doing business in ASEAN.

Thirdly, a robust regional surveillance mechanism is necessary to track emerging risks in the AEC and to deal with them in a timely manner. In this regard, the ASEAN Secretariat will soon be establishing a Macroeconomic and Finance Surveillance Office which will undertake surveillance on economic and financial integration issues. The office, as a start, will embark on trade, investment, and macroeconomic surveillance for the AEC.

Fourthly, financing the development of an ASEAN single market and production base will continue to be a challenge. In this regard, ASEAN countries should look at innovative and creative ways to augment the funds being provided by dialogue partners and donors to support ASEAN economic integration. While ASEAN Dialogue Partners are keen to support ASEAN integration, such assistance is mostly limited to the softer side of integration, such as capacity building, training, and sharing of best practices and experiences. The ASEAN Development Fund is undersized relative to what ASEAN intends to achieve by 2015. The Chiang Mai Initiative Multilateralisation (CMIM) and Credit Guarantee Investment

Facility (CGIF) are examples where ASEAN is starting to put in its own resources for its own development, but more has to be done to achieve the ambitious goal of the AEC.

One way forward would be to look at public-private partnership models. The participation of government in such high-cost endeavours will reduce the risks of investors and make investing in such long-term projects attractive. The multilateral development banks, including the World Bank and the Asian Development Bank, should also be actively engaged in such financing schemes. ASEAN's immediate neighbours, such as China, Japan, and the Republic of Korea, as well as India, Australia, and New Zealand, could be partners in some of these schemes as ASEAN's growth will also impact these economies positively.

Fifthly, the development divide within ASEAN certainly deserves more attention for the AEC to be realized by 2015. The assistance to the CLMV countries needs to be stepped up to enable them to catch up with the ASEAN-6 nations, so that they can effectively participate in building the AEC and benefit fully from it. Preliminary findings of a study on the impact of accelerating the AEC from 2020 to 2015 reveal that CLMV countries are benefiting in terms of increased trade and FDI flows amongst the CLMV countries, and with ASEAN-6, and East Asia.

New approaches are being examined to assist the CLMV countries. One is the "ASEAN help ASEAN approach" where the ASEAN-6 countries are sharing their expertise and experiences with these countries through bilateral development assistance. The second sees intra-ASEAN investments from ASEAN-6 to these countries increasing and this will help to transfer knowledge and technical know-how for their development and integration into the AEC. The third is to introduce targeted and tailored programmes for each of these countries to meet ASEAN economic integration goals such as the ongoing Laos Pilot Project (LPP). This tripartite cooperation model involves the Lao PDR as the recipient of aid, the Japan International Cooperation Agency (JICA) as the donor, and the ASEAN Secretariat as the facilitator.

Sixthly, the private sector of ASEAN must be better engaged in building the AEC as it is the principal driver of regional economic integration. There should be regular sector-specific dialogue with the business community so that ASEAN can address any concerns and create a more facilitating environment for doing business in the region. More technical meetings of ASEAN in the economic arena could also be opened up to the participation of the business community. More efforts are also needed to engage the peoples of ASEAN better, in particular, civil society, strategic think tanks, and economic institutes to tap their expertise and knowledge. A good intellectual foundation and the peoples' participation will provide a stronger underpinning for the development and consolidation of the AEC.

Finally, if the private sector in ASEAN is the "driver" of economic integration, the ASEAN Secretariat must be the "lubricant" of this integration. The ASEAN Economic Ministers at their last meeting have given their strongest endorsement yet for an enhanced role of the secretariat. A strengthened secretariat will contribute more to regional economic surveillance; compliance monitoring; economic dispute settlement; and implementing major economic integration programmes. ASEAN must explore the tremendous potential of developing the ASEAN Secretariat by investing in its human resources and systems.

## Concluding Remarks

The key challenge for ASEAN is to stay the course in community building as a whole. While readiness is important, it is not sufficient to deliver the AEC by 2015. The building of the AEC will need strong leadership, vision, political will, as well as strong mechanisms and institutions to support coordination and implementation, both at the national and regional levels. ASEAN must continue to stay open and engage its partners to maximize the gains from the AEC, given the region's outward-looking economic orientation. A transformation of mindset from "national interest to regional action" to "regional interest to national action" is also necessary for community building as a whole.

The time left for the establishment of the AEC is fewer than five years. A greater sense of urgency is therefore necessary to achieve the goal of AEC and maintain ASEAN's centrality.

# PART I

# Challenges for
# Member Countries

# 3

# Achieving the AEC 2015: Challenges for Brunei Darussalam

Lim Jock Hoi

Brunei Darussalam, being the smallest country in Southeast Asia in terms of its population,[1] stands out amongst its ASEAN peers as being one of the most unique. Although it has one of the highest gross domestic product (GDP) per capita in the world,[2] it remains an economy that is heavily reliant on its oil and gas exports. To maintain its relatively high standard of living and faced by the prospect of declining oil and gas reserves, the Government of Brunei Darussalam faces the challenge of setting out an ambitious economic diversification plan that will move Brunei's economy away from its heavy reliance on oil and gas, in line with its National Vision for 2035, or Wawasan 2035. Given these considerations, Brunei Darussalam's membership within ASEAN provides an opportunity for it to enhance its standing within the region, contribute to regional peace and prosperity efforts, and provides it with a platform for enhanced economic engagement, not only within ASEAN, but globally.

Brunei Darussalam became the sixth member of ASEAN on 7 January 1984, barely a week after being granted its independence. Since then, the former British protectorate has been part of all of ASEAN's efforts, and remains committed to the realization of achieving an ASEAN Community by 2015, under all three pillars: the ASEAN Economic Community (AEC), the ASEAN Political-Security Community (APSC), as well as the ASEAN Socio-Cultural Community (ASCC). In order to realize the ASEAN Economic Community by 2015, Brunei Darussalam, with its ASEAN counterparts, has agreed to work towards achieving the AEC's four key characteristics: (1) a single market and production base, (2) a highly competitive economic region, (3) a region of equitable economic development, and (4) a region that is fully integrated into the global economy.

This chapter will set out to identify some of the challenges that Brunei Darussalam faces in realizing the ASEAN Economic Community by 2015, by focusing on the unique challenges presented to realize the four key characteristics of the AEC.

## A Single Market and Production Base

In order to realize a single market and production base, ASEAN member states will seek to achieve the following: (1) free flow of goods, (2) free flow of services, (3) freer flow of investment, (4) free flow of capital, and (5) free flow of skilled labour. Additionally, a single market and production base includes two other important components: the priority integration sectors, and food, agriculture and forestry, which will not be discussed in this chapter. For Brunei Darussalam, each component brings its own challenges which need to be addressed.

### Free Flow of Goods

Brunei Darussalam operates under a relatively free trade environment, compared with other ASEAN member states. As per its World Trade Organization (WTO) commitments, nearly 97.2 per cent of Brunei Darussalam's tariffs lines are bound. Brunei Darussalam's applied MFN (most favoured nation) tariff rates are low, averaging approximately 93 per cent in 2010. The average bound rate is 24.12 per cent, and applied rates averaged 4.42 per cent in 2010. With the exception of a few products — including coffee, tea, tobacco, and alcohol — tariffs on agricultural products are zero. Roughly 130 products, including alcoholic beverages, tobacco, coffee, tea, petroleum oils, and lubricants, are subject to specific rates of duty and higher rates of overall protection. Under its commitments to ASEAN, Brunei has continued to reduce its low tariffs, with the Common Effective Preferential Tariff (CEPT) scheme seeing a reduction of preferential tariff rates.

As of 2011, Brunei Darussalam's largest trading partners were Japan, Korea, Australia, India, and Malaysia. However, the recent onset of the global financial crisis, and the hikes in the prices of food and gas which were experienced in late 2008, have seen a change in direction by the Government of Brunei Darussalam, where it has sought to move away from its reliance on goods and services from outside the region, and instead, leverage on the progress made within ASEAN to develop its single market and production base.

Intraregional trade between Brunei Darussalam and the rest of ASEAN has been rising progressively over the last few years. According to national figures, exports from Brunei Darussalam to other ASEAN countries rose 41.54 per cent between 2005 and 2008. At the same time, intra-ASEAN imports into Brunei Darussalam grew 37.90 per cent.

With ASEAN's aim to establish a single market and production base, the challenge for Brunei Darussalam is to ensure it can immerse itself in the regional supply networks by expanding business opportunities in economic clusters beyond the oil and gas industry and taking advantage of ASEAN's progress in cumulation rules under rules of origin for ASEAN products.

In this regard, a number of areas have already been identified as potential areas to diversify Brunei Darussalam's economy further, including tourism, Islamic banking, halal food production, fisheries, agriculture, and renewable energy, amongst others. The challenge for Brunei Darussalam, therefore, is to achieve full utility in realizing the ASEAN Economic Community by 2015 by leveraging commitments made within ASEAN in order to expand Brunei Darussalam's export of goods and services in these areas. In this regard, as many of these targeted areas are still in their very early stages of development, Brunei Darussalam must take a more proactive stance when dealing with ASEAN's commitments in areas of potential interest.

The country needs to strengthen its economic competitiveness vis-à-vis ASEAN member states. Given the relatively high value of the Brunei dollar (which is pegged to the Singapore dollar), as well as the high cost of living in Brunei Darussalam (when compared with its immediate neighbours of Malaysia, Indonesia, and the Philippines), operations costs in Brunei Darussalam tend to be higher than in other ASEAN member states, resulting in more expensive goods and services. In addition to this, given that its industrial development outside oil and gas remains minimal, Brunei Darussalam must work towards achieving the necessary economies of scale to ensure full utilization of resources and optimal supply. In this regard, the challenge for Brunei Darussalam is to carve out for itself niche markets where it can export high-quality products, the demand for which remain inelastic, and therefore, not affected by higher costs.

In order to take full advantage of the benefits of the ASEAN Trade in Goods Agreement (ATIGA) and the cumulation principles under agreements of ASEAN's rules of origin, another challenge for Brunei Darussalam is its ability to integrate itself into the regional supply networks. Given the small size of the country, and its limited capacity to utilize natural resources (e.g., non-abundant supply of metals, restrictions on felling trees for wood, and quarrying stone), Brunei Darussalam must import raw materials from external sources to ensure that it can manufacture products that can be exported to the region. However, this is one area that has yet to be given greater consideration.

Additionally, Brunei Darussalam has committed itself to improving the coordination of standards development, conformity assessment and accreditation, quality assurance, measurement, and productivity, through the establishment of the National Standards Council, which has identified these areas as being crucial to promoting greater efficiency and enhancing cost effectiveness of products of intraregional imports/exports. It should be noted that despite the lack of a developed standards body, Brunei Darussalam is a member of many international and regional standards and accreditation forums. As is evident from the high percentage of national standards adopted from international standards, Brunei Darussalam is also promoting adoption or direct use of international standards and the acceptance of certificates issued by certification and accreditation bodies in the regional and international arenas. This policy will facilitate trade and ensure that there are no unnecessary trade barriers introduced. In addressing the concerns of better national coordination, the Government of Brunei Darussalam is in the process of developing a "standards" law.

Another fundamental area that must be addressed is the implementation of ASEAN's commitments such as those under the ASEAN Trade in Goods Agreement and ensuring that there is enough publicity on the benefits of these agreements to Bruneian consumers. Initial studies on the utilization of certificate of origin forms for Brunei's preferential agreements tend to indicate that a large number of Brunei's exporters do not take advantage of the benefits conferred in its FTAs. As a result, Brunei Darussalam's Ministry of Foreign Affairs is embarking on a national communications plan to create awareness of the benefits of the country's preferential trade agreements, in a bid to increase the utilization of certificate of origin forms. Furthermore, work is also being undertaken to address soft infrastructure, such as national policies and frameworks, and to ease trade facilitation for products being imported into and exported out of Brunei Darussalam.

### Free Flow of Services

Under this chapter of the blueprint, ASEAN member states are required to liberalize substantially all four modes of services based on sectors in the WTO's GATS W/120 document, by 2015, albeit with certain pre-agreed measures and flexibilities in place. Brunei Darussalam has completed seven packages under AFAS to date. Presumably, the next package of commitments becomes increasingly difficult to achieve due to the further liberalization of commitments beyond the status quo that has provided regulators with some level of comfort over the years.

In 1995, Brunei's accession to the WTO marked its first foray into services liberalization, three years later in 1998, AFAS was introduced as a WTO-plus agreement on the regional track.

Services liberalization cannot be addressed in isolation from other forms of liberalization and economic cooperation. In addition to the lack of capacity and absence of policies/regulations related to services liberalization, there is a need to strengthen Brunei's infrastructure incidental to the services industry and to increase FDI inflows in tandem. Brunei will also have to review its policies on the movement of natural persons to ensure the free flow of services suppliers and tourists.

In the long run, Brunei's long-term development plan, Wawasan 2035, aims to establish Brunei as a knowledge-based economy, diversifying from the heavy reliance on the oil hydrocarbon industry into other industries. Brunei has since taken concrete steps towards prioritizing capacity building programmes through the recent establishment of the Department of Human Resources under the Department of Economic Planning and Development of the Prime Minister's Office. In ASEAN, numerous capacity building workshops have been held and there are ongoing studies to aid member states on their path towards AEC 2015.

### *Free Flow of Investment*

As Brunei Darussalam embarks on its path towards economic diversification away from the oil and gas sectors, the emerging Brunei Darussalam is predominantly outward looking and attractive to foreign direct investment. In addition to the country's open investment regime, with few limitations in sectors involving local natural resources and those relating to food security, many efforts to increase FDI inflows into Brunei have been taken through bilateral, plurilateral, and regional forums.

The AEC Blueprint calls for four strategic approaches to be taken to ensure the free flow of investments: liberalization, facilitation, promotion, and protection. Whilst Brunei Darussalam has no real difficulty in implementing the measures necessary for facilitation, promotion, and protection as prescribed in the blueprint, it may face some challenges in moving towards realizing a free and open investment regime with minimal restrictions by 2015.

Firstly, Brunei Darussalam is a developing economy with an embryonic private sector which mostly comprises small and medium enterprises (SMEs). In this regard, it is a challenge for the nation to guarantee a balance between its national interest in maintaining the growth of its local SMEs and increased foreign investment inflows into the country, without the latter crowding out local businesses. Secondly, investment activities are governed by administrative policies and guidelines as Brunei Darussalam does not have an investment law. This lack of a regulatory framework may present some difficulty as the country has to identify to what extent it can liberalize its sectors. It also realized that this may create a sense of unpredictability for investors as the absence of laws may leave some margin for administrative discretion.

Despite these drawbacks, Brunei Darussalam continuously endeavours to improve its business environment. Sectoral ministries and agencies have implemented several improved measures which facilitate the setting up of businesses. Information on doing business is also published and disseminated to the public through relevant agencies and the country's overseas foreign missions.

The respective agreements, including the ACIA, also aim to create a conducive environment for private sector development through ASEAN's commitment to promote and facilitate investments by, among other things, encouraging the growth of SMEs, enhancing industrial complementation and production networks, and streamlining and simplifying procedures for investment applications and approvals. There have also been simultaneous public outreach exercises which highlighted to the private sector these intentions as well as the benefits of FDI inflow into Brunei, which include transfer of technology and expertise, increased employment, and positive spillover effects.

### Freer Flow of Capital

Brunei Darussalam has progressed steadily towards liberalizing its capital account regime and financial services in tandem with the aspirations of the rest of the ASEAN member states.

With regard to financial services liberalization and capital account liberalization, Brunei Darussalam has already made some inroad into substantially removing restrictions for subsectors identified for liberalization by 2015. The rationale for this liberalization is in adherence to the main principle of the AEC Blueprint, which is to create a single market within an economic region that is highly competitive and fully integrated into the global economy. In this context, the challenges in meeting the commitments towards AEC by 2015 that relate to "free flow of capital" and "liberalisation of financial services commitments" that Brunei Darussalam faces are similar to those of developing countries. To meet these challenges it is important to ensure that liberalization is pursued in a systematic and orderly manner so as to sustain a sound and stable financial sector. To this end, Brunei Darussalam is building the necessary human and financial capacity as well as other associated infrastructure to address the impediments associated with liberalization in terms of regulations, supervision, monitoring systems, and ancillary services. Conversely, Brunei is also ready to reap the benefits of liberalization. However, above all, it still considers the interests of domestic industries of the utmost importance while remaining cognizant that they should not be detrimental to the development of the AEC.

### Free Flow of Skilled Labour

Like its neighbour, Singapore, Brunei Darussalam maintains a relatively open regime when dealing with the free flow of skilled labour. One of the underlying factors for having an open regime is that there remains a significant imbalance between the skills of the domestic labour force and the labour skills that are required. Brunei Darussalam's small population, while considered highly educated, does not necessarily have sufficient local experts in many specific fields, e.g., specialized doctors, and, as such, needs to maintain such an open regime. However, that said, to reduce the country's growing dependence on foreign labour and to address concerns of rising unemployment,[3] there has been a growing preference to hire Brunei nationals over foreign nationals. Despite this, there have not been any changes to national legislation or regulations which would restrict the free flow of skilled labour into the country.

## Competitive Economic Region

In order to develop the ASEAN region into a competitive economic region, ASEAN member states are to focus on six areas: competition policy, consumer protection, intellectual property rights (IPR), infrastructure development, taxation, and e-commerce. However, for the purposes of this chapter, focus will be placed on the challenges presented by competition policy, consumer protection, IPR, and infrastructure development.

### Competition Policy

Albeit small and developing, Brunei is an economy that is relatively open towards trade and foreign direct investment. The country acknowledges the positive benefits that can be garnered through having efficient competition, such as a more efficient market, variety in choices, as well as enhanced consumer welfare.

Efforts towards enhancing competition, or even more, towards promoting fair competition, still leave much to do. At present there is yet to be an overarching body that reviews the issue of competition and anticompetitive behaviour at the national level. Thus far, competition issues in Brunei have only been addressed on a sector-by-sector basis, with different bodies of authority being held responsible for monitoring and regulating the activities of players in their respective sectors. These include sectors such as banking and finance, oil and gas, as well as the telecommunications sector. In addressing competition, economic regulations, which are more administrative in nature, are more prevalent. These include the use of the Price Control Act, the control of entry and exit of firms through the issuance of licences, and other administrative measures.

Competition policy and law is a relatively new topic in Brunei. The major challenge is in advocating the benefits and opportunities arising from a national competition policy and law. Therefore, there is an urgent need to widen advocacy and awareness efforts among relevant stakeholders to allow them to understand better the issues revolving around competition policy and law (such as basic knowledge, benefits of competition, impact towards economic development, etc.).

The small and unique structure of the Brunei economy also warrants more preliminary research and studies to be done, as it may not be able to assimilate directly from the experiences of other economies that may have a more advanced or larger economic market. Further studies into the structure of the economy can hence help to determine the appropriate strategy and identify the right priorities in pursuing the development of a national competition policy and law for the country.

In addition, Brunei is also facing a lack of human resources in terms of numbers, skills, and expertise that would be required to establish a sound institutional foundation for a national competition policy and law.

Nonetheless, in recognizing the potential positive benefits of such, Brunei is progressing towards the development of a competition policy and law for the nation. Recent progress includes the implementation of the Privatization Master Plan (PMP) which was due to be completed by the end of 2010. The Master Plan will provide opportunities for the injection of more competition into the economy and will pave the way for a platform to review the "competition structure" of the Brunei economy.

Also, in line with its strong support for and commitment towards the achievement of the AEC Blueprint, Brunei has been taking an active role in the building of its capacity and knowledge for competition and competition-related matters. The country is an active member of the "ASEAN Experts Group on Competition (AEGC)" that has provided a much useful platform for enhancing skills and understanding, as well as for the sharing of related experiences among member states. In addition, Brunei has also been involved in initiatives towards the development of a competition policy and law in other international forums such as APEC, which also benefits Brunei, especially in terms of capacity building and the various forms of technical assistance currently offered.

### Consumer Protection

Brunei Darussalam's capacity in addressing the issue of consumer protection remains institutionally weak. Although the AEC Blueprint only calls for the formation of the ASEAN Coordinating Committee on Consumer Protection that would facilitate information exchange and consumer leaders, there is the realization that consumer protection is a vital part of the country's work to realize the ASEAN Economic Community, particularly in ensuring that the benefits of a single market and production base will flow on to local consumers. In this regard, it should be noted that the Emergency [Price Control Act] [Amendment] Order 1999 provides for the establishment of a National Advisory Council for Consumer Protection, although this has yet to be established. However, current laws do exist as they relate to fraud, advertising and marketing, sale of goods, and unfair contract terms. Furthermore, legislation is currently being drafted to establish consumer protection laws in Brunei Darussalam.

### E-Commerce

The AEC Scorecard commits ASEAN member states to lay the policy and legal infrastructure for electronic commerce, as well as to enable online trade in goods within ASEAN through the implementation of the e-ASEAN Framework Agreement, based on common reference frameworks. In response to this, a commercial code for electronic transactions was enacted in the Electronic Transactions Order 2000,[4] which draws from the UNCITRAL (United Nations Commission on International Trade Law) Model Law on Electronic Commerce and the Singapore Electronic Transactions Act, itself based on the U.S. Uniform Electronic Transactions Act.

However, the challenge for Brunei Darussalam is to enhance inter-agency coordination — given the cross-sectoral characteristics of e-commerce — to deal adequately with developments under e-commerce. Furthermore, there is a need to develop the private sector's interest in this area.[5] Factors that have been cited as deterrents to using e-commerce in Brunei Darussalam include a lack of perceived advantage of e-commerce over traditional means of commerce, lack of knowledge on how e-commerce is utilized, and perceived lack of trust. These are significant inhibitors, while environment characteristics such as competitive pressure and government support are significant motivators of electronic commerce in Brunei Darussalam. In light of this, the government is continuing to enhance its capacity in e-commerce to encourage uptake within the country.

### Intellectual Property Rights

Under the AEC Blueprint, Brunei Darussalam has focused on the creation, commercialization, and protection of intellectual property. The real challenge for the country is that it remains a net consumer as opposed to a net producer of intellectual property, and, as such, the gaps in development and incentives between Brunei Darussalam and the other ASEAN-6 countries must be bridged. This, admittedly, would be a difficult task as SMEs (which make up most of Brunei's private sector) which are most likely to create intellectual property assets and, therefore, would most likely benefit from intellectual property rights, lack the awareness of intellectual property protection. Furthermore, it should be noted that Brunei Darussalam is in the process of drafting amendments to its copyright law which was finalized in 2010.

That said, Brunei Darussalam is continuing to pursue its commitments under the AEC Blueprint, focusing on making the registration process more effective and convenient, as well as harmonizing its processes and supporting efforts to improve the effectiveness of intellectual property rights protection. It is expected that Brunei Darussalam will be able to achieve its commitments under the AEC Blueprint.

### Infrastructure Development

Under the AEC Blueprint, ASEAN member states are expected to engage in infrastructure development, which focuses on land transport, maritime and air transport, and information infrastructure. For Brunei

Darussalam, there is recognition that its infrastructure must be upgraded to ensure that the full benefits from the integrated ASEAN Economic Community are realized.

In this regard, the Government of Brunei Darussalam has been actively engaged in further enhancing its physical infrastructure development as part of its national development plan towards Wawasan 2035. Specific projects that have been identified and are in the process of being realized include the development of a world-class shipping port in Muara and an expansion of the existing Brunei International Airport.

Part of the challenge for Brunei Darussalam is to ensure the full use of the regulatory measures that have been agreed to at the regional level, specifically the agreements on multimodal transport and the facilitation of goods in transit. Furthermore, Brunei Darussalam needs to identify areas within its national boundaries where bottlenecks in transport and logistics infrastructure occur and work with its regional partners to overcome them. As such, the newly targeted ASEAN initiative to enhance connectivity within the region is seen as one way to overcome the challenges that have been presented. Through an agreement to enhance connectivity by addressing both soft and hard connectivity issues, it is thought that Brunei Darussalam can work further together with its neighbours and within its own government agencies to enhance the full benefits of ASEAN economic integration.

## Equitable Economic Development

Brunei Darussalam remains committed to achieving equitable economic development within ASEAN. Its interest in this area focuses on the importance of supporting its small and medium enterprises, as well as the need to address imbalances at a subregional level, specifically under the Brunei-Indonesia-Malaysia-Philippines–East ASEAN Growth Area (BIMP-EAGA).

### SME Development

As part of its commitments under the AEC, Brunei Darussalam is continuing to spearhead efforts to create opportunities for its local SMEs through integrating them within global supply networks. Despite SMEs constituting approximately 98 per cent of all firms within Brunei

Darussalam, the small size of its domestic market is one of the biggest challenges to developing the capacity and capabilities of SMEs within the country.

In the context of Brunei Darussalam, SMEs are defined as those enterprises having one to a hundred employees, which make up around 98.37 per cent of the nation's total business establishments, provide about 48.5 per cent of all businesses in the country, and 92 per cent of employment in the private sector.

Statistics show that 50 per cent of businesses in Brunei are made up of micro enterprises that have one to five employees; small enterprises (46 per cent) that have six to fifty employees, and 2.5 per cent of medium enterprises that have fifty-one to a hundred employees. According to the 2008 statistical information received from the Labour Department, Ministry of Home Affairs, there were 9,150 active business establishments in all sectors in the country compared with 7,716 in 2006. Thus SMEs have been recognized as an important partner in realizing the country's goal of economic diversification and a potential contributor to its socio-economic development.

Most SMEs within the country are family-run businesses that have neither the desire nor experience to expand their reach beyond Brunei Darussalam into global supply networks. However, the government is making strides to address this issue, particularly with regard to food security. The Ministry of Industry and Primary Resources plays a significant role in its economic diversification startegy by adopting the niche approach (high technology, high value, value adding, export oriented, import substitution, and environmentally friendly) through a priority list for preferred industrial activities such as agriculture, fisheries, forestry, manufacturing, services, hospitality, and tourism to achieve its vision to make Brunei Darussalam a diversified, competitive, and sustainable economy.

A strong, dynamic, and efficient SME sector will ensure sustainable, inclusive, and broad-based economic and social development. A vibrant SME sector is critical in supporting closer regional integration through the establishment of the ASEAN Community, particularly the AEC. Thus, the encouragement and promotion of competitive and innovative SMEs are necessary in contributing to greater economic growth and social development towards a more inclusive and broad-based integration of the ASEAN region.

The SME sector in ASEAN, however, is confronted with a wide range of structural, financial, and other challenges, among which are limited access to finance, technologies, and markets. There is also the question of entrepreneurial spirit and management skills among ASEAN SMEs. These problems are compounded by the lack of information, inadequate capacity for compliance with standards and certification, and the absence of a more conducive business and policy environment.

### Narrowing the Development Gap

Brunei Darussalam is supportive of ASEAN's efforts to narrow the development gap, which it does not only see as limited to the work undertaken for the Initiative for ASEAN Integration (IAI) that supports the productive capacity of the newer ASEAN member states. In addition to this, Brunei Darussalam, as a member of the subregional grouping of the BIMP-EAGA, has taken a keen interest in enhancing the welfare and income distribution within these areas as well.

However, despite the best efforts to realize the AEC goals within the BIMP-EAGA subregion, this goal is not without its own challenges. One common problem that Brunei Darussalam faces, being the only member with its entire territory as part of BIMP-EAGA, is that decisions which have been made at the regional level, among all ten ASEAN member states, have been difficult to apply within a subregional setting. For example, decisions by ASEAN member states to expand linkages and support greater participation in global supply networks, have often been met with a lack of political support within the subregion that, in turn, has stifled the impact of such reforms, hence reducing the ability to tackle adequately issues such as poverty and increase business opportunities as provided for under the AEC. This issue remains of particular concern for Brunei's desire to support its SMEs, which, when considering to expand their businesses, look to neighbouring areas.

## Integration with the Global Economy

Brunei Darussalam remains a strong supporter of ASEAN's integration with the global economy. While the small size of Brunei's economy results in little interest from many countries in engaging in free trade agreements with it on a bilateral basis, Brunei Darussalam's participation in ASEAN presents an opportunity to negotiate market access to many countries and regional groupings, which would otherwise remain difficult for the country to access.

The real challenge for Brunei Darussalam is to ensure that it can effectively enhance its participation in global supply networks, with a strong dedication to the adoption of best international practices and standards through ASEAN's integration into the global economy. While there remain a few barriers to adopting best international practices and standards, Brunei Darussalam needs to diversify its economy away from its reliance on oil and gas to ensure that it can participate in other areas of the global supply network. Although local industry outside of oil and gas remains small, Brunei Darussalam must find other areas in which it can participate in the global supply chain, and, as noted earlier, the development of its small and medium enterprises which are export oriented is one way for the country to enhance its participation further.

## Conclusion

Brunei Darussalam is working hard to achieve the ASEAN Economic Community by 2015; however, challenges to realize the benefits fully remain, both on a regulatory level as well as in implementation. While the small size of its economy and specialized areas of trade can be perceived as inhibiting factors for the country to realize the full benefits of economic integration, the small size of the economy also gives it an opportunity to overcome many of the regulatory hurdles to ensure the full benefits of the ASEAN Economic Community by 2015. Furthermore, prudent measures and initiatives being undertaken by the Government of Brunei Darussalam are expected to develop the country's capability further to engage actively within both regional and global supply networks, as well as position Brunei Darussalam as one of the most efficient markets within the region.

### NOTES

1. Approximately 390,000 people.
2. US$53,100 in 2008.

3. Estimated to be 3.7 per cent in 2010.
4. The Electronic Transactions Order 2000 was approved by His Majesty the Sultan of Brunei on 20 November 2000 and published by the government on 16 December 2000.
5. Hong Cheong Looi, "E-Commerce Adoption in Brunei Darussalam: A Quantitative Analysis of Factors Influencing its Adoption". Institut Teknologi Brunei.

# 4

# Achieving the AEC 2015: Challenges for Cambodia and its Businesses

Chan Sophal and Larry Strange*

## Cambodia's Economic Development

Over the past decade, Cambodia enjoyed high annual economic growth of around 8 per cent on average (Figure 4.1). More impressive, for four consecutive years (2004–07), the real gross domestic product (GDP) grew at a two-digit rate. The growth impetus chiefly came from the industry sector, which was supported by substantial increases in the garment and construction subsectors, and from the services sector. The services sector saw substantial increases in tourism and real estate until the impact of the global financial crisis and economic downturn. At times, the agriculture sector also contributed significantly to growth, and this had largely been driven by weather conditions.

**FIGURE 4.1**
**GDP Growth**

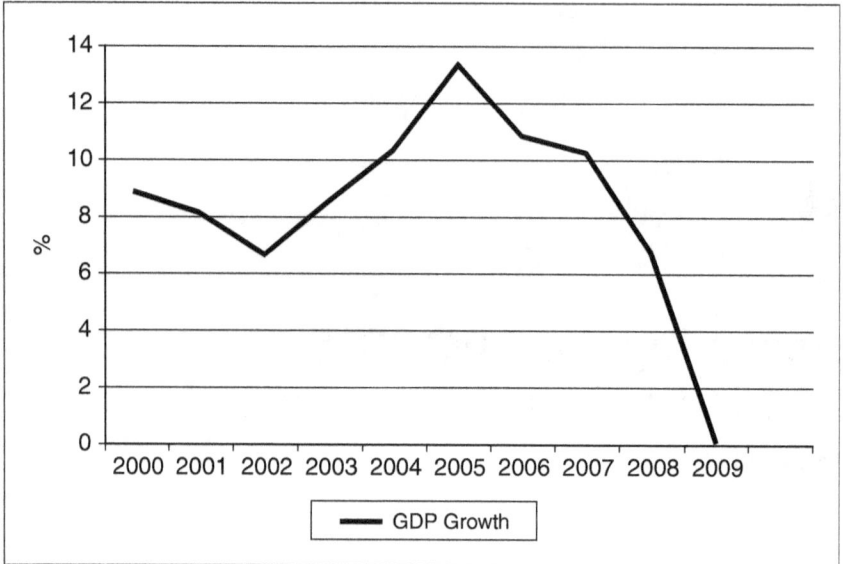

*Source:* Authors' calculations based on data from MEF.

Cambodia's agriculture accounted for about 30 per cent of GDP and employed more than half of the labour force from 2004 to 2007 (Table 4.1). The real value-added of this sector expanded by 6.2 per cent and contributed 1.1 percentage points to the overall GDP growth over the same period. In general, the growth rate of the agriculture sector remains highly variable, marked by peaks and troughs, reflecting the high reliance on adequate rainfall, which is erratic. However, it increasingly plays a significant role in supporting rural people, where most still rely on paddy cultivation for subsistence.

The industrial sector, which constitutes only about a quarter of GDP, given its small base, exhibited very high growth at an annual rate of 13.9 per cent from 2004 to 2007. The mining subsector, the manufacturing (mostly garments), the electricity, gas, and water, and the construction subsectors increased by 18.3 per cent, 13.4 per cent, 16.4 per cent, and 15.3 per cent, respectively.

The services sector, which accounts for about 45 per cent of GDP, rose by 11.6 per cent over the golden period of 2004–07, thanks to

TABLE 4.1
Sectoral Growth from 2004 to 2007

| | Growth Rate | | | | Share of GDP | | | |
|---|---|---|---|---|---|---|---|---|
| | 2004–07* | 2007 | 2008 | 2009 | 2004–07 | 2007 | 2008 | 2009 |
| Agriculture | 6.2% | 5.0% | 5.7% | 5.4% | 28.1% | 26.7% | 26.5% | 27.9% |
| Crops | 9.2% | 8.2% | 6.6% | 5.8% | 14.1% | 14.0% | 14.0% | 14.8% |
| Livestock & Poultry | 5.3% | 3.7% | 3.8% | 5.0% | 4.5% | 4.2% | 4.1% | 4.3% |
| Fisheries | 2.1% | 0.8% | 6.5% | 6.0% | 7.4% | 6.6% | 6.6% | 7.0% |
| Forestry & Logging | 3.5% | 1.1% | 0.9% | 1.1% | 2.1% | 1.9% | 1.8% | 1.8% |
| Industry | 13.9% | 8.4% | 4.0% | –9.5% | 27.7% | 28.2% | 27.5% | 24.8% |
| Mining | 18.3% | 7.7% | 15.8% | 20.0% | 0.4% | 0.4% | 0.4% | 0.5% |
| Manufacturing | 13.4% | 8.9% | 3.1% | –15.5% | 20.3% | 20.5% | 19.8% | 16.7% |
| Electricity, Gas & Water | 16.4% | 11.5% | 8.5% | 8.5% | 0.5% | 0.6% | 0.6% | 0.6% |
| Construction | 15.3% | 6.7% | 5.8% | 5.0% | 6.5% | 6.7% | 6.6% | 6.9% |
| Services | 11.6% | 10.1% | 9.0% | 2.3% | 38.4% | 38.3% | 39.1% | 40.0% |
| Trade | 7.7% | 9.5% | 9.4% | 4.2% | 8.6% | 8.4% | 8.6% | 8.9% |
| Hotel & Restaurants | 17.3% | 10.2% | 9.8% | 1.8% | 4.3% | 4.4% | 4.6% | 4.7% |
| Transport & Communications | 8.3% | 7.2% | 7.1% | 3.9% | 6.4% | 6.1% | 6.1% | 6.3% |
| Finance | 21.5% | 22.2% | 19.2% | 8.0% | 1.2% | 1.4% | 1.6% | 1.7% |
| Public Administration | –0.6% | 0.1% | 4.5% | 1.0% | 1.4% | 1.2% | 1.2% | 1.2% |
| Real Estate & Business | 12.3% | 10.7% | 5.0% | –2.5% | 7.7% | 7.6% | 7.5% | 7.3% |
| Other services | 16.4% | 12.1% | 12.0% | 2.9% | 8.7% | 9.1% | 9.6% | 9.8% |
| Taxes on Products less Subsidies | 20.7% | 45.7% | 9.1% | 6.1% | 6.8% | 8.0% | 8.2% | 8.6% |
| Less: Subsidies | –11.1% | –68.3% | 1.5% | 1.9% | 0.3% | 0.1% | 0.1% | 0.1% |
| Less: Finance Service Charge | 17.3% | 25.0% | 14.0% | 12.0% | 1.0% | 1.1% | 1.2% | 1.3% |
| Total GDP | 11.1% | 10.2% | 6.7% | 0.1% | 100% | 100% | 100% | 100% |

*Note:* * computed using geometric mean.
*Source:* Authors' calculation based on data from MEF.

the expansion in trade, real estate business, hotels and restaurants, and other services. These subsectors, which directly benefited from tourism growth, infrastructure development, and the overall boom in the economy, grew by 7.7 per cent, 17.3 per cent, and 16.4 per cent, respectively. The transport and communications subsector increased by 8.3 per cent, reflecting the increase in the number of tourists visiting Cambodia from 2004 to 2007. The finance subsector expanded by an annual rate of 21.5 per cent, showing a remarkable improvement in the credibility of Cambodia's banking system in recent years. Real estate became a lucrative business, posting a healthy annual growth of 12.3 per cent from 2004 to 2007.

Cambodia's balance of trade recorded a deficit of US$1,040 million per annum from 2004 to 2007. As in other years, this deficit was financed by capital inflow in the form of foreign aid and foreign direct investment (FDI). During this period, exports increased by 19.4 per cent per annum, averaging US$3,320 million or 48.2 per cent of GDP, of which domestic exports were US$3,160 million, and re-exports, US$160 million. It is important to note that only about 20 per cent of Cambodia's exports go to ASEAN countries, with the overwhelming majority of garment exports going to the United States and Europe. However, the percentage would increase substantially if the informal agricultural exports to Thailand and Vietnam were taken into account.

During the same period, total imports also increased by 18.8 per cent, reaching US$4,359 million per year, or 63.4 per cent of GDP. Retained imports were US$4,229 million, while imports for re-exports were US$131 million. As mentioned above, Cambodia's exports are underestimated because exports of agricultural products, which could be about 20 per cent of total exports, are mostly performed informally or without being recorded.[1] Total imports could also be well underestimated due to tax avoidance. So the actual openness of the Cambodian economy, which is measured by the total export volume divided by GDP, could be substantially above the 110 per cent of GDP normally reported.

To contextualize Cambodia in the region, Figure 4.2 shows that Cambodia lags behind neighbouring Vietnam, which had the same level of GDP per capita in 1993, and far behind China, which also started from a similar level in 1993. Among its neighbours, Thailand and Malaysia achieved higher economic growth for decades, while Cambodia was plunged into a devastating civil war and suffered from the Khmer regime and the impact of the international embargo from the

**FIGURE 4.2**
**Cambodia's GDP per capita in comparison with its neighbours**
(US$, at current prices)

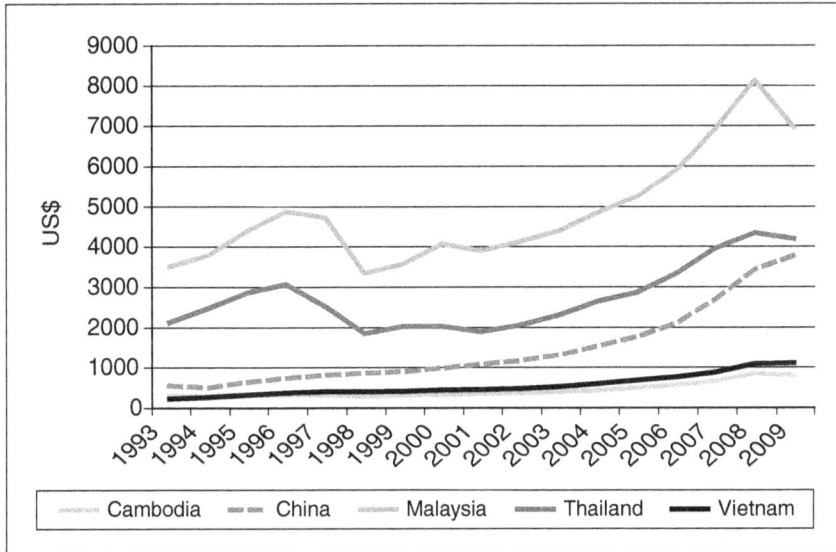

*Source: World Economic Outlook, IMF 2011.*

1970s to 1993.[2] It is projected that Cambodia needs to grow by at least 7 per cent per annum on average in order to move out of the World Bank International Development Assistance threshold (to be increased by 2 per cent annually) in the next decade, or by 2020 (Nelmes 2010).[3] It is therefore important that the Cambodian economy continues to grow at a high rate and it cannot afford a repeat of the decline of the garment industry, a fall of 16 per cent in 2009 due to the decline in U.S. consumption and demand.

## The Cambodian Economy, the Global Financial Crisis, and Recovery: Lessons and Imperatives, Opportunities and Constraints

The impact of the global economic crisis began to be felt in Cambodia in the fourth quarter of 2008. The country's narrow economic base and lack of diversification have been pointed out in many studies as a weakness in what is otherwise high growth.[4] The global crisis revealed Cambodia's vulnerability of relying too heavily on the garment industry, tourism services, and construction, all of which are too exposed to changes in foreign markets and capital flows. With demand for garments and the global tourism industry too much reliant on external factors, the Royal Government of Cambodia (RGC) has now increased attention on and investment in agricultural and rural development. An immediate achievement was the preparation of a rice production and export promotion policy, which is now being implemented. The rural sector has a lot to offer in terms of development potential because Cambodia's agriculture sector offers vast potential for increased productivity, the expansion of cultivated areas, and the improvement of processing capabilities.

As the impact of the global financial crisis deepened in Cambodia, the first semester of 2009 saw FDI, approved in terms of fixed assets, decrease to only 11 per cent of the total amount in 2008. It is, however, interesting to observe a significant increase in licensed FDI in the agriculture sector, while approvals for the industry and services sectors fell remarkably in 2009 and 2010. This supports the argument that Cambodia has a huge potential in developing its agriculture.[5]

The credit crunch in the international market and the loss of assets and capital among wealthy individual investors, as well as firms around the world, resulted directly in less capital being invested in Cambodia, although it is still regarded as a promising emerging economy. For instance, Leopard Capital, the first multisector investment fund in Cambodia, aimed and expected to raise US$100 million over the one-year period from April 2008 to April 2009. By the extended closing date of December 2009, the fund had managed to mobilize only US$34 million, although this was applauded as a success in the wake of the global financial and economic crisis. The global financial crisis had hit Korea hard and Cambodia had subsequently seen a large reduction or suspension of Korean investment projects. Some mega real estate projects by Korean firms were suspended, which was a setback for the construction industry in Cambodia.

The Royal Government of Cambodia was swift in responding to the negative impact of the global economic recession through both fiscal and monetary policy. In terms of fiscal policies, the RGC decided to run a high budget deficit of 4.8 per cent of GDP in 2009, and considered it a form of stimulus package. It ended up incurring a deficit of 6.4 per cent of GDP, much higher than planned, as revenue fell short of expectations. For similar reasons, the overall budget deficit continued to be high, at 5.9 per cent of GDP in 2010. Moreover, in order to save the garment industry, hard hit by the substantial fall of demand in the U.S. market, the RGC suspended the monthly turnover tax of one per cent on garment factory expenditures and extended the profit tax holiday, at least for garment factories established prior to 2006.

A special fund was set up to provide rice mills with more space to buy and process paddy for export. In addition to some other fiscal interventions, the RGC took monetary measures through the National Bank of Cambodia. A couple of examples are the decrease of the reserve requirements of commercial banks from 16 per cent to 12 per cent (after raising it from 8 per cent to curb the spiking inflation in the first half of 2008) and the lifting of the 15 per cent cap on real estate lending as conditions opened up some room for monetary easing. The RGC interventions seemed to work in preventing the Cambodian economy from contracting too seriously in 2009 and helping it recover well in 2010.

Nevertheless, there are important lessons to be learned from the global financial crisis, as pointed out in various previous studies. The World Bank has put forward three main messages for sustaining growth in Cambodia. Firstly, the economic growth of the past decade is unlikely to be sustainable in its current form. Secondly, with a focused growth strategy to increase competitiveness and diversify the economy, Cambodia can achieve sustainable growth. Thirdly, Cambodia is blessed with three important opportunities: harnessing the benefits of regional integration; managing natural resources in a sustainable way; and investing in its future (through agriculture, infrastructure, education, and higher savings).[6]

A recent UNDP study (2009) reveals that Cambodia's competitiveness indicators are among the lowest in the region in many fields, including skills and human resources, technology, infrastructure, regulations, and institutions. The study recommends that in addition to improving on these aspects, a new set of policies be established to consolidate growth in agriculture, the garment industry, tourism, and construction. These include embarking on a more proactive human resource development policy, a more targeted approach in industrial and investment policy (rethinking the Special Economic Zones or SEZs), a targeted infrastructure policy, and reducing corruption.[7]

The major development challenge facing Cambodia is how to broaden high economic growth and sustain it for a long period of time so that poverty reduction and human development can reach a robust level. Cambodia's poverty rate is still high at about 27 per cent in 2008, although it declined significantly from 47 per cent in 1993/4. However, about half of the population does not live far above the poverty line. For both quicker poverty reduction and more inclusive economic growth, agriculture has been identified as a promising sector. In this vein, a rice production and export policy has been prepared recently to realize the potential to process at least half of the paddy surplus for export. It is imperative that Cambodia successfully pass the transformation from resource-based growth to one that is based on capital accumulation and human resources improvement. For this purpose, quality education is indispensable. Currently the quality of education lags behind quantitative targets because the emphasis is on the "education for all" campaign to succeed.

Private sector development has been recognized as the engine of growth. However, it has been facing costly hurdles ranging from high energy costs to lack of property titles to bureaucracy costs. Infrastructure development, essential irrigation systems, roads, rails, bridges, energy, and ports are of paramount importance and a top priority for Cambodia. The energy sector remains largely undeveloped and thus access to electricity is restricted to mostly urban people. Due to its reliance on fossil fuels as the source of energy, electricity costs in Cambodia are way above those in neighbouring countries, making processing costs high and, in turn, fewer investment opportunities realized. Fortunately, however, a few hydropower projects have been constructed, mostly by Chinese aid, but have not been significant enough to reduce the price of electricity. Many rail, road, bridge, and irrigation projects are in the pipeline, thanks to aid and grants from both traditional and non-traditional donors (China and South Korea) and, to a certain extent, private sector investment in infrastructure projects. When infrastructure development speeds up, private sector and economic development will find it easier to realize their potential for expansion. It is crucially important to transform much of Cambodia's private sector, which is still characterized by the overwhelming presence of microenterprises, mostly informal. There should be increased incentives for firms to become formal, pay taxes, and have accounts and balance sheets that are properly audited. Efforts to transform the informal to formal ways of practising businesses will put Cambodia on the right track of a new phase of high economic growth and sustainable development.

## Cambodia's Private Sector: Its Role, Character, and Interaction with Government and Policymaking

The Cambodian Government regards the private sector as playing a key role in driving economic growth, reflecting a transition from a centrally planned to a market-oriented economy in the early 1990s. Twenty years later, the private sector in Cambodia is still generally characterized by micro, small-scale, and family-based enterprises, with the exception of the garment industry and a few large corporations. Micro-enterprises employing one to ten people accounted for 97 per cent of the 63,507 firms counted in the census commissioned by the World Bank's International Finance Corporation (IFC) and the Asia Foundation in 2008. The official nationwide Establishment Listing of Cambodia from 9 February to 8 March 2009 conducted by the National Institute of Statistics found 375,095 establishments in the whole country. Wage employment accounts for only 20 per cent of total employment. The overwhelming majority of micro and small enterprises poses a huge challenge for coordination in relation to ASEAN affairs, among other things. The informal nature of the businesses poses a constraint to banks and investment funds, which need sound paperwork and credible accounts against their lending or co-investment. The opportunities for increased trade and investment through regional integration and globalization are real if such constraints are reduced or removed.

The garment industry is by far the leading industry in terms of exports and coordination to reap benefits from a tax holiday from the government, global markets, and regional production chains within ASEAN countries. The industry picked up in 1998 and grew by more than two digits almost every year until 2008 when it declined sharply for the first time to –9 per cent due to the demand in the U.S. markets plummeting following the severe financial crisis and economic downturn. Cambodia's garment production and exports bounced back very well in 2010, although the industry was hindered by massive and prolonged strikes over low wages around mid-year. The main source of growth for the industry was initially the export market or the most favoured nations and Generalized System of Preferences granted by the United States in 1997 and by the European Union in 1996. The U.S. market has absorbed about 70 per cent of the total garments and textile exports from Cambodia, with the bulk of the rest going to the European Union, Canada, and Japan. At its peak in late 2008, the garment industry employed 360,000 workers, mostly young female workers from rural villages, in almost 300 factories.

The central mechanism for private sector interaction with the RGC is the Government–Private Sector Forum, which has been held biannually since 1999. Supported by and rated the best in the world by IFC, the forum is actively chaired by the Prime Minister of Cambodia, who may make decisions in the meeting in response to prepared requests by the eight working groups of the private sector.

The eight working groups listed below are each co-chaired by a prominent business leader and the most relevant minister. The business representatives in each working group meet among themselves a couple of times a year under the co-chairship of the private sector to report problems or obstacles in doing business and in ensuring a positive, enabling environment for private sector development and investment. They alternately meet with their government counterparts to report problems and recommendations and seek solutions from the responsible government institutions. If unsolved, outstanding issues are reported to the Prime Minister during the biannual Government Private Sector Forum. The eight government–private sector working groups are as follows.

1. Agriculture and Agro-industry
2. Tourism
3. Manufacturing and Small and Medium Enterprises
4. Law, Tax, and Governance
5. Banking and Financial Services
6. Export Processing and Trade Facilitation
7. Energy, Transport, and Infrastructure
8. Industrial Relations.

The forum and its working groups, supported by the IFC, have been very positively evaluated as an effective mechanism for government–private sector consultation and engagement on national regulatory and policy issues of central interest to the private sector. However, a review of the agendas and associated documents generated by the forum and its working groups, as confirmed by interviewees, reveals that ASEAN or GMS, regional or subregional, economic or business issues are seldom considered.

## Cambodian "Preparedness" for AEC 2015

Achieving the ASEAN Economic Community by 2015 involves progress in the implementation of reform measures in relation to specific "key deliverables" by ASEAN member state economies. These cover measures in relation to free flow of goods, free flow of services, the free flow of investment, freer flow of capital, and "hard and soft" transport and infrastructure development.

According to the Cambodian Ministry of Commerce, the latest status report, published in July 2010, on the implementation of key measures to be fully implemented by all ASEAN members states, for the period January 2008 to December 2009, assesses Cambodia as having achieved "70% compliance" with key deliverables of AEC, and being currently "ranked 3rd in ASEAN" in its implementation record. This excludes some special provisions under the free flow of goods measures for the CLMVs (Cambodia, Lao PDR, Myanmar, and Vietnam), such as the timetable for operationalizing a National Single Window as a building block for the ASEAN Single Window.

Cambodia's slowness in translating ASEAN legal documents into the Khmer language for ratification by its National Assembly has prevented Cambodia from achieving more on the scorecard. There are also some unresolved issues in its aviation industry, and, apart for the garment industry, still unresolved issues on the free flow of goods and people, both "formally" and "informally" across borders.

Officials of the Ministry of Commerce, while very positive about Cambodia's performance assessment against the AEC Scorecard, freely acknowledge that this strong performance is more the result of the general "openness" of the Cambodian economy, especially compared with some other ASEAN economies, Cambodia's 2004 accession to the World Trade Organization (WTO), and its very demanding compliance programme, rather than specific responses to AEC compliance measures.

## Cambodian Private-Sector Awareness and Engagement in ASEAN and AEC Processes

Despite effective national government–private sector consultation and engagement mechanisms in Cambodia, interviews with Ministry of Commerce senior officials responsible for ASEAN economic integration and AEC issues, IFC facilitators of the Government–Private Sector Forum working groups, and selected business leaders co-chairing the related working groups, suggest that private sector awareness and engagement in ASEAN and AEC processes, and the involvement of other relevant parts of the government, are, at best, very uneven and generally very weak. There is low or uneven knowledge on the implications of the AEC and its potential benefits, no reliable detailed analysis of Cambodian competitiveness by sector compared with other ASEAN economies, or where the most promising AEC benefits and opportunities might be found. This is a particularly critical factor for Cambodia and its private sector, given the imperatives of economic and industrial diversification and enhanced competitiveness discussed above.

Interviews with business leaders reveal that the private sector in Cambodia, except for the garment and tourism sectors, is not well networked, not well informed about ASEAN-AEC matters, and not effectively engaged in either ASEAN or GMS (Greater Mekong Subregion) processes. The few big conglomerate businesses are led by tycoons who are either playing a dual business and legislative role or are politically connected. Knowledge of ASEAN matters is very uneven among them. However, there is a strong desire to learn more about ASEAN issues and receive more accessible, useful information from relevant ASEAN bodies and their Cambodian Government focal points.

The Cambodian garment and tourism sectors, key sectors for economic growth and development, present important exceptions, with effective national leadership and coordination, and engagement with ASEAN sectoral processes. They can be seen as models for national and regional private sector collaboration and economic "community building", to be adopted by other key sectors, with resources and support from ASEAN and its development partners.

Interviews with senior officials and business leaders also reveal a "two way frustration" with current arrangements in ASEAN and GMS private sector mechanisms and issues. On the one hand, some business leaders who attend ABAC and other ASEAN and GMS meetings question their value and capacity for influencing good policy outcomes that are responsive to the day-to-day concerns of business, short notice of meetings, inaccessible and often too complex materials in English only, rather than national languages, and the lack of timely preparatory background briefings. On the other hand, senior officials complain that many business leaders have little interest or attention span on ASEAN and GMS issues, and a record of poor attendance and participation in both regional meetings and national and provincial workshops organized by the government to raise awareness of ASEAN and the GMS and their implications for business.

## The ASEAN-GMS Factor

The Cambodian private sector's engagement with and preparedness for the AEC is "complicated" by Cambodia's political membership of the GMS and its being a participant and beneficiary of the associated ADB-GMS development programme. The programme, established in 1992, comprises a complex set of initiatives to promote "connectivity", achieve socio-economic development, reduce poverty, and bridge the development gap in GMS and ASEAN in infrastructure and energy, transport, logistics and trade facilitation, environmental and natural resource management, and human resource capacity development, which are useful tools for GMS ASEAN members also in achieving the AEC. The GMS, like ASEAN, has its own complex set of multilateral government and private sector consultation and cooperation mechanisms, including a GMS Business Forum and sector-specific consultation processes.

A 2008–09 research study, "The Political Economy of Regional Integration in the GMS: A Stakeholder Analysis", hosted by UNESCAP-ARTNeT, involving research institutes in Cambodia, the Lao PDR, Thailand, Vietnam, and Yunnan province of China,[8] explored the effectiveness of these processes through a specific case study on the GMS Cross Border Transport Agreement (CBTA), and its transport and trade facilitation (TTF) aspects. It found that the complexity of ASEAN-GMS institutional arrangements, and regional economic integration strategies, priorities and initiatives, had fundamental implications for the pace and effectiveness of regional integration and for the "absorptive" and institutional capacity of GMS national and provincial governments and their private sectors, constituting "another noodle bowl" effect, which mirrors the proliferation of free trade agreements in ASEAN and the broader East Asia.

On the question of private sector awareness, consultation, and engagement on the GMS, and specifically on CBTA and associated cross-border transport and trade facilitation issues, it found a low or uneven awareness in the private sector of the value of regional and subregional integration of the CLVs in ASEAN and the GMS, and poor knowledge of mechanisms available for participation. It also found very uneven and often weak engagement in national consultative mechanisms and GMS activities for peak bodies such as national and provincial chambers of commerce and business associations, with a lack of easily accessible, up-to-date information on the value and benefits of subregional and regional integration and associated initiatives, a barrier to effective involvement and cooperation from stakeholders.

The study found uneven and often low capacity and poor resources both in the private sector (associations and peak bodies) and in some government agencies that are still working hard to build broader national institutional capacity that causes obstacles, delays, and uneven implementation of the CBTA. A strong common feature in all country cases was the finding that, if CBTA and related transport and trade facilitation were to be effective, there was a fundamental need to strengthen and seek private sector consultation and participation, with a focus on the key role of sectoral associations and chambers of commerce in regional and subregional integration mechanisms, including the GMS Business Forum. Many stakeholders also expressed concern at the limited relationship between and the integration of GMS subregional integration and TTF initiatives with the ASEAN Economic Community agenda, IAI initiatives and time frame, leading to confusion, duplication, and a waste of financial and human resources.

## Conclusion: Some Practical Measures

The experience of Cambodia suggests some practical measures that could be taken to raise private sector awareness of and participation in the achievement of an ASEAN Economic Community by 2015 and the associated subregional GMS integration and "connectivity". They include:

- The coordination and integration of ASEAN-AEC and GMS economic community, private-sector development, infrastructure and "connectivity" strategies, programmes, and initiatives — particularly the GMS programme and ASEAN's Initiatives for ASEAN Integration (IAI) — to ensure coherency and complementarity and ease the "absorptive burden" on national governments and the private sector;
- The production of easy-to-understand written and audiovisual materials on ASEAN-AEC in both English and national languages, disseminated widely to businesses in simple accessible forms and utilized in regular national business briefings for peak bodies and sectoral associations;
- Dissemination of these materials via workshops and the mass media, along with the development of ASEAN-AEC higher education curriculum materials focusing on business and management schools, in English and national languages;
- Regular, well resourced "genuine" consultation mechanisms or outreach exercises on ASEAN-AEC, using national experts and organizations in national languages wherever possible;
- The establishment of AEC sectoral coordination and support offices in the ASEAN Secretariat, building on the garment and tourism sector models and experience;
- The investment of ASEAN resources to build capacity of least developed country national peak private sector bodies and sectoral associations to participate in ASEAN-AEC processes, linked to the GMS programme where relevant.

## NOTES

* The views and errors, if any, are those of the authors, not of the institutions they represent. This chapter is an edited and expanded version of the authors' presentation to the ISEAS Brainstorming Session on this theme held in Singapore in September 2010. Its preparation included key informant interviews with senior officials of the Ministry of Commerce of the Royal Government of Cambodia and a small group of Cambodian private sector business leaders involved in the Cambodian National Government, ASEAN, and GMS private sector consultative processes.

1. For instance, the paddy surplus of two to three million tonnes, worth US$500 million–$1,000 million per year, is mostly exported informally and

not reported in trade statistics. Many other agricultural crops, though in less quantity, are in similar situations.

2.  In fact, despite the United Nations–run elections in 1993 resulting in a new constitution and government, Cambodia did not fully achieve peace until 1998, when the last stronghold of the Khmer Rouge forces were integrated with the government.

3.  John Nelmes, presentation of the IMF resident representative at the Cambodia Outlook Conference on 17 March 2010, at the Phnom Penh Hotel, Phnom Penh.

4.  See, for instance, UNDP, "Cambodia Country Competitiveness, Driving Economic Growth and Poverty Reduction", discussion paper no. 7, Insights for Action (UNDP Cambodia, 2009); World Bank, "Sustaining Rapid Growth in a Challenging Environment", Cambodia Country Economic Memorandum (2009); UNDP Cambodia, *Cambodia Human Development Report: Expanding Choices for Rural People (2007)*; World Bank, *Cambodia: Halving Poverty by 2015? Poverty Assessment (2006)*; CDRI Annual Development Review 2009–10.

5.  It should be noted, however, that approved FDI is only indicative of willingness to invest. The time taken to go from the investment proposal stage to actual implementation can be considerable. It may take years for projects worth hundreds of millions of dollars, if they do not get dropped in the process.

6.  World Bank, "Sustaining Rapid Growth in a Challenging Environment", Cambodia Country Economic Memorandum, Poverty Reduction and Economic Management Sector Unit, East Asia Pacific Region (prepared by the World Bank for the Royal Government of Cambodia, February 2009).

7.  UNDP, "Cambodia Country Competitiveness: Driving Economic Growth and Poverty Reduction", discussion paper no. 7, Insights for Action (UNDP Cambodia, 2009).

8.  The country case studies for this research project, including Cambodia, are accessible at <www.unescap.org/tid/artnet/>.

# 5

# AEC 2015, Cambodia, and the Lao PDR: View from the GMS

Pradeep Srivastava[1]

The ASEAN Economic Community (AEC) is an integral pillar of the ASEAN vision, envisaging the Southeast Asia region as an integrated community by 2015. The AEC Blueprint has set an ambitious agenda that seeks to establish ASEAN as a single market and production base, a highly competitive economic region, with equitable economic development and one that is fully integrated into the global economy. This is a vast canvas of integration, harmonization, and coordination activities, and its scope is matched by the complexity of the process.

The first element above, namely "ASEAN as a single market and production base", is critical to the development of the AEC, and includes in itself five core elements: (1) the free flow of goods; (2) the free flow of services; (3) the free flow of investments; (4) the freer flow of capital; and (5) the free flow of skilled labour. Recognizing the complexity and scale of the changes needed, the AEC Blueprint laid out action plans with targets and timelines that provided additional temporal flexibility for the CLMV (Cambodia, Lao People's Democratic Republic [PDR], Myanmar, and Vietnam) economies. However, the time targets for even the other ASEAN economies are considerably behind schedule and it is natural to expect that the deadlines for the CLMV countries, currently in the future, will likely also not be met.

This chapter looks at the readiness of two ASEAN economies, Cambodia and the Lao PDR (henceforth Laos), for the challenges of implementing the AEC. The approach adopted in doing so is to focus in detail on specific areas, rather than attempt to cover the broad range of areas listed in the AEC Blueprint, for which the space here is rather limited. The chapter consequently provides a relatively detailed look at a narrow, albeit central, component of the preparation for the AEC, namely transport and trade facilitation (TTF), which is of critical importance to the free flow of goods which, in turn, is crucial to the goal of ASEAN as a single market and production base. Solid progress on the TTF agenda is a prerequisite to the vision of the development of production networks to enhance ASEAN as a global production centre or as a part of the global supply chain.

ASEAN countries have done relatively well in reducing tariffs: ASEAN tariff levels are below world average, though there is considerable heterogeneity across the countries. The ASEAN region is also slightly more open than the world average by certain measures, but there is significant room for improvement in some areas, such as the number of documentary formalities and time taken for them, and the inter-country heterogeneity implies that indicators are much worse in some of the ASEAN economies (Shepherd and Wilson 2008). The heterogeneity among ASEAN member countries is well illustrated by the 2009 rankings of the World Bank's *Doing Business* surveys that rank Singapore first globally in terms of "trading across borders", defined as documents, time, and cost to import and export. Thailand (12th), Malaysia (35th), Indonesia (45th), and Brunei Darussalam (48th) also rank among the top 50 nations globally, while at the same time Cambodia (127th) and Laos (168th) are placed quite low out of the 183 nations ranked.[2]

The centrality of transport and trade facilitation in the AEC Blueprint is evident in the call in the blueprint for (1) continued reduction in tariffs, accompanied by actions to reduce non-tariff barriers; (2) the need to adopt simple, harmonized, and standardized trade and customs procedures, processes, and related information flows; (3) the integration of customs, modernizing tariff classification and valuation, and origin determination; (4) the development of National Single Windows in each member country to be integrated into an ASEAN Single Window; and the harmonization of standards, technical regulations, and conformity assessment procedures.

While this narrow slice of the AEC development is itself quite broad, it is easy to understand why TTF requires such emphasis. Asia's growth story over the past decades has been one of export-led growth. In more recent years, with increasing globalization, production networks have fragmented internationally and much of the growth of Asia's trade has been in various parts of these fragmented global value chains (the so-called Factory Asia). This trend has been an important avenue for SMEs (small and medium enterprises) in Asia (particularly in the electronics and auto parts sectors) to benefit from globalization (Brooks and Stone 2009). For all East Asian countries, the share of components in the exports and imports within the region has increased much faster than in trade with the rest of the world (Athukorala 2008). The increase in component intensity has been particularly noticeable in Southeast Asia's trade with the other developing East Asian economies, most notably the People's Republic of China (PRC). Following the global economic crisis, countries in ASEAN need to reconsider and rebalance their growth strategies, which will require increased intraregional trade to non-traditional markets. This will be of particular significance for the smaller ASEAN economies that will benefit from new markets within the region.

This chapter draws on the experience of the Greater Mekong Subregion (GMS) regional cooperation programme in assessing the TTF status in Cambodia and Laos. The GMS is an activity-based, subregional economic cooperation programme that began in 1992 and has been supported by the Asian Development Bank (ADB) as well as by several other donors. It covers six countries — Cambodia, Laos, Myanmar, Thailand, Vietnam, and the Yunnan Province and Guangxi Zhuang Autonomous Region of the PRC. The GMS programme has focused on three Cs: connectivity, competitiveness, and community; and its five strategic thrusts overlap strongly with the ASEAN Blueprint for the AEC, namely, strengthen physical infrastructure linkages; facilitate cross-border trade and investment with an emphasis on trade facilitation, trade financing, and investment promotion; enhance private-sector participation and improve its competitiveness; develop human resources skills and competencies, including capacity building to address cross-border human resource development and labour market issues; and, protect the environment and promote sustainable use of shared natural resources.[3] Both Cambodia and Laos have been very active participants in the GMS.

The outline of the chapter is as follows. In the second section, a brief description is provided of the TTF programme in the GMS, which is centred on the GMS economic corridors and the implementation of the Cross-Border Transport Agreement (CBTA). An assessment is provided in the next section of the implementation status of the CBTA, with a focus on Cambodia and Laos in particular. This discussion is used in the section that follows to outline the status of trade facilitation and the resulting challenges in Cambodia and Laos towards their meeting the AEC commitments. The final section concludes the chapter with lessons for the progress towards AEC 2015 in these two countries.

## GMS Corridors and CBTA

Improved infrastructure connectivity among its members has been a defining attribute of GMS cooperation since its founding in 1992.[4] Three major corridors have been developed as part of the GMS programme: the North-South Economic Corridor, the Southern Economic Corridor, and the East-West Economic Corridor.[5] These large investments in the transport corridors in the past years have led to increased physical connectivity of the GMS, which has created a need for improved TTF.

Despite rapid growth in intra-GMS trade in the past decade and generally low levels of tariffs in the region, non-tariff barriers to trade remain high among GMS members, particularly for trade in primary products. Agriculture remains a major sector for most GMS countries, and intra-GMS trade in agricultural products remains constrained by weak capacity of the sanitary and phytosanitary (SPS) regimes within and across the countries. In 2007 the total recorded export of agriculture, food, and forestry products by GMS countries came up to about US$65 billion, but only about US$7 billion of this was exported within the GMS region. About half of the latter were from Thailand, with Vietnam and China accounting for another US$1.6 billion and US$936 million respectively. The intra-GMS exports of Cambodia, Laos, and Myanmar were only US$241 million, US$230 million, and US$494 million respectively. The gains from increased trade within GMS economies, including for agricultural products, are quite large.

Recognizing the need for improved software to utilize the growing hardware connectivity to increase competitiveness of GMS economies, the countries gradually adopted the GMS Cross-Border Transport Agreement (CBTA) as the key platform for transport facilitation. The CBTA marked a pioneering landmark accord, which sought to consolidate, in a single legal instrument, all the key non-physical measures for efficient cross-border land transport. Three of the GMS countries signed the CBTA in 1999, and all had signed and ratified (and/or accepted it) by 2003, after which it went into force. Also, the GMS countries signed all of the CBTA's implementing guidelines (annexes and protocols[6]) between 2004 and 2007, and most GMS countries have now ratified and/or accepted all or nearly all of these annexes and protocols.

The need for improved TTF through CBTA implementation has also been emphasized at the highest levels of GMS leadership, at ministerial meetings, and summits. The 13th GMS Ministerial Conference in Vientiane in 2004 called for the initial implementation of the CBTA at selected border crossing pairs.[7] These pilot projects were intended to allow for the early identification of implementation-related issues and provide a demonstration of the efficacy of the CBTA. Subsequently the Joint Committee (established under Article 29 of the CBTA to monitor and facilitate CBTA implementation at the subregional level) at its second meeting in 2007 called for: (1) commencement of the initial implementation of the CBTA at seven or more border crossing pairs and their associated routes and corridors, by the end of 2008; (2) commencement of the full implementation of the CBTA and its annexes and protocols, along priority GMS Corridors, by the end of 2010; and (3) the formulation of sustainable subregional institutional coordination arrangements to monitor and oversee the full implementation of the CBTA and its annexes and protocols, by the end of 2010. The Third GMS Summit in 2008 stressed "the importance of making substantial and early progress" on measures to "[h]armonize and integrate procedures and systems to facilitate border crossing formalities, including customs, immigration, and quarantine, and promote the development of trade logistics".

## Status of TTF Implementation in GMS CBTA

The East-West highway is relatively the most advanced GMS corridor in terms of physical completion. The 1,450-kilometre-long transport corridor runs from Da Nang Port in Vietnam, through Laos, Thailand, to the

Mawlamyine Port in Myanmar. As part of TTF in the GMS, two border points on the East-West highway had been identified as pilot border crossing points for implementation of TTF: the Mukdahan-Savannakhet border between Thailand and Laos, and the Dansavanh–Lao Bao border between Laos and Vietnam. Relevant to Cambodia, two other border points for piloting TTF under the GMS CBTA on the southern routes were the Aranyaprathet-Poipet between Thailand and Cambodia and Bavet–Moc Bai between Cambodia and Vietnam.[8]

Table 5.1 summarizes the status of transport and trade facilitation measures at these pilot border crossing points. Approximate freight traffic volumes at these CBTA border crossings are still relatively low by international standards — 200 lorries cross the Thai/Cambodian border at Aranyaprathet/Poipet per day and approximately fifty per day at Moc Bai/Bavet. Cross-border trade and local resident traffic are comparatively more important, with about fifty local residents visiting the duty-free compound at Moc Bai daily and 250 private cars entering Thailand from Cambodia at Aranyaprathet.

Due to their visibility as pilots for GMS CBTA implementation, infrastructure at these border sites has received significant attention in recent years, with the result that border facilities are in good condition with some exceptions. Most of the pilot CBTA border stations have either been reconstructed, or are under various forms of rehabilitation, with the strategic objective of meeting CBTA operational principles (so called "Single Stop Inspection", through the use of a "Common Control Area", and with a focus on "Single Window Inspection"). The facilities are also comprehensive, incorporating all relevant agencies.

Nonetheless, it is also evident from the table that despite the signing of the CBTA agreement, as well as MOUs for its implementation at specific border crossing points, progress on the ground has proved difficult. A review of the practices shows considerable shortcomings in trade and transport facilitation at these sites, such as:

- *Infrastructure not used efficiently*: The notion of shared facilities has not developed, in part due to the need for legal changes required for border officials to work outside the border. Even though buildings on each side are sufficiently large to accommodate all agencies from both countries, separate structures are prepared on both sides. Similarly, where available, X-ray scans are considered an alternative to physical examination, with the risk that with

**TABLE 5.1**
**Status of TTF at Four Pilot CBTA Sites for Cambodia and Laos (as of April 2010)**

| Country Pair | Border Crossing | Status of TTF under CBTA |
|---|---|---|
| Laos-Thailand | Mukdahan-Savannakhet (Laos) | • Mukdahan (Thailand) facility has mostly outbound traffic with increasing transit to the PRC.<br>• Custom, immigration, and quarantine officials located in the same building each side of border, but capacities quite asymmetric.<br>• Common Control Area under construction, but no harmonization of customs information system and border crossing documents. Thai laws will need to be revised to accommodate extraterritorial exercise of jurisdiction by Thai officials, and to allow foreign officials to exercise jurisdiction in Thai territory.<br>• No exchange of advance information, though agreement reached in 2009 on types and fields of information to be exchanged and technique to be used. |
| Cambodia-Thailand | Aranyaprathet-Poipet (Cambodia) | • MOU on CBTA implementation signed in 2005 and another MOU signed in 2008 for exchange of traffic rights; neither MOU is being implemented. Discussions are ongoing on addendum to MOU on traffic rights at a quota of forty vehicles and to delink it from the other MOU. However, discussions were affected by other political issues between the countries in recent months.<br>• Agreement yet to be reached between the two countries on location of new border gate, and need for a new gateway or bypass.<br>• Single-window inspection not practised due to absence of designated agreed area. |
| Laos-Vietnam | Dansavanh–Lao Bao (Vietnam) | • Single-stop inspection in the country of entry (to be followed by joint processing of documents and joint inspection over time).<br>• Unbalanced border facilities on the Dansavanh side (Laos).<br>• Common Control Area on Laos side consists of makeshift facilities and is small on the Vietnam side.<br>• Harmonization of customs information system and border crossing documents yet to be done. Linking of information systems for customs constrained by security concerns.<br>• Need for capacity building on both sides of the border. |
| Cambodia-Vietnam | Bavet–Moc Bai (Vietnam) | • MOU on CBTA implementation signed in 2005, but not implemented yet.<br>• Exchange of traffic rights agreed at a quota of forty vehicles in 2006. Quota increased to 150 vehicles in May 2009.<br>• No Common Control Area.<br>• Single Window Inspection not agreed yet by both countries.<br>• Two customs agencies at Bavet border — Camcontrol and customs. |

*Source:* ADB staff reports.

the introduction of more scanners the percentage of physical examinations — which has been drastically reduced in recent years — will again increase. Up to 10 per cent of all shipments are randomly scanned before reaching the Dansavanh (Laos) border station, although the grounds for scanning exports on such a scale are not clear. There is also a scanner on the Vietnamese side (Lao Bao), though Vietnamese customs rarely carry out duplicate scans on imports. Vietnam is also planning to introduce one more scanner at Moc Bai. Scanners should also be shared amongst agencies, but that is not happening.

- *Interagency coordination weak:* Some interagency coordination exists at borders, but needs to be much more developed. In Laos, the Ministry of Agriculture relies on border guards, who patrol the border, to detect and prevent illegal movements of cattle herds across the border. In Thailand, customs use border police data for traffic statistics. More generally, however, interagency coordination is weak. Even in countries with electronic logging — China, Thailand, Vietnam — customs know in advance of most shipments expected at a border post, but there is no routine sharing of such information with other agencies. For Cambodia and Laos border crossings, there is even less interagency coordination. In some cases, different agencies collect and check the same information, which at best is a duplication of effort since there is no exchange of data between agencies. The justification is often that the purpose of the control is different for different agencies. For example, border guards want to keep track of vehicles entering and exiting the country, essentially for vehicle registration purposes, whereas customs is interested in the goods they carry. However, the base information is always the same. At Poipet (Cambodia), Camcontrol and customs officers collect the same data on lorries entering from Thailand.

- *Procedures at borders not modernized:* The focus of CBTA and related MOUs has been on local procedures at the pilot border crossings, whereas procedural reforms are centred on policies and decisions at headquarters. Capacity constraints at human and institutional levels have been addressed through training and workshops on CBTA (training manual) and the MOUs, but awareness and implementation have been modest. The appropriate implementation of border procedures will thus need extensive modernization of customs and SPS agencies in these countries to capture the spirit of TTF under the CBTA.

- *Network externalities of multilateral exchanges of traffic rights not utilized:* The CBTA trilateral exchanges of commercial traffic rights among Laos, Thailand, and Vietnam commenced in June 2009. However, the majority of goods and transport operators along the East-West Economic Corridor prefer to use bilateral road transport agreements between Laos and Thailand and between Laos and Vietnam than the CBTA trilateral exchanges of traffic rights since the former are perceived as more convenient, flexible, and extensive in terms of transport routes and roads.

- *Limited uptake of the GMS Custom Transit System (CTS):* Laos, Thailand, and Vietnam have each introduced agreements between their respective customs organizations and domestic institutions (Freight Forwarders Association in Laos and Vietnam and Board of Trade in Thailand) to be the CTS issuing and guaranteeing organizations. The three guaranteeing organizations have also reached interim agreement on the CTS along the East-West Economic Corridor. However, the CTS remains virtually unutilized by the private sector due to high costs of guarantees, inadequacies, and inefficiencies in trade facilitation as discussed above, and structural constraints in terms of limitations in choices of routes and roads available to operators using the CTS and related trilateral exchanges of traffic rights.

## Challenges and Constraints to Increased Integration

The review of TTF implementation under GMS CBTA at the pilot border sites shows there is considerable room for improvement in trade and transport facilitation in Cambodia and Laos. This section provides a broader view of trade facilitation at a national level (rather than GMS crossing points) in the two countries, including changes and initiatives that have been adopted in recent years to improve their trade facilitation regimes.

### Trade Facilitation in Cambodia

Trade policy and trade facilitation issues have been significant in Cambodia for several years for various reasons. Cambodia became a member of the World Trade Organization (WTO) in October 2004, ten years after it initiated the accession proceedings. The process included assessments and reviews of trade policies, measures, and their implementation. The country has also been an active participant in the Aid for Trade initiative and was one of the first three pilot countries under the revamped Integrated Framework for Trade-related Technical Assistance,[9] under which a Diagnostic Trade Integration Study was prepared in 2001 and updated in 2007 (ODI 2009). This study underpinned the development in 2005 of a Trade Sector-Wide Approach, under the leadership of the Ministry of Commerce, which provides the framework for channeling aid for trade into the country.

In part due to the priority given by the government, some progress has been evident in Cambodia's trade facilitation performance. For example, the average time to clear a shipment (between the port and the factory) has decreased for exports from 4.5 days in 2003 to 4.3 days in 2009 and from 6.5 days to 3.7 days for imports in the manufacturing sector (World Bank 2009). Nonetheless, as also evident in the previous section in the context of CBTA implementation, substantial problems remain. Much of the improvement in trade facilitation is confined more to the garment sector, whose exports have been of strategic importance to the country. The costs of shipping and getting an import licence remain high in other sectors, and uncertainty about processing times for exports and imports creates difficulty for businesses (World Bank 2009).

The modest improvements in Cambodia's trade facilitation regime can be attributed to commitments made as part of its accession to the WTO, political commitment of the government, and substantial support from development partners. A new Customs Law was enacted in 2007 and more than thirty supporting regulations have since followed. The ASEAN Harmonized Trade Tariffs were introduced in 2007, reducing the number of tariffs. A risk-management strategy was formulated for customs in 2006 and an audit and risk management unit created and staffed in the General Department of Customs and Excise (GDCE). The list of prohibited and restricted goods has been streamlined and risk and selectivity criteria have been set up along with the preparation of profiling of traders (World Bank 2008).

However, this process has largely been driven by the GDCE with relatively less ownership from other trade-related agencies, which need to create their risk management units. A critical issue underlying transport and trade facilitation — namely interagency coordination — is rendered more difficult in Cambodia due to the existence of two customs entities at the borders, customs and CamControl (under the Ministry of Commerce), and the need to coordinate both with the Transport Ministry. In November 2009, an Inter-Ministerial Joint Edict was signed between GDCE and CamControl on the Implementation of Trade Facilitation through risk management to move the implementation of risk management forward by mandating customs to be the lead agency on the border, and requiring customs to coordinate with CamControl, based on the policy mandate of CamControl. Subsequently, other inter-ministerial agreements/joint edicts have been signed between the MEF (Ministry of Economy and Finance)/GDCE and the Ministry of Health, and the MEF/GDCE with the Ministry of Industry, Mines and Energy (MIME). GDCE has contacted the Ministry of Agriculture, Forestry and Fisheries (MAFF) to finalize the Inter-Ministerial Joint Edict, and is still awaiting confirmation from MAFF. The inter-ministerial agreements/joint edicts represent substantive and important positive steps for strengthening the institutional arrangements for promoting trade and transport facilitation. However, much work has to be done before these joint edicts can be operationalized. Many of the policy and technical issues with regard to the functions and responsibilities of agencies will need to be defined clearly, first with customs, but also with the SPS agencies. In particular, there will be the need to define and clarify lists of items and associated procedures for specific SPS agencies and customs.

As of 24 February 2010, the Cambodian Government has established the National Cross-Border Transport Facilitation Committee (NCTFC) which upgrades the NTFC by transferring the overall implementation of both trade and transport facilitation to be under the leadership of the Minister of Economy and Finance or representative. The NCTFC will have the customs director general as the permanent vice-chair, in addition to three vice-chairs from the Ministries of Interior, Commerce, and Public Works and Transport. According to the Ministry of Economy and Finance, it is proposed that four subcommittees under the NCTFC will respectively cover the areas of transport, customs, immigration, and SPS facilitation. The operationalization of the new sub-decree establishing the NCTFC will require further clarification of the interface between the NCTFC and the NTFC, including the possibility of effectively integrating the NTFC into the NTCFC as one of the proposed subcommittees.

Cambodia decided in 2006 to move towards the ASEAN Single Window by 2012, based on the ASYCUDA (Automated System for

Customs Data) platform. The ASYCUDA system was launched in 2008, funded by a World Bank loan (World Bank 2009b), but progress has been somewhat limited. The ASYCUDA system is operational at Sihanoukville Port, with further roll-out planned for the Phnom Penh International Airport and dry ports. However, the system has not been set up as a centralized system operating through a wide area network but, instead, through separate local area networks. Automation of other trade-related agencies has also not moved significantly, with the minor exception of the Ministry of Commerce, which has introduced a Trade Information Gateway with the goal of automating Ministry of Commerce related processes. The government has decided it will not proceed with the institutional model originally envisaged for the creation of the Single Window. A National Single Window Steering Committee was set up in 2008 that will develop the vision for Cambodia's National Single Window in due course.

### Trade Facilitation in Laos

Trade facilitation is clearly of high importance to Laos, which is a landlocked country that shares borders with five countries — Cambodia, the PRC, Myanmar, Thailand, and Vietnam. As a "Least Developed Country", Laos also faces several challenges to promoting trade and investment, including a difficult geographical terrain, sparse population, and long recovery from an extended period of war. Trade flows are also constrained by tariff and non-tariff barriers, but Laos's growth strategy views exports as a key driver. The country is in the process of accession to the WTO.

The government has undertaken efforts to enhance trade facilitation during this decade through some simplification of trade documentation; improving coordination between line agencies by placing officers for trade, customs, quarantine, and food and drug control at most major checkpoints; and gradual elimination of licensing for imports and exports. Up to ten agencies used to be operating at the border, but the government took a decision to limit the number of agencies present to three in 2007. Checking posts and checking of goods for domestic trade were also phased out and the registration of new enterprises simplified under a new enterprise law. Nonetheless, the clearance of imports, exports, and transit goods remains administratively complex, dependent on inefficient physical inspections, reliant on manual processing and paper-based documentation, and subject to physical interface between traders and officials endowed with discretionary decision making.

Effective institutional coordination remains a constraint for improving TTF and a barrier towards meeting the goals of the AEC Blueprint since the latter builds upon the approach of modern coordinated border management (CBM), which is an approach to simplify border handling procedures and integrate roles of different stakeholders with responsibilities on the border, such as the customs and sanitary and phytosanitary standards (SPS) agencies. Customs is under the jurisdiction of the Ministry of Finance while transport and logistics comes under the Ministry of Communication, Transport, Post and Construction. In addition, several agencies are involved in managing the SPS aspects of border trade. Under the CBTA, a National Transport Facilitation Committee (NTFC) was established, chaired by the Ministry of Transport with representatives from customs and SPS agencies. However, ownership of this committee is low amongst trade agencies. The government is now considering restructuring the national institution for trade facilitation, as distinct from transport facilitation. To address the institutional needs for sound transport and trade facilitation better, it is desirable to strengthen the trade facilitation mechanism through such restructuring, and the government has agreed to establish the National Trade Facilitation Committee.

According to the WTO Trade Facilitation National Self-Assessment of Lao PDR, several areas need improvement, including coordination and cooperation between border agencies; adoption and use of international standards; simplification of procedures and formalities linked to export and import; development and adoption of an effective risk management system; and, improvement in post-clearance audit in compliance with international best practices.[10] Other necessary measures include greater transparency in laws and regulations, including trade measures, greater consultation amongst stakeholders, including the private sector, on new or amended rules and regulations and advance rulings, and an appeals procedure.

The situation on the improvement of SPS trade regime for Laos is even more challenging since the country lacks a well-functioning SPS management system. It has insufficient ability to assess the situation on plant pests, animal diseases and food hazards and to provide basic data on these hazards for trading partners.[11] The ability to control agrochemicals and imported genetic material is also very limited. The components of the SPS management system — regulatory and institutional frameworks, standards, diagnostic capacity, surveillance, inspection, and quarantine — still have major gaps and are not well integrated, which, in combination with the general lack of awareness about good agricultural and hygiene practices, sets formidable challenges to the growth of exports and imports.

For example, the ability of the government to monitor food safety is inadequate, and the productivity of crops and livestock is negatively affected by insufficiently controlled pests and diseases. Animal husbandry of buffalo, pigs, poultry, and cattle is a growing sector, but the animal disease status of Laos everely limits its opportunities for formal livestock and meat trade, which is thus confined to informal trade across porous borders. Food-and waterborne diseases, the prevalence of contaminants in foodstuffs, and the misuse of agrochemicals represent a threat not only to export opportunities, but also to domestic consumers.

To integrate SPS agencies successfully into effective trade facilitation and CBM agencies, Laos will need to address substantial gaps in the national SPS system, in terms of institutional capability, regulations and standards, diagnostic capacity, surveillance, inspection, and quarantine. There is also a need to improve collection and evaluation of basic data on pests, diseases, and food hazards and to conduct basis risk management.

More broadly, substantial technical and financial resources and time will be needed to address the institutional and human resource constraints to improving TTF, such as the lack of expertise, insufficient manpower, the lack of training, lack of well-developed policy framework and guidelines, limited infrastructure, and the lack of effective coordination mechanisms. Several development partners are involved in assisting the government in enhancing trade facilitation. The ADB has been assisting with CBTA implementation and is currently preparing a multi-year technical assistance programme to support TTF. AusAID (Australian Government Overseas Aid Programme) is supporting enhancing analytical support for policymaking, research capacity, and capacity building. The European Commission is facilitating the export of valuable flora of the country by promoting best practices, and facilitating the development of a modern intellectual property system. Capacity building support is being provided by France, Switzerland, and Singapore. The UNDP is supporting measures to help Laos integrate with the international trading system as well as into ASEAN. A World Bank loan is financing customs modernization through the installation of the ASYCUDA system, including translation, modification, and training; the implementation of the WTO Valuation Agreement, which governs the methods to be used when valuing goods for import and export; the development of a post-audit mechanism; and advance rulings and an appeals procedure.

## Lessons and Conclusions

The above discussion drew upon the CBTA implementation in GMS to look at issues related to the TTF, which is a core component of the AEC Blueprint for the emergence of the ASEAN region as a single market and production base. The CBTA has strong overlaps with the AEC Blueprint and with the commitments the countries have made for the TTF, including single-window inspection, single-stop inspection, common control areas, and transit of goods and vehicles.[12] The CBTA implementation has also been ongoing for several years, with substantial support from the ADB and other donors. Nonetheless, the experience of the CBTA for Cambodia and Laos shows that substantial implementation challenges remain on the ground. The broader review of trade facilitation initiatives and status at the national level in each of these two countries highlights the complexity of the various constraints faced by Cambodia and Laos as they seek to meet their commitments under the AEC.

Some of the clear messages emerging from this review can be briefly noted. First, while agreements and related MOUs are necessary, and sometimes quite time-consuming, they are simply the first step in a long process of actually implementing what is agreed. The latter is neither automatic nor straightforward, and the details of implementation can be more challenging than the negotiation of the agreement. Second, the area of trade and transport facilitation is quite complex, requiring legal, regulatory, and institutional changes, as well as difficult coordination across agencies, both within the country and across borders. Patience is thus needed, as are substantial resources and technical support, in areas where development partners can be useful. Third, and related to the above, there is considerable need for building capacity, both in terms of human capital and institutional strengthening. This is also an area where development partners can play an important role in assisting the countries to meet the challenges of the AEC. Fourth, it is important to recognize the achievements, even if seemingly small and slow, on the part of the countries facing complex challenges intrinsic to enhancing trade facilitation. Modernization of customs is well known from experience around the world for its complexities and difficulties. The obstacles associated with reforming the other border agencies that can mitigate non-tariff barriers, namely the SPS entities, are equally daunting, perhaps even more so, due to the lack of awareness in parts of the government and also the private sector on the role of these agencies in reducing the costs of trading. Given adequate resources, technical support, and adequate time, both countries have shown enough political commitment to ensure they will continue to increase their integration into global trade and the AEC. Whether this will beat the AEC Blueprint clock is of course a separate matter.

## NOTES

1. Views expressed in this chapter are only those of the author and do not in any way represent those of the ADB or its Board of Governors. I appreciate the comments from participants at the roundtable on ASEAN integration at the Institute of Southeast Asian Studies.
2. See "Philippines and Vietnam rank 68 and 74 respectively" <http://www.doingbusiness.org/economyrankings/?direction=Asc&sort=9>.
3. For additional information on the GMS, see <www.adb.org/gms>.
4. As of December 2009, the ADB had provided investments totalling nearly US$4 billion dollars in the GMS programme, and catalyzed additional co-financing of almost US$7 billion from development partners and governments; a large majority of the investment is in the transport sector.
5. The North-South Economic Corridor comprises three different routes: (1) the Western Sub-Corridor: Kunming–Chiang Rai–Bangkok; (2) the Central Sub-Corridor, Kunming–Ha Noi–Hai Phong, running from northern to southern Vietnam; and (3) Eastern Sub-Corridor: Nanning (PRC)–Ha Noi. The Southern Economic Corridor also has three routes: (1) the Central Sub-Corridor, Bangkok–Phnom Penh–Ho Chi Minh City–Vung Tau; (2) the Northern Sub-Corridor, Bangkok–Siem Reap–Stung Treng–Rattanakiri–Pleiku–Quy Nhon; and (3) Southern Coastal Sub-Corridor, Bangkok-Kampot (Cambodia)–Nam Can (Vietnam). The East-West Economic Corridor runs

from Da Nang Port in Vietnam to Mawlamyine Port in Myanmar. For more information on the GMS corridors, see ADB (2009*a*, 2009*b*, and 2009*c*).

6. An annex is an attachment to the CBTA that contains technical details; a protocol is an attachment to the CBTA that contains time, and/or site specific variable elements.

7. Including (1) Bavet (Cambodia)–Moc Bai (Vietnam); (2) Poipet (Thailand)–Aranyaprathet (Thailand); (3) Mukdahan (Thailand)–Savannakhet (Lao PDR); and (4) Dansavanh (Lao PDR)–Lao Bao (Vietnam).

8. For more details on the status of CBTA implementation in GMS, see ADB (2009*d*).

9. The integrated framework process is based on the formulation of a diagnostic trade integration study that is intended to function as the basis for mainstreaming trade into national development strategies and formulating an action plan for trade-related assistance.

10. "Technical Report: Lao PDR WTO Trade Facilitation National Self-Assessment of Needs and Priorities", World Trade Organization, February 2010. The objective of the assessment is to identify areas needing attention to comply with existing GATT Articles V (relating to freedom of transit), VIII (relating to import and export fees and formalities), and X (relating to publication and administration of trade regulations).

11. See <http://www.standardsfacility.org/files/Briefings/Final_Lao.pdf>.

12. However, the terms are not identical between ASEAN and CBTA.

## REFERENCES

Asian Development Bank (ADB). "Toward Sustainable and Balanced Development: A Strategy and Action Plan for the GMS North-South Economic Corridor", Draft. Manila: Asian Development Bank, Manila, February 2009*a*.

———. "East-West Economic Corridor Strategy and Action Plan", Draft. Manila: Asian Development Bank, May 2009*b*.

———. "Sharing Growth and Prosperity: A Strategy and Action Plan for the Southern Economic Corridor", Draft. Manila: Asian Development Bank, November 2009*c*.

———. "Preliminary Strategic Review of the GMS CBTA", TA 6450-REG. Manila: Asian Development Bank, 2009*d*.

Athukorala, P. C. "Recent Trends in Asian Trade and Implications for Infrastructure Development". Background paper prepared for the ADB/ADBI Flagship Study on Infrastructure and Regional Cooperation, 2008 <www.adbi.org/research. infrastructure.regional.cooperation>.

Brooks, D.H. and S.F. Stone. "Accelerating Regional Integration: Issues at the Border", ADBI Working Paper 200. Tokyo: Asian Development Bank Institute, 2010.

Overseas Development Institute (ODI). "An Integrated Approach to Aid for Trade: Cambodia Trade Sector-Wide Approach". London, 2009.

Shepherd, B. and J.S. Wilson. "Trade Facilitation in ASEAN Member Countries: Measuring Progress and Assessing Priorities". Policy Research Working Paper #4615. Washington, DC: World Bank, May 2008.

The World Bank. "Project Appraisal Document for Trade Development Support Program". Report No. 46752-KH. Washington, D.C., December 2008.

————. "Cambodia: A Better Investment Climate to Sustain Growth". Report No. 49371-KH. Washington, D.C., April 2009a.

————. "Cambodia: Trade Facilitation and Competitiveness Project — Project Paper Supporting the Restructuring of Grant H165-KH". November 2009b.

# 6

# Deadline 2015: Assessing Indonesia's Progress towards the AEC

Hadi Soesastro and Raymond Atje*

On 1 January 2010, ASEAN entered yet another important phase in its advance towards the implementation of the ASEAN Economic Community (AEC) in 2015. On that day, the ASEAN Six members, including Indonesia, was to eliminate all tariffs under the inclusion list (AEC), except for those phased in from the sensitive list and highly sensitive list (SL), some of which, according to the schedule, may be eliminated at a later date. Similarly, they should remove all quantitative restrictions and non-tariff barriers on goods in the SL. In Indonesia, this event has gone by almost unnoticed.

This chapter attempts to assess Indonesia's compliance with AEC liberalization schedules. In particular it tries to answer whether Indonesia is well positioned to fulfil all its commitments by 2015. The difficulty that arises in trying to address this issue stems from insufficient information to carry out the assessment. But it is also because the evolution of the AEC is by its nature a dynamic process. One cannot simply do a linear extrapolation of the progress to date into the future. There are other unforeseen, endogenous as well as exogenous, factors that may influence the future implementation of the blueprint.

With regard to trade liberalization, Indonesia's performance to date is at best mixed. On the one hand, in the goods trade sector, Indonesia has done relatively well. As a result of more than two decades of liberalization programmes, the country's average MFN (most favoured nation) tariff is now fairly low. Similarly, Indonesia has removed most of the non-tariff barriers and quantitative restrictions that were once widespread. In the services sector, on the other hand, Indonesia's performance is rather poor. Unlike the goods sector, the liberalization of the services sector has proceeded only slowly. In this respect, it seems that Indonesia's commitments to the General Agreement on Trade in Services (GATS) and the ASEAN Framework Agreement on Services (AFAS) do not provide enough incentive for further liberalization in the services sector.

This chapter argues that the ability of Indonesia to meet its commitments under the AEC will be influenced by developments in the country's trade sector. In particular, it argues that, given the progress to date, Indonesia will most likely be able to meet its commitments in the goods sector, but it has to do a lot more to liberalize the sector. This argument rests on the assumption that the more open the country's trade, the easier for it to meet the AEC deadline.

In addition, there is an external factor, namely the opposition to the ASEAN-China FTA (ACFTA), that may become a stumbling block for Indonesia in its effort to meet the AEC deadline. The implementation of the ACFTA has generated anxieties in Indonesia and some other ASEAN countries, such as the Philippines and Thailand. In Indonesia the government has come under pressure to renegotiate some of the terms of the agreement. This might explain why its people have hardly paid any attention to the removal of tariffs for intra-ASEAN trade. The opposition against the implementation of the ACFTA is likely to have some repercussions on the ability of the Indonesian Government to implement its future commitments under the AEC.

## Reviewing the Progress

### Government Commitments

To its credit the Indonesian Government has taken the necessary steps to incorporate its commitments to the AEC into the country's national economic development programmes. In particular, Presidential Instruction no 5/2008 explicitly contains, among other things, provisions concerning all the necessary steps, including presidential and ministerial regulations that the government would issue, to ensure that Indonesia meets its commitments as stated in the AEC Blueprint. The government had pursued a similar approach in the past. In the 1990s, it used its commitments, especially to the Common Effective Preferential Tariff (CEPT)-AFTA, to maintain the momentum of its deregulation programmes. Similarly, after the 1997/98 East Asian financial crisis, it made use of its commitments to the International Monetary Fund (IMF) for the same purpose.

With regard to its commitments to the AEC, there is, unfortunately, no simple way to verify the degree of the Indonesian Government's compliance. The ASEAN Secretariat has prepared and issued the AEC Scorecard to keep track of each member country's compliance with the AEC Blueprint schedules. Nevertheless, the report, at least the one that is available to the general public, is too general to be useful for the purpose of this chapter. Meanwhile, the Economic Research Institute for ASEAN and East Asia (ERIA) is also preparing an ASEAN scorecard of its own, but it is still in its early stage and far from being completed. As such, one can only gauge the government's compliance indirectly, using all available data and information that are relevant to the objective of this chapter.

### Tariff Reduction

Ever since Indonesia initiated trade liberalization in the mid-1980s, it has significantly reduced tariff rates, more or less across the board. Indonesia's participation in the World Trade Organization (WTO) and ASEAN Free Trade Area (AFTA) and other free trade arrangements has helped it to keep the momentum of tariff reduction. As some have argued (for example, Chen and Petri 2009), tariff reduction negotiated with FTA partners tended to lead to the reduction of the MFN tariffs as well.

In 2004 Indonesia introduced a two-phase tariff harmonization programme with the main objectives of moving towards low and uniform tariff rates and avoiding tariff escalation. The first phase was implemented in 2005 and covered 1,964 tariff lines on six groups of products: agriculture, fishery, mining, pharmaceutical, ceramics, and steel. The second phase covered over 9,100 tariff lines on products not included in the first phase. As a result of the programme, the weighted average tariff rate has fallen to 7.7 per cent in 2010. About 87 per cent of the tariff lines fall into two bands, that is, 5 per cent and 10 per cent.

On the other hand, the number of products that are subject to zero tariff has fallen to only 5.5 per cent in 2010 from 20.9 per cent in 2004. In addition, while Indonesia has relatively low applied MFN tariffs, it has bound tariff levels that are well above the applied tariffs. The average bound tariff is 37 per cent, more than four times the average applied tariff. In agriculture the average bound tariff is 48 per cent compared with the applied tariff of 12 per cent (Chen and Petri 2009).

Meanwhile, as noted earlier, under CEPT-AFTA, Indonesia had to remove all the tariffs on products under the inclusion list by 1 January 2010. This includes products previously under the sensitive list and the highly sensitive list that had subsequently been phased into the inclusion list during the interim period. As a result, Indonesia had been expected to reduce tariffs on 1,690 additional products to zero per cent on 1 January 2010, to bring the total number of products with zero tariff to 8,632. The remaining products under the sensitive list were scheduled to have 0–5 per cent tariff rates, and the remaining products under the highly sensitive list were due to have ending rates of 20 per cent by January 2010.

In addition, Indonesia is also making use of the general exclusion list (GEL) on a number of products (ninety-six tariff lines), especially rice and sugar. With regard to rice and sugar, Indonesia has made use of the Protocol to Provide Special Consideration for Rice and Sugar. Under the protocol, tariffs on rice (nine tariff lines), raw sugar and refined sugar (seven tariff lines), will be reduced gradually to 30 per cent, 5 per cent, and 10 per cent respectively by 2015. Note that GEL can be sustained as long as it is consistent with Article 9 of CEPT, which allows any member state to take "action and adopting measures, which it considers necessary for the protection of its national security, the protection of public morals, the protection of human, animal or plant life and health, and the protection of articles of artistic, historic and archaeological value".

### Non-Tariff Measures

Before the 1997/98 East Asian financial crisis, the use of non-tariff measures (NTM) in Indonesia was pervasive. In the 1990s around 1,192 tariff lines were subject to import restrictions, prohibitions, and special licensing. During the crisis, Indonesia, as a part of its commitment to the IMF, removed many of the measures. After the crisis the government continued to remove the existing non-tariff barriers and by early 2008 the number had dropped to 141 products that were subject to import licensing, covering primarily alcoholic beverages, explosives, lubricants, textiles, and some dangerous chemical products. However, at the end of 2008, in response to the global financial crisis, the government introduced import control measures on a wide range of products. Under CEPT Indonesia had to remove all the quantitative restrictions and non-tariff barriers by January 2010.

## *Investment*

In 2007 Indonesia introduced a new investment law aimed at making Indonesia more attractive to foreign investors. The law provides for legal certainty, that is, a non discrimination principle (national treatment); protection against appropriation; and the right of fund transfer and repatriation. In addition, in the event of a dispute between the government and any foreign investors, the law allows for a settlement through international arbitration. It should be noted that not all sectors are open to foreign investors. The government has issued a negative list of investment which provides a list of sectors that are open with conditions, or closed, to foreign investors, as well as sectors that are completely closed to all investors. The main objective of issuing the negative list is to provide investors with greater transparency. Nevertheless there is a sense that the list has been defined in a somewhat arbitrary way. Arguably the list has not been based on sound economic considerations.

In a study on investment in ASEAN, Urata and Ando (2009) make an assessment about, among other things, foreign direct investment (FDI) flows in ASEAN. They find that the FDI policy regime in Indonesia is relatively open, comparable to that of Thailand and the Philippines, more open than Malaysia's, but less open than Singapore's. However, in certain respects, Indonesia does poorly. For example, with regard to screening and appraisal, Indonesia has the worst performance of all the ASEAN countries. Indonesia is also relatively highly restrictive with regard to the movement of investors.

*Competition Policy*

Indonesia is one of the few countries in ASEAN that has promulgated a competition law and has established an independent agency in charge of competition policy — the Commission for the Supervision of Business Competition (Komisi Pengawas Persaingan Usaha — KPPU). Among the objectives of the competition law are to improve economic efficiency and people's welfare, to regulate the business climate so as to ensure equal opportunities for all firms, regardless of their size, and to foster competition and best business practices. It needs to be added that KPPU has to do a lot more to improve its efficiency and effectiveness.

## Services Sector as a Potential Hurdle

The traditional view that services are important to an economy only when it reaches a relatively advanced stage of economic development is being challenged as recent evidence suggests that services are a prerequisite for economic development rather than just its final demand. In particular, the inadequate provision of intermediate services — that is, services that contribute to the production of other goods and services — could inhibit the growth of other sectors. The Indonesian experience also shows that the existence of a dynamic manufacturing base alongside a relatively weak services sector results in a heavy reliance on imported services and contribute to a huge outflow of foreign exchange.

The potential for growth in commercial services has expanded with rising incomes. Likewise, the demand for services inputs over the last three decades has also risen with the increase in the level of maturity in Indonesia's manufacturing. The increase in demand from the goods-producing sector for commercial services is partly fuelled by the trend to outsource their services rather than providing them in-house. Finally, the demand for services provided by the public sector, commonly termed non-commercial services, has expanded with the rising population and a higher standard of living.

Indeed, the services sector plays an increasingly important role in Indonesia's economy. The share of the services sector in GDP has increased steadily from 44 per cent in 2000 to 52 per cent in 2009. During the period, its share grew by 9.2 per cent per annum, compared with four per cent per annum and 3.9 per cent per annum for agriculture and manufacturing, respectively. The average growth of trade in services between 2000 and 2008 is 15.8 per cent, higher than the average growth of trade in goods of 12 per cent during the same period.

Despite these figures, the country's balance of payment data suggest that the share of the country's trade in services is far below that of its trade in goods. In addition, unlike the goods sector, the liberalization of services industry has been very slow. Before the 1997/98 East Asian financial crisis, only the financial sector had undergone noticeable liberalization. After the crisis, a few other sectors, most notably telecommunications and air transportation have, to a significant extent, also been liberalized. But most of the other services sectors are being liberalized only slowly.

As a member of WTO and ASEAN, Indonesia has submitted to commitments for services liberalization at the global and regional levels to the General Agreement on Trade in Services (GATS) and the ASEAN Framework Agreement on Service (AFAS). Indonesia joined GATS in 1995 and AFAS in 1997. At the national level, the services sector liberalization is regulated by the new investment law promulgated in 2007 and the negative investment list published in conjunction with the promulgation of the law, as well as by various sectoral rules and regulations.

## Commitments in GATS

For the GATS, Indonesia requires commercial presence to take the form of joint venture and/or representative office (i.e., limited liability enterprise with foreign equity of not more than 49 per cent) in terms of market access. Foreign services providers do not have the right to own land, but their local partners in joint ventures have that right. The rules for foreign labour is based on the Indonesian labour and immigration laws and regulation which allow only directors, managers, and technical experts a maximum stay of two years, with a one-year extension. The person in question must hold a valid working permit issued by the Ministry of Manpower.

In specific sectors, Indonesia has made various commitments regarding market access and national treatment. In the telecommunications sector, Indonesia offers maximum foreign equity of up to 35 per cent and limits the number of foreign managers and technical experts to twenty people.[1] In the financial sector, Indonesia offers the "grandfather clause" to existing branches of foreign banks, permitting foreign shareholding in joint ventures, capping the purchase of existing banks at 49 per cent, and allowing up to 100 per cent foreign ownership for foreigners offering non-bank financial services through subsidiaries. In the tourism sector, particularly for hotel services, foreign capital is permitted up to 100 per cent in the eastern part of Indonesia — in Kalimantan, Bengkulu, Jambi, and Sulawesi.

### Commitments in AFAS

In the regional context, Indonesia has joined AFAS and offered its commitments since the first-round negotiation in 1997. There have been seven rounds of negotiations in AFAS and Indonesia has so far committed to nearly all services subsectors, except for the health care sector. In the first-round negotiation, Indonesia offered its commitment on only the tourism and transportation sector. The business, communication, financial, and construction sectors were committed in the second round negotiation, followed by distribution, education and recreation in the fifth-round negotiation. In the sixth-round negotiation, Indonesia made commitments on environmental services, while another important sector, namely health care, is still following the GATS commitment.

For the financial sector, general commitment in the banking sector includes permission for a foreign bank to establish or acquire locally incorporated banks (in cooperation with an Indonesian institution); permission to open branches in other capitals of all provinces in Indonesia; and increasing foreign ownership of up to 51 per cent. General entry into non-banking financial institutions has also been introduced, such as elimination of market access and national treatment limitations on non-banking sectors by 2020; and permission of foreign ownership of up to 100 per cent of companies listed on the stock exchange.

In the telecommunications sector, there are restrictions on foreign equity with up to 35 per cent allowed for local services and 40 per cent for other telecommunication services. Regarding the movement of people, all the telecommunications subsectors may employ up to only twenty foreigners at the management and technical expert levels.

In other services sectors, Indonesia's commitments in AFAS are mostly unbound, implying that Indonesia makes no commitment in those sectors (Harms et al. 2003). For consumption abroad and cross-border supply, Indonesia makes no restrictions for all sectors and subsectors.

A study by Thanh and Bartlett (2006) finds that Indonesia's (and other ASEAN members') commitment in AFAS is not significantly deeper or more liberal than its commitment in GATS. In terms of sector coverage, Indonesia has committed in more sectors in GATS than in AFAS, thus achieving only little benefit from the regional negotiations. The study also finds that Indonesia's commitment in AFAS is less restrictive by only 13 per cent than its commitment in GATS. It concludes, based on five criteria, namely, governance effectiveness, regulatory quality, voice and accountability, rule of law, and control of corruption, that in general the degree of transparency and predictability of ASEAN members' commitments in service liberalization (including Indonesia) is poor.

### *The Negative Investment List*

As mentioned earlier, in conjunction with the enactment of the investment law (Law No 25/2007), the government issued Presidential Regulation No. 77/2007 regarding the list of business fields that are closed, or open with certain conditions, for investment (hereafter, negative list). The investment law stipulates that essentially all business fields are open for investment, except those listed as closed, or open with certain conditions. The negative list will be reviewed every three years.

The original negative list comprises 658 sectors, based on five-digit standard classification of business fields or KBLI (about 58 per cent of total KBLI).[2] It suggests that 42 per cent of Indonesia's business fields are open to all investors. The list is divided into two groups: absolutely closed and open with conditions. About 4 per cent of the sectors in the list are closed to all investors. Of all the sectors in the list, only 32 per cent are open with conditions to foreign investors, 33 per cent are open to domestic investors only, and 17 per cent of the sectors are reserved for small and medium enterprises (SME).[3] The rest of the list comprises restrictions such as partnerships only with the government, and special permission from the ministry to establish the business.

With regard to foreign equity limitation, the list covers a wide range of foreign equity limitations, from 25 per cent to 99 per cent. From the breakdown of foreign equity limitations, it appears that the government offers rather limited foreign equity participation. About 36 per cent of the sectors in this group have a maximum foreign equity participation of 49 per cent, and only about 18 per cent of the sectors may have foreign equity participation of 95 per cent or above. The rest are somewhere in between.

In addition, Indonesia restricts all types of foreign investment in casinos/gambling, buses and taxis, marine vessel certification, private television and radio broadcasts, and film-making. Foreign investment in other sectors should be in the form of joint ventures, with foreign capital of up to 49 per cent (unless specified otherwise), and all foreign workers are subject to a 20 per cent withholding tax. Below are examples of sectors that have become less open under the current investment regime.

### Health Care

Prior to the promulgation of the negative list, the health care sector was open to joint ventures with no specified maximum on foreign equity. In this case, the common interpretation of the hitherto valid government regulation on foreign investment was that a foreigner could own up to 95 per cent equity. However, in practice it was up to relevant officials to decide the amount of foreign equity they would allow.

The negative list offers less foreign equity participation in medical services than before. Some subsectors are closed to foreign investors (for example, general medical clinics, ambulance services, and other medical services), or require special permission from the Ministry of Health (for example, pharmaceutical retailers, particularly for narcotics), or are open to foreign investment with maximum foreign equity of 65 per cent, as in the case of specialized medicine and dental clinics.

### Telecommunications

As with the health care sector, the telecommunications sector has become less open under the negative list regime. Up until 2007, the sector was open to joint ventures, with maximum foreign ownership of 95 per cent. The negative list provides a more disaggregated classification for the sector, but none of the subsectors is open to foreign capital of up to 95 per cent. For fixed line service, foreign capital is limited to 49 per cent, whereas for the cellular service, the maximum foreign capital participation is 65 per cent.

### Some Evidence

As with most ASEAN countries, Indonesia has been slow in liberalizing its services sector partly because it has doubts over the benefits of such liberalization. In an attempt to measure the progress in services liberalization in ASEAN, ERIA has undertaken a number of survey-based studies. One such study was conducted by Dee (2009) on ASEAN health care and banking sectors. With regard to Indonesia's health care and financial sectors, the findings of the study confirm the assertion made earlier about the degree of liberalization in those two sectors.

In particular, Dee finds that in the health care sector, Indonesia is more restrictive than the average ASEAN country. She nevertheless argues that, given the current condition, ASEAN as a whole is likely to be able to meet the AEC deadline in the health care sector. Meanwhile, in banking and insurance services, the study finds that Indonesia is relatively free of restrictions compared with other members and applies a non-discriminatory regulation for foreign services.

Another study by the New Zealand Institute of Economic Research (2009) finds that Indonesia imposes severe restrictions on business services, especially accounting and legal services. The restrictions include limitations on foreign workers, licensing requirements, and the scope of services to be supplied by foreign providers. Meanwhile, in the maritime services, the same study finds that most of the restrictions are in the form of prohibitions on foreign shipping companies to provide cabotage services, requirements to establish a commercial presence in the form of joint ventures, and exemption from competition policy, mainly the allowance of shipping conferences (cartels).

### Opposition to ACFTA

On the 1 January 2010, the ASEAN-China Free Trade Agreement (ACFTA) came into force. A closer look at the nature of trade between ASEAN and China during the past decade reveals that ASEAN-China trade has been growing rapidly, particularly since 2002, when the growth rates of both ASEAN exports to China, and its imports from China, began to accelerate. In 2004, the year when ACFTA was signed, ASEAN exports to China reached US$41.1 billion, while its imports from China were even higher, reaching US$46.5 billion, leaving ASEAN with a trade deficit of close to US$5.5 billion. By 2008 ASEAN trade deficit vis-à-vis China had swelled to about US$22 billion.

Since 2000 almost all the ASEAN Five countries have a negative trade balance with China, except for Indonesia and the Philippines. In 2000, only Indonesia had a trade surplus, while all the others had trade deficits, with China. Indonesia continued to experience trade surplus between 2000 and 2007, sustained largely by the high prices of commodities.

However, by 2008, the trade balance turned negative and preliminary data suggests that the same was true for 2009.

A recent paper by Huang (2010) suggests that Chinese Government intervention in the country's factor markets is pervasive. The Chinese Government's interventions repress prices of labour, capital, land, and resources so as to increase profits and improve the international competitiveness of Chinese products. If one takes Huang's assessment at face value, then one unintended consequence of it is that Indonesian producers may have been put at a disadvantage vis-à-vis Chinese producers when it comes to trade. In a way it may not be entirely incorrect to say that the Chinese Government provides implicit subsidies to Chinese producers.[4]

For any country, the idea of having an FTA with China will undoubtedly generate both great expectations as well as anxieties. Indonesia is no exception. On the one hand, China, with a population of over 1.3 billion, offers a huge potential market for its products. This might explain the excitement expressed by many Indonesians when the ACFTA was signed in 2004.

On the other hand, in a relatively short period, China has established itself as a global manufacturing powerhouse. Moreover, one often hears an expression that China has a comparative advantage in everything. While every economist can easily refute the argument, yet, in general, the anxiety associated with the rise of China as a global economic power is hard to dispel. This is partly because the Chinese economy and its trade are already very large. It is partly also because China and Indonesia produce similar products and casual observation seems to suggest that China's products are highly competitive.

It is not so surprising, therefore, that the implementation of ACFTA has generated anxieties in Indonesia and some other ASEAN countries such as the Philippines and Thailand. In Indonesia the government has come under pressure to renegotiate some of the terms of the agreement. This is one reason people hardly paid any attention to the event concerning ASEAN mentioned above. This chapter argues that the opposition against the implementation of ACFTA is likely to have some repercussions on the ability of the Indonesian Government to implement its commitments under the AEC. If Indonesia continues to experience a trade deficit with China, then the government will be under pressure to postpone, or, at least, slow down the implementation of its commitments to various FTAs that it is involved in, including AFTA.

## The Way Forward

This chapter argues that Indonesia's ability to fulfil all its commitments to the AEC by 2015 hinges on a number of factors. First, it depends on its ability to speed up liberalizing its services sector. Unfortunately, as Hapsari (2010) points out, neither its participation in GATS nor its participation in AFAS is of any help in this respect. They do not provide enough incentives for further liberalization in the services sector. As such, Indonesia may have to rely on domestic pressure to further the services liberalization. There is increasing recognition in Indonesia on the importance of services to the economy as a whole; services are important inputs to the production of goods and services. The absence of the efficient provision of services will make production costs of goods and services higher than otherwise.

There is also a need for ASEAN to put a greater emphasis on trade and investment facilitation, as well as other behind-the-border liberalization. While the implementation of all the commitments matters a lot, it is not sufficient to ensure the creation of a truly single market where the law of one price prevails. Similarly, the establishment of a single production base depends on the ability of investment to move freely within the region. However, investment will flow to a place where the return is the highest. Many investment-related, behind-the-border measures, such as the prolonged screening and appraisal process in Indonesia mentioned earlier, will increase the cost of investment and, hence, reduce the return to investment. A single production base is possible only if returns on investment are more or less equalized across ASEAN.

### NOTES

\*   The authors would like to thank Indira Hapsari for helping with the research.
1.  Based on the GATS document, S/GBT/W/1/Add.15/Rev.1, for Indonesia on basic Telecom Services Commitments.
2.  KLBI stands for Klasifikasi Baku Lapangan Usaha Indonesia.
3.  It is based on the analysis of sectoral coverage in the new negative investment list.
4.  One wants to be very careful, however, in using Huang's study to analyse the implications of the policy described therein on ASEAN–China trades. Furthermore, more in depth studies are necessary to examine the actual nature of such trades.

## REFERENCES

Australia-Japan Research Centre, Crawford School of Economics and Government, ANU. *Service Liberalization in East Asia: Financial, Logistics, and Distribution Services*. ERIA Related Joint Research Project Series 2007, no. 3. Tokyo: IDE-JETRO, 2008.

Chen, Tze-Wei and Pete A. Petri. "Indonesia 2009 IAP Study Report". Report prepared for the Asia-Pacific Economic Cooperation Secretariat. Singapore, 2009 <aimp.apec.org/Documents/2009/SOM/SOM1/09_som1_008anx2.pdf>.

Corbett, Jenny and So Umezaki. *Deepening East Asian Economic Integration*. ERIA Research Project Report 2008, no. 1. Jakarta: ERIA, 2009.

Dee, Philippa. "Services Liberalization toward the ASEAN Economic Community". In "Deepening East Asian Economic Integration", edited by Corbett and Umezaki, ERIA Research Project Report 2008, no. 1. Jakarta: ERIA, 2009.

Hapsari, Indira. "Financial Services Trade Liberalization and its Effects on ASEAN Member Countries". *Indonesian Quarterly* 38, no. 1 (2010): 54–76.

Huang, Yiping. "Dissecting the China Puzzle: Asymmetric Liberalization and Cost Distortion", Working Paper Series No E201003. China Center for Economic Research, Peking University, 2010.

Indonesia's Schedule of Specific Commitments in GATS, 1995.

Indonesia's Schedule of Specific Commitments in AFAS, 1st–6th-Round Negotiations, 1997.

Indonesia's Presidential Regulation 77/2007, on Negative Investment List.

Harms, Philipp, Aaditya Mattoo, and Ludger Schuknecht. "Explaining Liberalization Commitments in Financial Services Trade". *Review of World Economics* 139, no. 1 (2003): 82–113.

New Zealand Institute of Economic Research. "Service Liberalization in East Asia: Business, Postal/Courier and Maritime Services". ERIA Related Joint Research Project Series 2007, no. 2. Tokyo: IDE-JETRO, 2008.

Thanh, Vo Tri and P. Bartlett. "Ten Years of ASEAN Framework Agreement on Services (AFAS): An Assessment". REPSF Project no. 05/004. Jakarta: ASEAN Secretariat, 2006.

Urata, Shujiro and Mitsuyo Ando. "Investment Climate Study on ASEAN Member Countries". In *Deepening East Asian Economic Integration*, edited by Corbett and Umezaki. ERIA Research Project Report 2008, no. 1. Jakarta: ERIA, 2009.

World Bank. "Indonesia Trade Note June 2006". Jakarta: World Bank, 2006.

# 7

# Towards an Integrated AEC: Where is Malaysia?

Rajah Rasiah

The Association of Southeast Asian Nations (ASEAN) was founded in 1967 with Indonesia, Malaysia, the Philippines, Singapore, and Thailand as the original members, and was subsequently enlarged to include Brunei and the transition economies of Vietnam, Laos, Cambodia, and Myanmar. Although political interests were important in the initiation of ASEAN, economic interests have carried the regional body over the last few decades. The launching of the ASEAN Free Trade Area (AFTA) in 1992 — which preceded the formation of the World Trade Organization in 1995 — became the initiator that subsequently led to the adoption of Vision 2020 in 1997 to turn it into a stable, prosperous, and competitive region (Mikic 2009, p. 11). It was then formalized through the signing of the Bali Concord II declaration in 2003, with the deadline subsequently brought forward to 2015. At the ASEAN 2007 summit in Singapore the ASEAN members accepted the AEC as a blueprint.

The AEC aims to become a single market and production base, and a highly competitive economic region, characterized by equitable economic development and fully integrated into the global economy by 2015. This chapter seeks to examine developments to evaluate Malaysia's preparations to meet the four objectives outlined above.

## Critical Issues

While the political processes leading to the formation of the AEC appear irreversible and are not in the hands of economists such as me, it is pertinent that I revisit its arguments here before proceeding to examine Malaysia's preparations. The four objectives set out appear sound and do not invoke anything seriously controversial. However, some of the strategies that both economists and policymakers have set out to pursue appear contradictory. Hence, an attempt to review them is necessary to reconcile national and ASEAN goals against the strategies pursued to create a single economic region by 2015.

The integration of the AEC as a major market offers individual members a much larger market to appropriate economies of scale and to access labour and capital. Indeed, the catastrophic effect of a recession in the United States and other countries dragged in by its whirlpool led the Malaysian Government to review potential opportunities to reduce trade dependence on the developed countries by targeting Malaysia and the AEC markets.

AEC members have streamlined their investment regulations to attract foreign direct investment (FDI) inflows from the rest of the world, as well as to stimulate flows between members. China's sheer size and rapid growth, and the emergence of India and its liberalization efforts, have increasingly driven Southeast Asian countries to review their own policies. FDI inflows to Malaysia, which was the main driver of industrialization from the 1970s until the 1990s (Rasiah 1995), has slowed down considerably since the millennium, after recording an annual average growth rate of 11.1 per cent over the period 2000–2008 (Malaysia 2010a, Appendix 6.1). Net FDI actually hit negative figures since 2006 as FDI outflows grew faster than inflows. Concerns over its potential deleterious impact have led the government to review its policy. Unlike the least developed countries of Cambodia, Laos, and Myanmar, where much of the focus is confined on attracting FDI to resource- and labour-intensive operations, Malaysia and Thailand are facing serious labour shortages alongside their initiatives to stimulate technological upgrading. Another pertinent point to make is that unless local or national governments actively support local capability building, the freeing of capital movements will accentuate rather than narrow economic inequality between the member countries (Lall 2001; Cimoli, Dosi, and Stiglitz 2009).

Clearly a major instrument of integration pursued in single markets is the removal of tariffs and, in the case of regions such as the European Monetary Union (EMU), policymakers successfully legislated to implement even a common monetary policy with a single currency and common interest rates. The developments in the AEC suggest that initiatives are in place to establish a tariff free region through the Common Effective Preferential Tariff blueprint, but without any common monetary and fiscal instruments. By and large there have been significant strides to achieve this, but initiatives to remove the thorny issue of preferential national treatment remains a problem in particular industries.

While it is good to remove national treatment obstacles to drive the formation of a single market, the achievement of the third goal of ensuring that the AEC becomes more equitable cannot simply be met by blanket removal of tariff walls and the withdrawal of government support that removes the stimulating role of selective interventions to support technological capability development (see Kaldor 1979; Lall 1986; Amsden 1989, Wade 1990; Chang 2003; and Reinert 2008). The evidence of globalization shows that countries that evolved national capabilities such as Korea, Singapore, and Taiwan have benefited from the process, while those that did not, such as the sub-Saharan African countries, have continued to face depletion of their resources (Lall 2001). It is here that the flag bearers of the AEC have addressed little to the third objective of engendering more equitable development. Unlike in the United States where labour mobility is fairly fluid, it is rigid in other regions seeking to establish integration, including in the EMU. Despite the relaxation of immigration controls and the free movement of trade and services and investment in such regions, a wide range of problems have reduced the propensity to hire foreign workers in jobs other than those where wages in informal labour markets are much lower than in formal labour markets. There is recognition in the EMU over the relatively underdeveloped status of the newly integrated members from the former Eastern European bloc, and it has hence launched initiatives to ameliorate such problems.

In as much as markets must be a key institution of governance, the goal of achieving equitable distribution between member countries will not be possible if the concept of free markets is embraced as the prime driver of governance — *à la* the new institutional arguments of Coase (1937), North (1994), and Williamson (1985). The high per capita incomes enjoyed by Singapore was achieved with the strong leveraging role played by the government to create the capabilities necessary to support high wages. Singapore achieved rapid technological catch-up in the industries of shipbuilding and repair, electronics and petrochemicals by selectively intervening in markets. Consistent with the evolutionary argument of Nelson (2008), each industry experienced a different type of intervention. Electronics faced largely governance procedures using multinational participation. On the one hand, the government strengthened high-tech infrastructure by building R&D labs, and attracting high-end human capital, on the other hand the government filtered FDI inflows to allow only high-end activities and offered R&D grants to stimulate upgrading. In shipbuilding and repair, and in petrochemicals, the government directly owned a number of the firms, imposed tariffs in the incipient phase, and drove technological catch-up.

While it is politically expedient, AFTA's principles of allowing members to retain certain industries that are excluded from the normal deregulation does not help ensure economic efficiency if a clear time frame cannot be established. For example, if a country that chooses to protect an industry to stimulate technological catch-up, using the scale and learning requirements as necessary conditions, they should be given a time frame to end it. Otherwise, not only will the country face deadweight loss in economic benefits, but will also contribute to unproductive drag and friction in the region.

While skilled labour movement has been discussed in the assessments of gains the AEC can appropriate from the process of integration, there has been little institutional development to address immigration and visa issues involving workers from other ASEAN countries. Unlike in the United States where the one-country national border has facilitated free mobility of labour, the same cannot be said of the AEC. What constitutes labour demanded may quickly fade as firm-level demand often fluctuates with the vicissitudes of markets. Besides, countries seeking to stimulate technological upgrading may actually attract skilled labour thereby creating a technical division of labour between countries in the AEC. Singapore has managed to leverage its policies to develop its high-tech infrastructure so that it continues to attract high value added operations, which has attracted skilled and professional human capital from other AEC members. While Singapore has earned its position at the apex of the AEC, the freeing of labour movement — even if it does not generate xenophobic reactions from local populations — may perpetuate the uneven development patterns in the region. If this continues it is unlikely to help achieve economic convergence among the countries in the AEC. The freeing of labour will complete the relaxation of both the factors of production (including capital) and, with that, will only aggravate the inequality between countries as skilled workers seeking higher wages and better living conditions migrate to the more advanced countries in the region.

Finally, economic integration would require the streamlining of a range of legal provisions where enforcement will be far more important than simply adopting a common regulatory framework across the region. There must be greater implementation surveillance to prevent goods and services recording low value addition in Southeast Asia from being either traded in member countries, or exported with the AEC as the region of origin. The main concern here is over dumping practices that can undermine productive operations in the AEC member countries.

## Drivers and Barriers Facing Integration Initiatives

Trade liberalization has taken place in the export-oriented industries to the extent that tariffs for all of them with respect to other AEC countries have been reduced to zero per cent. As noted earlier, that has been the case with the ASEAN Six countries. However, inward-oriented industries and services still face problems. Coming in the wake of proclamations by the Malaysian Government in 2010 that the new economic model of Malaysia will seek to quicken the country's transformation into a high-income country by 2020, the road to achieve it may not be exclusively through unbridled liberalization.

### Trade

Driven by the need to scale down the deficit, the government has taken initiatives to remove subsidies on goods and services, which should remove the moral hazard of free-rider problems enjoyed by non-target groups — both rich nationals and foreigners. At least against Singapore there will be common prices on basic and essential goods such as rice, oil and gas, and sugar. This development will remove Malaysia's concerns over the subsidy enjoyed particularly by Thais, Indonesians (in Borneo), and Singaporeans travelling to Malaysia, and worries of firms located in these three countries over dumping caused by smuggling. It should also remove Bruneian concerns about free riding by Malaysians from Sarawak.

Apart from industries where government-linked companies are involved, tariffs facing the rest of the industries have been liberalized in Malaysia. The country's trade with AEC members actually increased over the period 2005–09 despite the financial crisis (see Table 7.1). Apart from with Indonesia, and Laos until 2007, Malaysia enjoyed a positive trade balance with the remaining members. Brunei absorbed the most exports of Malaysia to the AEC countries, followed by Singapore. Even the trade deficit with Indonesia has improved.

However, Malaysia's initiatives to quicken economic development to achieve its 2020 goals require that its key industries must lead technological catch-up. The value added content of these industries must rise faster than that of Singapore for economic convergence between the two countries. Such an initiative may contradict rather than concur with the AEC framework, which is dominated by liberalization initiatives, rather than efforts to establish a horizontal division of labour in the region. Also, Malaysia's framework appears eclectic here as liberalization in itself will not provide the impetus for technological upgrading. Unless capabilities are quickly evolved to match Singapore's successful leveraging strategy, the targeted strategic industries in the country will continue to face a hollowing out, which has characterized the electronics industry from the mid-1990s.

While smuggling activities can be expected to fall as subsidies and duties are removed, not much is clarified to date on the protected industries of automobiles and telecommunication services. There is a road map that stipulates the evening out of tariffs and duties facing imported and assembled vehicles, but there are no details differentiating support given to national and non-national firms. Within the AEC, the deregulation road map in automotives of Malaysia has remained sensitive to the massive build-up in capabilities within a

**TABLE 7.1**
**Importance of Trade with AEC Members, Malaysia, 2005–09**
(Malaysian ringgit in millions)

|  | 2005 | 2006 | 2007 | 2008 | 2009 |
|---|---|---|---|---|---|
| *Exports* | | | | | |
| Brunei | 139519 | 153024 | 155560 | 171216 | 89317 |
| Cambodia | 414 | 397 | 461 | 551 | 375 |
| Indonesia | 12540 | 14925 | 17749 | 20736 | 11206 |
| Laos | 24 | 21 | 32 | 29 | 19 |
| Myanmar | 930 | 607 | 721 | 1044 | 474 |
| Philippines | 7517 | 7992 | 8739 | 9760 | 4443 |
| Singapore | 83596 | 90199 | 88508 | 97784 | 47983 |
| Thailand | 28746 | 31148 | 29984 | 31735 | 18589 |
| Vietnam | 4390 | 6461 | 7966 | 8083 | 5130 |
| *Imports* | | | | | |
| Brunei | 110432 | 121508 | 128320 | 126420 | 68925 |
| Cambodia | 30 | 74 | 73 | 48 | 37 |
| Indonesia | 16553 | 18122 | 21379 | 24185 | 14188 |
| Laos | 49 | 166 | 122 | 10 | 0.2 |
| Myanmar | 506 | 459 | 476 | 592 | 292 |
| Philippines | 12191 | 10640 | 9775 | 6942 | 2397 |
| Singapore | 50586 | 55844 | 57955 | 57326 | 29061 |
| Thailand | 22857 | 26269 | 27000 | 29275 | 18242 |
| Vietnam | 3862 | 5181 | 6304 | 7703 | 5064 |
| *Trade Balance* | | | | | |
| Brunei | 32838 | 35995 | 32139 | 44796 | 20392 |
| Cambodia | 384 | 323 | 388 | 503 | 338 |
| Indonesia | −4013 | −3197 | −3630 | −3449 | −2046 |
| Laos | −25 | −145 | −90 | 19 | 18.8 |
| Myanmar | 424 | 148 | 243 | 452 | 182 |
| Philippines | −4674 | −2648 | −1036 | 2818 | 2048 |
| Singapore | 33010 | 34355 | 30553 | 40458 | 18922 |
| Thailand | 5889 | 4679 | 2978 | 2460 | 2327 |
| Vietnam | 528 | 1280 | 1682 | 380 | 66 |

*Note:* 2009 figures until August 2009.
*Source:* Malaysia 2010, Appendix 3.3.

liberal framework in Thailand, and, to a smaller extent, in Indonesia and the Philippines.

Given the long period of protection starting from the time the first Proton cars rolled on the roads of Malaysia in 1985, it can be argued that the case for infant protection does not exist anymore for automotive products. Heterodox economists would argue that the case for intervention is persuasive when scale economies and increasing returns are involved and hence the solution should rest on the formulation and execution of the right institutional and govern-ance framework to make it work, rather than the discontinuation of protection (Young 1928; Amsden 1989; Chang 2003; Reinert 2008). However, state intervention in Malaysia has been driven by unproduc-tive rent seeking rather than productive rent transformation (see Jomo 2006). There has been little evidence to suggest that state capacity in the country has evolved to instil dynamic catch-up, as well as to with-draw rents when particular industries fail. Hence, I would argue that it is undesirable to pursue such an expensive project that continues to impose heavy costs on the government. Indeed, this is one of the key problems that has prevented the Government of Malaysia from signing any bilateral free trade agreements (FTAs) despite several at-tempts. The agreement signed with Japan in 2006 is a watered down one that carries the title, Economic Partnership Agreement (Basu Das and Aekapol 2010).

The Malaysian Government's New Economic Model (NEM) launched in 2010 calls for further liberalization (Malaysia, 2010*b*). Although the Prime Minister of Malaysia has been calling for liberalization, protection and subsidies faced by industries such as automotives have remained an obstacle to greater integration in the AEC. Indeed, Datuk Seri Najib Tun Razak has maintained that the 30 per cent equity for bumiputra corporate interests will remain an objective (Izatun 2009).[1] The messages contained, however, remain ambiguous as government-linked companies are considered to be important for socio-economic restructuring purposes. The NEM simply appears to carry forward the problems that afflicted the New Economic Policy (NEP) of 1971 and the New Development Model of 1990. Although the NEM asserts that affirmative action strategies that will be taken will be market friendly, the lack of a clear, non-ethnic slant offers no assurance that unproductive rent seeking will not dominate the execution of the model.

### Foreign Direct Investment

Malaysia has removed almost all obstacles facing foreign direct investment in the manufacturing sector. Regulations still apply in the automotive, banking, and services sector. Initiatives to filter investment to stimulate upgrading were removed following the Asian financial crisis of 1997–98. The traditionally large foreign investors of the United States and Japan occupied second and third places behind Australia in 2008 (see Table 7.2). Korea, Taiwan, and Hong Kong became important investors from the late 1980s until the 1990s. However, investment from these countries contracted over the period 2008–10.

The imminent contraction of FDI inflows to Malaysia was already reported from the mid-1990s, following growing labour shortages, human capital deficiency, and the lack of support for designing and R&D activities (Rasiah 1999). The NEM declared the need to stimulate technological upgrading of industries to higher value added activities. The government produced a high technology report with a road map to encourage technological catch-up in strategic high-tech industries (Malaysia 2009). The achievement of this goal will help integrate Malaysia horizontally with Singapore. A more equitable regional per capita income distribution requires that technological capabilities of firms, institutions, infrastructure, and governance capacities evolve to become equally strong. The successful transition of Malaysian industrialization to high

**TABLE 7.2**
**FDI Inflows, Malaysia, 2000–08**
(Malaysian ringgit in millions)

| | 2000 | 2005 | 2008 | 2000–08 Annual Average Growth Rate |
|---|---|---|---|---|
| United States | 7491.9 | 5155 | 8669 | 1.8 |
| Australia | 129.9 | 155.9 | 13105.8 | 78.0 |
| The Netherlands | 2174.8 | 1674 | 1795.7 | −2.4 |
| Hong Kong | 345.3 | 105.4 | 83.6 | −16.2 |
| Indonesia | 66.3 | 52.5 | 22.1 | −12.8 |
| Japan | 2880.5 | 3671.7 | 5594.9 | 8.7 |
| Germany | 1655.9 | 387.7 | 4438.3 | 13.1 |
| Korea | 722.8 | 673.6 | 197.6 | −15.0 |
| Singapore | 1788.5 | 2919.9 | 2004.3 | 1.4 |
| Taiwan | 916.1 | 430.7 | 911.6 | −0.1 |
| United Kingdom | 771.6 | 99.2 | 850.5 | 1.2 |
| Others | 914.9 | 2557.3 | 8425.5 | 32.0 |
| Total | 19858.5 | 17882.9 | 46098.9 | 11.1 |

*Source:* Malaysia 2010, Appendix 6.1.

value added activities will attract strong inflows of FDI back, but in high tech activities.

However, the governance framework to achieve this goal remains loose. The government does not have a mechanism to assist the technology transfer unit at the Ministry of International Trade and Industry (MITI) to vet, monitor, or appraise technology transfer experiences, which was so critical in the Japanese, Korean, and Taiwanese catch-up miracles (see Johnson 1982; Amsden 1989; Fransman 1986). In addition, the government also lacks a technical advisory council *à la* Taiwan comprised of experts with world-class tacit and experiential knowledge to guide such a mechanism (see Lin 2009).

### Competition Policy

Competition policy targeted at eliminating monopolistic conduct that arise from high levels of concentration would be useful, but there are no signs yet that the act, which was gazetted in 2010 and came into effect in 2012, will effectively curb unproductive monopoly practices (see Malaysia 2010c). Although previously the government acted to allow more firms in industries where scale is important — for example, automobiles, telecommunications, power suppliers, and cement — the spirit of checking monopolistic behaviour cannot be achieved simply through increasing participants in such industries.

The initiative to implement a competition policy among the countries is a good one to prevent unfair monopolistic conduct by sellers and buyers. However, for competition policy to be effective, the Government of Malaysia will have to also enact anti-monopoly laws. Instead, the government has encouraged the entry of a few firms into lucrative, inward-oriented services — for example, telecommunications — where national providers such as Maxis and Digi have entered the market to compete with Celcom. Clearly, the entry of more firms has raised competition, leading to improved service and greater choice for customers. However, an AEC may require eventually allowing firms from other member states to compete in the Malaysian market.

### Skilled Labour

Malaysia has attempted to attract foreign human capital to overcome the growing demand-supply deficits from the mid-1990s. Although member countries are unlikely to complain if individual members fail to formulate and execute policies to offer same treatment conditions on skilled labour, it is worth discussing this initiative further as it figures prominently in Malaysia's technological upgrading drive. Despite recognizing the benefits that brain gain and brain circulation strategies are providing to Taiwan, Korea, Singapore, and India, poorer members may remain concerned with their ability to attract their diaspora back to participate in the technological catch-up programmes in their own countries. However, only Singapore appears to have a cogent framework and the mechanisms to execute it effectively.

Unlike Singapore, Malaysia has largely failed to attract not only sufficient numbers of foreign human capital, but also its own diaspora back. Between 1994 and March 2010, only 650 Malaysians returned under the three brain gain programmes in place (Rasiah 2010). Although Malaysia has tried to simplify and quicken the procedures for hiring foreign skilled workers, surveys show that bureaucratic problems have thwarted their efforts to hire professionals from the Philippines.

In fact, the lack of human capital has been reported as the single most important factor causing a hollowing out of electronics manufacturing in Malaysia. Growing labour shortage and rising production costs in the face of emerging sites with an abundance of labour (for example, China, the Philippines, and Vietnam) have forced the relocation of low-end operations out of Malaysia. The limited pool of engineers and scientists has allowed only some firms to upgrade into designing and fabrication activities (for example, Intel, Motorola, Alterra, Agilent, OSRAM, Silterra, and AMD) (see Rasiah 2010). A recent memorandum of understanding between the Indian Institute of Technology (Kanpur) and Universiti Sains Malaysia (Penang) brokered by Khazanah Holdings has raised the potential for producing the human capital and research support to feed technological upgrading.[2] However, much needs to be done to facilitate the quick hiring of human capital to support the transition to higher value added activities in Malaysia.

Taken together, by and large Malaysia's initiatives remain spot on to meet the obligations it has set to integrate within the AEC by 2015. However, a number of concerns still threaten to hold back deregulation in particular industries. On the one hand, under the guise of quickening structural transformation and poverty alleviation, industries such as automotives remain protected, but with no dynamic framework to make them competitive. On the other hand, the misapplication of resources for political motives is draining the country of them.

Given the typical ASEAN style of engagement, it is unlikely these barriers will hold back the culmination of the AEC by 2015. However, it is also unlikely that the AEC will take on a full blown integrated structure in the next decade.

## Conclusions and Implications

Typical of ASEAN initiatives, Malaysia has been a strong driver as well as an executor of the AEC road map. The already liberal environment of the country has ensured that most of the obligations are easily met. Indeed, the ASEAN Six have already brought tariffs down to zero on 99 per cent of goods. However, a few barriers can potentially reduce the synergies that could be appropriated from an integrated ASEAN. Firstly, within ASEAN the overriding pursuit of liberalization does not recognize that its benefits can only be increased once individual members put in place effective mechanisms to stimulate technological capabilities. The evolution of technological capabilities is paramount to the appropriation of integration benefits. Secondly, there is a serious lack of urgency in implementing regulatory changes to prevent predatory monopolistic competition in the region. Because scale is important, dynamic regulations are necessary rather than simply an adoption of liberalization to effect anti-monopoly predatory conduct. Thirdly, Malaysia has not shown the drive to liberalize ethno-policy coloured industries that have drained competitiveness. Fourthly, ethno-coloured policies also appear to hold back Malaysia's execution of brain gain policies. Not only has the number of returnees been dismal, but their roles have hardly connected dynamically in synergizing technological catch-up.

The main positive policy implication that can be drawn from Malaysia's initiatives within ASEAN is that integration efforts will not be derailed as long as national preferences are allowed to remain, even if they may not be identical in other member countries. Indeed, as the Secretary-General of ASEAN, Surin Pitsuwan, often envisaged, the constructive engagement principle that drives its initiatives will see to the realization of the AEC by 2015. However, will the AEC achieve the four objectives sought at its launch in 2003? With the exception of economic convergence — which I argue cannot happen without serious capability building efforts — the AEC can be expected to broadly achieve the rest. There can be some shortfalls though, in forcing the removal of protection and subsidies in politically sensitive industries such as automotives in Malaysia, and in ensuring that skilled labour can indeed freely relocate to meet demand. Besides, because human capital is the only active driver of technological advancement, problems can emerge if individual members seek to pursue "poaching" or "brain gain" strategies aggressively from a limited pool within the region.

## NOTES

1. Despite the use of the term "macro objective", the Prime Minister's statement in no way removes the objectives of NEP and NDP.
2. The author assisted with the establishment of the initial links between the two universities for Khazanah.

## REFERENCES

Amsden, A. *Asia's Next Giant: South Korea and Late Industrialization.* New York: Oxford University Press, 1989.

Basu Das, Sanchita and C. Aekapol. "Free Trade Agreements in Southeast Asia". In *The New Political Economy of Southeast Asia*, edited by R. Rasiah and J.D. Schmidt. Cheltenham: Edward Elgar, 2010.

Chang, H.J. *Kicking Away the Ladder.* London: Anthem Press, 2003.

Cimoli, M., G. Dosi, and J. Stiglitz. *Industrial Policy and Development: The Political Economy of Capabilities Accumulation.* Oxford: Oxford University Press, 2009.

Coase R. "Nature of the Firm". *Economica* 16, no. 4 (1937): 386–405.

Fransman, M. "International Competitiveness, Technical Change and the State: The Machine Tool Industry in Taiwan and Japan". *World Development* 14, no. 2 (1986): 1375–96.

Izatun, S. "PM Announces a Slew of Liberalization Measures". *The Star*, 30 June 2009.

Johnson, C. *MITI and the Japanese Miracle.* Stanford: Stanford University Press, 1982.

Kaldor, N. "Equilibrium Theory and Growth Theory". In *Economics and Human Welfare: Essays in Honor of Tibor Scitovsky*, edited by M. Boskin. New York: Academic Press, 1979.

Lall, S. *Learning to Industrialize: The Acquisition of Technological Capability by India.* London: Macmillan, 1987.

———. *Competitiveness, Technology and Skills.* Cheltenham: Edward Elgar, 2001.

Lin, Y. "The Contribution of the Diaspora to Taiwan's High Tech Industrialization". In *Brain Gain Review*, edited by R. Rasiah and K. Thiruchelvam. Putra Jaya: MOSTI, 2009.

Malaysia. *The Second Malaysia Plan 1971–1975*. Kuala Lumpur: Government Printers, 1971.

———. *Malaysia High Technology Industry Report*. Putra Jaya: MIGHT, 2009.

———. *Annual Report*. Kuala Lumpur: Bank Negara, 2010a.

———. *The New Economic Model*. Putra Jaya: Finance Ministry, 2010b.

———. "Competition Act 2010", Laws of Malaysia Act 712. Putrajaya: Government Printers, 2010c.

Mikic, M. "ASEAN and Trade Integration". Trade and Investment Division Staff Working Paper 01/09. Bangkok: Economic and Social Commission for Asia and Pacific (ESCAP), 2009.

Nelson, R. "Economic Development from the Perspective of Evolutionary Theory". *Oxford Development Studies* 36, no. 1 (2008): 9–21.

North, D. "Economic Performance through Time". *American Economic Review* 84, no. 3 (1994): 359–68.

Rasiah, R. *Foreign Capital and Industrialization in Malaysia*. Basingstoke: Macmillan, 1995.

———. "Malaysia's National Innovation System". In *Technology, Competitiveness and the State*, edited by K.S. Jomo and G. Felker. London: Routledge, 1999.

———. "Are Electronics Firms in Malaysia Catching Up in the Technology Ladder?" *Journal of Asia Pacific Economy* 15, no. 3 (2010).

Reinert, E. *How Rich Countries Got Rich ... and Why Poor Countries Stay Poor*. London: Anthem Press, 2008.

Wade, R. *Governing the Market*. Princeton: Princeton University Press, 1990.

Williamson O.E. *The Economic Institutions of Capitalism*. New York: Free Press, 1985.

Young, A. "Increasing Returns and Economic Progress". *Economic Journal* 38, no. 152 (1928): 527–42.

# 8

# Achieving the AEC 2015:
# Challenges for the Philippines

Jenny D. Balboa, Fatima Lourdes E. Del Prado,
and Josef T. Yap[1]

ASEAN member countries are moving towards achieving the ASEAN Economic Community (AEC) by 2015. Recent studies have shown the benefits of the AEC. For example, the study edited by Plummer and Chia (2009) presents estimates that ASEAN economic welfare will rise by 5.3 per cent or US$69 billion relative to the baseline. It is therefore important for policymakers in the region to sustain the momentum — or perhaps even accelerate the pace — towards establishing the AEC.

Policy measures are being implemented based on the AEC Blueprint agreed on in 2007. However, progress among the ASEAN member countries in meeting their commitments has been uneven. Moreover, many difficult regional issues have not yet been resolved. Among these are wide development gaps and entrenched domestic interests.[2] Hence, achieving the AEC in 2015 may be on the optimistic side. The theme of 2010's ASEAN Summit, "From Vision to Action", is therefore quite appropriate.

This chapter reviews the progress of the Philippines in meeting its commitments. The progress is largely reflected in the AEC Scorecard, an analytical tool in tracking the achievements of member countries that was developed by ASEAN for this purpose. The framework of the AEC Blueprint is described in Box 1 of the Preface. As of this writing, only the Philippine scorecard for the first batch of priority actions was available. The official data is supplemented by a study conducted by the Economic Research Institute for ASEAN and East Asia (ERIA; Corbett and Umezaki 2009).

In the next section, the current Philippine economic situation is described by comparing it with other economies in terms of indicators of competitiveness. Many of the latter are components of the AEC Blueprint. This is followed by a section where the Philippine performance in terms of the ASEAN Scorecard is presented and discussed. As mentioned earlier, the official data will be supplemented by results from the ERIA studies. The penultimate section attempts to explain the progress of the Philippines in meeting its AEC commitments, particularly vis-à-vis the more developed ASEAN countries. The last section looks at structural problems in the Philippines that may prevent it from benefiting from the AEC. These problems also explain the relatively poor performance of the Philippines in terms of competitiveness.

## Competitiveness of the Philippine Economy

The AEC Blueprint calls for creating a single market and production base that will improve the competitiveness of the region. In this context, the Philippines stands to benefit a great deal since its level of competitiveness lags those of many economies, including its ASEAN neighbours. For example, the World Bank's *Doing Business* report shows a deteriorating performance for the Philippines in its latest survey on the ease of doing business. The country fell by three notches, from its rank of 141th in 2009 to its rank of 144th in 2010. The same survey also shows the country's global ranking weakening in all areas of doing business, particularly in the areas of ease of paying taxes, starting a business, dealing with construction permits, and protecting investors (Table 8.1).

Factors that can explain this poor performance are shown in Figure 8.1. Latest surveys show that corruption, an inefficient government, and the inadequate infrastructure remain the main obstacles for doing business in the Philippines.

The Philippine situation highlights two key issues related to the AEC and economic integration in general. First, the factors that hamper progress towards implementing the country's commitments have to be explained. Some of these factors may overlap with a second category: factors that prevent the Philippines from benefiting fully from the implementation of these commitments, in particular (from previous policies under the banner of liberalization, privatization, and deregulation, in general). These factors will be discussed in turn in the last two sections of the chapter.

### TABLE 8.1
### Ease of Doing Business in the Philippines

|  | Doing Business 2010 rank | Doing Business 2009 rank | Change in rank |
|---|---|---|---|
| Starting a Business | 162 | 155 | −7 |
| Dealing with Construction Permits | 111 | 106 | −5 |
| Employing Workers | 115 | 114 | −1 |
| Registering Property | 102 | 101 | −1 |
| Getting Credit | 127 | 125 | −2 |
| Protecting Investors | 132 | 127 | −5 |
| Paying Taxes | 135 | 126 | −9 |
| Trading Across Borders | 68 | 66 | −2 |
| Enforcing Contracts | 118 | 116 | −2 |
| Closing a Business | 153 | 153 | 0 |
| Doing Business Report Rank | 144 | 141 | −3 |

Source: *Doing Business* report <http://Doing Business in Philippines — Doing Business — The World Bank Group.htm> (accessed 10 April 2010).

**FIGURE 8.1**
**The Most Problematic Factors for Doing Business in the Philippines**

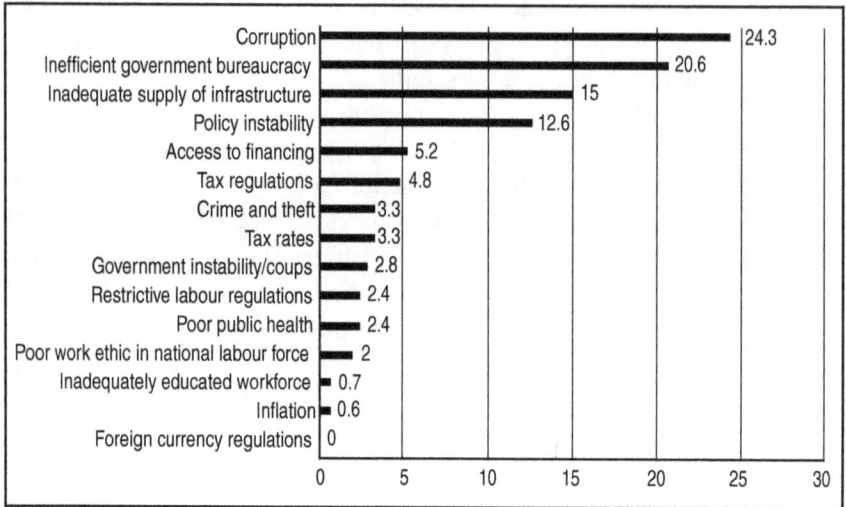

| Factor | Value |
|---|---|
| Corruption | 24.3 |
| Inefficient government bureaucracy | 20.6 |
| Inadequate supply of infrastructure | 15 |
| Policy instability | 12.6 |
| Access to financing | 5.2 |
| Tax regulations | 4.8 |
| Crime and theft | 3.3 |
| Tax rates | 3.3 |
| Government instability/coups | 2.8 |
| Restrictive labour regulations | 2.4 |
| Poor public health | 2.4 |
| Poor work ethic in national labour force | 2 |
| Inadequately educated workforce | 0.7 |
| Inflation | 0.6 |
| Foreign currency regulations | 0 |

*Source: Global Competitiveness Report, 2009–10.*

## Progress of the Philippines with its AEC Commitments

### The AEC Scorecard

To monitor the timely implementation of the AEC Blueprint, an AEC Scorecard was developed to serve as a tool to keep track of the progress of member states in implementing the commitments. The scorecard has two major goals: (1) to provide qualitative and quantitative indications of the ratification, adoption, and transposition into domestic laws, regulations, and administrative procedures of agreed obligations, and commitments within the prescribed timeframes as specified in the AEC Blueprint; and (2) to track the implementation of agreements/commitments and achievement of milestones in the AEC Strategic Schedule.

The scorecard monitors the timely implementation of the Priority Actions based on the AEC Blueprint. The Priority Actions are derived from the four primary objectives and seventeen core elements of the AEC. The four primary objectives are: (1) a single market and production base; (2) a highly competitive region; (3) a region of equitable economic development; and (4) a region fully integrated into the global economy.

The ASEAN single market and production base has seven core elements: (1) free flow of goods, (2) free flow of services, (3) free flow of investment, (4) freer flow of capital, (5) free flow of skilled labour, (6) priority integration sectors, and (7) food, agriculture and forestry.

With respect to creating a competitive economic region, six core elements are included, namely: (1) competition policy, (2) consumer protection, (3) intellectual property rights, (4) infrastructure development, (5) taxation, and (6) e-commerce.

Two core elements are included in the equitable economic development objective, and are as follows: (1) SME development and (2) initiative for ASEAN integration (IAI).

Finally, in creating a region fully integrated into the global economy, ASEAN is aware that it needs to take into account external rules and regulations. In this regard, two elements are included in this objective: (1) developing a coherent approach towards external economic relations, (2) enhanced participation in global supply networks.

Priority actions under these core elements are to be undertaken within four implementation periods: 2008–09, 2010–11, 2012–13, and 2014–15.

The ASEAN Secretariat keeps track, evaluates, and rates the performance of member countries. While the scorecard can benefit from further refinement, the current format gives a picture of the achievement of ASEAN member states in incorporating the strategic actions of the AEC Blueprint.

## The Philippine Scorecard: Tentative Results

Preliminary estimates show that the Philippines generated a score of 45.71 per cent, indicating thirty-two measures implemented out of seventy-two for the first set of priority actions. The score can still improve as several commitments under transport (9/25) already complied but are yet to be implemented. At least eleven protocols from the transport sector are pending for executive ratification as of April 2010.

### *Highlights of Results of AEC Scorecard for the Philippines (Tentative Results)[3]*

Listed below are the highlights of the AEC Scorecard results of the Philippines as of May 2010:

### Implemented Measures

A. Single Market and Production Base

1.  Free Flow of Goods
    *   CEPT-AFTA — Full implementation of the AFTA CEPT Scheme.
    *   Tariff Liberalization, except for the end rate for Highly Sensitive Product (rice).
    *   Rules of Origin — Approved revised CEPT ROO Scheme had been reviewed and implemented.
    *   ASEAN Trade Facilitation Work Programme — Comprehensive Work Programme on Trade Facilitation had been finalized.
    *   ASEAN Single Window (Bureau of Customs) — the National Single Window was launched recently and included standardized data elements for digitalized processing and exchange. However, it is still to be fully operationalized.
    *   Standards and Conformance (Bureau of Product Standards) — ASEAN Reference Laboratories had been established and the ASEAN Cosmetic Directive had been implemented. The bureau still has not implemented the following: (1) ASEAN Common Technical Dossier and ASEAN Harmonized Common Technical Requirement; (2) Signing of ASEAN Sectoral MRA on GMP of Inspection of Manufacturers of Medicinal Products.

2.  Free Flow of Services
    *   Scheduled maximum of three types of non-equity market access limitations for twelve subsectors under the Other Sectors area.
    *   Scheduled "none" for modes 1 and 2 market access and national treatment, with exceptions due to bona fide regulatory reasons.
    *   Complete compilation of inventory of barriers to services.
    *   Completed negotiations and signed MRA on accountancy services.
    *   Completed negotiations and signed MRA on medical practitioners.
    *   Completed negotiations and signed MRA on dental practitioners.

3. Free Flow of Investment
   - Discussed, drafted, negotiated, and signed the new ASEAN Comprehensive Investment Agreement (ACIA).
   - Publication of ASEAN Investment Report.
   - Publication of Statistics of FDI in ASEAN.
   - Commenced Phase 1 of progressive reduction/elimination of investment restrictions and impediments.

4. Priority Integration Measures
   - Automotive — A regional strategy study on the automotive industry is being developed; other measures, such as an ASEAN database on automotive products, as well as an ASEAN portal for ASEAN automotive components, are also being developed.
   - Textile/Apparel — Initiated a study to assess the impact of the Multi-Fibre Agreement expiry on ASEAN textile industry and a study on the impact in ASEAN of China's export of textiles and apparel products in Asia.

B. Creating a Competitive Region

   - Competition Policy — Carrying out a foundation-laying study, review of study findings and recommendations, and convening a regional meeting on study findings and recommendations; Establishment of the ASEAN Expert Group on Competition.
   - Consumer Protection — Establishment of the ASEAN Coordinating Committee on Consumer Protection.
   - Infrastructure — Several protocols and initiatives under the transport sector.

C. Equitable Economic Development

   - Initiative for ASEAN Integration (IAI) — Endorsement of the IAI Strategic Framework and Work Plan 2.

## Priority Actions Pending for Implementation

A. Single Market and Production Base

1. Free Flow of Goods
   - End rate for HSL products (rice).
   - ASEAN Single Window (to be fully operationalized).

- Standards and Conformance — Implementation of ASEAN Common Technical Dossier and ASEAN Harmonized Common Technical Requirement; Signing of ASEAN Sectoral MRA on GMP of Inspection of Manufacturers of Medicinal Products.

2. Free Flow of Services
   - Schedule of ten new subsectors.
   - Schedule at least 51 per cent of foreign equity allowed in the priority services sector.
   - Schedule at least 49 per cent of foreign equity allowed in logistics services and other sectors.
   - Schedule a maximum of two types of non-equity market access limitations for all twenty-nine subsectors of the four priority services sector.
   - Schedule maximum of three types of non-equity market access limitations for all logistics services subsectors.

3. Free Flow of Capital
   - Assess and identify top five rules for liberalization, listing of existing rules and measures on FDI, and review, evaluate and assess existing rules and measures.

4. Priority Integration Measures
   - E-ASEAN — Facilitate MRAs for qualifications in IT professionals.
   - Electronics — Institutionalize Rosettanet compatibility in ASEAN for the exchange of trade documents; Implement 24/7 customs operations, as may be applicable or deemed necessary, through operationalization of the systems of electronic processing and those similar on the basis of the ASEAN Cargo Processing Model.
   - Health care — Set up "one stop centre" in each ASEAN country responsible for facilitating investments including health care projects.
   - Food, Agriculture, and Forestry — Define legality standards for timber (elements and indicators for legal timber).

B. Creating a Competitive Region

- Consumer Protection — Terms of Reference and Work Programme for the development of a rapid alert system and information exchange.

- Transport — Eleven Protocols covering issues on trade facilitation pending ratification.
- Energy — Ratify MOU on ASEAN Power Grid.

C. Initiative for ASEAN Integration

- Conduct study to determine the impact of accelerating the AEC from 2020 to 2015 on CLMV.

## Recent Achievements: The National Single Window Project

An important strategic action under the AEC Blueprint is the international Single Window Project. This is part of the initiative to improve import/export and customs operations in ASEAN. The main idea of this project is to have a single customs portal for ASEAN by interconnecting the Single Window of member economies for easier and more efficient import and export processing in the region. The ASEAN Single Window Project is due to be completed by 2012.

In 2010, the Philippines had the soft launching of the National Electronic Single Window. Planning and implementation of the project are overseen by a steering committee led by the Department of Finance and composed of agencies linked to the Bureau of Customs (BOC). The National Single Window project is expected to speed up customs processing for importers and exporters substantially and enhance transparency and efficiency in transactions with the BOC.

## Results of Selected ERIA Studies

To complement the ASEAN Scorecard, the Economic Research Institute for ASEAN and East Asia (ERIA) has embarked on a series of studies under the banner "Deepening East Asian Economic Integration". The initial set of studies (Corbett and Umezaki 2009) focused on developing quantitative measures to "provide several snapshots of the progress in selected key policy pillars in the AEC Blueprint. The quantitative measures were designed (1) to visualize the process of policy reforms consistent with the AEC Blueprint, (2) to provide a framework under which milestones and end goals for each element can be defined, and (3) to evaluate the current status and the progress towards the milestones and end goals".

Urata and Ando (2009) conducted a study to examine and evaluate the restrictiveness/openness of the FDI policy regime and environment for ASEAN countries. They examined FDI policies found in legal documents that are related to six aspects: market access or right of establishment; national treatment; screening and approval of procedure; restrictions on boards of directors; movement of foreign investors; and performance requirement.

Since it is common in developing countries that the existence of a law does not necessarily imply its implementation, Urata and Ando used information on barriers to FDI from the survey compiled by the Japan Machinery Center for Trade and Investment (JMC). The survey looked into the obstacles faced by Japanese firms operating in ASEAN countries.

The scoring system used shows a high score for a relatively open FDI regime and the various factors are given different weights. The results of their evaluation, which are shown in Table 8.2, indicate that the FDI policy regime in Singapore is very open and those in the Philippines, Thailand, Indonesia, and Cambodia are relatively open, while those in Myanmar, Malaysia, Brunei, and the Lao PDR are relatively closed. The said study ranks the Philippines as the second-most open economy in ASEAN.

A study conducted by Urata, Ando, and Ito (2007), which is related to the aforementioned JMC survey, shows that the FDI performance in a country is not only determined by liberalization policies, but also facilitation issues. Ten major categories of issues were identified, with four issues relevant to FDI liberalization and six issues relevant to facilitation, as indicated below:

FDI liberalization:

1. Restrictions on foreign entry
2. Performance requirements
3. Restrictions on overseas remittances and controls on foreign currency transactions
4. Restrictions on the movement of people and employment requirements

FDI facilitation

5. Lack of transparency in policies and regulations concerning investment (institutional problems)

**TABLE 8.2**
**Assessment of FDI Policy Regimes of ASEAN Countries**

| | Market Access | National Treatment | Screening and Appraisal | Board of Directors | Movement of Investors | Performance Requirements | Total Score |
|---|---|---|---|---|---|---|---|
| Weight | 0.40 | 0.20 | 0.10 | 0.10 | 0.10 | 0.10 | 1.00 |
| Brunei | 0.76 | 0.20 | 0.57 | 0.41 | 0.82 | 0.82 | 0.61 |
| Cambodia | 0.86 | 0.60 | 0.25 | 1.00 | 0.25 | 0.88 | 0.70 |
| Indonesia | 0.69 | 0.95 | 0.24 | 0.95 | 0.48 | 0.95 | 0.73 |
| Lao PDR | 0.60 | 0.70 | 0.34 | 0.67 | 0.54 | 0.79 | 0.61 |
| Malaysia | 0.59 | 0.17 | 0.76 | 0.62 | 0.89 | 0.91 | 0.59 |
| Myanmar | 0.55 | 0.61 | 0.30 | 0.61 | 0.24 | 0.61 | 0.52 |
| Philippines | 0.74 | 0.81 | 0.89 | 0.48 | 0.96 | 0.89 | 0.78 |
| Singapore | 0.83 | 0.95 | 0.86 | 0.75 | 0.95 | 0.95 | 0.88 |
| Thailand | 0.58 | 1.00 | 0.91 | 0.98 | 0.37 | 0.90 | 0.75 |
| Vietnam | 0.66 | 0.74 | 0.64 | 0.71 | 0.53 | 0.85 | 0.69 |
| Average | 0.69 | 0.67 | 0.58 | 0.72 | 0.60 | 0.85 | 0.69 |
| Standard deviation | 0.11 | 0.29 | 0.28 | 0.20 | 0.28 | 0.10 | 0.11 |

*Source:* Urata and Ando 2009, Table 3.2.

6. Complicated and/or delayed procedures with respect to investment related regulations (implementation problems)
7. Insufficient protection of intellectual property rights
8. Labour regulations and related practices excessively favourable to workers
9. Underdeveloped infrastructure, shortages of human resources, and insufficient investment
10. Restricted competition and price controls

The survey conducted in 2008 shows that FDI liberalization policies in the Philippines, as perceived by Japanese firms, on average are at par, or even better, than other ASEAN countries. However, it is in FDI facilitation measures that the Philippines is outperformed by other ASEAN countries. Comparing the results of the survey with 2005 figures show that the number of problems pertaining to FDI facilitation in the Philippines even increased sharply (Table 8.3). This was attributed to a growing number of issues related to implementation problems for investment-related policies and regulations and a perceived labour regulation excessively favourable to workers (Urata and Ando 2009).

Meanwhile the survey of Findlay (2009) on trade facilitation shows that there are large differences in the regulatory environment for logistics of the ASEAN+6 economies. Both the domestic measures that apply to all entrants and measures that apply only to foreign providers were evaluated. Citing a study of Hollweg and Wong (2009), Findlay reports that Vietnam, Lao PDR, India, and the Philippines have relatively high scores, that is, relatively restrictive regimes — on the domestic index. The countries with high scores for the foreign index are Indonesia, the Philippines, China, and Malaysia. Only the Philippines appears on both lists.

## Explaining the Progress with AEC Commitments

### Trends in the Philippines

The Philippine AEC Scorecard reveals that the Philippines is committed to be part of the ASEAN Economic Community and to contribute to regional integration goals. It shows positive results in trade liberalization, with the CEPT-AFTA in full implementation and tariff barriers

**TABLE 8.3**
**Investment Climate in the Philippines, 2005, 2008**

| | Philippines | |
|---|---|---|
| | 2005 | 2008 |
| a) The number of Japanese affiliates in each country | | 419 |
| b) Issues to be solved for FDI liberalization and facilitation | | |
| **FDI liberalization** | **11** | **9** |
| 1) Restriction on foreign entry | 6 | 6 |
| 2) Performance requirements | 2 | 0 |
| 3) Restrictions on overseas remittances and controls on foreign currency transactions | 1 | 2 |
| 4) Restrictions on the movement of people and employment requirements | 2 | 1 |
| **FDI facilitation** | **37** | **48** |
| 5) Lack of transparency in policies and regulations concerning investment (institutional problems) | 10 | 11 |
| 6) Complicated and/or delayed procedures with respect to investment related regulations (implementation problems) | 12 | 16 |
| 7) Insufficient protection of intellectual property rights | 1 | 3 |
| 8) Labour regulations and related practices excessively favourable to workers | 6 | 10 |
| 9) Underdeveloped infrastructure, shortages of human resources, and insufficient investment incentives | 8 | 8 |
| 10) Restricted competition and price controls | 0 | 0 |
| **Total** | **48** | **57** |

*Source:* Urata and Ando 2009, Tables 4.2 and 4.3.

reduced or eliminated, allowing the free flow of goods in the country. The Philippines' commitment to free trade is more or less reflective of the general pattern of trade liberalization in the region. Table 8.4 shows tariff and non-tariff barriers (NTBs) in ASEAN and other East Asian countries. Average tariff rates had been either removed for some member countries or lowered to 0.1. Average tariff weight for non-agricultural products had been likewise brought down to the same level. Tariff rates for agricultural products are higher, but had been generally brought down to 0–0.5. The Philippines is at 0.1 average tariff rate.

TABLE 8.4
Tariff and Non-tariff Barriers Indicators

| Country | Trade weighted average tariff rate | Trade weighted average tariff rate for non-agricultural products | Trade weighted average tariff rate for agricultural products | Non-tariff barriers |
|---|---|---|---|---|
| Australia | 0.1 | 0.1 | 0.0 | 20.2 |
| Brunei | | | | |
| Cambodia | 0.1 | 0.1 | 0.2 | 4.2 |
| China/PRC | 0.1 | 0.1 | 0.2 | 22.6 |
| Hong Kong | 0.0 | 0.0 | 0.0 | n/a |
| Indonesia | 0.1 | 0.1 | 0.1 | 45.0 |
| Japan | 0.0 | 0.0 | 0.2 | 65.4 |
| Korea (Rep. of) | 0.1 | 0.1 | 0.5 | n/a |
| Lao PDR | | | | |
| Malaysia | 0.1 | 0.1 | 0.2 | 17.1 |
| Myanmar | | | | |
| New Zealand | 0.0 | 0.0 | 0.0 | 23.7 |
| **Philippines** | **0.0** | **0.0** | **0.1** | **64.5** |
| Singapore | 0.0 | 0.0 | 0.0 | 23.8 |
| Taiwan | 0.1 | 0.0 | 0.2 | 23.0 |
| Thailand | 0.1 | 0.1 | 0.3 | 26.9 |
| Vietnam | 0.1 | 0.1 | 0.4 | 34.9 |

*Source: Global Competitiveness Report, 2010.*

However, non-tariff barriers remain high in the region, with Japan having the most number of NTBs at 65.4, and the Philippines following closely at 64.5. Non-tariff measures (NTMs) were also observed to be significantly increasing in the Philippines in the past decade, with more technical barriers to trade being imposed (Basu 2010). One of the reasons cited for the increase in NTMs is that with the reduction or removal of tariffs, NTMs have been resorted to so as to provide some protection to local industries to help them survive competition against imports. Nonetheless, based on its AEC commitment, the Philippines NTBs will be reduced by 2012. Compliance to this commitment will address the issue of rising NTMs.

With tariffs removed and the remaining ones gradually reduced and removed, and with efforts towards eliminating non-tariff barriers, ASEAN and East Asia will be creating a huge open market as the economies move closer to the target date of creating an ASEAN Economic Community in 2015. The next step would be to move to create an open business environment that would facilitate the free flow of trade and accelerate transactions between and among economies. As discussed in the earlier section, the Philippines has a lot of catching up to do in improving its competitiveness and in making the country an attractive trade and investment destination.

For the Philippines, an important area that has to be addressed is enhancing transparency and efficiency of customs procedure. Based on the latest survey conducted by the World Economic Forum, the Philippines is perceived to be the most inefficient, corrupt, and costly (by middle-income country standards) customs service in East Asia (Table 8.5). Full operation of the BOC's National Single Window could potentially be the solution to this problem. Reducing human interface in customs transactions could reduce the agency's vulnerability to corrupt practices and also substantially reduce transaction costs.

The Philippine AEC Scorecard likewise reflects the country's weakness in the area of free flow of investment and freer flow of capital. This is consistent with the study of Urata and Ando discussed earlier. Inadequate government policies to facilitate these two key areas resulted in smaller investment and capital flows to the country relative to other middle-income economies in ASEAN. A recent survey shows that the Philippines is perceived to be the least open in foreign participation in the region (Table 8.6). The government is bound by

**TABLE 8.5**
**Customs Procedures**

| Country | Burden of Customs procedures[1] How would you rate the level of efficiency of customs procedures (related to the entry and exit of merchandise) in your country? (1 = extremely inefficient; 7 = extremely efficient), I 2008–09 weighted average | | Time for Import | Documents for Import | Cost to Import | Time for export | Documents for export | Cost to export | Trading across borders |
| --- | --- | --- | --- | --- | --- | --- | --- | --- | --- |
| | Score | Rank (out of 133 Countries) | Number of days required to import/2009 | Number of documents required to import/2009 | (US$ per container) | Number of days required to export/2009 | Number of documents required to export/2009 | (US$ per container) | Rank out of 183 countries, 2009 |
| Australia | 4.9 | 24.0 | 8.0 | 5.0 | 1119.0 | 9.0 | 6.0 | 1060.0 | 27.0 |
| Brunei | 4.6 | 36.0 | 19.0 | 6.0 | 708.0 | 28.0 | 6.0 | 630.0 | 48.0 |
| Cambodia | | | 30.0 | 11.0 | 872.0 | 22.0 | 11.0 | 732.0 | 127.0 |
| China/PRC | 4.6 | 41.0 | 24.0 | 5.0 | 545.0 | 21.0 | 7.0 | 500.0 | 44.0 |
| Hong Kong | 6.1 | 2.0 | 5.0 | 4.0 | 583.0 | 6.0 | 4.0 | 625.0 | 2.0 |
| Indonesia | 3.7 | 83.0 | 27.0 | 6.0 | 660.0 | 21.0 | 5.0 | 704.0 | 45.0 |
| Japan | 4.4 | 49.0 | 11.0 | 5.0 | 1047.0 | 10.0 | 4.0 | 989.0 | 17.0 |
| Korea (Rep. of) | 4.6 | 42.0 | 8.0 | 3.0 | 742.0 | 8.0 | 3.0 | 742.0 | 8.0 |
| Lao PDR | | | 50.0 | 10.0 | 2040.0 | 50.0 | 9.0 | 1860.0 | 168.0 |
| Malaysia | 4.8 | 28.0 | 14.0 | 7.0 | 450.0 | 18.0 | 7.0 | 450.0 | 35.0 |
| Myanmar | | | | | | | | | |
| New Zealand | 5.9 | 4.0 | 9.0 | 5.0 | 850.0 | 10.0 | 7.0 | 868.0 | 26.0 |
| Philippines | 3.0 | 117.0 | 16.0 | 8.0 | 819.0 | 16.0 | 8.0 | 816.0 | 68.0 |
| Singapore | 6.4 | 1.0 | 3.0 | 4.0 | 439.0 | 5.0 | 4.0 | 456.0 | 1.0 |
| Taiwan | 5.0 | 23.0 | 12.0 | 7.0 | 732.0 | 13.0 | 7.0 | 720.0 | 33.0 |
| Thailand | 4.1 | 60.0 | 13.0 | 3.0 | 795.0 | 14.0 | 4.0 | 625.0 | 12.0 |
| Vietnam | 3.6 | 91.0 | 21.0 | 8.0 | 940.0 | 22.0 | 6.0 | 756.0 | 74.0 |

*Note:* 1. World Economic Forum, *World Competitiveness Report: 2009.*
*Source:* World Bank, *Doing Business Report: 2009.*

## TABLE 8.6
## Openness to Foreign Participation

| Country | Openness to Foreign Participation | Ease of hiring foreign labour | Prevalence of foreign ownership[1] | | Business impact of rules on FDI[1] | |
|---|---|---|---|---|---|---|
| | This variable is calculated as the average of four variables: Ease of hiring foreign labour, Prevalence of foreign ownership, Business Impact of rules on FDI, & Capital controls, 2007, 2008 (1 = least open, 7 = most open) | Labour regulation in your country (1 = prevents your company from employing foreign labour, 7 = does not prevent your company from employing foreign labour), 2007, 2008 | How prevalent is foreign ownership of companies in your country? (1 = very rare; 7 = highly prevalent), 2008–09 weighted average | | To what extent do rules governing foreign direct investment (FDI) encourage or discourage it? (1 = strongly discourage FDI; 7 = strongly encourage FDI), 2008–09 weighted average | |
| | | | Score | Rank (out of 133 countries) | Score | Rank (out of 133 countries) |
| Australia | 5.2 | 4.5 | 5.6 | 26.0 | 5.1 | 55.0 |
| Brunei | 5.0 | | 4.2 | 108.0 | 4.8 | 78.0 |
| Cambodia | 4.5 | 4.6 | 4.9 | 77.0 | 5.2 | 47.0 |
| China/PRC | 4.5 | 5.1 | 4.4 | 98.0 | 5.6 | 23.0 |
| Hong Kong | 6.3 | 5.4 | 6.6 | 1.0 | 6.5 | 3.0 |
| Indonesia | 5.5 | 5.3 | 5.3 | 41.0 | 5.3 | 41.0 |
| Japan | 4.6 | 4.0 | 4.4 | 93.0 | 4.5 | 98.0 |
| Korea (Rep. of) | 5.2 | 4.9 | 5.1 | 62.0 | 4.9 | 65.0 |
| Lao PDR | | | | | | |
| Malaysia | 5.1 | 4.9 | 5.0 | 68.0 | 5.3 | 43.0 |
| Myanmar | | | | | | |
| New Zealand | 5.5 | 4.8 | 5.9 | 14.0 | 5.0 | 61.0 |
| **Philippines** | **4.5** | **4.0** | **4.3** | **102.0** | **4.5** | **97.0** |
| Singapore | 6.3 | 5.9 | 6.4 | 3.0 | 6.7 | 1.0 |
| Taiwan | 4.8 | 4.2 | 5.3 | 51.0 | 5.4 | 39.0 |
| Thailand | 4.6 | 4.3 | 4.8 | 80.0 | 5.3 | 44.0 |
| Vietnam | 4.8 | 4.8 | 4.2 | 107.0 | 5.5 | 27.0 |

*Note:* 1. World Economic Forum, *World Competitiveness Report: 2009.*
*Source:* World Economic Forum, *Executive Opinion Survey 2007, 2008.*

constitutional restrictions to legislate policies that will facilitate foreign investment in certain areas. The Foreign Investment Negative List (FINL) (RA 8179, as amended) specifies the areas restricted to Filipinos and areas opened to foreigners, and the corresponding investment equity restrictions. The FINL includes, among other restrictions on its use, management and ownership of certain utilities and infrastructure (for example, the cabotage law in shipping), and imposes foreign equity restriction of up to 40 per cent in BOT projects and government procurement. In retail trade, a minimum of US$7.5 million equity is required, which is much higher than the requirement for Thailand (at US$250,000). Meanwhile, Singapore and Hong Kong have no such requirement.

In terms of creating a competitive region, the Philippines needs to strengthen efforts in this area. Amidst fear of market domination of large foreign companies with a more liberalized investment regime, developing an effective competition policy, aligned with regional guidelines, has even become more expedient. This is an area that needs urgent attention and for which the government, for a long time now, has failed to come up with decisive actions due to strong private-sector lobby. Also, in relation to creating a competitive region, the government needs to enact better policies to protect intellectual property rights and improve tax regulation policies in the country.

The Philippines is also sorely lagging in infrastructure and logistics and needs to catch up with the other East Asian economies (Table 8.7). This is an important area since infrastructure and logistics affect the country's attractiveness as an investment destination.

The Philippine AEC Scorecard did not include actions to strengthen SMEs to make it at par with best practices in SMEs in East Asia. As the biggest employer in the country and the source of employment of the poor, the SME is a critical sector for growth and development and therefore needs full support in terms of access to financing and product and skills development to enable them to compete with domestic and international players. SME development should be considered a top priority and its progress should be closely tracked at both the domestic and regional levels. The Department of Trade and Industry, through the Bureau of Micro, Small and Medium Enterprise Development (BMSMED), is in charge of this sector. The BMSMED has launched several initiatives to spur SME growth in the country.

**TABLE 8.7**
**Infrastructure**

| Country | Paved Roads[1] — Paved roads as percentage of total roads/2005 | Road — Motor vehicles per km of road/2005 | Quality of port infrastructure — Score | Quality of port infrastructure — Rank (Out of 133 Countries) | Quality of air transport infrastructure — Score | Quality of air transport infrastructure — Rank (Out of 133 Countries) | Quality of railroad infrastructure — Score | Quality of railroad infrastructure — Rank (Out of 114 Countries) | Quality of roads — Score | Quality of roads — Rank (Out of 133 Countries) | Quality of Overall Infrastructure — Score | Quality of Overall Infrastructure — Rank (Out of 133 Countries) |
|---|---|---|---|---|---|---|---|---|---|---|---|---|
| Australia | 38.7 | 17.0 | 4.6 | 50.0 | 5.8 | 28.0 | 4.1 | 29.0 | 5.0 | 37.0 | 5.0 | 38.0 |
| Brunei | | | 4.8 | 42.0 | 5.2 | 47.0 | | | 5.2 | 29.0 | 3.4 | 82.0 |
| Cambodia | 6.3 | 37.0 | 3.5 | 89.0 | 4.1 | 88.0 | 1.6 | 94.0 | 3.3 | 77.0 | 4.0 | 66.0 |
| China/PRC | 81.6 | 16.0 | 4.3 | 61.0 | 4.3 | 80.0 | 4.1 | 27.0 | 4.2 | 50.0 | 6.7 | 3.0 |
| Hong Kong | 100.0 | 254.0 | 6.8 | 2.0 | 6.9 | 2.0 | 6.5 | 3.0 | 6.6 | 3.0 | 3.1 | 96.0 |
| Indonesia | 55.3 | 62.0 | 3.4 | 95.0 | 4.7 | 68.0 | 2.8 | 60.0 | 2.9 | 94.0 | 5.8 | 17.0 |
| Japan | 77.7 | 63.0 | 5.2 | 34.0 | 5.1 | 53.0 | 6.6 | 2.0 | 5.6 | 22.0 | 5.8 | 20.0 |
| Korea (Rep. of) | 76.8 | 151.0 | 5.1 | 36.0 | 6.0 | 21.0 | 5.7 | 8.0 | 5.8 | 14.0 | 5.4 | 27.0 |
| Lao PDR | | | | | | | | | | | | |
| Malaysia | 81.3 | 72.0 | 5.5 | 19.0 | 5.8 | 27.0 | 4.8 | 19.0 | 5.5 | 24.0 | 4.7 | 45.0 |
| Myanmar | | | | | | | | | | | | |
| New Zealand | 64.9 | 32.0 | 5.5 | 22.0 | 6.1 | 17.0 | 3.7 | 37.0 | 4.6 | 43.0 | **3.1** | **98.0** |
| **Philippines** | **9.9** | **14.0** | **3.0** | **112.0** | **3.7** | **100.0** | **1.7** | **92.0** | **2.8** | **104.0** | 6.7 | 2.0 |
| Singapore | 100.0 | 183.0 | 6.8 | 1.0 | 6.9 | 1.0 | 5.7 | 9.0 | 6.7 | 1.0 | 5.8 | 19.0 |
| Taiwan | n/a | n/a | 5.6 | 16.0 | 5.5 | 41.0 | 5.8 | 7.0 | 5.8 | 18.0 | 4.8 | 41.0 |
| Thailand | 98.5 | n/a | 4.7 | 47.0 | 5.9 | 26.0 | 3.0 | 52.0 | 5.0 | 35.0 | 2.8 | 111.0 |
| Vietnam | 25.1 | n/a | 3.3 | 99.0 | 4.1 | 84.0 | 2.8 | 58.0 | 2.8 | 102.0 | | |

*Quality of port infrastructure:* How would you assess port facilities in your country? (1 = extremely underdeveloped; 7 = well developed and efficient by international standards), 2008–09 weighted average

*Quality of air transport infrastructure:* How would you assess passenger air transport infrastructure in your country? (1 = extremely underdeveloped; 7 = extensive and efficient by international standards), 2008–09 weighted average

*Quality of railroad infrastructure:* How would you assess the railroad system in your country? (1 = extremely underdeveloped; 7 = extensive and efficient by international standards), 2008–09 weighted average

*Quality of roads:* How would you assess roads in your country? (1 = extremely underdeveloped; 7 = extensive and efficient by international standards), 2008–09 weighted average

*Quality of Overall Infrastructure:* How would you assess general infrastructure (e.g., transport, telephony, and energy) in your country? (1 = extremely underdeveloped; 7 = extensive and efficient by international standards), 2008–09 weighted average

*Note:* 1. World Economic Forum, *Executive Opinion Survey 2007, 2008*
*Source:* World Economic Forum, *World Competitiveness Report: 2009*

Finally, the Philippine AEC Scorecard did not explicitly include a strategy on external economic relations under the Priority Action on Full Integration in the Global Economy. The Philippines is an active participant in FTAs, both at the bilateral and plurilateral levels (as part of its commitment with ASEAN). However, the country still needs to improve its technical and administrative capacity in implementing the various FTAs.

### Political Economy Considerations

The slow pace in ASEAN economic integration has been attributed traditionally to a number of factors that relate mostly to imperfect market conditions, non-binding regional trade agreements, and the futility of state-led growth. Of late, observers however noted how economic policies may be pursued at variance with the official commitment to regional economic integration. The wide dissonance between ASEAN's official commitments and the practices of its members has led some to view its statements with some misgivings, dismissing them as mere rhetoric (Tantikulananta n.d.; Jetschke and Rüland 2009; Jones and Smith 2002; 2007; and Nabers 2003).

Under the guise of "national interest", domestic politics and domi-nant interest groups seek to maintain trade barriers and economic restrictions. These protection measures by individual countries serve to obstruct ASEAN economic integration (Tantikulananta n.d.). At the helm of the crisis in 2008, the Indonesian Trade Ministry issued Decree 56 restricting imports amidst fears of becoming a dumping ground of unsold merchandise. Malaysian Prime Minister Abdullah Ahmad Badawi has been quoted in an interview to profess anti-protectionist sentiments but was quick to add that "protectionism was a ... 'normal reaction' for countries to resort to at a time of crisis". The government, he said, had to protect the people. Campaigns reflecting domestic protectionist sentiments persist in other countries as well. Cambodia and Laos had "Buy Local" slogans and the Philippines had its "Buy Pinoy, Buy Local", all notable examples of "normal reactions" that defy ASEAN's "assertive action" against trade protectionism (Nair 2011). Moreover, the persistent calls of Indonesia's Chamber of Commerce (Kadin) for renegotiations in the ASEAN-China agreement and the Philippines' appeal for deferment of tariff cuts on sugar, to give the sugar industry more time to adjust to liberalized trade under AFTA, are manifestations of what Ravenhill (2008) called "negotiated protectionism". In the Philippines, this trade distorting practice takes many forms and persists in highly sensitive sectors. Allegations of institutional weakness, regulatory capture, and cases of abuse of market power have been reported in the power sector, the aviation industry, and telecommunications.

## Structural Problems in the Philippines

Structural problems continue to plague the Philippines economy, which also slows down the process of achieving regional goals. These were discussed extensively by Balboa et al. (2007). The major factors that have prevented the Philippines from maximizing its gains from globalization can be traced to policy shortcomings, and can be summarized as follows:[4]

1. Low investments in infrastructure. According to World Bank estimates, a middle-income country in East Asia will need to spend at least 5 per cent of its GDP on infrastructure to meet its needs in the next ten years. Infrastructure expenditure in the Philippines is far below this benchmark as it only accounts for 2.8 per cent of its GDP. In addition, resources allotted for infrastructure development are spent inefficiently. Infrastructure upgrading is necessary to improve the economic performance of the country as it would help attract more investments and reduce production costs. The lack of an infrastructure programme is largely related to the fragile fiscal situation of the government.

2. Lack of political will to implement a sustained and credible fiscal reform programme. Weak fiscal institutions created policies that increased debt burden and inherently put a bias towards deficit spending. They are also responsible for the fiscal blunders created, such as politicized spending and delayed fiscal consolidation during crises — as epitomized during the aftermath of the 2008 global financial crisis. To be effective, fiscal reforms should aim at creating stronger fiscal institutions that adhere to rules and do not easily give in to populist demands. Reforms should also create accountable and more transparent institutions that will implement revenue

generation programmes and include capability enhancement measures to reinforce the technical capacity of these institutions to mobilize revenues for the country's needs fully.

3. High Transaction Costs. Transaction costs refer to market-related infrastructure, facilities, and services needed to conduct business, including logistics. They also include costs in acquiring and exchanging information in transactions and contract enforcement. If transaction costs are high, these become a disincentive to producers to participate in any market exchange. It has been argued that the relatively poor performance of Philippine exports may be explained by high transaction costs in the country rather than market access issues. Logistical cost disadvantages — as pointed out earlier in this chapter — have hindered domestic industries from benefiting fully from the effects of trade liberalization and have discouraged foreign investors from considering the Philippines in their production and logistical networks.

4. Lack of a coherent industrial policy. This is an area that has been overlooked because of the controversy it generates. However, recent work has attempted to provide a pragmatic approach that eschews ideological prescriptions and instead looks more closely at historical experience. The basic argument is that industrial policy is as much about eliciting information from the private sector on significant externalities — primarily information and coordination externalities — and their remedies, as it is about implementing appropriate policies. However, the capacity to apply industrial policy is also important, which leads to the importance of governance and institutions. Since 1972, Philippine economic managers followed a programme that largely mimicked the Washington Consensus and did not allow for strategic intervention on the part of the government.

There were also gaps in the implementation of reforms and this is related to the failure to address issues in good governance. This focuses on anti-corruption initiatives and the institutionalization of corporate governance practices. The Philippines has always been cited as a country whose potential for growth has been eroded by corrupt institutions.

Hence, it is of utmost importance that measures to curb corruption are undertaken. An anti-corruption strategy should be reinforced by a committed leadership with able management skills to implement the programmes and sustain the progress made. Continued re-engineering of the bureaucracy is necessary, with reforms focused not only on achieving efficiency and effectiveness, but also instilling a culture of adherence to rules.

The Philippines has to work on addressing governance issues that hinder the country from taking advantage of opportunities from regional integration. A committed leadership that has the political will to pursue genuine reforms would be critical. The Philippine experience has shown that elite groups, at their will, could impede the implementation of reforms. Hence, mechanisms towards reducing opportunities for the monopoly of power that undermine reform efforts should be installed.

## Concluding Remarks

The economic reform process in the Philippines can be depicted in Figure 8.2. Political economy factors largely explain the slow progress

**FIGURE 8.2**
**Depiction of the Reform Process in the Philippines**

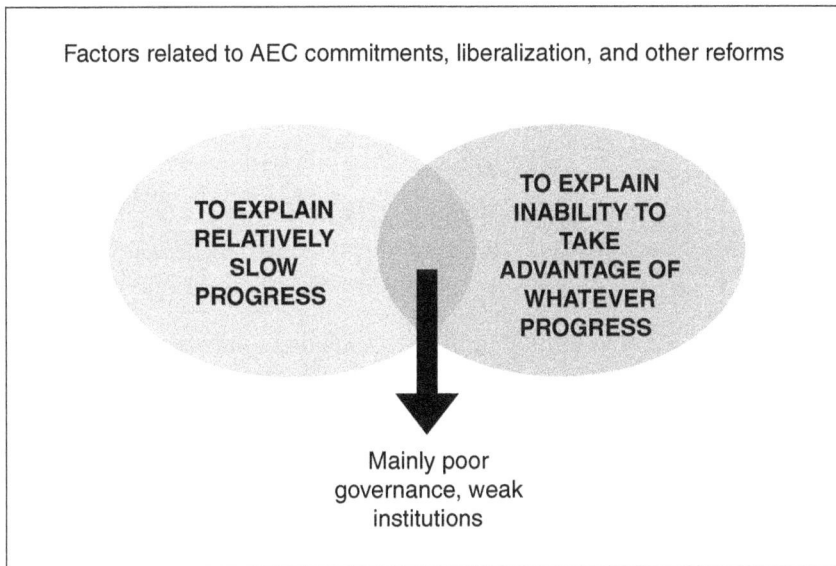

Factors related to AEC commitments, liberalization, and other reforms

TO EXPLAIN RELATIVELY SLOW PROGRESS

TO EXPLAIN INABILITY TO TAKE ADVANTAGE OF WHATEVER PROGRESS

Mainly poor governance, weak institutions

in implementing economic reforms, including the AEC commitments. These factors include the need to adhere to the democratic process and the presence of entrenched domestic interests.

Meanwhile, even if reforms are implemented, economic agents — especially private firms — are unable to take advantage of the opportunities presented. This can be explained by structural factors, including supply-side constraints. Poor infrastructure and the absence of a strategic and effective industrial policy are the main elements of supply-side constraints.

The intersection of these two sets of factors reveal aspects related to poor governance and weak institutions. Unfortunately, economists do not have the ready answer to the question of how to strengthen institutions. This would require a multidisciplinary approach. But definitely credible and visionary leadership is an important consideration.

## NOTES

1. The authors would like to acknowledge the valuable inputs of Dr Rafaelita M. Aldaba and Dr Erlinda M. Medalla. The excellent research assistance of Susan Pizarro is also acknowledged. The usual disclaimer applies.
2. For example, see "Regional Bloc's 2015 Deadline a 'Stretch Goal'?" *Business World*, 5 April 2010, p. 1.
3. Preliminary draft provided by the Bureau of International Trade Relations–Department of Trade and Industry. Updated commitments are still under embargo at time of writing.
4. Balboa et al. (2007), pp. 133–34.

## REFERENCES

Aldaba, R.M. "Assessing Competition in Philippine Markets". PIDS Discussion Paper No. 2008–23, Philippine Institute for Development Studies, Makati City, 2008.

ASEAN Secretariat. The ASEAN Economic Community Blueprint 2008.

Balboa, J.D., E.M. Medalla, and J.T. Yap. "Closer Trade and Financial Cooperation in ASEAN: Issues at the Regional and National Level with Focus on the Philippines". In *Bridging the ASEAN Developmental Divide: Challenges and Prospects*, edited by Lorraine Carlos Salazar and Sanchita Basu Das. Institute of Southeast Asia Studies, 2007.

Basu, S. "Non-tariff Measures and Protectionism". Powerpoint slides, PIDS Brownbag Presentation, Makati City, Philippines, 16 March 2010.

Bureau of International Trade Relations. AEC Scorecard of the Philippines (Preliminary Draft), 2009.

Corbett, J. and Umezaki, S. "Deepening East Asian Economic Integration". ERIA Research Project Report 2008 No. 1, Economic Research Institute for ASEAN and East Asia, Jakarta, 2009.

Findlay, C. "Trade Facilitation". In *Deepening East Asian Economic Integration*, edited by Corbett and Umezaki. Economic Research Institute for ASEAN and East Asia, Jakarta, 2009.

Hollweg, C. and H.M. Wong. "Measuring Regulatory Restrictions in Logistics Services". ERIA Discussion Paper Series No. 2009–14, Economic Research Institute for ASEAN and East Asia, Jakarta, 2009.

Jetschke, A. and Jurgen Rüland. "Decouplig Rhetoric and Practice: The Cultural Limits of ASEAN Cooperation. *Pacific Review* 22, no. 2 (2009): 179–203.

Jones, D.M. and Smith, M.L.R. "Making Process, Not Progress: ASEAN and the Evolving East Asian Regional Order. *International Security* 32, no. 1 (2007): 148–84.

Nabers, D. "The Social Construction of International Institutions: The Case of ASEAN+3". *International Relations of the Asia-Pacific* 3 (2003): 113–36.

Nair, Deepak. "ASEAN's Core Norms in the Context of the Global Financial Crisis". *Asian Survey* 51, no. 2 (2011): 245–67.

Plummer, M.G. and S.Y. Chia. *Realizing the ASEAN Economic Community: A Comprehensive Assessment*. Singapore: Institute of Southeast Asia Studies, 2009.

Ravenhill, J. "Fighting Irrelevance: An Economic Community with ASEAN Characteristics". *Pacific Review* 21, no. 4 (2008): 469–88.

Senate Economic Planning Office. "Regulating Competition". Policy Brief PB 09-04, Senate Economic Planning Office, Manila, 2009 <http://www.senate.gov. ph/publications/PB%202009-04%20-%20Regulating%20competition.pdf>.

Soesastro, Hadi. "Implementing the ASEAN Economic Community (AEC) Blueprint". In *Deepening East Asian Economic Integration*, edited by Corbett and Umezaki. Jakarta: Economic Research Institute for ASEAN and East Asia, 2009.

Tantikulananta, Chulanee. "Government-Business Relations and ASEAN Economic Integration in the Post Financial Crisis: A Case Study of Thailand. School of Political Science and International Studies, The University of Queensland, Brisbane, Australia <http://www.pol.mq.edu.au/apsa/papers/ Refereed%20papers/Tantikulanata%20Government-business%20relations%20 and%20ASEAN.pdf> (accessed: 11 April 2010).

Urata, S. and M. Ando. "Investment Climate Study on ASEAN Member Countries". In *Deepening East Asian Economic Integration*, edited by Corbett and Umezaki. Jakarta: Economic Research Institute for ASEAN and East Asia, 2009.

Urata, S., M. Ando and K. Ito. "Survey on Investment Liberalization and Facilitation". In "Obstacles to FDI in the APEC Economies: A Study Based on the JMC Firm Survey". Japan Machinery Center for Trade and Investment, Japan <http://www.apec.org/apec/publications/free_downloads/2007.html>.

The World Bank. *Doing Business Report*. Washington, D.C.: The World Bank, 2010. Accessed on 10 April 2010.

————. *Worldwide Governance Indicators*. Washington, D.C.: The World Bank, 2008.

World Economic Forum. *Global Competitiveness Report*.

# 9

# ASEAN Economic Integration: Perspectives from Singapore

Ong Keng Yong

When the leaders of five countries in Southeast Asia decided to come together and form the Association of Southeast Asian Nations (ASEAN) almost forty-three years ago, the Cold War was being fought and the military conflict in Vietnam was escalating beyond the country's borders. Indonesia, Malaysia, the Philippines, Singapore, and Thailand perceived a common threat to their survival as non-communist sovereign states. Launching ASEAN was an instinctive response to immediate fears and passing problems generated by the convulsions of the war in Vietnam. Some saw ASEAN as no more than an anti-communist front. However, ASEAN was more than that and its subsequent development has transformed the grouping's apparent mission.

## From Politics to Economics

In the Bangkok Declaration of 1967 that brought ASEAN into being, economic cooperation was held out as one of the organization's key objectives and specific actions were taken to move ASEAN towards this goal. Tariff reduction was regarded as the first step to increasing trade and strengthening economic ties, but negotiations were protracted. By 1977 ASEAN produced its first-ever preferential trading arrangements. Singapore's open economy was a pathfinder. Multinational companies and foreign direct investment (FDI) were warmly welcomed in Singapore. They led to a rapid expansion of the economy and helped Singapore to industrialize quickly. Gradually the other ASEAN countries were also attracted to such a policy. At the same time, the notion of developing a larger market beyond the national boundary through economic cooperation with neighbouring states was articulated as a way forward, not just for Singapore, but for the rest of ASEAN as well. Malaysia and Thailand were opened up and their economic development accelerated, with noticeable benefits for their business and people sectors.

In the 1970s and 1980s, external developments, particularly what was happening in China, Europe, Japan, and the United States, and the dramatic increase of oil prices, pushed the ASEAN countries to coalesce as a more substantive regional body. Brunei joined ASEAN in 1984, after its formal independence. In 1995, Vietnam was admitted into ASEAN. In 1997, Laos and Myanmar entered the grouping, and in 1999, Cambodia became an ASEAN member. This completed the Southeast Asian footprint of the organization and firmly established ASEAN's role as the collective enterprise for managing challenges and opportunities affecting the region. The Cambodian crisis from 1978 to the 1990s further strengthened ASEAN's habit of consultation and cooperation. The perceived common threat rallied the ASEAN countries into joint actions to secure peace and stability, from which economic prosperity was derived.

The geography of ASEAN is also important. Being in the middle between the huge continental economies of China and India, and straddling the major sea lanes and shipping routes connecting Europe/Middle East with Asia/Australia and New Zealand, ASEAN is situated in a strategic location impinging on the interests of all the major powers of the world, especially those that dominate the global economy. This central position was adroitly capitalized on by ASEAN to play a prominent role in managing stakeholders' interests in Southeast Asia and the immediate neighbourhood. Various ASEAN-centric mechanisms (such as the ASEAN Plus One and ASEAN Plus Three processes, the ASEAN Regional Forum, and the East Asia Summit) were set up to engage those interested in the region, and top-level meetings were held on an annual basis. Consequently, ASEAN is at the centre of the regional architecture and ASEAN's relations with all the major powers and big neighbours have been positive and mutually beneficial.

As globalization snowballed into an all-pervasive development and the emerging economies in Asia, Central/Eastern Europe, and Latin America became more attractive to foreign investors, ASEAN's economic competitiveness seemed under threat. The ASEAN Free Trade Area (AFTA) initiative was seen as too slow moving. The fear was that ASEAN would lose out in the competition for FDI and the region would be sidelined and become irrelevant in the globalization process.

As the grouping entered the twenty-first century, ASEAN leaders decided to commission a landmark study by the private sector consultancy, Mckinsey and Company. The conclusion of the study persuaded ASEAN leaders to accelerate market integration and trade liberalization. The key was providing a substantial economy of scale and exploiting ASEAN's potential as a huge market of 550 million consumers. By developing a single market, ASEAN could reduce business costs by 20–30 per cent which would serve as an incentive for foreign investors to put money in ASEAN. To obtain quick results, priority sectors were designated. The Mckinsey study was accepted by ASEAN leaders and paved the way for the promulgation of the ASEAN Economic Community (AEC) as we know it today.

## China and Globalization

In 2000, China offered to negotiate a free trade area with ASEAN. This was to protect China's own political, strategic, and economic interests. Still, a free trade area comprising ASEAN and China would be a market of almost 1.7 billion people. The Chinese initiative came with an extraordinary "early harvest" package. In essence, this meant that even as negotiations were undertaken, designated goods from ASEAN countries could enter China tariff-free. This was an enormous inducement to ASEAN and it opened the way for ASEAN to advance its free trade strategy significantly. A boost also came from the entry of Vietnam and Cambodia into the World Trade Organization (WTO) and their respective domestic economic reforms which attracted an increased inflow of FDI.

China's move for a free trade area with ASEAN triggered off similar ventures between ASEAN and Japan, South Korea, India, Australia, and

New Zealand. By the end of 2008, ASEAN had signed and operationalized free trade agreements (FTAs) with all these major trade partners and had reinforced the positive relationships between ASEAN and these powers. These agreements have added a new dimension to the ASEAN-centric mechanisms in the region and buttressed the role of ASEAN as a hub for multilateral engagement and open regionalism.

Once again it was the external factor that pushed ASEAN into collective undertakings in response to new challenges. The later developments had revolved around economic issues, in contrast to the political and security imperatives of the early years of ASEAN's evolution. Globalization and its attendant developments have left ASEAN leaders with limited choices to maintain the organization's prominence and relevance in regional and international affairs. The economy was the driver of intra-ASEAN diplomacy and dominated ASEAN's engagement with the outside world.

The creation of a single market for trade and investment is now the underpinning of ASEAN's future. ASEAN leaders have concretized their free trade vision into the realization of the AEC. The establishment of the ASEAN Charter has also facilitated the building of the AEC as it has strengthened the rule of law in ASEAN and brought about more accountability and predictability. It is unlikely that ASEAN leaders would let the AEC implementation slip and undermine ASEAN's credibility and long-term interests. Indeed, their preoccupation in the past few ASEAN Summits clearly demonstrated their commitment to realizing the AEC. Ideas such as the AEC Blueprint, the AEC Scorecard, and the ASEAN Connectivity initiative were adopted by ASEAN leaders to fast forward the AEC.

## ASEAN Connectivity

Let us take this opportunity to examine the ASEAN Connectivity initiative in more detail as it has not been well deliberated in its entirety outside government circles. In their public statement on the subject, ASEAN leaders had observed that ASEAN was located at the crossroads of an economically vibrant and growing region bounded by India in the west, China, Japan, and South Korea in the northeast, and Australia and New Zealand in the south. ASEAN thus has the potential to anchor itself physically as the transportation, information and communication technology (ICT), and tourism hub of this vast region.

Enhancing intraregional connectivity within ASEAN and its subregional groupings would benefit all ASEAN countries through enhanced trade, investment, tourism, and development. As all the overland transport linkages will have to go through continental Southeast Asia, Cambodia, Laos, Myanmar, and Vietnam would stand to benefit the most through infrastructure development and the opening up of remote inland and less-developed areas. All these efforts would significantly narrow the development gap within ASEAN. In addition to the tangible economic benefits of ASEAN connectivity, the linkages created would intensify and strengthen ASEAN community building efforts, not only in terms of enhanced regional cooperation and integration, but also through people-to-people contacts. In this regard, the concept of ASEAN connectivity would also complement the ongoing regional efforts to realize a people-oriented ASEAN Community by 2015, with a focus on fostering a sense of shared cultural and historical linkages.

ASEAN leaders have agreed that it is vital to complete the physical road, rail, air, and sea linkages within ASEAN. The development of infrastructure and multimodal transport projects such as, *inter alia*, the ASEAN Highway Network and the Singapore-Kunming Rail Link, should be expedited in parallel with addressing software related issues within relevant existing work plans of ASEAN. Given the importance of the Internet in business, education, and development, it is also crucial to complete the ASEAN launched ICT Master Plan 2015 to enhance intraregional ICT linkages.

As ASEAN leaders see it, the deepening and widening of connectivity in the region would reinforce ASEAN's position as the hub of East Asia, which could be further strengthened through realizing the potential of a broader connectivity in the longer term with ASEAN's partners in the wider region. In this regard, ASEAN leaders view that this concept of ASEAN Connectivity would complement and support integration within ASEAN and within the broader regional framework in East Asia. ASEAN should seek the support of all its dialogue partners and other international agencies and development partners to realize the vision of ASEAN Connectivity, including the establishment of an infrastructure development fund for ASEAN. It should also explore ways to capitalize effectively on existing cooperation funds for infrastructure development with its dialogue partners, and remain open to future cooperation with other interested parties, as appropriate.

An ASEAN High Level Task Force, comprising relevant experts, and supported by the ASEAN Secretariat and relevant sectoral bodies, in cooperation with relevant international organizations such as the Asian Development Bank (ADB), the United Nations Economic and Social Commission for Asia and the Pacific (UNESCAP), and the Economic Research Institute for ASEAN and East Asia, was established to study ASEAN's internal and external connectivity, and to develop an ASEAN Master Plan on regional connectivity, that includes, among other things, innovative infrastructure financing mechanisms, taking into account the work done and planned to ensure optimum synergy rather than duplication of work. In devising the Master Plan, the task force, ensured that the limited resources from ASEAN, dialogue partners, and international development banks and agencies are employed in the most efficient and effective manner to realize the vision of ASEAN leaders. The ASEAN High Level Task Force submitted its recommendations to the 17th ASEAN Summit in Vietnam in October 2010, and it has been adopted by the ASEAN leader during the same summit.

A well-connected ASEAN will be a tremendous boost for the AEC as well as the ASEAN Community. The ASEAN Connectivity initiative takes regional economic integration efforts a step further by providing the necessary physical infrastructure to make Southeast Asia the conduit through which regional interactions take place, thereby anchoring ASEAN's centrality in the regional architecture. Economically, this physical network will help ASEAN realize the full potential of its FTAs with China, Japan, South Korea, India, and Australia/New Zealand.

## Obstacles to Integration

The urgent task now is to implement what ASEAN countries have already agreed to, and not let local problems and certain misgivings in some ill-informed quarters distract the AEC from its settled course. Many challenges lie ahead, but almost all of these are internal issues which ASEAN leaders can resolve through a determined exercise of political will. Let us consider some of these difficulties.

The inherent bureaucratic culture in the ASEAN countries is not yet conducive to the promotion of a region-wide agenda for economic integration. The tendency of officials in the respective capital cities and provinces is to focus on local requirements and narrow interests. In this respect, ASEAN leaders need to motivate their officials to proceed quickly and implement the agreed plans. Otherwise the leaders should intervene to drive the process more directly. The decision to have two ASEAN Summits a year (with effect from 2009) signifies the intention of the leaders to pay more attention to the implementation of ASEAN plans.

The harnessing of technology can contribute significantly to such decisive actions. For example, the computerization of customs clearance of goods has increased the speed of processing through national borders. Standardized rules have been pushed out to far-flung government agencies across ASEAN through the use of computers and other electronic equipment. Innovative ideas such as the AEC Scorecard have assisted the relevant authorities to review performance and remove bureaucratic obstacles. AFTA and the ASEAN Plus FTAs have come into force at the beginning of 2010, and the technological advancements and innovations will help in the monitoring and compliance of their provisions.

Undoubtedly, more administrative reforms and mindset transformation are needed, but ASEAN leaders are constantly looking for creative ways to overcome bureaucratic inertia. In some ASEAN countries, a systematic modernization of bureaucratic practices is being pursued. With better training and more exposure to the ASEAN agenda, officials are beginning to make a more positive impact.

Another form of inertia is found in the business sector. There seems to be lukewarm support of the AEC, particularly from indigenous business quarters. The usual feedback is that the local business community is not familiar with the details of the AEC and its implementation process. The inclination of most domestic companies is also to carry on business as usual as they find the standardization of ASEAN processes and procedures a costly adjustment and, therefore, not something they would readily comply with. In some cases, the inadequate communication about the AEC and its coverage are at fault. However, very often, it is due to the lack of willingness to change. Hence, public awareness and education, as well as the simplification of the process, are crucial in consolidating the AEC. ASEAN leaders are trying to strengthen the sense of ASEAN identity and to bring the benefits of ASEAN integration into more public consciousness.

## Singapore's Position

Singapore remains committed and continues to work closely with the other ASEAN countries to achieve the goals of the AEC as set out in the AEC Blueprint. Singapore's tariffs for all products under the Inclusion List for the Common Effective Preferential Tariffs (CEPT) of the AFTA were eliminated well before the stipulated deadline of 1 January 2010. According to the latest AEC Scorecard, Singapore has registered more than 93 per cent implementation of the requirements in the AEC Blueprint for the period 2008 to 2009.

Beyond CEPT AFTA, Singapore has also completed the seventh package of services liberalization under the ASEAN Framework Agreement on Services (AFAS) and is consulting relevant domestic agencies for the eighth package as stipulated under the Strategic Schedule of the AEC Blueprint. Similarly, it has ratified the enhanced ASEAN Comprehensive Investment Agreement. Singapore was urging the other ASEAN countries to do so by August 2010. On the trade facilitation front, among ASEAN's key initiatives is the establishment of the respective National Single Windows (NSWs) and thus creating the environment for the ASEAN Single Window (ASW). Singapore has implemented its NSW — TRADENET — and is continuously improving the system. It is also working with the rest of ASEAN to develop the ASEAN Master Plan on regional connectivity, which is another critical element of ASEAN economic integration.

Singapore believes that a strong and competitive ASEAN is important in the face of growing challenges posed, not just to the Southeast Asian economy, but the global economy. Thus, while Singapore acknowledges that some problems are faced by the ASEAN countries in implementing the AEC Blueprint, there is an urgent need to persevere in order for the region to remain competitive and relevant to the global economy. While it fully supports efforts taken to accelerate internal integration towards AEC 2015, ASEAN needs to deepen its engagement with key trading partners in parallel. To this end, Singapore participates actively in the various negotiations of the ASEAN Plus FTAs. For example, Singapore co-chaired the ASEAN–South Korea FTA talks, as well as the various working groups under the other FTAs. Furthermore, in support of ASEAN's overall outreach efforts, Singapore continues to collaborate with relevant domestic agencies, dialogue partners, business organizations, and relevant stakeholders, to implement the various economic agreements/initiatives. Outreach activities such as seminars for the business community on the various FTAs, with the most recent one on the ASEAN-India FTA, also provide an avenue to obtain useful feedback from stakeholders. This is necessary and extremely helpful for the formulation of appropriate policies for the benefit of the business community.

Going forward, Singapore will focus on capacity building and human resource development in the ASEAN countries to help them prepare for the 2015 deadline. In this respect, Singapore has spent more than US$120 million cumulatively in various initiatives and training programmes to help narrow the gaps among ASEAN economies.

## Gains from Economic Integration

According to a number of studies conducted by experts and scholars, ASEAN countries will benefit from the AEC in various ways. In the book *Realising the ASEAN Economic Community — A Comprehensive Assessment*, edited by Michael Plummer and Chia Siow Yue, the costs and benefits of this ambitious enterprise by ASEAN have been scrutinized and evaluated. I am extracting several conclusions from the book to illustrate the generic gains from economic integration as the specific numbers vary from year to year, and country to country. In sum, the net gains from the AEC will be significant, even though the initial costs to some sectors in some ASEAN countries are likely to be high.

The AEC will expand ASEAN's trade in goods with exports outpacing imports in almost all sectors. There are many opportunities in these areas for ASEAN producers to join global production chains. Production networks will be particularly advantageous to small and medium-sized enterprises throughout ASEAN. As the AEC Blueprint is implemented, the single open market can be a boon for the ASEAN Plus FTAs signed with China, Japan, South Korea, India, and Australia/New Zealand. More trade can be transacted and this means more benefits accruing to the ASEAN countries. More importantly, ASEAN's centrality is enhanced, and ASEAN's voice in regional and global affairs is also strengthened.

Another benefit is the greater inflow of FDI into Southeast Asia as investors want to establish more businesses and manufacturing operations in the region to take advantage of the economies of scale and the enlarged consumer base. The implementation of the ASEAN Comprehensive Investment Agreement (ACIA) will also remove barriers for investors. In particular, foreign companies that have been operating in the region for a long time are treated like ASEAN companies. The AEC could increase FDI stocks in the respective ASEAN countries. The annual income growth of the ASEAN countries will rise at between 0.5 and 1 per cent of GDP per annum. Over time, this effect could be considerable, given the potential of ASEAN countries to expand in existing production value chains and enter new ones. The creation of opportunities for production networks and the spreading of best practices that raise productivity will also help narrow the development gap. Productivity improvements will be greatest in the less-developed countries of ASEAN, and the AEC will help them converge with the rest of ASEAN.

The liberalized regime for the movement of skilled workers in the AEC is also beneficial to ASEAN countries. It will contribute to making ASEAN attractive to foreign investors, encouraging mutual recognition of professional qualifications, and engendering regional cooperation among training institutes, universities, and research institutions. ASEAN countries with shortages of labour may benefit most, and professional and skilled workers will be able to seek better jobs and higher earnings. Greater efficiency stemming from a less-restricted movement of skilled labour will also boost GDP growth.

Consumer markets will be more competitive in the AEC as a cheaper and wider range of imported goods and services is available. The domestic competition will be more intense, but there will be more extensive consumer protection and other institutional improvements under the AEC. The net result is more efficiency in both the private and public sectors.

## Insufficient Institutionalization

One area which ASEAN leaders need to address is the limited number of entities championing ASEAN and the AEC. So far, there is only the ASEAN Secretariat based in Jakarta, which employs no more than 300 personnel. Across the region, there are few agencies and facilities to promote and strengthen ASEAN's causes and programmes. The ASEAN Biodiversity Centre outside Manila, the ASEAN Foundation and the ASEAN Energy Centre in Jakarta, the ASEAN University Network in Bangkok, and the ASEAN Specialised Meteorological Centre in Singapore are the only outfits helping to carry out ASEAN initiatives and projects.

Most of them, however, are confined to their specific areas of expertise and have limited budgetary allocations. They cannot conduct wider outreach programmes essential to galvanizing popular support for the AEC.

Frequently the ASEAN agenda is left to officials in selected ministries who are not full-time implementers of the ASEAN plans and are often distracted by other bureaucratic responsibilities. The national coordinating mechanisms in ASEAN countries have been overstretched. Inevitably these bodies have to pay attention to national concerns and the national ego will always be dominant. The ad hoc task forces established by ASEAN leaders from time to time are not enough to sustain the championing of ASEAN and its region-wide agenda.

The ASEAN Secretariat can be expanded and its professional mandate enlarged so that it can organize more activities to complement ASEAN's political vision and economic goals, monitor implementation of ASEAN agreements and plans, and report non-compliance to ASEAN leaders. The spread of more suitable ASEAN institutions in different cities across Southeast Asia will also raise public visibility of the grouping and increase the sense of ownership of ASEAN's projects and programmes. The numerous business chambers and related industry bodies in the member states of ASEAN could be empowered to do more for the ASEAN agenda.

The path to the AEC is not the work of one person, one committee, or even one nation. It stems from the clear vision of ASEAN leaders and their commitment towards realizing the goals they have set out to achieve. Only then will the drive these leaders exemplify be passed down to the thousands of officials and private individuals who matter within ASEAN countries. Furthermore, belief in not only individual member states, but also ASEAN's capabilities as a whole must be present. Each country's strength should be leveraged, so as to add value to various processes already in place. The lack of sufficient institutionalization has to be dealt with sooner than later.

## Conclusion

Even if not everything ASEAN leaders have set out to achieve in the AEC is accomplished by 2015, the establishment of the AEC Blueprint, the timeline, and now the AEC Scorecard will have transformed ASEAN. It is important to remember that the AEC is not a European Union–type economic integration in Southeast Asia. The AEC constitutes the most ambitious programme of economic cooperation in the developing world, and implementing this agenda will be technically and politically difficult.

For ASEAN Leaders, the AEC is the strategic imperative. They have anticipated the trends and embarked on a long-term strategy to keep ASEAN open and be a single market. It is a response to globalization and the rise of the giant economies of China and India. The challenge is to have ASEAN survive as a viable regional organization that matters to the member countries and their friends. The alternative is ASEAN becoming adrift and fading into irrelevance and eventual oblivion. The AEC will forever be influenced by external developments, particularly the state of the global economy. However, the AEC must also reflect the diversity, *raison d'être*, and will of the ASEAN nations. It has to be uniquely Southeast Asian and not simply a replication of another model from elsewhere in the world.

The evidence suggests that the AEC implementation is intensifying. Firstly, the commitment to overcome the obstacles has been demonstrated, albeit in spasmodic fashion. Secondly, the standardization and harmonization of practices and rules are ongoing and the increasing volume of such ASEAN-centric practices and rules bears testimony to the currency of the AEC initiative. Thirdly, the ASEAN Charter has laid down the rule of law in ASEAN and there is more accountability and predictability even as the provisions for dispute settlement mechanisms and the protection of intellectual property rights are being developed. Most encouraging is the fact that several ASEAN and non-ASEAN multinational companies are already operating production networks based on the envisaged ASEAN single-market model. The AEC process is evolving in an ulcerative manner, but picking the low-hanging fruit and getting the first 50 per cent of targeted results are achievable within the next two to three years.

While the AEC Scorecard show that implementation of AEC requirements is around an average of 72 per cent across the whole of ASEAN, the prognosis is that the AEC is happening. There is constant pressure to avoid giving in to the ASEAN agenda as political considerations surface from time to time to force a delay or review. Nevertheless, with a skilful balance of interests, the demonstrated visionary leadership, and the proven track record of tackling common challenges in a collective manner, ASEAN can deliver the AEC.

At the meeting of ASEAN leaders in Hanoi, Vietnam, in April 2010, the participants reviewed progress made and repeated their commitment to realize the AEC by 2015. Indonesian President Susilo Bambang Yudhoyono was emphatic in moving his country towards the AEC. He said that he was optimistic about achieving the goal, and stressed that Indonesia needed to take various steps, such as improving legislation and economic competitiveness. Such timely review and signalling of ASEAN leaders' determination has generated more propulsion. The grumbling and fumbling witnessed so far should not be mistaken as buyer's remorse and a clawback of ASEAN economic integration.

# 10

## Achieving the AEC 2015: Challenges for Thailand

Nipon Poapongsakorn

The main objectives of this chapter are to discuss some progress in Thailand's commitments and implementation of the ASEAN Economic Community (AEC) Blueprint and the challenges it faces in pursuing the AEC commitments. The chapter will discuss five issues. After summarizing the road map of the AEC Blueprint and some liberalization milestones in the first part, the second part will explain the progress in Thailand's implementation of the AEC Blueprint with regard to the four characteristics of the AEC. The third part is a brief assessment of the impact of AFTA and remaining barriers in Thailand's services sector, while the fourth part focuses on the challenges faced by Thailand in pursuing the liberalization commitments under the AEC Blueprint. Finally, the chapter will conclude by discussing some possible policies for ASEAN to achieve its goal of economic integration.

## The ASEAN Economic Community

The ASEAN vision 2020 envisaged "a stable, prosperous and highly competitive ASEAN economic region in which there is a free flow of goods, services, investment and freer flow of capital, equitable economic development and reduced poverty and socio-economic disparities" by the year 2020, which was later brought forward to 2015. To realize the goal, ASEAN leaders in October 2005 signed the Declaration of the Bali Concord II, which aims at an ASEAN Economic Community.

In 2007, ASEAN leaders adopted the AEC Blueprint, which laid out a road map to accelerate economic integration and included action plans, targets, and timelines to facilitate the process. The AEC Blueprint is organized along four characteristics: (1) a single market and production base; (2) a highly competitive economic region; (3) a region of equitable economic development; and (4) a region fully integrated into the global economy.

The road map spells out the core elements and action plan for each of the key characteristics of the AEC. For example, a single market and production base vision comprises five core elements: the free flow of goods, services, investment, capital, and skilled labour. In addition, given the scarce resources, ASEAN identified twelve priority integration sectors for accelerated economic integration. It also includes the action plans to enhance trade and long-term competitiveness of ASEAN's food, agriculture, and forestry products/commodities.

The following are some liberalization milestones for the objective of the free flow of goods:

- Eliminate tariffs on all products by 2010 for the ASEAN Six and by 2015 for the CLMV (Cambodia, Laos, Myanmar, and Vietnam) countries, except products on the Sensitive List and Highly Sensitive List.
- Eliminate tariffs on products in the Priority Integration Sectors by 2007 for the ASEAN Six, and 2010, for CLMV.
- Remove all non-tariff barriers (NTBs) by 2010 for the ASEAN Five, by 2012 for the Philippines, and by 2015 with flexibilities to 2018 for CLMV.
- Enhance transparency of NTBs.
- Continuous reform of and enhance rules of origin (ROO).
- Implement ASEAN e-Customs.
- ASEAN Single Window.

- Harmonize standards, technical regulations, and conformity assessment procedures.
- Develop and implement trade facilitation work programme.
- Implement the 2005–10 Strategic Plan of Customs Development.

The liberalization milestones for the free flow of services are:

- Complete inventory of ASEAN barriers to services by 2008.
- ASEAN equity participation of not less than 51 per cent in four priority services sectors (air transport, e-ASEAN, health care, and tourism) and 49 per cent for other services by 2008.
- Complete MRAs for architected services and accountancy.
- Liberalization of the following services subsectors: surveying qualification and medical practitioners by 2008; dental services by 2009; develop MRAs for other professional services by 2012; and complete all MRAs by 2015.
- ASEAN equity participation of not less than 70 per cent in four priority services sectors; 51 per cent for other services sectors by 2010, and 70 per cent by 2015; and 70 per cent for logistics by 2013.
- Progressively remove other mode-3 market access limitations by 2015.
- Allow for flexibilities, i.e., sectoral exclusion and partial liberalization.
- Liberalization through ASEAN — X is allowed, etc.

## Progress in Thailand's Commitments and Implementation of the AEC

Table 10.1, shows that Thailand's implementation status of AEC measures is slightly above the average for ASEAN as a whole for most measures. The country's most progressive area of implementation is in the free flow in goods. There are also some areas where Thailand's implementation rates are only as good as the average rate for ASEAN, for example, for the ASEAN Trade in Goods Agreement (ATIGA), and the free flow of investment and capital. However, the aggregate scorecard fails to reveal the true rates of implementation at the disaggregate level, especially the implementation of AFAS commitments (Table 10.1).

The following shows progress in selected areas of the AEC Blueprint commitments: The Thai Parliament will soon ratify ATIGA and the Product Specific Rules for ROO. It already signed an MOU with the Philippines

**TABLE 10.1**
**Implementation Status of AEC Measures**
(for the Period 1 January 2008–30 September 2009)

| AEC Measures | Implementation Rate (%) | | | | | |
|---|---|---|---|---|---|---|
| | ASEAN-10 | Thailand | Malaysia | Philippines | Indonesia | Vietnam |
| A. Towards a Single Market and Production Base | 82.0 | 88.7 | 94.3 | 88.4 | 87.1 | 90.0 |
| A1. Free Flows of Goods | 70.0 | 84.6 | 100.0 | 100.0 | 75.0 | 100.0 |
| 1. ATIGA | 50.0 | 50.0 | 100.0 | 100.0 | 50.0 | 100.0 |
| 2. Tariffs Liberalization | — | — | — | 0.0 | — | — |
| 3. Elimination of NTBs | 100.0 | 100.0 | 100.0 | — | — | 100.0 |
| 4. Rules of Origin | 100.0 | 100.0 | 100.0 | 100.0 | 100.0 | 100.0 |
| 5. Trade Facilitation Work Programme | 100.0 | 100.0 | 100.0 | 100.0 | 100.0 | — |
| 6. Customs Integration | — | — | — | — | — | — |
| 7. ASEAN Single Windows | 66.7 | 50.0 | 100.0 | 100.0 | 100.0 | — |
| 8. Standards & Conformance | 53.9 | 100.0 | 75.0 | 61.5 | 66.7 | 100.0 |
| A2. Free Flow of Services | 66.7 | 76.9 | 100.0 | 66.7 | 76.9 | 61.5 |
| A3. Free Flow of Investment | 50.0 | 66.7 | 50.0 | 50.0 | 66.7 | 83.3 |
| A4. Free Flow of Capital | — | 50.0 | — | — | 50.0 | 50.0 |
| A5. Free Flow of Skilled Labour | — | — | — | — | — | — |
| A6. Priority Integration Sectors | 100.0 | 100.0 | 100.0 | 100.0 | 100.0 | 100.0 |
| A7. Food, Agriculture & Forestry | 100.0 | 100.0 | 100.0 | 100.0 | 100.0 | 100.0 |
| B. Competitive Economic Region | 50.0 | 57.1 | 55.9 | 61.8 | 64.7 | 61.8 |
| B1. Competition Policy | 100.0 | 100.0 | 100.0 | 100.0 | 100 | 100.0 |
| B2. Consumer Protection | 100.0 | 100.0 | 100.0 | 100.0 | 100 | 100.0 |

**TABLE 10.1** *(Cont'd)*

| AEC Measures | Implementation Rate (%) | | | | | |
|---|---|---|---|---|---|---|
| | ASEAN-10 | Thailand | Malaysia | Philippines | Indonesia | Vietnam |
| B3. Intellectual Property Rights | — | — | — | — | — | — |
| B4. Infrastructure Development | | | | | | |
| Transport | 34.6 | 42.3 | 42.3 | 50.0 | 53.9 | 50.0 |
| Energy | 100.0 | 100.0 | 100.0 | 100.0 | 100.0 | 100.0 |
| ICT | 100.0 | 100.0 | 100.0 | 100.0 | 100.0 | 100.0 |
| Minerals | — | — | — | — | — | — |
| B5. Taxation | — | — | — | — | — | — |
| B6. e-Commerce | 100.0 | 100.0 | 100.0 | 100.0 | 100.0 | 100.0 |
| C. Towards a region of equitable economic development | 100.0 | 100.0 | 100.0 | 100.0 | 100.0 | 100.0 |
| C1. SME Development | 100.0 | 100.0 | 100.0 | 100.0 | 100.0 | 100.0 |
| C2. Initiative for ASEAN Integration (IAI) | 100.0 | 100.0 | 100.0 | 100.0 | 100.0 | 100.0 |
| D. Integration into the Global Economy | — | — | — | — | — | — |
| D1. Coherent Approach towards External Economic Relations | — | — | — | — | — | — |
| D2. Enhanced Participation in Global Supply | — | — | — | — | — | — |
| Total | 72.4 | 78.9 | 82.2 | 80.2 | 80.4 | 81.3 |

*Source:* AEC Scorecard (*SEOM 1/41*, 19–20 January 2010, Da Nang, Vietnam).

Government after the latter agreed to compensate Thailand for not reducing the tariff on rice. The Philippines will allow the tariff-free import of 367,000 tonnes of Thai rice, 50,000 tonnes of which will be of high quality.

In the transition from the AIA to the ACIA, Thailand submitted three agricultural subsectors into the "reservation list". In the original AIA, Thailand did not have any reservation list. Moreover, ASEAN investors who want to do business in one subsector of the fisheries sector in Thailand, i.e., marine animal products, must obtain the permission and licences from the Foreign Business Committee and they must have a minimum capital of 3 million baht. There are two reasons for the backtracking: strong opposition from non-governmental organizations and some producer associations (orchids), and the fact that the AIA has not yet been approved by its parliament. In addition, Thailand and a few ASEAN members have not yet committed to extending non-discrimination treatment to ASEAN-based foreign investors, citing security and other reasons. These reservations will compromise the single market objective of the AEC.

In contrast to its commitment on the free flow of goods, Thailand's commitment to AFAS is lagging behind that of other ASEAN members. Table 10.2 shows that according to the threshold of sixty-five subsectors for liberalization commitments in the seventh package, Thailand is the only country that has failed to provide any commitment to priority sectors with the requirement of foreign ownership being at least 51 per cent. So Thailand has to provide commitments in other services subsectors that are not in the priority sectors for its commitment to satisfy the threshold of sixty-five subsectors.

### Market Access for the Priority Services Sector

Table 10.3 calculates the points (number of subsectors) that each ASEAN member has committed to provide market access to in the priority integration sector and other service sectors. Each ASEAN member submits its market access commitments according to three modes of service provision, that is, modes 1, 2 and 3.

There is not yet any commitment for mode 4 by ASEAN members, including Singapore, the free trader, because they still have serious concerns about the free flow of foreign skilled labour which will have a negative impact on the income of local professional workers.

**TABLE 10.2**
**Consolidated Commitments under AFAS (7th package)**

| ASEAN Countries | No. of Threshold Sectors | No. of priority integration sectors that can be opened (at least 51%) | No. of other service sectors that can be opened (at least 49%) |
|---|---|---|---|
| Brunei | 65 | 21 | 44 |
| Cambodia | 67 | 25 | 42 |
| Indonesia | 68 | 13 | 55 |
| Laos | 67 | 14 | 51 |
| Malaysia | 65 | 23 | 42 |
| Myanmar | 66 | 26 | 40 |
| Philippines* | 54 | 9 | 39 |
| Singapore | 73 | 24 | 49 |
| Thailand | 65 | 0 | 65 |
| Vietnam** | 58 | 28 | 30 |

*Notes:* * The Philippines cannot yet fully commit up to the threshold.
　　　** Vietnam has recently completed the threshold commitments, but the data was not available at the time of press.
*Source:* Consolidated Commitments under AFAS (7th package).

As shown in Table 10.3, Thailand barely meets the minimum threshold of 65 points. The Philippines is the only country with lower points of commitments than Thailand.

### National Treatment

Since ASEAN does not yet agree on the modalities of national treatment for the priority services subsectors, we cannot prepare a table comparative to that of Table 10.3. Yet it is possible to assess the extent of Thailand's liberalization commitments under AFAS, compared with commitments under GATS, in eleven main sectors, excluding other services not included elsewhere. Table 10.4 shows the continuous expansion of subsectors under AFAS from the first package to the seventh package of commitment schedule. The cumulative number of liberalized subsectors increased from 52.6 per cent of the total number of W/120 subsectors in the sixth package, to 71.4 per cent in the seventh package.

What are Thailand's commitments in mode 4 on market access and national treatment in eleven service sectors under AFAS? Tables 10.5 to 10.6 show that Thailand made commitments in mode 2 (consumption

## TABLE 10.3
## Number of Subsectors that Comply with Market Access Commitments under AFAS (Seventh Package)

| Sector or Subsector | Brunei | Cambodia | Indonesia | Laos | Malaysia | Myanmar | Philippines | Singapore | Thailand | Vietnam* |
|---|---|---|---|---|---|---|---|---|---|---|
| 1. Business Services | 29 | 23 | 20 | 23 | 24 | 20 | 28 | 29 | 28 | 23 |
| A. Professional Services | 7 | 7 | 8 | 5 | 4 | 8 | 5 | 7 | 5 | 10 |
| B. Computer and Related Services | 5 | 5 | 0 | 5 | 5 | 5 | 5 | 4 | 0 | 5 |
| C. Research and Development services | 3 | 0 | 1 | 3 | 3 | 0 | 3 | 3 | 3 | 1 |
| D. Real Estate Services | 0 | 0 | 0 | 0 | 0 | 0 | 2 | 0 | 2 | 0 |
| E. Rental/Leasing Services without Operator | 2 | 1 | 1 | 2 | 3 | 1 | 2 | 2 | 4 | 0 |
| F. Other Business Services | 12 | 10 | 10 | 8 | 9 | 6 | 11 | 13 | 14 | 7 |
| 2. Communications Services | 12 | 16 | 7 | 10 | 14 | 18 | 3 | 13 | 2 | 16 |
| A. Post | 0 | 0 | 0 | 0 | 0 | 0 | 0 | 0 | 0 | 0 |
| B. Services Document | 0 | 1 | 0 | 1 | 0 | 1 | 0 | 0 | 0 | 1 |
| C. Telecommunications Services | 12 | 15 | 7 | 6 | 13 | 13 | 0 | 11 | 0 | 15 |
| D. Audiovisual Services | 0 | 0 | 0 | 3 | 1 | 4 | 3 | 2 | 2 | 0 |
| E. Other Communication Services | 0 | 0 | 0 | 0 | 0 | 0 | 0 | 0 | 0 | 0 |
| 3. Construction Services | 5 | 5 | 5 | 5 | 5 | 5 | 5 | 5 | 5 | 5 |
| 4. Distribution Services | 0 | 5 | 2 | 3 | 2 | 3 | 5 | 4 | 4 | 1 |
| 5. Education Services | 4 | 3 | 4 | 5 | 3 | 3 | 0 | 1 | 5 | 0 |
| 6. Enviromental Services | 0 | 4 | 2 | 4 | 2 | 3 | 1 | 2 | 4 | 3 |
| 8. Health Related and Social Services | 1 | 1 | 2 | 0 | 2 | 3 | 2 | 3 | 0 | 2 |
| 9. Tourism and Travel Related Services | 2 | 3 | 2 | 3 | 2 | 3 | 2 | 4 | 0 | 3 |
| 10. Recreational, Cultural and Sporting Services | 3 | 2 | 2 | 0 | 2 | 2 | 1 | 3 | 5 | 0 |
| 11. Transport Services | 11 | 5 | 22 | 13 | 9 | 6 | 11 | 9 | 11 | 5 |
| A. Maritime Transport Services | 3 | 0 | 5 | 6 | 5 | 3 | 4 | 5 | 5 | 4 |
| B. Intrariver Transport | 0 | 0 | 5 | 4 | 0 | 0 | 0 | 0 | 0 | 0 |
| D. Air Transport | 1 | 0 | 0 | 0 | 0 | 0 | 0 | 0 | 0 | 0 |
| E. Rail Transport Services | 4 | 0 | 5 | 0 | 0 | 0 | 1 | 0 | 0 | 0 |
| F. Road Transportation Services | 0 | 5 | 3 | 1 | 1 | 0 | 3 | 3 | 2 | 0 |
| G. Transport by Pipeline | 0 | 0 | 0 | 0 | 0 | 0 | 0 | 0 | 0 | 0 |
| H. Services Auxiliary to All Modes of Transport | 3 | 0 | 3 | 2 | 3 | 3 | 3 | 1 | 2 | 1 |
| I. Other Transport Services | 0 | 0 | 0 | 0 | 0 | 0 | 0 | 0 | 0 | 0 |
| 12. Other services that are not included in listed sectors | 0 | 0 | 1 | 1 | 0 | 0 | 1 | 0 | 1 | 0 |
| Total Subsectors (Excluding services related to agriculture and fisheries production, forestry and mining, financial services, and air transport services) | 65 | 67 | 68 | 67 | 65 | 66 | 54 | 73 | 65 | 58 |

*Note:* * Vietnam achieved the minimum threshold (65 commitments) recently.

*Source:* Compiled from the Consolidated Commitments under AFAS (seventh package).

**TABLE 10.4**

**Cumulative Number of Subsectors Liberalized under AFAS**

| CPC Code Under GATS | Sector | 6th package | | | 7th package | |
|---|---|---|---|---|---|---|
| | | W/120 | AFAS | Extension of Commitments (%) | AFAS | Extension of Commitments (%) |
| 1 | Business Services | 46 | 24 | 52.17 | 36 | 78.26 |
| 2 | Communication Services | 24 | 11 | 45.83 | 16 | 66.67 |
| 3 | Construction and Related Engineering Services | 5 | 5 | 100 | 5 | 100 |
| 4 | Distribution Services | 5 | 1 | 20 | 4 | 80 |
| 5 | Educational services | 5 | 3 | 60 | 5 | 100 |
| 6 | Environmental Services | 4 | 4 | 100 | 4 | 100 |
| 7 | Financial Services | 17 | 11 | 64.71 | 11 | 64.71 |
| 8 | Health Related and Social Services | 4 | 1 | 25 | 2 | 50 |
| 9 | Tourism and Travel Related Services | 4 | 3 | 75 | 3 | 75 |
| 10 | Recreational Cultural and Sporting Services | 5 | 3 | 60 | 5 | 100 |
| 11 | Transport Services | 35 | 15 | 42.86 | 19 | 54.29 |
| | **Total** | **154** | **81** | **52.60** | **110** | **71.43** |

*Sources:* (1) Compiled by Nikomborirak (2009) from *Thailand: Schedule of Specific Commitments for the 6th Package of Commitments under the ASEAN Framework Agreement on Services.*
(2) *Thailand: Schedule of Specific Commitments for the 7th Package of Commitments under the ASEAN Framework Agreement on Services*

## TABLE 10.5
## Market Access Commitments of Thailand under AFAS (7th Package)

### National Treatment (%)

| Services Sectors | Mode 1 | | | | | | Mode 2 | | | | | | Mode 3 | | | | | | Mode 4 | | | | | |
|---|---|---|---|---|---|---|---|---|---|---|---|---|---|---|---|---|---|---|---|---|---|---|---|---|
| | N | B | U | H | Total (%) | Sub-sectors (No.) | N | B | U | H | Total (%) | Sub-sectors (No.) | N | B | U | H | Total (%) | Sub-sectors (No.) | N | B | U | H | Total (%) | Sub-sectors (No.) |
| 1. Business | 81 | 0 | 19 | 0 | 100 | 36(25*) | 100 | 0 | 0 | 0 | 100 | 36(25*) | 86 | 14 | 0 | 0 | 100 | 36(25*) | 0 | 0 | 53 | 47 | 100 | 36(25*) |
| 2. Communication | 62 | 23 | 15 | 0 | 100 | 13(6*) | 100 | 0 | 0 | 0 | 100 | 13(6*) | 54 | 46 | 0 | 0 | 100 | 13(6*) | 0 | 0 | 15 | 85 | 100 | 13(6*) |
| 3. Construction | 0 | 0 | 100 | 0 | 100 | 1(1*) | 100 | 0 | 0 | 0 | 100 | 1(1*) | 100 | 0 | 0 | 0 | 100 | 1(1*) | 0 | 0 | 0 | 100 | 100 | 1(1*) |
| 4. Distribution | 75 | 0 | 25 | 0 | 100 | 4(3*) | 100 | 0 | 0 | 0 | 100 | 4(3*) | 100 | 0 | 0 | 0 | 100 | 4(3*) | 0 | 0 | 100 | 0 | 100 | 4(3*) |
| 5. Education | 100 | 0 | 0 | 0 | 100 | 6(5*) | 100 | 0 | 0 | 0 | 100 | 6(5*) | 33 | 67 | 0 | 0 | 100 | 6(5*) | 0 | 0 | 67 | 33 | 100 | 6(5*) |
| 6. Enviroment | 33 | 0 | 67 | 0 | 100 | 6(6*) | 100 | 0 | 0 | 0 | 100 | 6(6*) | 100 | 0 | 0 | 0 | 100 | 6(6*) | 0 | 0 | 0 | 100 | 100 | 6(6*) |
| 7. Finance | 100 | 0 | 0 | 0 | 100 | 6(6*) | 100 | 0 | 0 | 0 | 100 | 6(6*) | 100 | 0 | 0 | 0 | 100 | 6(6*) | 100 | 0 | 0 | 0 | 100 | 6(6*) |
| 8. Health | 100 | 0 | 0 | 0 | 100 | 5(5*) | 100 | 0 | 0 | 0 | 100 | 5(5*) | 0 | 100 | 0 | 0 | 100 | 5(5*) | 0 | 0 | 20 | 80 | 100 | 5(5*) |
| 9. Tourism/Travel | 89 | 0 | 11 | 0 | 100 | 9(8*) | 100 | 0 | 0 | 0 | 100 | 9(8*) | 89 | 11 | 0 | 0 | 100 | 9(8*) | 0 | 0 | 0 | 100 | 0 | 9(8*) |
| 10. Recreation | 40 | 0 | 60 | 0 | 100 | 5(4*) | 100 | 0 | 0 | 0 | 100 | 5(4*) | 100 | 0 | 0 | 0 | 100 | 5(4*) | 0 | 0 | 40 | 60 | 100 | 5(4*) |
| 11. Transportation | 67 | 0 | 33 | 0 | 100 | 18(9*) | 100 | 0 | 0 | 0 | 100 | 18(9*) | 61 | 22 | 17 | 0 | 100 | 18(9*) | 0 | 0 | 39 | 61 | 100 | 18(9*) |

*Notes:* N = None
B = Bound (partial)
U = Unbound
H = As indicated in the horizontal section
* = Number of subsectors with 4 or 5 CPC-digits

*Source: Thailand: Schedule of specific commitments for the 7th Package of Commitments under the ASEAN Framework Agreement on Services*

## TABLE 10.6
## National Treatment Commitments of Thailand under AFAS (7th Package)

National Treatment (%)

| Services Sectors | Mode 1 | | | | | | Mode 2 | | | | | | Mode 3 | | | | | | Mode 4 | | | | | |
|---|---|---|---|---|---|---|---|---|---|---|---|---|---|---|---|---|---|---|---|---|---|---|---|---|
| | N | B | U | H | Total (%) | Sub-sectors (No.) | N | B | U | H | Total (%) | Sub-sectors (No.) | N | B | U | H | Total (%) | Sub-sectors (No.) | N | B | U | H | Total (%) | Sub-sectors (No.) |
| 1. Business | 67 | 14 | 19 | 0 | 100 | 36(25*) | 100 | 0 | 0 | 0 | 100 | 36(25*) | 97 | 3 | 0 | 0 | 100 | 36(25*) | 0 | 0 | 53 | 47 | 100 | 36(25*) |
| 2. Communication | 85 | 0 | 2 | 0 | 100 | 13(6*) | 100 | 0 | 0 | 0 | 100 | 13(6*) | 54 | 46 | 0 | 0 | 100 | 13(6*) | 8 | 0 | 15 | 77 | 100 | 13(6*) |
| 3. Construction | 0 | 0 | 100 | 0 | 100 | 1(1*) | 100 | 0 | 0 | 0 | 100 | 1(1*) | 100 | 0 | 0 | 0 | 100 | 1(1*) | 0 | 0 | 0 | 100 | 100 | 1(1*) |
| 4. Distribution | 75 | 0 | 25 | 0 | 100 | 4(3*) | 100 | 0 | 0 | 0 | 100 | 4(3*) | 100 | 0 | 0 | 0 | 100 | 4(3*) | 0 | 0 | 100 | 0 | 100 | 4(3*) |
| 5. Education | 100 | 0 | 0 | 0 | 100 | 6(5*) | 100 | 0 | 0 | 0 | 100 | 6(5*) | 33 | 67 | 0 | 0 | 100 | 6(5*) | 0 | 0 | 100 | 0 | 100 | 6(5*) |
| 6. Enviroment | 33 | 0 | 67 | 0 | 100 | 6(6*) | 100 | 0 | 0 | 0 | 100 | 6(6*) | 100 | 0 | 0 | 0 | 100 | 6(6*) | 0 | 0 | 0 | 100 | 100 | 6(6*) |
| 7. Finance | 100 | 0 | 0 | 0 | 100 | 6(6*) | 100 | 0 | 0 | 0 | 100 | 6(6*) | 100 | 0 | 0 | 0 | 100 | 6(6*) | 100 | 0 | 0 | 0 | 100 | 6(6*) |
| 8. Health | 100 | 0 | 0 | 0 | 100 | 5(5*) | 100 | 0 | 0 | 0 | 100 | 5(5*) | 0 | 100 | 0 | 0 | 100 | 5(5*) | 0 | 0 | 20 | 80 | 100 | 5(5*) |
| 9. Tourism/Travel | 89 | 0 | 11 | 0 | 100 | 9(8*) | 100 | 0 | 0 | 0 | 100 | 9(8*) | 100 | 0 | 0 | 0 | 100 | 9(8*) | 0 | 0 | 0 | 100 | 0 | 9(8*) |
| 10. Recreation | 40 | 0 | 60 | 0 | 100 | 5(4*) | 100 | 0 | 0 | 0 | 100 | 5(4*) | 100 | 0 | 0 | 0 | 100 | 5(4*) | 0 | 0 | 40 | 60 | 100 | 5(4*) |
| 11. Transportation | 72 | 0 | 28 | 0 | 100 | 18(9*) | 100 | 0 | 0 | 0 | 100 | 18(9*) | 78 | 5 | 17 | 0 | 100 | 18(9*) | 0 | 0 | 33 | 67 | 100 | 18(9*) |

*Notes:* N = None
    B = Bound (partial)
    U = Unbound
    H = As indicated in the horizontal section
    * = Number of subsectors with 4 or 5 CPC-digits

*Source: Thailand: schedule of specific commitments for the 7th Package of Commitments under the ASEAN Framework Agreement on Services*

abroad) on both market access and national treatment in every service sector. Commitments in the more politically sensitive mode 3 (commercial presence) are more limited, but show signs of increasing liberalization between various packages of commitments. Commitments in mode 1 (cross-border trade) are not yet made for every "main" service sector, but all the priority subsectors have no limitations in mode 1. Mode 4 (movement of natural persons) commitments are determined mainly by its horizontal counterparts that concern domestic rules and regulations governing immigration and work permits for foreign nationals.

## Assessment of the Impact of the AEC

This section will assess the trade impact of AFTA and describe the barriers in the services sector. It is useful to assess the trade impact of AFTA for two reasons: AFTA-CEPT has been implemented for more than sixteen years and the tariff reduction programmes were completed by 2003. Moreover, the tariffs for ASEAN Six were also eliminated by 2007. Tariff elimination accounts for 80 per cent of eight-digit tariff lines in 2009, up from 54 per cent in 2006 (SCB 2010). Yet the actual trade impact of the free trade agreements, which grant preferential treatment only to the FTA members, are an empirical issue because it depends on the rules of origin and the existing margin between the MFN and preferential tariff rates.

In addition to the tariff reduction under AFTA-CEPT, five ASEAN economies had taken the initiative of unilateral liberalization in the early 1990s, which resulted in a substantial reduction of the MFN tariffs for ASEAN Five. As a result the ASEAN preferential margins are not high, averaging only 4–14 per cent. More than 60 per cent of tariff lines have a margin of less than 5 per cent (Table 10.7). Yet the tariff margins for export to and import from each ASEAN economy vary widely for different products categories (Table 10.8).

Exporters who want to exploit the preference margin have to comply with the rules of origin (ROO), thus incurring some transaction costs. The ROO are based on the 40 per cent regional value added, except for textiles and garments (which use substantial transformation).

Thanks to the small preferential margins (SCB 2009; Somkiat 2008) and high cost of complying with ROO (Kohpaiboon 2009), the utilization rates for both Thai exports to ASEAN and Thai imports from ASEAN have been relatively low. The utilization rates for exports were 15.4 per

## TABLE 10.7
### General and AFTA-Preferential Tariffs and Distribution of Preference Margins of Selected ASEAN Member Countries (%)

| | Thailand | Indonesia | Malaysia | Philippines | Vietnam |
|---|---|---|---|---|---|
| **MFN Tariff** | | | | | |
| 1995 | 23.1 | 19.4* | 13.0* | 20 | 12.8 |
| 2006 | 11.1 (5.3) | 6.9 (5.3) | 7.2 (4.0) | 6.2 (3.4) | 16.8 (12.4) |
| Preferential Tariffs in 2006 | 1.9 (1.3) | 2 (1.6) | 2 (1) | 2.1 (2.1) | 2.5 (2.3 |
| **Distribution of the margin between general and preferential tariffs (% of total tariff lines)** | | | | | |
| $\Delta t = 0$ | 11.0 | 34.1 | 59.4 | 9.5 | 34.1 |
| $0 < \Delta t \leq 5$ | 54.9 | 41.9 | 12.7 | 70.7 | 18.3 |
| $5 < \Delta t \leq 10$ | 7.2 | 15.2 | 6.8 | 16.9 | 6.2 |
| $10 < \Delta t \leq 20$ | 8.5 | 8.3 | 15.4 | 1.7 | 9.8 |
| $20 < \Delta t \leq 30$ | 15.0 | 0.2 | 4.4 | 0.7 | 9.7 |
| $30 < \Delta t$ | 3.4 | 0.3 | 1.2 | 0.6 | 21.9 |
| #tariff lines | 5,225 | 5,391 | 5,222 | 5,390 | 5,219 |

*Notes:* * Data for 1994; The number in parentheses indicate weighted tariff rates calculated using import values in 2005; General tariff rates are MFN rates for all countries except Thailand for which applied rates are used.

*Source:* Kohpaiboon 2009. "Exporters' Response to AFTA Tariff Preferences: Evidence from Thailand". Faculty of Economics Discussion Paper, Thammasat University

**TABLE 10.8**
**Top 10 items Traded between Thailand and ASEAN-10 During the Period 2003–06**

Exports

| SITC | Description | Tariff Margin (%) | | | |
|---|---|---|---|---|---|
| | | Indonesia | Malaysia | Philippines | Vietnam |
| 776 | Thermionic, cold cathode or photocathode valves and tubes; diodes, transistors and semiconductor devices; integrated circuits, etc.; parts | 0.0 | 0.0 | 1.0 | 1.4 |
| 784 | Parts and accessories for tractors, motor cars and other motor vehicles, trucks, public transport vehicles and road motor vehicles n.e.s. | 3.3 | 16.8 | 5.7 | 23.5 |
| 759 | Parts and accessories suitable for use solely or principally with office machines or automatic data processing machines | 0.6 | 0.0 | 1.0 | 0.7 |
| 713 | Internal combustion piston engines and parts thereof, n.e.s. | 4.4 | 2.9 | 2.4 | 20.3 |
| 752 | Automatic data processing machines and units thereof; magnetic or optical readers; machines transcribing coded media and processing such data, n.e.s. | 0.2 | 0.0 | 0.0 | 4.1 |
| 785 | Motorcycles (including mopeds) and cycles, motorized and not motorized; invalid carriages | 14.7 | 7.9 | 10.6 | 44.1 |
| 772 | Electrical apparatus for switching or protecting electrical circuits or for making connections to or in electrical circuits (excluding telephone etc.) | 4.1 | 4.9 | 1.6 | 8.6 |
| 775 | Household type electrical and non-electrical equipment, n.e.s. | 5.9 | 12.6 | 4.2 | 29.0 |
| 764 | Telecommunications equipment, n.e.s.; and parts, n.e.s., and accessories of apparatus falling within telecommunications, etc. | 5.4 | 3.1 | 2.3 | 10.4 |
| 778 | Electrical machinery and apparatus, n.e.s. | 3.6 | 2.9 | 2.6 | 7.4 |

**TABLE 10.8** *(Cont'd)*

Imports

| SITC | Description | Tariff Margin (%) | (%) Share of Import for which Board of Investment Tariff Exemption applies |
|---|---|---|---|
| 776 | Thermionic, cold cathode or photocathode valves and tubes; diodes, transistors and similar semiconductor devices; integrated circuits, etc.; parts | 2.2 | 72.9 |
| 759 | Parts and accessories suitable for use solely or principally with office machines or automatic data processing machines | 3.3 | 70.3 |
| 772 | Electrical apparatus for switching or protecting electrical circuits or for making connections to or in electrical circuits (excluding telephone etc.) | 4.6 | 62.1 |
| 752 | Automatic data processing machines and units thereof; magnetic or optical readers; machines transcribing coded media and processing such data, n.e.s. | 0.0 | 16.9 |
| 778 | Electrical machinery and apparatus, n.e.s. | 4.1 | 47.4 |
| 764 | Telecommunications equipment, n.e.s., and parts, n.e.s., and accessories of apparatus falling within telecommunications, etc. | 6.3 | 24.1 |
| 784 | Parts and accessories for tractors, motor cars and other motor vehicles, trucks, public transport vehicles and road motor vehicles n.e.s. | 34.7 | 29.6 |
| 773 | Equipment for distributing electricity, n.e.s. | 8.7 | 68.1 |
| 743 | Pumps (not for liquids), air or gas compressors and fans; ventilating hoods incorporating a fan; centrifuges; filtering etc. apparatus; parts thereof | 5.0 | 35.5 |
| 716 | Rotating electric plant and parts thereof, n.e.s. | 5.4 | 35.9 |

*Source:* Kohpaiboon (2009).

cent–20.3 per cent from 2003–06. For imports, they were 11–16 per cent (see Table 10.9).

The utilization rates are the highest for Thailand's trade with Indonesia and the Philippines, and lowest for with Singapore and Malaysia (for imports) (see Table 10.9 and Figures 10.2 and 10.2).

Econometric analysis (Kohpaiboon 2009) also confirms that tariff concessions are significantly underutilized by exporters because of the binding ROO. Secondly, due to the presence of tariff exemption schemes (especially the tax incentive granted by the Board of Investment), manufacturers who import parts and components from ASEAN do not need to make use of the preferential tariffs (Table 10.8). Indonesia's imposition of NTBs on agricultural imports (Fane and Warr 2006) also impedes the ASEAN trade.

But the good news is that the utilization rate is greater among local firms, particularly large, local conglomerates, compared with foreign firms. High rates of AFTA tariff concession utilization are explained by the fact that all vehicle trade among ASEAN members qualifies for AFTA

**FIGURE 10.1**
**Tariff Preferential Utilization Rates of Thai Exports to ASEAN**

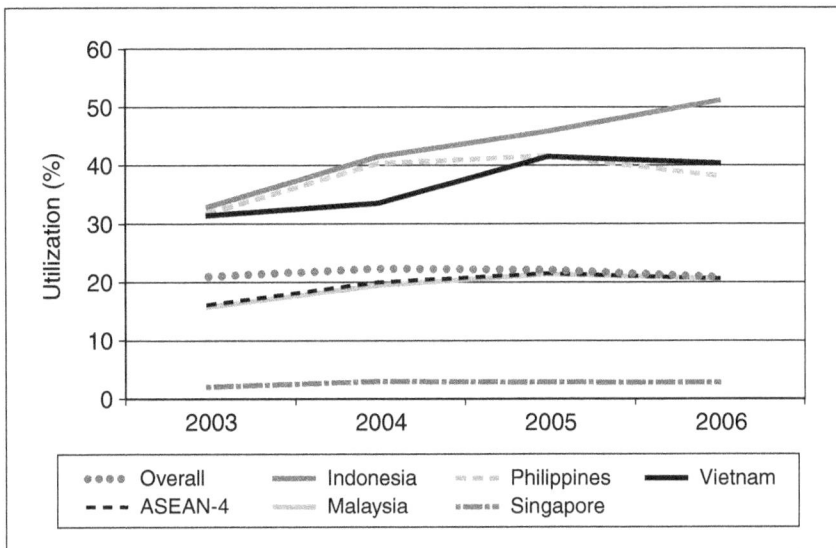

## TABLE 10.9
### Thailand's Trade under AFTA Tariff Concessions: Value ($ million) and Concession Utilization Rates, 2003–06

|  | 2003 | 2004 | 2005 | 2006 |
|---|---|---|---|---|
| **Exports** | | | | |
| Value of exports approved under AFTA ($ mil) | 2,560 | 4,075 | 5,146 | 5,509 |
| Market share (%) | | | | |
| ASEAN-4 (1 + 2 + 3 + 4) | 84.4 | 94.0 | 80.5 | 77.0 |
| 1. Indonesia | 29.0 | 32.6 | 35.3 | 30.6 |
| 2. Malaysia | 31.3 | 28.7 | 24.7 | 24.7 |
| 3. Philippines | 20.0 | 18.1 | 16.6 | 17.8 |
| 4. Singapore | 4.2 | 4.7 | 4.0 | 3.8 |
| Vietnam | 15.4 | 15.5 | 19.0 | 22.4 |
| Other ASEAN countries | 0.2 | 0.5 | 0.5 | 0.6 |
| **Utilization* (%)** | | | | |
| Overall | 15.5 | 19.2 | 21.1 | 20.3 |
| ASEAN-4 | 15.9 | 19.7 | 21.2 | 20.3 |
| 1. Indonesia | 32.7 | 41.3 | 45.6 | 50.9 |
| 2. Malaysia | 20.7 | 22.0 | 21.8 | 20.6 |
| 3. Philippines | 31.6 | 40.1 | 41.4 | 37.9 |
| 4. Singapore | 1.8 | 2.7 | 2.6 | 2.5 |
| Vietnam | 31.2 | 33.6 | 41.3 | 40.1 |
| **Imports** | | | | |
| Value of imports approved under AFTA ($ mil) | 1,459 | 2,458 | 3,540 | 3,077 |
| Import source (%) | | | | |
| ASEAN-4 (1 + 2 + 3 + 4) | 97.1 | 96.8 | 96.0 | 94.7 |
| 1. Indonesia | 30.4 | 33.6 | 33.1 | 31.9 |
| 2. Malaysia | 28.8 | 28.3 | 27.6 | 27.1 |
| 3. Philippines | 23.2 | 17.8 | 16.1 | 15.7 |
| 4. Singapore | 14.7 | 17.1 | 19.2 | 19.9 |
| Other ASEAN countries | 2.9 | 3.2 | 4.0 | 5.3 |
| **Utilization* (%)** | | | | |
| Overall | 11.7 | 15.5 | 16.4 | 13.2 |
| ASEAN-4 | 13.1 | 17.6 | 18.4 | 14.9 |
| 1. Indonesia | 25.3 | 35.8 | 37.4 | 28.8 |
| 2. Malaysia | 9.3 | 12.6 | 12.1 | 10.0 |
| 3. Philippines | 25.4 | 28.3 | 30.2 | 23.0 |
| 4. Singapore | 6.6 | 10.1 | 12.7 | 10.8 |

*Note:* * Value of trade approved by the Bureau of Preferential Trade, Ministry of Commerce under AFTA as a percentage of total trade.
*Source:* Kohpaiboon 2009. "Exporters' Response to AFTA Tariff Preferences: Evidence from Thailand".

**FIGURE 10.2**
**Tariff Preferential Utilization Rates of Thai Imports from ASEAN**

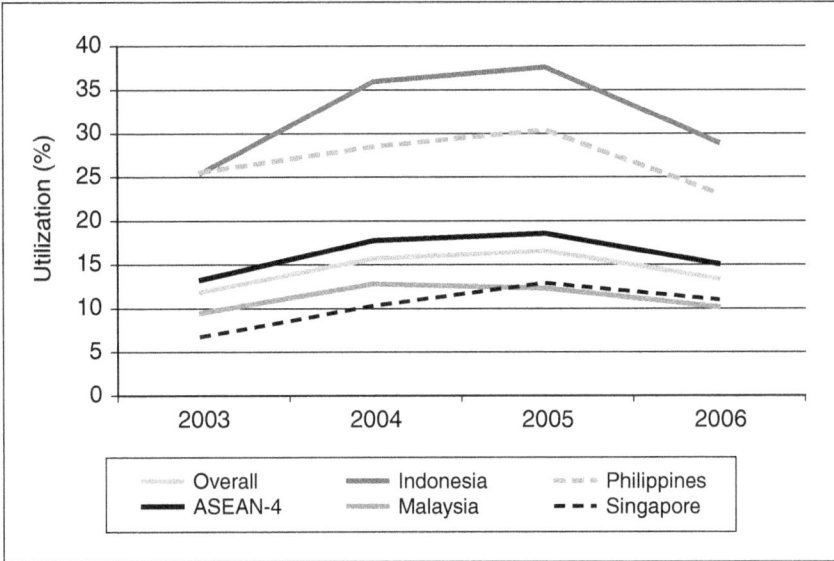

preferential terms, except in Malaysia. High tariff margins for Vietnam are another reason for high utilization rates of Thai exports to Vietnam (Tables 10.8 and 10.9).

In conclusion, the key policy inference is that AFTA is unlikely to play a significant role in promoting intraregional trade because of the high administrative cost of ROO and the already low levels of protection achieved through unilateral liberalization over the years (Kohpaiboon 2009). Moreover, since some ASEAN economies are already part of the global production network in automotive and electronics industries, ASEAN should consider using the "trade-investment link" strategy to promote interregional trade, which will enable every (or most) ASEAN economies to become an integral part of the value chain in the global production network (more discussion below).

### Remaining Barriers to Services Trade

It is still too early to assess the impact of AFAS on services trade because most commitments made under AFAS are not beyond the status quo, except in some trivial sectors, and liberalization has been made conditional (Nikomborirak 2009). In addition, there is not enough disaggregated data on the services trade by countries to carry out the analysis. Therefore, this chapter will discuss the remaining barriers in the services trade, most of which are domestic laws and regulations. The description is drawn from Nikomborirak (2009).

## Capital

The Foreign Business Act 1999 prohibits foreign entities from holding majority equity in the services sector, with some exemptions to be considered by the Cabinet and Board of Investment. But the Board of Investment cannot grant exemptions for business on "list 1" of businesses prohibited to foreigners (for example, services involving *sui generis* law such as the Telecom Act and Commercial Banking Act (Mode 3).

## Labour

There are cumbersome processes for obtaining a work permit and minimum requirements for the undertakings that employ foreign workers (mode 3). The Alien Employment Act also prohibits foreigners in certain professions (e.g., civil engineering, legal services) (mode 4). Other professions are regulated by professional associations (mode 3).

## Land

The ownership of land is prohibited to foreigners, but the Board of Investment and the Industrial Estate of Thailand can grant waivers to promoted businesses (mode 3).

## Production Process

Certain businesses require licences or permission, such as businesses reserved for state monopoly (e.g., public transport) or regulated services (telecom, energy, utilities) or exploitation of natural resources (mode 3). Some domestic rules do not allow the granting of a permit to foreign entities at all, for example, for exploiting economic forest land.

## Marketing and Distribution

Some specific regulatory bodies can impose price regulation, for example, the National Telecom Commission, the National Energy Commission, and Bank of Thailand (mode 3).

## Other Areas

The Trade Competition Act 1999 has not yet been effectively enforced.

## What Are the Challenges Faced by Thailand in Pursuing the Liberalization Commitments under the AEC Blueprint?

Since the manufacturing sector has been liberalized for decades, the issue of free flow of goods is no longer a main concern, except for a few issues of customs administration and trade facilitation. Since the services sector is still tightly regulated, this chapter will address the major challenges in service liberalization.

In the Thai economy, the services sector accounts for the largest share of GDP (49 per cent) and employment (45 per cent). Yet its GDP share declined recently and productivity growth has stagnated (Nikomborirak 2008). The main reason is that the major subsectors are still monopolized by state enterprises, while others are dominated by large firms as a result of regulatory barriers.

Despite the commitments to the AEC, Thailand has not yet been able to fulfil its liberalization obligations under the AEC Blueprint. The foreign equity share cap in four priority sectors has not been raised to at least 51 per cent. An important question is why service liberalization is so difficult.

First, although the blueprint recognizes the need to tackle the issue of domestic regulations and mandates the compilation of an inventory of barriers to services by 2008, there is not yet a concrete framework for negotiation. Secondly, the author agrees with Nikomborirak (2009) that without the reform of a myriad of domestic regulations, AFAS will not lead to actual investment in the liberalized sectors. In addition, services sector liberalization is difficult because it also requires coordination across many government agencies which have different interests. Fourthly, unlike the manufacturing sector, which has a clear industrial policy, there is no clear policy for the services sector. Perhaps the most important reason is the entry barriers stipulated both in the general law (that is, Foreign Business Act) and the specific laws (Telecom Act, Commercial Bank Act, etc.). These laws must be repealed before the foreign equity share cap can be raised. Finally, Thailand and many ASEAN countries still maintain a relatively protectionist stance for the services sector. As yet the scope of quid pro quo negotiations for service sector liberalization is limited.

Perhaps a weak government and interests of government agencies are the most important factors affecting the effort to liberalize the services sector. The AEC Blueprint, strategic schedule, and commitments are a mammoth task to be achieved by 2015. Without clear government position on the liberalization issues of each sector and serious efforts on domestic regulation reforms by each government, bureaucrats will be left to play their own game for the benefit of their organizations, but which is not in the national interest. In response to the businessmen's lobby, they will maintain the status quo, rather than open up the services sector, which may put their careers at risk.

Other challenges are as follows: customs valuation problems, transit shipment problems (that is, too many customs rules), unofficial payments and corrupt practices of some officials involved in the clearance and release of imported goods, the inconvenience of movement between countries for investors (visa and work permits), and difficulty of movements of goods across borders (for example, no exchange of traffic rights, trucks cannot cross the border).

## How Can ASEAN Achieve its Goal of Economic Integration?

To achieve ASEAN's goal of economic integration which will bring about prosperity to its citizens, it is of utmost importance that ASEAN members vigorously make an effort at further liberalization of the services sector and get rid of the remaining barriers to trade and investment. This chapter suggests two policy implications.

Since the services sector in most ASEAN economies is still highly regulated, its liberalization will be a major factor boosting its productivity and hence the standard of living of ASEAN people. First, liberalization must be comprehensive, rather than piecemeal. The comprehensive package should remove major obstacles — domestic as well as at-the-border — throughout the supply chain. Secondly, each country should concentrate on the liberalization and deregulation of a few "key" sectors such as telecoms. The priority should be domestic regulatory reforms. Thirdly, individual bilateral agreements of each ASEAN member state may help pave the way for broader liberalization. Finally, there is an urgent need for much more information on the services sector if effective policymaking is to be achieved.

The second policy implication is how to make ASEAN a truly open market place, that is, explore the linkage between trade and investment. Some studies using the gravity model find evidence to support the argument that ASEAN as a group has been a significant determinant of international trade flows after serious ASEAN economic integration began to take off (Plummer 2006; Elliot and Ikemoto 2003). Yet intra-ASEAN trade is only one-fourth of its total trade as many ASEAN members are highly integrated globally (Plummer 2006). In addition, a large part of intra-industry trade in ASEAN and East Asia is vertical as it involves the regional production network (Aldaba, Yap, and Petri 2009). This is attributed to the diversity in the economic development between East Asian economies and ASEAN. Given the fact that ASEAN economies are so diverse, "the AEC should be concerned not merely with increasing intra-regional trade but rather global economic integration more generally" (Plummer 2006) because of the link between trade and investment. Trade and investment integration policies should be the means to achieve results.

As mentioned above, the nature of ASEAN trade has also been characterized by the product fragmentation phenomenon, especially the dramatic increase in the trade share of electronics components and transport equipment (SITC 7). But when SITC 7 is excluded, ASEAN members are not Thailand's major trading partners, as opposed to the United States and the European Union. The evidence points to the importance of the FDI-export link. One policy implication is that ASEAN should revise its ROO agreement to allow the parts and components that are produced and assembled in one ASEAN economy to enjoy the AFTA tariff preferential. The change will allow the less-developed ASEAN members to specialize in products at the low end of the global supply chain and thus be integrated into the regional production network of vertical integration. As a consequence, ASEAN as a region will become a larger global production network.

The fragmentation theory also suggests that the difference in development stages may hasten fragmentation and FDI at the production level. The right policy environment, which will lower the costs of service link and network set-up costs, requires a stable legal system, upgrading of industry, one-stop shops for foreign investors, and efficient logistics infrastructure.

Plummer (2006) also recommends the creation of a Common External Commercial Policy (CECP, a modified customs union) to minimize trade diversion. The CECP could be adopted by a few ASEAN members initially.

Last, but not least, the ASEAN Four, namely Malaysia, the Philippines, Indonesia, and Thailand, should begin to open their domestic markets for agricultural products from the CLMV countries, especially the CLM. With the stage of development of the CLM economies being what it is, agricultural trade will be the most effective means of growth and higher income for poor farmers.

## REFERENCES

Aldaba, Rafaelita M., Josef T. Yap, and Peter A. Petri. "The AEC and Investment and Capital Flows". In *Realizing the ASEAN Economic Community*, edited by M.G. Plummer and Chia Siow Yue. Singapore: Institute of Southeast Asian Studies, 2009.

Elliott, Richard J.R. and K. Ikemoto. "AFTA and the Asian Crisis: Help or Hindrance to ASEAN Intra Regional Trade". *The School of Economics Discussion Paper Series* 0311, Economics, University of Manchester, 2003.

Fame, G. and Peter Warr. "Distortions to Agricultural Incentives in Indonesia". Agricultural Distortions Research Project. World Bank, 2006.

Kohpaiboon, A. "Exporters Responses to AFTA Tariff Preferences: Evidence from Thailand". *ERTC Discussion Paper No. 17*. Faculty of Economics, Thammasat University, 2009.

Nikomborirak, Deunden, W. Paiboonjit-aree, and B. Sumano. "Interim Report — Thailand Trade in Service". Thailand Development Research Institute, 2009.

———. "Service Sector Strategic Plum". A research project prepared for the National Economic and Social Development Board. Thailand Development Research Institute, 2008.

Plummer, Michael G. "The ASEAN Economic Community and the European Experience". *Working Paper on Regional Economic Integration*. Asian Development Bank, 2006.

SCB-Economic Intelligence Center. "FTAs: What Are the Impacts on Thailand?" *Insight*. January–February 2010.

Tankitwanit, Somkiat. "Seeking the Benefits from the Free Trade Agreements". A research project commissioned by the Office of Industrial Economics. Thailand Development Research Institute, 2008.

# 11

# Achieving an Efficient AEC by 2015: A Perspective from Vietnam[1]

Vo Tri Thanh

In December 1997, the Association of Southeast Asian Nations (ASEAN) adopted a vision till 2020, aimed at "transforming ASEAN into a stable, prosperous, and highly competitive region with equitable economic development, and reduced poverty and socio-economic disparities". In October 2003, the ASEAN member countries agreed on the establishment of the ASEAN Community by 2020, resting on the three pillars of security community, economic community, and sociocultural community. In order to accelerate the realization of the vision, the ASEAN leaders in 2007 expressed their commitment to establish an ASEAN Economic Community (AEC) by 2015 as a single market and production base. In line with this, ASEAN agreed to develop "a single and coherent blueprint for advancing the AEC" and the AEC Blueprint as an action plan was signed by ASEAN leaders in November 2007.

For such a big move, ASEAN member countries certainly have a sizeable workload. There remain challenges and impediments to each country and the region as a whole, the most pressing of which lies in whether the less-developed members can catch up with more advanced ones. Yet the progress of ASEAN so far, particularly in amalgamating themselves as a single block in negotiating and implementing free trade agreements (FTAs) with other major trading partners, brought about hopes for on-time realization of the AEC goal.

This chapter attempts to provide a Vietnam perspective of the progress and challenges for ASEAN in establishing the AEC. Apart from the introduction, the chapter consists of four sections. The first briefly reviews the achievements ASEAN has recorded on the way from Vision 2020 to the AEC. The second describes the progress and the challenges in realizing the goal of the AEC. The third section covers Vietnam's experience and challenges in ASEAN integration. Finally, the author draws some concluding remarks on realizing the AEC by 2015.

## Achievements on the Way from Vision 2020 to the AEC

Thanks to the measures to liberalize regional trade and investment, trade growth of ASEAN countries has been impressive. The average growth rate of ASEAN trade reached 1.3 per cent per annum in 1995–2000, and 7.9 per cent per annum in 2000–2007. The corresponding figures for ASEAN Six member countries are 0.9 per cent per annum and 7.3 per cent per annum, whilst those for CLMV (Cambodia, Laos, Myanmar, Vietnam) are 11.9 per cent per annum and 16.5 per cent per annum respectively.[2] An investigation into the pattern of intra-ASEAN trade growth meanwhile yields more impressive results. Intra-ASEAN trade growth averaged 2.8 per cent per annum in the period 1995–2000 and 9.3 per cent per annum in the years 2000–2007. The corresponding figures for the ASEAN Six (2.6 per cent per annum and 8.9 per cent per annum respectively) differ markedly from those of the CLMV (6.7 per cent per annum and 16 per cent per annum respectively) (Austria 2010).

ASEAN has also proven to be a more attractive investment destination. Foreign direct investment (FDI) into the region increased quite considerably from 2002 to 2008. In the years from 2006 to 2008, FDI inflows to ASEAN member countries went up by 8.6 per cent. Intra-ASEAN FDI rose even faster — by 42.6 per cent. In 2008 alone, FDI into ASEAN reached almost US$59.7 billion, while intra-ASEAN FDI equalled US$10.8 billion, or approximately 18.2 per cent of total FDI into ASEAN.[3] Together with trade performance, this reflects stronger economic ties between ASEAN members.

The expansion of trade and investment has made a significant contribution to ASEAN economic growth. Moreover, the newer ASEAN member countries in general registered faster GDP growth than the older ones, albeit GDP growth decelerated in all countries in 2009 due to the impact of the global financial crisis and economic recession. For the period 2000–2009 as a whole, average GDP growth rates of Cambodia, the Lao PDR, Myanmar, and Vietnam were higher than those of other ASEAN member countries (Figure 11.1).

In relative terms, there has been a tendency for income convergence between the ASEAN Six and CLMV. Table 11.1 indicates that the

**FIGURE 11.1**
**GDP Growth of ASEAN Countries, 2000–09**

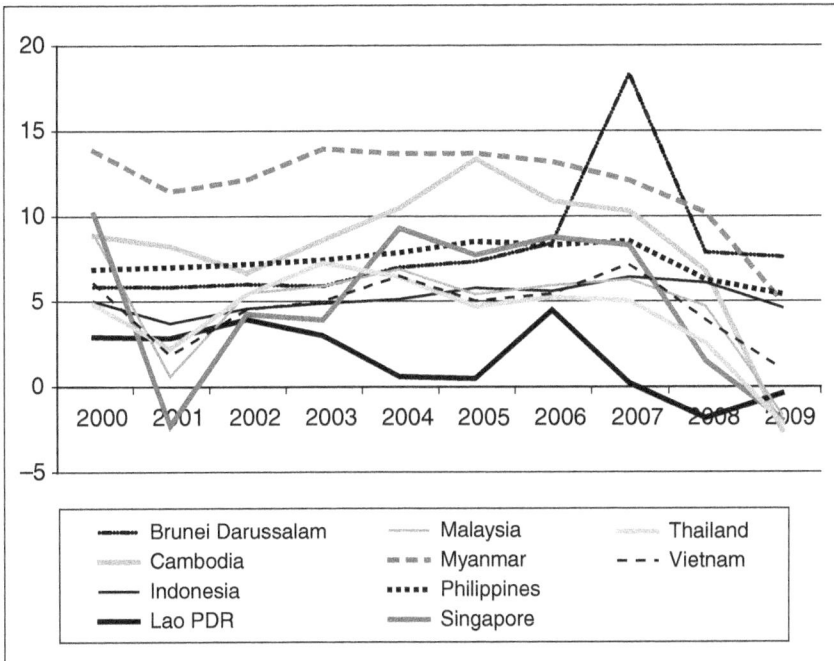

Source: Author's compilation from various sources.

**TABLE 11.1**
**PPP-Income Gaps between Asian Countries**

|              | 2000 | 2005 | 2008 |
|--------------|------|------|------|
| **Cambodia** | 0.6  | 0.7  | 0.7  |
| Indonesia    | 1.6  | 1.4  | 1.4  |
| **Lao PDR**  | 0.8  | 0.8  | 0.8  |
| Malaysia     | 6.0  | 5.3  | 5.1  |
| Philippines  | 1.7  | 1.5  | 1.4  |
| Singapore    | 23.7 | 19.9 | 17.8 |
| Thailand     | 3.3  | 3.1  | 2.2  |
| **Vietnam**  | 1.0  | 1.0  | 1.0  |
| China        | 1.7  | 2.0  | 2.2  |

*Note:* Vietnam's PPP-income is set at unity.
*Source:* MPI (2010).

PPP-income gap between CLV and the higher-income ASEAN members has generally been reduced in the years from 2000 to 2008. More specifically, the income gaps between Cambodia and Vietnam, and between the Lao PDR and Vietnam, have been unchanged. At the same time, this may not be the case between the ASEAN Six countries.

However, such an income convergence has been insufficient. Notwithstanding the attempts to facilitate trade and investment liberalization, and the pledged commitments towards an AEC, in the years from 2000 to 2009, the development gap within ASEAN was still huge (especially between CLMV, and even Indonesia and the Philippines and Malaysia and Singapore in terms of PPP-income, and between CLM and the ASEAN Six in terms of the human development index — HDI) (Table 11.1 and Table 11.2).

Notably, the PPP-income gap between CLV countries and China has widened and living standards in Indonesia and the Philippines are now lower than in China. CLMV and Indonesia generally had a HDI ranking of 100th or over. The decline in HDI rankings of the Philippines was dramatic, from 77th to 105th, a result of the fall in HDI score even in absolute terms. This reflects the lack of progress in accessing basic services in many ASEAN countries.

TABLE 11.2
HDI of ASEAN Countries

|  |  | 2000 | 2005 | 2007 |
|---|---|---|---|---|
| **Ranked countries** |  | 173 | 177 | 182 |
| Vietnam | Value | 0.688 | 0.733 | 0.725 |
|  | Rank | 109 | 105 | 116 |
| Brunei | Value | 0.871 | 0.894 | 0.920 |
|  | Rank | 32 | 30 | 30 |
| Indonesia | Value | 0.684 | 0.728 | 0.734 |
|  | Rank | 110 | 107 | 111 |
| Malaysia | Value | 0.782 | 0.811 | 0.829 |
|  | Rank | 59 | 63 | 66 |
| Singapore | Value | 0.885 | 0.922 | 0.944 |
|  | Rank | 25 | 25 | 23 |
| Cambodia | Value | 0.543 | 0.598 | 0.593 |
|  | Rank | 130 | 131 | 137 |
| Lao PDR | Value | 0.485 | 0.601 | 0.619 |
|  | Rank | 143 | 130 | 133 |
| Myanmar | Value | 0.552 | 0.583 | 0.586 |
|  | Rank | 127 | 132 | 138 |
| Thailand | Value | 0.762 | 0.781 | 0.783 |
|  | Rank | 70 | 78 | 87 |
| Philippines | Value | 0.754 | 0.771 | 0.751 |
|  | Rank | 77 | 90 | 105 |

*Source:* UNDP.

# Realization of the AEC by 2015: Progress and Challenges

ASEAN member countries have been ambitious about their AEC targets. The realization of the AEC as a single market and production base with free flow of goods, services, investments, capital, and skilled labour is made available via a number of instruments, including the liberalization of trade, investment, development of twelve priority sectors, development cooperation, and regional financial cooperation (Figure 11.2). ASEAN adopted the AEC Blueprint in 2007, which is binding for advancing the AEC establishment. In addition, in 2008 ASEAN approved the ASEAN Charter, which can be seen as a breakthrough for strengthening ASEAN institutions, which, in turn, reinforces the implementation of the ASEAN Blueprint.

The realization of the AEC should, besides, be viewed in the broader perspective of East Asian integration in which ASEAN serves as a hub. The existing ASEAN-plus FTAs and those under negotiation may exert pressure on promoting further ASEAN integration itself. Yet the complexity of various FTA commitments, that is, the so-called "spaghetti-bowl" syndrome, and their ambiguous impacts on ASEAN member countries, could hinder ASEAN's consensual move towards deeper integration. Eventually, deeper FTA-based integration must be accompanied by the harmonization of integration routes. The success

**FIGURE 11.2**
**Ambitious Targets of the AEC**

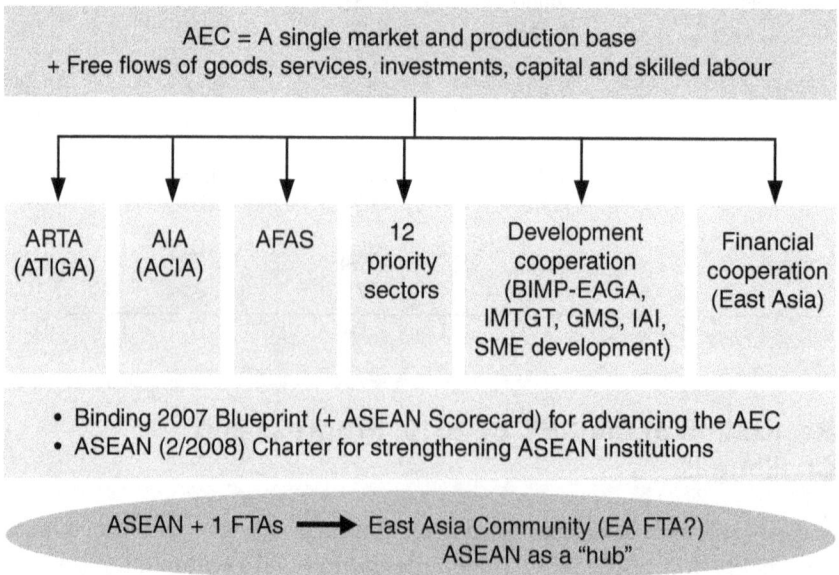

AEC = A single market and production base
+ Free flows of goods, services, investments, capital and skilled labour

| ARTA (ATIGA) | AIA (ACIA) | AFAS | 12 priority sectors | Development cooperation (BIMP-EAGA, IMTGT, GMS, IAI, SME development) | Financial cooperation (East Asia) |

• Binding 2007 Blueprint (+ ASEAN Scorecard) for advancing the AEC
• ASEAN (2/2008) Charter for strengthening ASEAN institutions

ASEAN + 1 FTAs ⟶ East Asia Community (EA FTA?)
ASEAN as a "hub"

*Source:* Author's compilation.

of ASEAN integration is therefore the single first step, but crucial to realizing the vision of an East Asian Community.

The efforts of ASEAN so far to realize the AEC have deepened the people's perception of the integration of ASEAN countries into — rather than just a free trade area — an economic community. From the trade perspective, the AFTA (ASEAN Free Trade Area; ATIGA [ASEAN Trade in Goods Agreement] in February 2009) took significant leaps towards the achievement of its goals. Tariffs were sharply reduced, with the ASEAN Six setting 0 per cent tariff rates for 99.11 per cent of lines, and the CLMV setting 98.86 per cent of lines to between 0 and 5 per cent.

However, relatively rapid tariff reduction seems to have been the single most notable achievement. Meanwhile, the region as a whole is left with a number of challenges. Firstly, regional tariff harmonization needs to be further improved, while some countries have difficulties in dealing with sensitive items. In addition, the rate of utilization of tariff preferences is low, at below 10 per cent.

Secondly, in the areas of services trade and investment liberalization, the progress has been slow. As argued by the Joint Expert Group on EAFTA (2009), "for many countries [in East Asia], no meaningful service liberalization has been achieved" and the room for expanding the coverage of the AFAS, ACFTA (ASEAN-China Free Trade Area), AKFTA (ASEAN-Korea Free Trade Agreement), and AJCEP (ASEAN-Japan Comprehensive Economic Partnership), remains ample. This is not surprising as the services and investment liberalization progress depends to a large extent on the deepness of domestic reforms dealing with the behind-the-border issues.

For example, Figure 11.3 depicts the restrictiveness in terms of logistics in a range of Asian and Oceania countries. Malaysia, China, Indonesia, the Lao PDR, the Philippines, and Vietnam are the most restrictive economies for logistics services in the region.

FDI inflows to ASEAN also encounter enormous impediments from FDI policies, as well as in their implementation and enforcement. Table 11.3 summarizes the evaluation of FDI policy regimes in ASEAN countries. The highest average scores are for screening and approval, and movement of investors. In particular, screening and appraisal procedures could be a major hindrance as they often embody lack of transparency and complicated processing. Meanwhile, the single smallest average score is with performance required. It may be wrong to assess that ASEAN countries are not so much different in terms of restrictiveness to FDI as

**FIGURE 11.3**
**Logistic Restrictiveness Indices for Some Countries**

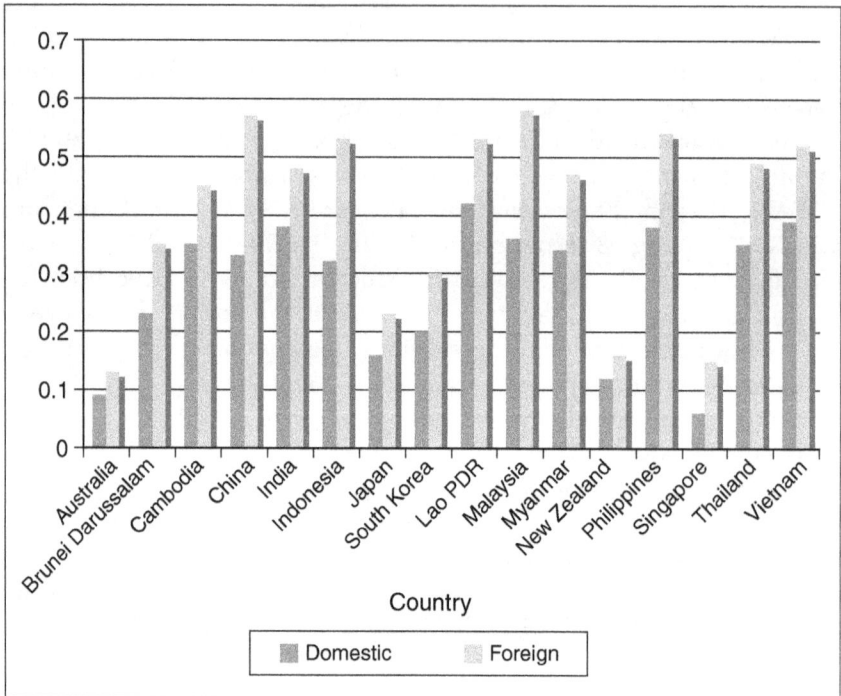

Source: Hollweg and Wong (2009).

the standard deviation is only 0.100. In fact, for the areas of movements of investors, screening and appraisal, national treatment, board of directors, and market access, ASEAN countries are vastly heterogeneous, as indicated by rather high standard deviations.

Another example is the adoption by ASEAN countries of restrictions on foreign ownership in a range of sectors. As can be seen in Table 11.4, the number of sectors under restrictions differ considerably among East Asian countries. In Southeast Asia, Singapore and Indonesia exercise restrictions on the smallest numbers of sectors — in ten and fifteen, respectively. Thailand, Malaysia, the Philippines, and Vietnam restrict foreign ownership in the largest range of sectors. Cambodia, the Lao PDR, and Myanmar only apply relatively modest sectoral restrictions on foreign ownership, which are almost comparable to that in Korea.

TABLE 11.3
FDI Policy Regime of ASEAN Countries

| | Total score | Market access | National treatment | Screening & approval | Board of directors | Movement of investors | Performance required |
|---|---|---|---|---|---|---|---|
| Weight | 1 | 0.4 | 0.2 | 0.1 | 0.1 | 0.1 | 0.1 |
| Brunei | **0.394** | 0.243 | 0.795 | 0.434 | 0.590 | 0.180 | 0.180 |
| Cambodia | **0.242** | 0.140 | 0.183 | 0.622 | 0.000 | 0.750 | 0.117 |
| Indonesia | **0.375** | 0.364 | 0.198 | 0.789 | 0.308 | 0.546 | 0.255 |
| Lao PDR | **0.428** | 0.392 | 0.410 | 0.608 | 0.250 | 0.793 | 0.245 |
| Malaysia | **0.438** | 0.320 | 0.833 | 0.250 | 0.397 | 0.562 | 0.227 |
| Myanmar | **0.481** | 0.378 | 0.401 | 0.921 | 0.399 | 0.714 | 0.463 |
| Philippines | **0.237** | 0.257 | 0.279 | 0.112 | 0.519 | 0.043 | 0.107 |
| Singapore | **0.175** | 0.197 | 0.143 | 0.154 | 0.356 | 0.074 | 0.091 |
| Thailand | **0.310** | 0.423 | 0.000 | 0.500 | 0.000 | 0.805 | 0.100 |
| Vietnam | **0.315** | 0.305 | 0.350 | 0.475 | 0.310 | 0.494 | 0.194 |
| *Average* | *0.339* | *0.305* | *0.350* | *0.475* | *0.310* | *0.494* | *0.194* |
| Standard dev. | 0.100 | 0.092 | 0.272 | 0.266 | 0.193 | 0.296 | 0.113 |

*Source:* Urata and Ando (2010).

**TABLE 11.4**
**Number of Sectors with Restrictions on Foreign Ownership**

|  | Number of restricted sectors |
|---|---|
| Brunei | 18 |
| Cambodia | 23 |
| Indonesia | 15 |
| Lao PDR | 29 |
| Malaysia | 59 |
| Myanmar | 23 |
| Philippines | 50 |
| Singapore | 10 |
| Thailand | 63 |
| Vietnam | 45 |
| **China** | **40** |
| **Japan** | **12** |
| **Korea** | **21** |

*Source:* Joint Expert Group on EAFTA (2009).

This means, while being progressive in trade liberalization, ASEAN member countries fail to phase out barriers to services and foreign investment significantly. The extent of restrictions generally differs markedly across the countries. More importantly, higher economic growth and a more advanced economy are by no means accompanied by a more liberalized business environment.

Thirdly, further attempts towards the AEC are also challenged by regional institutional inadequacy. The regional institutions for implementation, albeit having improved, fail to keep up with the pace of de facto integration. The ASEAN institutionalized integration process has so far followed a "top-down" approach, giving little emphasis on the roles of people, social, and business communities. The monitoring and evaluation of the integration progress remain a critical task. The AEC Scorecard demonstrates its importance as an instrument to support the implementation of the ASEAN Blueprint; it is, however, less than fully satisfactory on its own. Instead, the instrument needs to be complemented by some others which can trace the state, performance, and impact of trade and investment liberalization in the ASEAN region.

Moreover, given the regional development gap and member countries' specific internal problems, ASEAN's core principles (namely, consensus, non-intervention, consultation-based) are sometimes not really flexible for ASEAN to move forward to realize the goal of the AEC. Apparently, less-advanced economies find it hard to realize the same goals via the same road maps as those of more advanced counterparts.

Finally, ASEAN also comes under the challenges of new arising issues. At this stage, the world and the East Asian region are undergoing a "transition period" of reallocation/redistribution of geopolitical and geo-economic powers. The newly emerging economies, particularly BRIC (Brazil, Russia, India and China), have a greater voice in the aftermath of the global financial crisis and economic restructuring. The major trade and investment partners of ASEAN member countries are also experiencing drastic changes. The new transnational and non-traditional securities issues, such as energy security, food security, and climate change, are also confronting the region. Without sufficient well-coordinated efforts at both the regional and country levels, ASEAN can hardly realize its goal of establishing on time the ASEAN Community in general, and the AEC, in particular.

## Vietnam and the Establishment of the AEC

Vietnam became the seventh member of ASEAN in July 1995. Since then, the country has found itself deeply involved in the ASEAN integration process, which has been well in line with the market-oriented reforms and proactive "open-door" policy that Vietnam has been pursuing since the start of *doi moi* (renovation) in 1986.

For a country in transition such as Vietnam, ASEAN integration is of vital importance in various aspects. This process provides favourable conditions, including regional stability, for Vietnam's socio-economic development. It also serves as a stepping stone to the wider liberalization and economic integration of Vietnam. After joining ASEAN and its agreements, Vietnam became a member of APEC (1998) and the WTO (2007), and a signatory to various agreements such as the Vietnam-U.S. Bilateral Trade Agreement, and ASEAN-plus FTAs. Moreover, being a member of ASEAN strengthens Vietnam's bargaining power in the international arena. Most importantly, Vietnam can no longer stay out of the events happening in/to the ASEAN region. In fact, ASEAN has proved itself to be a key trading and investment partner of Vietnam.

Since its ASEAN accession, Vietnam has also seen its trade with the region increasing almost continuously in absolute terms, from US$4.8 billion in 1996 to around US$29.7 billion in 2008 (Table 11.5). Even with the impact of the global financial crisis and economic recession, bilateral trade between the country and ASEAN still amounted to US$22 billion. This reflects the robustness of ASEAN as a key trading partner of Vietnam.[4] The FDI tie between ASEAN and Vietnam has also been strengthened. Over the period from 1990 to 2009, the accumulated (registered) FDI from ASEAN to Vietnam totalled US$40 billion (1,517 projects), accounting for 26 per cent of total FDI inflows (13.8 per cent of total projects) to Vietnam. Conversely, FDI from Vietnam to ASEAN reached US$4.8 billion (269 projects), mostly during the years 2006–09, and to the CLM.

The performance of ASEAN-Vietnam trade and investment has by no means been automatic. In fact, it was largely attributed to Vietnam's implementation of ASEAN integration commitments. Since the start of the *doi moi* process, Vietnam has always acknowledged international integration as an integral part of the whole reform process. The positive connection between the extent of integration and economic development has enhanced the country's confidence in making further regional integration attempts. In general, Vietnam has

### TABLE 11.5
### Vietnam's Trade with ASEAN

|  | 1996 | | 2008 | | 2009 | |
|---|---|---|---|---|---|---|
|  | Value (US$ b.) | Share of total | Value (US$ b.) | Share of total | Value (US$ b.) | Share of total |
| Export to ASEAN | 1.8 | 24.5 | 10.2 | 16.3 | 8.6 | 15.2 |
| Import from ASEAN | 3.0 | 25.8 | 19.5 | 24.2 | 13.4 | 19.5 |
| (Export + Import) | 4.8 | 25.3 | 29.7 | 20.7 | 22.0 | 17.5 |

*Source:* Data provided by General Statistics Office and author's estimates.

seriously implemented international commitments (Murray et al. 2009) despite facing several challenges like other ASEAN countries do (see the next section).

Vietnam also has to confront some specific issues in undertaking further regional integration commitments. The country has to negotiate reducing tariffs and getting oil and petroleum items out of the General Exclusion List. Even though participation in the experimental Programme on Self-recognition of Origin is not compulsory at this stage, the target for implementing such a mechanism by 2012 necessitates enormous preparation. As part of its services liberalization process, Vietnam, in another instance, will become involved in making an offer for the eighth package. Like in other ASEAN member countries, these issues present practical difficulties in integration at the country level. Thus, striking a balance between the flexibility needed for each country to deal with its own specific issues and enforcing mechanisms for on-time realization of the AEC (and more broadly, the Vision of the ASEAN Community) should be of crucial importance. This also means that there exists room for further meaningful liberalization, provided the challenges can be dealt with effectively.

From Vietnam's perspective as a low middle-income economy, some major challenges remain. Firstly, the country has to take full advantage of labour/resources while moving up the value chain for higher value added and avoiding the "low-cost labour trap". This, however, depends crucially on how the country can improve its own institutions (administration and factor production markets), human resources (education and training systems), and infrastructure systems (transportation, energy supply). These have been set out as key areas for breakthrough in the Socio-Economic Development Strategy 2011–20 (MPI 2010). Still, more specific measures need to be identified to address the challenges.

Secondly, Vietnam must strive to harmonize the integration tracks/ routes. The WTO commitments have so far been the most comprehensive. Trade and investment agreements with key partners (East Asian countries, the European Union, the United States, etc.) have either been signed or are under negotiations and are essential for Vietnam's development. However, risks may arise from the discrepancy in commitments that Vietnam has made under those different agreements. As such, harmonizing the integration tracks emerges as an important need, to prevent any unwanted inducement of distorted resource allocation. Furthermore,

Vietnam has to attach liberalization to international cooperation, aiming not only at economic reforms, but also deeper relations with partners for stability and a sustainable win-win partnership.

Finally, Vietnam has to minimize adjustment and environmental costs, as well as macroeconomic instability and social risks during the integration process. Integration is more than just eliminating all the barriers. As it eventually seeks to enhance socio-economic development, the integration process should incorporate adjustments in a way that improves the people's participation, and that prevents rising environmental costs or social risk. Vietnam's failure to manage effectively the flux of capital inflows just after its accession to the WTO, which subsequently sparked high inflation and macroeconomic instability, remains a good lesson (Vo and Nguyen 2009).

Several lessons can be learnt from Vietnam's recent implementation of its international integration commitments (HLAG 2008). After its accession to the WTO, the country has adopted a new way of implementing international commitments. The Communist Party of Vietnam first promulgated Resolution No. 08-NQ/TW in February 2007. The government then prepared and enforced its own action plan, with support from donors (The Beyond WTO Programme 2007–12), and consultation with the independent High Level Advisory Group (HLAG). The new approach has brought about major positive outcomes, having facilitated a better understanding of the role and significance of integration. All ministries and provinces have subsequently had their own action plans in compliance with their specific contexts and demands. Some actually have new ideas for attaining major breakthroughs in their development process. Taking advantage of integration, several provinces have improved their local business and investment environment. Thanks to the public administrative reform programme on reducing administrative procedures, the administrative costs of doing business have become a smaller burden to firms.

However, there have also been weaknesses. In fact, most action plans submitted by ministries and provinces are too spread out, with a lack of priorities. Apparently, with limited resources, they can hardly realize all the objectives and/or targets. The ministries and provinces also demonstrate poor attempts at handling cross-cutting issues (linkages by sector and by region) and interaction between the WTO and other regional/bilateral arrangements. Also, the monitoring and necessary adjustments of action plans when needed failed to be presented with sufficient details. Also, the action plans in general reflect the weak voice of the business community.

## Concluding Remarks

ASEAN as a whole has made commitments to regional integration with a rather wide scope. Significant progress has been made mainly in the liberalization of merchandise trade, but investment and services liberalization remain relatively slow. In particular, higher economic growth and a more advanced economy are by no means accompanied by a more liberalized business environment. Future attempts towards the AEC are also challenged by institutional inadequacy, considerable diversification among ASEAN member countries, as well as the emergence of new issues, including non-traditional security ones.

Past experience presents significant implications. Most importantly, it may be hard to achieve an AEC in real economic terms. As argued by Lloyd (2005), with the definition of a single market as one in which the Law of One Price must hold for all goods, services, and factor markets, the progress towards ASEAN economic integration so far has been limited and far from the ASEAN single market that has been envisioned.

However, even if a "true" single market cannot be realized, it is crucial to make a breakthrough to ASEAN economic integration by the agreed time frame. One should ask whether ASEAN as a whole can really have a sense of community by 2015. This is very much dependent on how ASEAN can effectively enforce its commitments, moving "from action to decisive action" rather than just "from vision to action". ASEAN cooperation should also be enhanced in a way that facilitates connectivity through regional infrastructure development and service-link cost reduction. Monitoring of the ASEAN Blueprint implementation should be strengthened, with support from a more effective scorecard system. ASEAN integration should also allow for the active participation of the people and social and business communities.

ASEAN has proved its vital importance to Vietnam — a country making progressive moves in the integration process to accelerate its transition to a market-oriented economy. Yet Vietnam also has to confront several common issues to further ASEAN economic integration, as well as the problems of a low middle-income economy like itself. These problems have persisted for quite some time, rather than being new. In this regard, the successful integration experience over the past years only marked a profound start. Vietnam, like other ASEAN member countries, still has room for more meaningful integration. Vietnam continues to commit to being proactive and responsible for further ASEAN integration. As a country moving from a low-income to a middle-income economy, Vietnam can serve as a good "bridge" for better mutual understanding between the newer and older members in ASEAN. In turn, this contributes to further ASEAN integration and the realization of an effective AEC.

## NOTES

1. Paper prepared for the ASEAN Round Table in 2010 on "Achieving the AEC 2015: Challenges for Member Countries" in Singapore on 29 April 2010.
2. The ASEAN Six consists of Brunei, Malaysia, Indonesia, the Philippines, Singapore, and Thailand; and CLMV are Cambodia, the Lao PDR, Myanmar, and Vietnam.
3. Data of FDI are provided by Vietnam's Ministry of Planning and Investment (MPI).
4. The decrease of bilateral trade with ASEAN in relative terms (i.e., as a percentage of Vietnam's total trade) results largely from the more rapid expansion of Vietnam's trade with other partners such as the United States, the European Union, and China, which reflects the sequencing of Vietnam's economic integration with the region and the world

## REFERENCES

Austria, Myrna S. "Trade and Investment Issues in ASEAN". In ASEAN Studies Centre, ASEAN-Canada Forum 2008, Report No. 9. Singapore: Institute of Southeast Asian Studies, 2010.

High Level Advisory Group (HLAG). "Institutions for Implementing and Monitoring Government's Action Plan (Resolution 16/2007/NQ-CP for WTO commitments implementation)". July 2008 (in Vietnamese).

Hollweg, Claire and Marn-Heong Wong. "Measuring Regulatory Restrictions in Logistics Services". ERIA discussion paper series DP 14, 2009 <www.eria. org>.

Joint Expert Group on EAFTA. "Desirable and Feasible Option for an East Asia FTA". Final Report on EAFTA Phase II Study, June 2009.

Lloyd, Peter J. "What is a Single Market? An Application to the Case of ASEAN". *ASEAN Economic Bulletin* 22, no. 3 (December 2005).

Ministry of Planning and Investment (MPI). "Vietnam's Socio-Economic Development Strategy 2011–2020" (Draft), Hanoi, April 2010 (in Vietnamese).

Smith, Murray et al. "Vietnam's Economic Integration and Development: Final Report". Project 2007/146105, E.U. Commission, December 2009.

Urata, Shujiro and Mitsuyo Ando. "Investment Climate Study on ASEAN Member Countries". Paper presented at the ERIA Workshop, Jakarta, 22 February 2010.

Vo Tri Thanh and Nguyen Anh Duong. "Vietnam after Two Years of WTO Accession: What Lessons Can Be Learnt?" *ASEAN Economic Bulletin* 26, no. 1 (April 2009).

# PART II

# Challenges for the Private Sector

# 12

# ASEAN Economic Integration: Challenges to Brunei Businesses

Pushpa Thambipillai

Within ASEAN (Association of Southeast Asian Nations), Brunei Darussalam occupies a distinct position mainly as a result of its domestic characteristics. Thus its actions towards the ASEAN Economic Community (AEC) and regional economic integration are guided in some instances, and hindered in other instances, by those special features inherent in its political, sociocultural, and economic systems (see Table 12.1).

Being one of the original six of the ASEAN grouping, Brunei has never wavered in its support for common political-security, economic, and social policies that could contribute towards ensuring a peaceful and developed region. However, the nature of its own environment does not render it a lead player, let alone an active player. Brunei is the smallest member, with an area of 5,765 square kilometres and a population of only about 400,000. In addition, its economy is dependent on the oil and gas sectors which together accounted for about 96 per cent of its total export earnings in 2009. This overreliance on the hydrocarbon contribution has had a negative impact on the general trend of economic

### TABLE 12.1
### Brunei Darussalam Key Indicators, 2010

| | |
|---|---:|
| Area (square kilometres) | 5,765 |
| Population | 414,000 |
| Citizen | 268,000 |
| No. of Permanent Residents | 33,000 |
| No. of Temporary Residents | 112,000 |
| No. of Labour, Employed | 199,000 |
| Unemployment (%) | 2.7 |
| GDP per capita (2009) | B$40,700 |

*Source:* Department of Economic Planning and Development, Brunei Darussalam, Brunei Darussalam Key Indicators 2011 <www.depd.gov.bn>.

activity in the state, and Brunei has only in the last few years taken serious steps to reduce its dependence by seeking a more diversified economic base. Non-oil exports are negligible, and thus Brunei may not be able to enjoy the full advantage of the regional economic integration. On the other hand, as a country with little agricultural and manufacturing of its own, it is able to enjoy all the benefits of a free trade area as it imports a wide variety of goods, about 51 per cent of which come from its ASEAN partners. It also stands to gain from the trade in services as local and foreign firms will be able to operate under the AEC initiative if they are located in Brunei.

Government interest in and support for the AEC have been way ahead of the economic realities of the country and at times it appears that the public enthusiasm and business participation are two different carriages running along parallel tracks. Both public and private sectors are of course committed to increasing economic activity and contributing to increased income. Next only to Singapore within ASEAN in its openness and low or zero tariff rates, there were nevertheless muted murmurings among  local entrepreneurs when AFTA first came into force among the original six. When the China-ASEAN Free Trade Agreement was introduced, there was initial excitement, which dissipated later when it was perceived to be an unequal engagement, dominated by the bigger and more experienced partner state, leaving the local enterprises exposed even before they had claimed a viable status within the Brunei context.

## The Brunei Economy

Brunei is yet to establish itself either as an agricultural, industrial, or service-centred economy. If not for its exports of crude oil and gas that expanded significantly since the 1970s, it would not have been able to afford the increasing demands for imported goods and services, in the absence of substantial foreign or local direct investments. Non-tariff barriers in some sectors have also discouraged external participation in certain industrial sectors, while the small home market and the absence of economies of scale are further discouragements. Thus the government has become the largest domestic player, including being the sole source of national income by holding a joint ownership with the Royal Dutch Shell Company in exploiting hydrocarbon resources. The World Economic Forum's Global Competitiveness Index groups Brunei in what it refers to as Stage 2 economies, where states are dependent on product exports. Brunei ranks an admirable 28th out of 139 states on its overall performance, despite averaging low points for certain fundamental indicators.[1]

Since 2007 Brunei has been promoting its long-term development plan (Wawasan 2035, or Vision 2035) that should alter some of the sluggish aspects of its economic development. The current five-year National Development Plan (2007–12) aims to, along with other programmes, widen the economic base and strengthen the foundations for a knowledge-based economy that would support its diversification goals. Nevertheless, policy planners have an uphill task in ensuring positive economic growth each year by emphasizing both public and private-sector involvement. The national strategy does recognize the development of local businesses that will enhance the expansion of small and medium enterprises (SMEs) with the supportive role of the government in infrastructure development. Brunei's SMEs have remained largely small or micro size, while the medium ones are in the construction or hydrocarbon-related sectors. The emergence of a handful of enterprises in the productive industries is an encouraging sign; they are mostly related to the agricultural, fisheries, and meat-based food processing sectors that cater to the consumer market.

Muslim consumers are particular about their products being halal,[2] and Brunei's certification will satisfy domestic and foreign markets. Brunei's own halal food brand which it hopes to market internationally is already recognized in the region and is thus an opportunity for local food and services sectors to be promoted. The global market for the halal industry is enormous, given the total Muslim population of at least a billion. However, the actual increase in business enterprises, especially in the export sector, is marginal since most of them are domestically oriented and not yet engaged in producing extensively for external consumers.

The structure, composition, and direction of trade for the latest period are generally similar in pattern to previous years, except for differences in the value of total trade recorded due to global price shifts. For instance, total trade decreased by 25 per cent in 2009 compared with 2008, and the trade surplus was lower than that of the previous year (Table 12.2). The major export commodities, crude oil and natural gas, affect the total trade receipts as a result of prevailing lower global prices, coupled with Brunei's voluntary reduction of production. In 2009 both commodities accounted for 96 per cent of its total exports, amounting to B$10,023.5 million. Thus the remaining exports were negligible in comparison, accounting for about B$700 million, of which garments fetched only B$57 million. In 2009 the non-oil and gas sector grew by 0.9 per cent, while the oil and gas

**TABLE 12.2**
**Brunei's External Trade**
(B$ million)

|                  | 2008     | 2009     | % Decrease in trade |
|------------------|----------|----------|---------------------|
| Exports f.o.b    | 14,941.9 | 10,431.7 | 30.2                |
| Imports c.i.f    | 3,647.3  | 3,491.9  | 4.3                 |
| Total trade      | 18,589.2 | 13,923.6 | 25.1                |
| Balance of trade | 11,294.7 | 6,939.9  |                     |

*Source:* Department of Economic Planning and Development, Brunei Darussalam, *Brunei Darussalam Key Indicators 2009*, p. 7. Additional information is from the media release by the said department, August 2010 <www.depd.gov.bn>.

sector declined by 4.6 per cent, thereby causing a negative GDP growth of 1.8 per cent.

Of the total exports, Japan absorbed 46 per cent, Korea 12 per cent, and ASEAN states 17 per cent. ASEAN led the major import partners, accounting for 52 per cent (dominated by Singapore with 26 per cent and Malaysia with 19 per cent), followed by the United States at 13 per cent, the European Union at 10 per cent, Japan at 9 per cent, and China at 6 per cent, ahead of other smaller sources. Brunei imports a wide variety of food, machinery, electronic, and other necessities as it does not have an indigenous manufacturing or import substitution industrial infrastructure. It does contribute a certain amount of home-grown rice, fruits, vegetables, and poultry, in addition to part of the local requirements of the building industry.

As the above discussion on Brunei's economic features and trade statistics indicates, the country has high trade dependence, dominated by oil and gas exports, while imports are equally crucial (Table 12.3). In such circumstances it is important to review Brunei in the ASEAN context, and its role in the AEC, its contributions, and expected benefits for the private sector in the coming years.

### TABLE 12.3
### Brunei's Trade Pattern, 2009

| Exports | |
| --- | --- |
| LNG and Crude Oil | 96.1% |
| LNG | 48.4% |
| Oil | 47.7% |
| Garments | 0.5% |
| Others | 3.4% |
| **Imports** | |
| Machinery, transport equipment | 41.3% |
| Manufactured, miscellaneous goods | 33.5% |
| Food and live animals | 12.4% |
| Chemicals | 7.1% |
| Others | 5.7% |

*Source:* <www.depd.gov.bn>.

## Brunei's Business Sector

The public sector dominates the local economic environment, employ-ing about 60 per cent of the labour force. Except for the hydrocarbon and financial services sector, the domestic business environment is limited to only a few players of any significant size. SMEs (defined as an enterprise that employs between six and 100 workers) are considered the backbone of the private sector in Brunei Darussalam; in fact, most of the enterprises fall under the "micro" category, for example, in the food, tailoring, and trade services sectors. In addition, a main characteristic is that almost all of the businesses cater to domestic needs, whether they are in the product or services areas, and thus tend to exhibit characteristics of limited size, capital, output, and peculiar local tastes. Thus it is no surprise that over 9,000 enterprises are registered as business organizations, each engaged in some form of activity, even though the oil and gas sector dominates Brunei's GDP (Table 12.4).

According to data from the Department of Economic Planning and Development (DEPD), in 2009 there was a decline in the oil and gas sector, a growth in the primary resources and services sector, and a decline in the industrial sector that included manufacturing and construction.

### TABLE 12.4
### Brunei's Gross Domestic Product

|  | 2008 | 2009 | 2010 |
|---|---|---|---|
|  | B$ million | B$ million | B$ million |
| GDP at current prices | 20.397.9 | 15.6 | 16.9 |
| Oil and gas sector | 14,300.0 | 9,410 | 10,460 |
| Non-oil and gas sector | 6,097.9 | 5,190 | 6,400 |
| Government sector | 2,152.2 | 2,180 | 2,310 |
| Private sector | 3,945.7 | 4,000 | 4,090 |
| GDP per capita ($B thousand) | 51.3 | 38.4 | 40.7 |

*Notes:* The decline in the oil and gas sector caused the negative growth of GDP of 1.8 per cent. The exchange rate in 2011 was about US$1:B$1.28.
*Source:* Department of Economic Planning and Development, Brunei Darussalam, Brunei Darussalam Key Indicators, 2009, p. 6; 2011, p. 7.

Brunei, being a small, vulnerable economy, may have suffered the national decline as a result of global economic recession that affected both its hydrocarbon-based trade and the limited size of its incoming foreign direct investments.

Despite the discouraging signs, there are several silver linings in Brunei's private sector. For instance the following have been the leading business sectors: restaurant and catering services, light manufacturing (foodstuff, beverages, cables, wires, nails and screws, roofing, wood products), forwarding and shipping, retail and wholesale, and heavy industry (methanol, cement). The Brunei Industrial Development Agency (BINA), under the Ministry of Industry and Primary Resources, and the Brunei Economic Development Board, have been involved in the attempt to diversify the economy by identifying potential areas for industries, seeking potential investors, and by establishing appropriate industrial sites in various localities. In fact BINA has been promoting the investment potential in areas such as silica sand–based products, textile and apparel, building products, metal products, footwear, leather products, selected wooden furniture, clay products, and ceramic pottery. These are products whose inputs can be sourced locally and thus can qualify under ASEAN CEPT (Common Effective Preferential Tariffs) for export to ASEAN and other partner countries. To date a number of enterprises have taken advantage of the facilities provided.[3]

## Brunei in the ASEAN Context

Several governmental policies are already in place in support of ASEAN's promotion of a regional free trade area, and specifically towards achieving the AEC by 2015. However, as some in the private sector point out, the pro-regional enthusiasm generally represented by the Ministry of Foreign Affairs and Trade, is not usually translated into specific action at the implementation level by the national agencies concerned. Thus, the Brunei business sector is not only faced with a number of hurdles in starting and operating businesses under a wide range of unnecessary and decentralized procedures (as revealed by studies of the World Bank or the World Economic Forum) and in the relative cost of doing business, but they also face higher costs compared with neighbouring economies[4] (Table 12.5).

**TABLE 12.5**
**Starting a Business in Brunei**

| Indicator | Brunei | OECD states |
|---|---|---|
| Procedures | 15 | 5.6 |
| Time (days) | 105 | 13.8 |
| Cost (% income per capita) | 13.5 | 5.3 |
| Min. capital (% income per capita) | 0.0 | 15.3 |

*Notes:* The start-up procedures from company registration, inspection, etc., until the licence is ready for collection by a potential entrepreneur takes about 105 days — compared with 14 days in the OECD countries — and the total costs amount to about BD$5,000. Brunei had in fact jumped +19 points for this category — on starting a business — from 152 to 133 in the latest survey for 2011. But it is still considered unsatisfactory in its overall score.
*Source:* <www.doingbusiness.org>.

Not only are there delays and complicated procedures in starting a business, but there are also several obstacles when established enterprises wish to export their products, going beyond their limited domestic demand. Thus the local entrepreneurs face the challenges of an "infant", domestic non-oil and gas sector that is not well geared towards making the country more productive through manufacturing and knowledge-based services, even if certain policies are already in place. There are also problems in getting engaged at the next level of productive activity, that is, at the regional level, through participation in the ASEAN economic integration process. Most businessmen still concentrate on their own limited activities of economic "survival" and profitability, and have not yet explored beyond their shores as they are unsure of its viability due to factors such as inexperience, the lack of adequate knowledge and information, and a general aversion to risk taking. The latter is an important ingredient in the cultural make-up of the Brunei Malay and may be a crucial determinant when compared with the business acumen of immigrant communities in most of the ASEAN states that extend informal networks of business linkages, which the Brunei businessman cannot normally tap into.

However, the few businesses that seem interested in venturing into the region realize that there are opportunities. Brunei's private sector participation in the regional process is not as sophisticated or as aggressive as, for example, Singapore's. Nevertheless, businesses acknowledge that even for the most rudimentary of trade matters, there are challenges to overcome, as Brunei is not yet participating to its optimum capacity in accordance with its medium-term economic strategies. To private-sector players, their successful development within the local business environment seems to be the priority (despite its smallness), before they are prepared to consider moving further afield; presently that appears more formidable and challenging, and is thus to be sidelined till they gain their business acumen and confidence.

Brunei's export driven economy has become so specialized in catering to the hydrocarbon industry that it has not been adequately prepared to accommodate other emerging sectors. No doubt it constitutes, on average, 70 per cent of the GDP, and 90 per cent of export earnings, and the government and residents are conscious of the implications of energy security — in terms of falling national income during times of poor global prices and the potential depletion of the non-renewable resource. The fossil fuel sector has attracted both foreign and local investment, while its international linkages have become highly specialized in terms of capital investment, human resource professionalism, and marketing strategies. Consider the latter for example. Both crude oil and liquefied natural gas have their own export mechanism, with their special export tankers that deliver directly to their international buyers in Japan and Korea, and, in future, in China. The recently established methanol industry is also similarly organized, with its export sector targeting extra-ASEAN markets. It is precisely for this reason that export and shipping requirements of other products have not been adequately developed. One of the hurdles for a local producer is in exporting his products where only coastal shipping (mostly barge service) is available, while most exports (and imports) are outsourced through major ports in Singapore and Peninsular Malaysia (whether it is to fellow ASEAN member such as Vietnam, or to China (under CAFTA, the China-ASEAN Free Trade Area). Inevitably, one of the reasons for the lack of shipping is the small volume of Brunei products, that render it uneconomical for any major line to connect Brunei to the export markets. Air cargo is of course more costly, with only one main carrier servicing the regional and selected Asia Pacific airports. But the general belief is that for the current level of trade, the air freight service is good and reliable, but that more has to be explored in shipping services.

Another economic activity that could have taken advantage of the AFTA initiatives would have been the re-export services; but owing to poor shipping facilities, and the lack of a free trade or processing zone, there is no current interest in exploring this sector beyond a limited undertaking. Some businessmen are still keen to explore the re-export sector to take advantage of CEPT. One of the products cited was new or used automobile tyres for which there is apparently a healthy demand and which would make a viable economic activity.

Domestic policies in relation to the export of certain items, such as agricultural or meat and chicken products, may need specific export permits that are coordinated by various agencies, including the departments of agriculture and health. Some of those products may seek a halal endorsement, others, a specific clearance required by an importer. Some business operators felt that the coordination by the various issuing agencies needed improvement to enable a speedier process for exporters. Others feel that their potential exports are hampered by the domestic policy environment, in addition to the externally originating NTB (non-tariff barrier) that required stringent procedures, especially for meat products, such as hot dogs, that some companies are already producing for the local market and apparently has a ready market outside Brunei. External NTBs are difficult to overcome despite the AFTA or CEPT rules. One local product, cement, which has potential importers from neighbouring countries, faces several obstacles from the importing side and as a result could not be exported.

Brunei's businessmen acknowledge that its import sector is doing well as there is a good demand for machinery, automobiles, chemicals, food and agricultural products, electronics and other consumer items. With several FTAs in operation, there is increased incentive to import from regional partners. They do not face too many hurdles, as long as they meet Brunei's halal and other specific requirements under the prohibitive list. ASEAN partners, especially Malaysia and Singapore, are the biggest sources of imports, and thus promote the AFTA ideals of integration. Geographical proximity, political and cultural familiarity, and the readily available sources of products have forged a closer market link.

**TABLE 12.6**
**Brunei Public Institutions Facilitating Business**

- Ministry of Foreign Affairs and Trade
  Regional Policies, ASEAN agreements, Certificates of Origin
- Ministry of Industry and Primary Resources
  Business facilitation services
  Investment promotion, industrial sites — role of BINA
  Export, import facilitation, agro and meat products
- Ministries of Health, Religious Affairs, Home Affairs
  Certification for halal products; business set-up licensing from Municipal
  Board; Foreign labour applications from Department of Labour
- Prime Minister's Office, Department of Economic Planning and
  Development
  General policy direction and development plans; compilation of national
  statistics
- Brunei Economic Development Board
  Promotion of local business development; seek foreign direct investment
  implement economic diversification strategies

## Towards AEC 2015

The AEC envisages creating a single market and production base, with free flow of goods, services, investments, capital, businesses, and professional and skilled labour. Several road maps are already in place for intraregional economic integration for the ten member states. A recently issued ASEAN Economic Scorecard has further evaluated the journey towards the AEC. Through various FTAs with China, Japan, Korea, India, Australia, and New Zealand, ASEAN states hope to widen the economic linkages. However, each ASEAN member state's private sector is at a distinct level of integration into the regional economy. As this study has indicated, the domestic political and economic environment is as much a factor as external variables in promoting that integration.

In the case of Brunei, it is not only the logistics and connectivity, but also policy execution that has not been geared for a regionally oriented business community, especially in the exports of products, never mind the trade in services. Brunei has been for too long a consumer of imports and externally sourced service providers. It is only just developing to be an exporting country, and is experiencing inevitably the associated problems of being a new entrant. It is thus significant in such a situation that the public sector be ready, aware, and realizes the urgency in order to be technically and logistically committed to assist the private sector in dealing with the external market. The government has several broad-based regimes in place, but it is the specifics that seem to discourage the business community.[5]

Equally responsible in realizing Brunei's role in regional economic integration is the private sector itself. It is generally weak and fractured. The various business groups are dispersed, despite the presence of several chambers of commerce, established along ethnic lines that promote their particular group's vested interests (as is common in other parts of Southeast Asia as well).[6] Thus there is no unified representation to the national government to promote a consensual policy stand, for example, on AFTA or the AEC, other than ad hoc interactions. Most of the business group members have been continuing the traditional interests in commerce, retail or the wholesale business, and other service-oriented activities, building and mining, or in merely enjoying rents for the use of their business licences by non citizen and foreign entrepreneurs without being directly involved. The business community is represented to some extent at the national level. However, some view the ASEAN Business Council or the APEC Business Council as not largely representing their interests and thus stay clear of such institutions. There appears to be a better level of identity with the BIMP-EAGA Business Council as the region it represents is geographically and culturally closer to the interests of the Brunei business community and it seems to have generated more direct results. Some of the local business enterprises participate regularly in the trade expos within and outside Brunei and claim beneficial outcomes. The EAGA business membership follows on the agreements under AFTA as all facilities are streamlined under regional procedures; however, it too faces some credibility issue as the "big boys" are not interested in it, and at times it cannot make its voice heard.

Another interesting phenomenon that is slowly emerging is the success story of a handful of enterprises which, on their own initiatives — but nevertheless due to ASEAN dialogue partner arrangements — have managed to establish economic links, either in investment or in trade. This is specifically with the Plus Three partners, China, Japan, and Korea. Brunei businessmen are able to utilize the preferential arrangements with those partners and establish new markets.[7] This may be good for Brunei, but may not instil the spirit towards regional integration that ASEAN seeks.

**TABLE 12.7**
**AEC Readiness of Brunei Businesses**

- Public sector support for AEC not translated to effective implementation
- Private sector not yet integrated into the ASEAN economy
- Business sector not into regional integration, priority in national level success
- Multinationals have own extra-ASEAN schemes with established markets
- The SMEs need government support in facilitating exports to ASEAN states
- Imports from AFTA region are increasing
- Exports in services are still underexploited
- Need concerted effort in coordination of national AEC-related action
- Complex set of challenges, given Brunei's special economic characteristics
- Dominance of the oil/gas sector has a large impact on the development of non-oil sector

## Wake-up Call?

For Brunei, the AEC and 2015 is an opportune time and an appropriate incentive to restructure its domestic economic priorities and policies. For the past two decades the government has emphasized the importance of diversifying away from hydrocarbon dependence and creating a more broad-based economy. There is the chance, through ASEAN, to grab the regional road map that will provide some of the initiatives towards achieving its domestic goals; on its own, it will be an even more difficult task. What the business community seeks from the public sector is to improve the infrastructure, establish the connectivity that the private sector needs, and be the supporter of the business community that has not been in the forefront of taking risks. Within the business community, there are several experienced and enthusiastic entrepreneurs for whom the AEC will provide greater opportunities, provided that the economic environment is conducive at the national and external levels. They are aware of the several niche areas that they can be involved in to reap the benefits, being engaged either at the subregional (EAGA) context or at the regional (ASEAN) level. Of the twelve priority areas identified by the policymakers, there are opportunities in the fields of agro-based, fisheries and wood-based industries.[8] But the average Brunei business person in the food, wood, or agro industry is not entirely aware or, even if enlightened, not too impressed by such concepts as the "score card". The crucial factor is, can he expand his business and how much profit can he make.

Not all within the private sector may be ready to take full advantage of the 2015 timeline, but the sector is slowly being made aware of the potentials. The next time leaders meet at the regional or international levels to expound the positive aspects of ASEAN regional cooperation, they should each return to their countries and engage in megaphone public diplomacy to get the message back to their peoples, and then set about reassessing the supportive institutions in place. Only then will the opportunities and the urgency be transmitted to the masses within their own constituencies.

## NOTES

The writer would like to thank the individuals from Brunei's public and private sectors who provided interesting insights into the local business environment. However, responsibility of interpretation and analyses lie solely with the writer.

1. See <www.weforum.org> on country reports for 2010–11.
2. Halal — that which is permissible according to Islam.
3. Some of the popular products include food products such as chips, biscuits, savoury, sauces, fisheries products, sausages, high-end furniture and building materials, and crystal products.
4. In the latest study, *Doing Business 2011: Making a Difference for Entrepreneurs*, Singapore, Hong Kong, and New Zealand were the leading three out of 183 economies. Brunei was at 112, but fared well as one of the 10 most improved economies compared with the previous year's study when it was at 117. Although this study does not measure all aspects of the business environment, such as macroeconomic stability or corruption, it "analyses regulations that apply to an economy's businesses during their life cycle, including start-up and operations, trading across borders, paying taxes and closing a business".
5. The ASEAN Secretariat announced the Pilot Project for the Implementation of a Regional Self-Certification System which would streamline the rules of origin procedure and reduce the documentation processes by exporters. Brunei is one of three (with Malaysia and Singapore) ASEAN states that endorsed the Plan Towards Self Certification at the AFTA Council Meeting in August 2009 and agreed to implement it beginning 1 November 2010, ahead of the other seven states that will follow it by 2012.

6. These are the Brunei Malay Chamber of Commerce and Industry, the Chinese Chamber of Commerce, the National Chamber of Commerce and Industry, Brunei Darussalam, and the Brunei Darussalam International Chamber of Commerce and Industry.
7. Some of the local business enterprises that have participated in the China-ASEAN Expo in Nanning claim to be making some progress, especially in the potential export of food products. Others have successfully exported selected items to Japan, while wood-based industries have found buyers in South Korea.
8. ASEAN has identified twelve priority areas in its regional economic integration strategy: agro-based, air transport, automotive, electronics, e-ASEAN/ICT, fisheries, health care, logistics, rubber-based, textile and apparel, tourism, and wood-based industries. See *ASEAN Economic Community Scorecard* at <www.aseansec.org>.

## REFERENCES

*Borneo Bulletin. Borneo Bulletin Brunei Yearbook.* Bandar Seri Begawan: Brunei Press, 2010.

*Brunei Darussalam Long Term Development Plan: Wawasan Brunei 2035.* Bandar Seri Begawan: Government Printers, 2007.

Brunei Darussalam, Department of Economic Planning and Development. *Brunei Darussalam Key Indicators 2009* and *2011.*

Brunei Darussalam, Ministry of Industry and Primary Resources. *Directory of Brunei Darussalam Exporter/Importer Lists, English/French.*

# 13

## Perspective of the Indonesian Business Sector on the Regional Integration Process

Widdi Mugijayani and Pratiwi Kartika

In recent years, Indonesia has engaged itself in a number of free trade agreements (FTA) and other initiatives, such as the Indonesia-Japan Economic Partnership Agreement (IJEPA; 2008), ASEAN-China Free Trade Agreement (ACFTA; 2010), and ASEAN Economic Community (AEC; 2015). With regard to the AEC, ASEAN leaders agreed in January 2007 to move forward the establishment of the AEC from 2020 to 2015. One main objective of the AEC is to establish ASEAN as a single market and production base, which, according to the AEC Blueprint, shall comprise five core elements: free flow of goods, free flow of services, free flow of investment, freer flow capital, and free flow of skilled labour. The objectives of establishing the AEC are to make ASEAN a more dynamic and competitive region, with new mechanisms and measures to strengthen the implementation process of its existing economic initiatives; accelerate regional integration in the priority sectors;

facilitate movement of business persons, skilled labour and talents; and strengthen the institutional mechanism of ASEAN.

In the implementation process, an effective public-private sector engagement would be mutually reinforcing. Pushpanathan (2010c) asserted that ASEAN ministers agreed on the importance of engaging the private sector more intensively, not only during the implementation phase of economic integration initiatives, but also during the formulation exercise of ASEAN economic policies. However, there are many obstacles, including the lack of awareness particularly in the private sector in most of the ASEAN countries. Meanwhile, many multinational companies perceive the ASEAN market as "too fragmented" and not integrated.

The aim of this chapter is to assess the effectiveness of the ASEAN economic integration, based on the business sector's point of view and the prospects of the AEC to achieve its stated objectives by 2015. The study uses the survey or in-depth interview method with selected business communities and associations to gauge the level of their awareness concerning the AEC. While the questionnaire also asks respondents about other FTAs, the main focus of this study is about the AEC.

This study concludes that there are different levels of awareness within the private sector regarding the AEC and other FTA measures; as a result, the business community cannot get engaged fully in the implementation process. They also cannot utilize the FTA privileges optimally. In general, bigger companies or major players are more aware and more optimistic about implementation of the AEC. However, the number of major players in Indonesia is very small, less than 1 per cent of the total members of the country's business community. The respondents pointed out that regardless of the proliferation of FTAs in the region, many forms of trade protectionism remain prevalent, which, in one way or another, restricts the implementation of various ASEAN FTAs. Improvement in competitiveness, infrastructure development, policy coordination, and legal certainty are key factors to achieve an effective AEC by 2015.

The first part of this chapter addresses the development of ASEAN trade and investment and is followed by a section on the status/progress in the ASEAN economic community. The subsequent section discusses the survey findings and focuses on issues such as general awareness concerning the AEC, the impact of the AEC, the degree of utilization of FTA privileges, and obstacles and strategies towards AEC. The chapter ends with a conclusion and policy recommendations.

## ASEAN Trade and Investment

From 1990 to 2008, ASEAN's exports to the world exhibited an increasing trend, jumping from around US$130 billion to more than US$960 billion. Imports also went up from US$145 billion to US$927 billion over the same period (World Integrated Trade Solution n.d.). Subsequently, due to the 2008 global financial crisis, exports fell dramatically by 24 per cent, and imports by 30.6 per cent in 2009. As for foreign direct investment (FDI), while it had steadily increased before the 1997–98 financial crisis. It dropped in 1997–98, then recovered rapidly in 2003–4. FDI dropped again in the 2008 global financial crisis.

There have also been several significant developments in ASEAN's trade and investment relations since 2009. First, China has replaced Japan as the top trading partner; its trade with ASEAN was around

**TABLE 13.1**
**Top Ten ASEAN Trade Partner Countries/Regions, 2009**
As of 15 July 2010 (value in US$ billion; share in per cent)

| Trade Partner Country/Region[1] | Value | | | Percentage of total ASEAN trade | | |
|---|---|---|---|---|---|---|
| | Exports | Imports | Total Trade | Exports | Imports | Total Trade |
| ASEAN | 199.6 | 176.6 | 376.2 | 24.6 | 24.3 | 24.5 |
| China | 81.6 | 96.6 | 178.2 | 10.1 | 13.3 | 11.6 |
| European Union-27 | 92.9 | 78.8 | 171.8 | 11.5 | 10.8 | 11.2 |
| Japan | 78.1 | 82.8 | 160.8 | 9.6 | 11.4 | 10.5 |
| United States | 82.1 | 67.4 | 149.6 | 10.1 | 9.3 | 9.7 |
| Republic of Korea | 34.3 | 40.4 | 74.7 | 4.2 | 5.6 | 4.9 |
| Hong Kong | 56.7 | 11.2 | 67.9 | 7.0 | 1.5 | 4.4 |
| Australia | 29.0 | 14.8 | 43.8 | 3.6 | 2.0 | 2.9 |
| India | 26.5 | 12.6 | 39.1 | 3.3 | 1.7 | 2.5 |
| United Arab Emirates | 10.6 | 13.8 | 24.4 | 1.3 | 1.9 | 1.6 |
| Total top ten trade partner countries | 691.5 | 595.0 | 1286.6 | 85.3 | 81.9 | 83.7 |
| Others[2] | 118.9 | 131.3 | 250.2 | 14.7 | 18.1 | 16.3 |
| Total | 810.5 | 726.3 | 1536.8 | 100.0 | 100.0 | 100.0 |

*Notes:* 1. Identified/ranked based on share of total trade.

2. Includes trade of all other countries and those that could not be attributed to specific countries.

Some figures may not add up to totals, due to rounding off errors.

*Source:* ASEAN Trade Database.

US$178 billion in 2009 (Table 13.1). It should be noted that the top ten ASEAN trade commodity groups with the world include electric machinery, equipment and parts, sound equipment, television equipment (HS code 85); and mineral fuels, mineral oils and products of their distillation, bitumin substances, mineral wax (HS code 27) (full list in Table 13.2). Secondly, in investment area, the top sources of the investment in ASEAN are the European Union, Japan, followed by intra-ASEAN, and the United States. China is in fifth position (Table 13.3).

Meanwhile, the share of intra-ASEAN trade in each member's total trade has also increased during the past decade. From 1998 to 2008, the share of intra-ASEAN import in total ASEAN import increased from 21 per cent to 29 per cent, while that of export rose from 17 per cent to 26 per cent. In some industries (or sub-industries) there is a high degree of intra-industry trade (IIT), implying the region's specialization in those sectors. For instance, Austria (2004) asserts that intra-ASEAN trade in ICT and electronics products is highly concentrated in a few products. This is also evident from the fact that ASEAN countries are exporting and importing the same products to and from each other, which implies that each country is specializing in a particular segment of the production chain. Austria further argues that the pattern of intra-ASEAN trade was the result of the liberal policy environment in the relevant sectors. Meanwhile, Intal, Narjoko, and Simorangkir (2010) find that the intra-ASEAN trade is higher than those of the Latin American Integration Association (LAIA), Asia-Pacific Trade Agreement (APTA), and the Black Sea Economic Cooperation (BSEC). One possible explanation is, as noted, the increasing importance of intra-industry trade in ASEAN. Another possible explanation is the relatively freer trade, i.e., lower rate of preferential tariffs among the ASEAN countries than those of the other regional trade arrangements.

Among the ASEAN members, the Lao PDR has the highest percentage of intra-ASEAN trade with 83.7 per cent in 2009, followed by Myanmar with 51.6 per cent; while, the lowest was Vietnam with 17.6 per cent (Table 13.4). The size of the ASEAN share in a country's trade implies the relative importance of the region to that particular country's trade. The higher the share the more important is ASEAN to that country. For Indonesia, intra-ASEAN trade rose from less than 10 per cent in 1990 to around 20 per cent in 2009 (World Integrated Trade Solution n.d.).

As for bilateral trade among the ASEAN members, trade between the Lao PDR and Thailand was the highest at 50.78 per cent; in this case Thailand functions as a platform for the Lao PDR's products to

## TABLE 13.2
### Top Ten ASEAN Trade Commodity Groups, 2009
As of 15 July 2010 (value in US$ billion; share in per cent)

| Rank in 2007 | Rank in 2009 | 2-digit HS code | Commodity group[1] Description | Value | | | Percentage of total ASEAN trade | | |
|---|---|---|---|---|---|---|---|---|---|
| | | | | Exports | Imports | Total trade | Exports | Imports | Total trade |
| 1 | 1 | 85 | Electric machinery, equipment and parts; sound equipment; television equipment | 175.8 | 154.2 | 330.0 | 21.7 | 21.2 | 21.5 |
| 3 | 2 | 27 | Mineral fuels, mineral oils and products of their distillation; bitumin substances; mineral wax | 112.8 | 128.1 | 240.9 | 13.9 | 17.6 | 15.7 |
| 2 | 3 | 84 | Nuclear reactors, boilers, machinery and mechanical appliances; parts thereof | 109.2 | 105.8 | 215.0 | 13.5 | 14.6 | 14.0 |
| 8 | 4 | 87 | Vehicles, (not railway, tramway, rolling stock); parts and accessories | 20.4 | 21.6 | 42.0 | 2.5 | 3.0 | 2.7 |
| 4 | 5 | 39 | Plastics and articles thereof | 21.6 | 19.8 | 41.4 | 2.7 | 2.7 | 2.7 |
| n.a. | 6 | 71 | Natural or cultured pearls, precious or semi-precious stones, precious metals and metals clad therewith and articles thereof; imitation jewellery; coin | 20.2 | 15.2 | 35.4 | 2.5 | 2.1 | 2.3 |
| 6 | 7 | 29 | Organic chemicals | 19.2 | 15.2 | 34.4 | 2.4 | 2.1 | 2.2 |

**TABLE 13.2** (Cont'd)

| Rank in 2007 | Rank in 2009 | 2-digit HS code | Description | Value Exports | Value Imports | Value Total trade | % Exports | % Imports | % Total trade |
|---|---|---|---|---|---|---|---|---|---|
| | | | | | | | **Percentage of total ASEAN trade** | | |
| 9 | 8 | 90 | Optical, photographic, cinematographic, measuring, checking, precision, medical or surgical instruments/apparatus; parts and accessories | 15.5 | 16.4 | 32.0 | 1.9 | 2.3 | 2.1 |
| 7 | 9 | 15 | Animal or vegetable fats and oils and their cleavage products; prepared edible fats; animal or vegetable waxes | 25.6 | 2.9 | 28.5 | 3.2 | 0.4 | 1.9 |
| 5 | 10 | 40 | Rubber and articles thereof | 20.8 | 6.6 | 27.4 | 2.6 | 0.9 | 1.8 |
| **Top Ten Commodities** | | | | **541.2** | **485.8** | **1,027.0** | **66.8** | **66.9** | **66.8** |
| **Others[2]** | | | | **269.3** | **240.5** | **509.8** | **33.2** | **33.1** | **33.2** |
| **Total** | | | | **810.5** | **726.4** | **1,536.8** | **100.0** | **100.0** | **100.0** |

*Note:* Data in italics are the latest updated/revised figures from previous posting.

1. identified based on the share of the 2-digit classification (section) of the Harmonized System (HS) to total trade.

2. includes products with unspecified codes and/or products that could not be explicitly classified according to the current HS. Some figures may not add up to totals due to rounding off errors.

*Source:* ASEAN Trade Database (compiled from data submission and/or websites of ASEAN member countries' national statistical offices and other relevant agencies.

**TABLE 13.3**

**FDI Net Inflows to ASEAN from Selected Partner Countries/Regions**

As of 15 July 2010 (value in US$ billion; share in per cent)

| Partner country/region | Share to total net inflow | | | | Value | |
|---|---|---|---|---|---|---|
| | 2007 | 2008 | 2009 | 2007–2009 | 2009 | 2007–2009 |
| ASEAN | 13.0 | 21.1 | 11.2 | 15.0 | 4.4 | 24.6 |
| United States | 10.8 | 10.4 | 8.5 | 10.1 | 3.4 | 16.6 |
| Japan | 11.9 | 9.4 | 13.4 | 11.5 | 5.3 | 18.8 |
| European Union (EU)-25[1] | 23.9 | 19.2 | 18.4 | 21.1 | 7.3 | 34.6 |
| China | 2.3 | 4.3 | 3.8 | 3.2 | 1.5 | 5.3 |
| Republic of Korea | 3.7 | 3.2 | 3.6 | 3.5 | 1.4 | 5.7 |
| Australia | 2.0 | 1.9 | 1.8 | 1.9 | 0.7 | 3.1 |
| India | 2.0 | 1.4 | 2.5 | 1.9 | 1.0 | 3.1 |
| Canada | 0.5 | 1.6 | 0.8 | 0.9 | 0.3 | 1.5 |
| Russia | 0.0 | 0.2 | 0.4 | 0.2 | 0.2 | 0.3 |
| New Zealand | 0.1 | (0.3) | 0.6 | 0.1 | 0.2 | 0.2 |
| Pakistan | 0.0 | 0.0 | 0.0 | 0.0 | 0.0 | 0.0 |
| Total selected partner countries/regions | 70.2 | 72.3 | 64.9 | 69.6 | 25.7 | 113.8 |
| Others[2] | 29.8 | 27.7 | 35.1 | 30.4 | 13.9 | 49.7 |
| **Total FDI inflow to ASEAN** | **100.0** | **100.0** | **100.0** | **100.0** | **39.6** | **163.5** |

*Notes:* 0.0 value is below 0.1 per cent.

1. Includes Austria, Belgium, Cyprus, Czech Republic, Denmark, Estonia, Finland, France, Germany, Greece, Hungary, Ireland, Italy, Latvia, Lithuania, Luxembourg, Malta, the Netherlands, Poland, Portugal, Slovakia, Slovenia, Spain, Sweden, and the United Kingdom.

2. Includes inflow from all other countries and unspecified countries as well as total reinvested earnings and inter-company loans in the Philippines.

*Sources:* ASEAN Foreign Direct Investment Statistics Database (compiled/computed from data submission, publications and/or websites of ASEAN Member States' central banks, national statistics offices, and relevant government agencies through the ASEAN Working Group

**TABLE 13.4**
**Intra- and Extra-ASEAN Trade, 2009**
As of 15 July 2010 (value in US$ billion; share in per cent)

| Country | Intra-ASEAN exports (% of total exports) | Extra-ASEAN exports (% of total exports) | Total exports | Intra-ASEAN imports (% of total imports) | Extra-ASEAN imports (% of total imports) | Total imports | Intra-ASEAN trade (% of total trade) | Extra-ASEAN trade (% of total trade) | Total trade |
|---|---|---|---|---|---|---|---|---|---|
| Brunei Darussalam | 17.1 | 82.9 | 7.2 | 51.8 | 48.2 | 2.4 | 25.8 | 74.2 | 9.6 |
| Cambodia | 12.9 | 87.1 | 5.0 | 37.3 | 62.7 | 3.9 | 23.6 | 76.4 | 8.9 |
| Indonesia | 21.1 | 78.9 | 116.5 | 28.7 | 71.3 | 96.8 | 24.5 | 75.5 | 213.3 |
| Lao PDR | 80.6 | 19.4 | 1.2 | 85.8 | 14.2 | 1.7 | 83.7 | 16.3 | 3.0 |
| Malaysia | 25.7 | 74.3 | 156.9 | 25.7 | 74.3 | 123.3 | 25.7 | 74.3 | 280.2 |
| Myanmar | 50.4 | 49.6 | 6.3 | 53.7 | 46.3 | 3.8 | 51.6 | 48.4 | 10.2 |
| Philippines | 15.2 | 84.8 | 38.3 | 25.4 | 74.6 | 45.5 | 20.7 | 79.3 | 83.9 |
| Singapore | 30.3 | 69.7 | 269.8 | 24.0 | 76.0 | 245.8 | 27.3 | 72.7 | 515.6 |
| Thailand | 21.3 | 78.7 | 152.5 | 20.0 | 80.0 | 133.8 | 20.7 | 79.3 | 286.3 |
| Vietnam | 15.1 | 84.9 | 56.7 | 19.6 | 80.4 | 69.2 | 17.6 | 82.4 | 125.9 |
| **ASEAN** | **24.6** | **75.4** | **810.5** | **24.3** | **75.7** | **726.4** | **24.5** | **75.5** | **1,536.8** |

*Sources*: ASEAN Merchandise Trade Statistics Database (compiled/computed from data submission, publications and/or websites of ASEAN member states' national statistics offices, and ASEAN Free Trade Area (AFTA) units, customs departments/agencies, or central banks).

enter the global market. Indonesia and Malaysia have a relatively high dependency on Singapore (Table 13.5). As Intal, Narjoko and Simorangkir (2010) note, ASEAN intraregional trade has two hubs, that is, Singapore for Malaysia and Indonesia, and Thailand for Cambodia, the Lao PDR, and Myanmar.

In addition, the trade similarity index provides useful information on distinctive export patterns from one country to another. Table 13.6 presents the trade similarity index for selected countries for such industries as agriculture resource intensive (ARI), mineral resource intensive (MRI), unskilled-labour intensive (ULI), technology intensive (TI), and human capital intensive (HCI). Major competitor countries for Indonesia are Malaysia (for ARI), China (HCI), and Singapore (for TI). In general Indonesia's trade similarity index exhibits an increasing trend from 2000 to 2005 in all sectors, indicating higher competition for Indonesia's products (Table 13.6).

Table 13.7 presents the intra-industry index for Indonesia; intra-industry exchange produces extra gains from international trade over and above those associated with the comparative advantage of larger markets. By engaging the IIT, a country can simultaneously reduce the number of similar products it produces while increasing the variety of goods available to domestic consumers. In 2005 the TI sector in Indonesia was the most integrated sector with the world, mainly because Indonesia was part of East Asia's industrial production network. The data also suggest that Indonesia and Malaysia have a high degree of intra-industry trade in such sectors as MRI and ULI.

For Indonesia, maintaining its position in the production network can improve its competitiveness in general. According to the World Bank's *Doing Business 2010* report, to start a new investment in Indonesia, investors need forty-seven days, coupled with nine procedures; this shows it was simpler and faster than in 2008 when it needed 105 days with twelve procedures. However, it is still slow compared with other ASEAN countries such as Malaysia, where it takes only seventeen days with nine procedures; Thailand, which requires only thirty-two days with seven procedures; and the Philippines, which needs thirty-eight days with fifteen procedures.

With regard to trade across borders, Indonesia is relatively more competitive than the Philippines, but less so than Thailand, Malaysia, and Singapore. To export a product, it needs twenty days coupled with five documents and costs around US$704 per container. To import, it

TABLE 13.5
Average Trade Share of Bilateral Intra-ASEAN Trade: 2000–08 (per cent)

| | Reporting Country | | | | | | | | | |
| | Brunei Darussalam | Cambodia | Indonesia | Lao PDR | Malaysia | Myanmar | Philippines | Singapore | Thailand | Vietnam |
|---|---|---|---|---|---|---|---|---|---|---|
| Brunei D. | | 0.002 | 0.49 | 0.00 | 0.155 | 0.004 | 0.02 | 0.20 | 0.21 | 0.002 |
| Cambodia | 0.002 | | 0.07 | 0.06 | 0.05 | 0.00 | 0.009 | 0.13 | 0.43 | 0.88 |
| Indonesia | 8.51 | 1.73 | | 0.16 | 2.93 | 1.79 | 1.53 | 5.24 | 2.67 | 1.98 |
| Lao PDR | 0.00 | 0.02 | 0.002 | | 0.01 | 0.00 | 0.00 | 0.01 | 0.46 | 0.33 |
| Malaysia | 5.70 | 1.97 | 4.21 | 0.60 | | 4.61 | 4.39 | 14.79 | 5.37 | 3.04 |
| Myanmar | 0.00 | 0.003 | 0.09 | 0.00 | 0.14 | | 0.011 | 0.20 | 1.02 | 0.06 |
| Philippines | 0.20 | 0.11 | 1.11 | 0.02 | 1.96 | 0.14 | | 2.17 | 1.75 | 1.35 |
| Singapore | 10.77 | 5.77 | 11.03 | 2.09 | 14.17 | 10.83 | 7.45 | | 5.89 | 9.57 |
| Thailand | 5.87 | 10.37 | 3.31 | 50.78 | 4.71 | 27.06 | 3.36 | 4.04 | | 4.04 |
| Vietnam | 0.02 | 6.55 | 0.88 | 10.40 | 0.84 | 0.55 | 0.98 | 1.33 | 1.26 | |

*Source:* Intal, Narjoko, and Simorangkir (2010).

## TABLE 13.6
### Indonesia's Trade Similarity Index

| | Agriculture Resource intensive | | Mineral Resource intensive | | Unskilled Labour intensive | | Technology intensive | | Human Capital intensive | |
|---|---|---|---|---|---|---|---|---|---|---|
| | 2000 | 2005 | 2000 | 2005 | 2000 | 2005 | 2000 | 2005 | 2000 | 2005 |
| World | 58.07 | 69.70 | 53.72 | 55.34 | 50.27 | 52.62 | 58.46 | 63.20 | 51.08 | 57.87 |
| ASEAN | 91.01 | 94.34 | 65.87 | 44.70 | 40.61 | 36.77 | 70.96 | 72.26 | 70.86 | 63.91 |
| Cambodia | 69.31 | — | 57.23 | — | 43.13 | — | 13.97 | — | 2.07 | — |
| China | 41.87 | 65.83 | 72.36 | 73.76 | 76.56 | 75.05 | 67.66 | 59.85 | 61.94 | 56.11 |
| European Union | 52.68 | 64.27 | 53.20 | 57.28 | 49.80 | 48.43 | 49.56 | 54.95 | 47.95 | 55.88 |
| India | 8.09 | 14.74 | 14.64 | 12.70 | 45.80 | 43.43 | 45.02 | 48.31 | 32.61 | 41.79 |
| Japan | 39.94 | 44.76 | 46.14 | 47.84 | 23.21 | 29.39 | 52.05 | 53.13 | 41.41 | 47.70 |
| Korea, Rep. of | 10.41 | 13.31 | 12.58 | 73.62 | 23.35 | 32.45 | 22.80 | 67.28 | 20.46 | 45.97 |
| Malaysia | 87.51 | 79.36 | 11.16 | 59.12 | 12.68 | 19.02 | 16.95 | 52.10 | 11.09 | 21.28 |
| Philippines | 33.56 | 51.14 | 2.21 | 13.99 | 9.92 | 14.36 | 5.99 | 16.06 | 1.53 | 3.14 |
| Singapore | 55.31 | 52.14 | 7.92 | 17.12 | 14.16 | 21.42 | 27.37 | 68.85 | 10.69 | 27.44 |
| Thailand | 40.46 | 60.13 | 56.24 | 75.53 | 58.41 | 23.97 | 58.70 | 38.37 | 58.12 | 20.03 |
| United States | 57.31 | 30.19 | 46.44 | 42.68 | 33.89 | 35.50 | 49.45 | 50.45 | 50.53 | 54.61 |
| Vietnam | 33.09 | — | 32.91 | 61.66 | 39.53 | 48.67 | — | — | — | — |

*Source:* Ministry of Finance, 2007.

TABLE 13.7
IIT Index between Indonesia and Major Countries, 2000 and 2005

| | Agriculture Resource Intensive | | Mineral Resource Intensive | | Unskilled Labour Intensive | | Technology Intensive | | Human Capital Intensive | |
|---|---|---|---|---|---|---|---|---|---|---|
| | 2000 | 2005 | 2000 | 2005 | 2000 | 2005 | 2000 | 2005 | 2000 | 2005 |
| World | 0.825 | 0.801 | 0.680 | 0.952 | 0.912 | 0.992 | 0.990 | 0.971 | 0.944 | 0.907 |
| United States | 0.220 | 0.765 | 0.517 | 0.840 | 0.917 | 0.904 | 0.964 | 0.938 | 0.993 | 0.844 |
| Japan | 0.563 | 0.980 | 0.638 | 0.843 | 0.974 | 0.891 | 0.997 | 0.917 | 0.878 | 0.981 |
| European Union | 0.914 | 0.998 | 0.597 | 0.849 | 0.767 | 0.989 | 0.958 | 0.978 | 0.998 | 0.971 |
| China | 0.973 | 0.595 | 0.677 | 0.846 | 0.911 | 0.696 | 0.975 | 0.997 | 0.782 | 0.909 |
| Korea, Rep. of | 0.063 | 0.131 | 0.537 | 0.767 | 0.932 | 0.952 | 0.961 | 0.994 | 0.912 | 0.948 |
| ASEAN | 0.805 | 0.981 | 0.890 | 0.979 | 0.945 | 0.966 | 0.991 | 0.944 | 0.995 | 0.985 |
| Cambodia | 0.986 | N/A | — | N/A | 0.971 | N/A | 0.743 | N/A | 0.162 | N/A |
| Malaysia | 0.925 | 0.577 | 0.747 | 0.904 | 0.997 | 0.999 | 0.994 | 0.998 | 0.989 | 0.998 |
| Philippines | 0.696 | 0.035 | 0.138 | 0.077 | 0.964 | 0.669 | 0.987 | 0.974 | 0.913 | 0.941 |
| Thailand | 0.879 | 0.783 | 0.937 | 0.862 | 0.961 | 0.997 | 0.898 | 0.975 | 0.955 | 0.938 |
| Vietnam | 0.509 | N/A | — | N/A | 0.961 | N/A | 0.929 | N/A | 0.745 | N/A |
| Singapore | 0.779 | 0.494 | 0.367 | 0.920 | 0.809 | 0.996 | 0.968 | 0.983 | 0.932 | 0.912 |

Source: Ministry of Finance, 2007.

takes twenty-seven days with six documents and costs around US$660 per container.

## Status/Progress in the ASEAN Economic Community

To achieve the ASEAN Economic Community, ASEAN countries need to have strong political will. According to Scorecard I for the period 1 January 2008–30 September 2009, on average 72.38 per cent of the targeted measures were implemented by every ASEAN country. The unimplemented ones were mainly measures such as ratification of important economic agreements concerning trade in goods, investment, transport, and the cosmetics directive. During the period under consideration, of the 124 economic agreements under the AEC, only 73 per cent have been ratified by all ASEAN member states. Indonesia was in the seventh position and has implemented 80.37 per cent of the total measures (107 measures). Singapore occupied the highest position with 93.52 per cent and Brunei Darussalam the lowest with 74.57 per cent. The progress occurred in several areas such as the ratification of the ASEAN Trade in Goods Agreement (ATIGA); the improvement in trade facilitation through the ASEAN Single Windows (ASW) programme; and improvement in standard and conformity assessment, for example, the Mutual Recognition Arrangements (MRAs) in the electrical and electronics sector and the cosmetic sector. In addition, the AFAS seventh package and the ASEAN Comprehensive Investment Agreement (ACIA) have been completed. In the transportation sector, three frameworks on the facilitation of goods in transit, multimodal transit, and facilitation of interstate transport were concluded in 2010.

Even though some notable progress has been achieved, the degree of utilization of the AEC and, previously, AFTA privileges, is still quite low. As Hayakawa et al. (2009) note, the utilization of AFTA is low by international standards because of three reasons. The first is the active use of investment incentive schemes in ASEAN. Enjoying such schemes, firms do not need to use FTA schemes in order to trade at zero tariff rates. Second, the major trade in ASEAN is in the electrical machinery industry, for which MFN tariff rates are already low. The third reason is the existence of fixed costs such as administrative costs due to the cumbersome procedures for obtaining tariff exemption.

Hayakawa et al. (2009) also enumerated various kinds of firms/ affiliates in ASEAN that are more likely to use FTAs in exporting. They found that the larger the firm, the more likely it is to take advantage of an FTA scheme in its export activities. Second, firms that export actively to countries with higher MFN tariffs are more likely to use FTAs. Third, there are clear differences in FTA utilization depending on a firm's location and sector.

Hiratsuka et al. (2008) also find that the larger the firm's size, the more likely it would utilize the FTA scheme. Moreover, FTA privileges are selectively utilized depending on the industry: textile and automobile utilize them well, while electrical machinery does not. This in turn depends on the margin between the MFN and FTA preferential tariff. The larger the margin, the more likely that exporters will make use of the preferential scheme. Moreover, firms in the Philippines and Vietnam are less likely to utilize the FTA scheme because the procedure to obtain the certificate of origin in those countries may be more cumbersome than in other countries.

## The Survey

### The Questionnaire

The questionnaire was designed to serve the objective of the study and consists of six parts: (1) the company's general information; (2) export status (for manufacturing firms); (3) knowledge about trade-related agreements in ASEAN, including: the ASEAN Free Trade Agreement (AFTA), the ASEAN Framework Agreement on Services (AFAS), the ASEAN Investment Agreement (AIA), MRA on a few selected professionals, the ASEAN Economic Community (AEC), the ASEAN-China Free Trade Agreement, and ASEAN-Japan FTA; (4) utilization of AFTA preferential treatments, with special emphasis on the companies' response to AFTA and the utilization of AFTA/FTA privilege; (5) obstacles of AFTA and the impact of the National Single Window (NSW); and (6) policy recommendations for the ASEAN Economic Community (AEC) 2015.

### Survey Samples

We contacted ten companies and associations from various sectors in Jakarta in November 2010; the response rate was quite good, eight of them were willing to be interviewed. They comprise four business associations, three firms in logistic services and poultry, and one official of the Indonesian Chamber of Commerce and Industry/Kadin.[1] Their opinions are believed to represent their respective firms or associations.

Since the survey method was the face-to-face interview, most of the respondents answered all questions, whether or not they had knowledge of the AEC or other agreements. Each interview took around 40–50 minutes.

### Survey Findings

### General Awareness of AEC

In general, knowledge and perceptions about the benefit of an FTA are closely associated with the size of the firm in question. Larger firms tend to have better knowledge about the existing FTAs and, in general, are more optimistic than smaller ones. This is true also with regard to the AEC. Larger firms perceive the implementation of AEC as an opportunity to expand their markets. In contrast, small and medium enterprises tend to view the implementation of the AEC as a threat, not only because of their limited knowledge of the AEC, but also because of their own weaknesses, that is, they tend to be less efficient and less competitive than the larger companies. This is in line with the findings of a JETRO (Japan External Trade Organization) study (2010) which states that the lack of awareness of FTAs is the most common reason for non utilization of FTAs among small and medium enterprises (SMEs). The JETRO study also notes that, in general, the firms in the IT sector and the precision industries do not take advantage of FTAs' preferential tariffs because import duties have been waived through other schemes rather than FTAs. Similarly, many firms in the electrical equipment industry also asserted that they had no plans to utilize FTAs since, in general, duties at their export destinations are non-existent. Meanwhile, a relatively large number of firms in the cars/car parts/other transportation machinery industry argued that they had difficulties in satisfying the rules of origin requirements.

Most of interviewees in this survey are aware of the existing FTAs, particularly the ASEAN Free Trade Agreement/AFTA (1993), the China-ASEAN Free Trade Agreement/CAFTA (2010), and the ASEAN Economic Community/AEC 2015 (Figure 13.3). This might be because the interviewees are large companies, business associations, and a chamber of commerce and are all located in Jakarta. As such they are well informed about developments at the national, regional, as well as

**FIGURE 13.3**
**Private Sector Awareness of Several FTAs/Agreements**

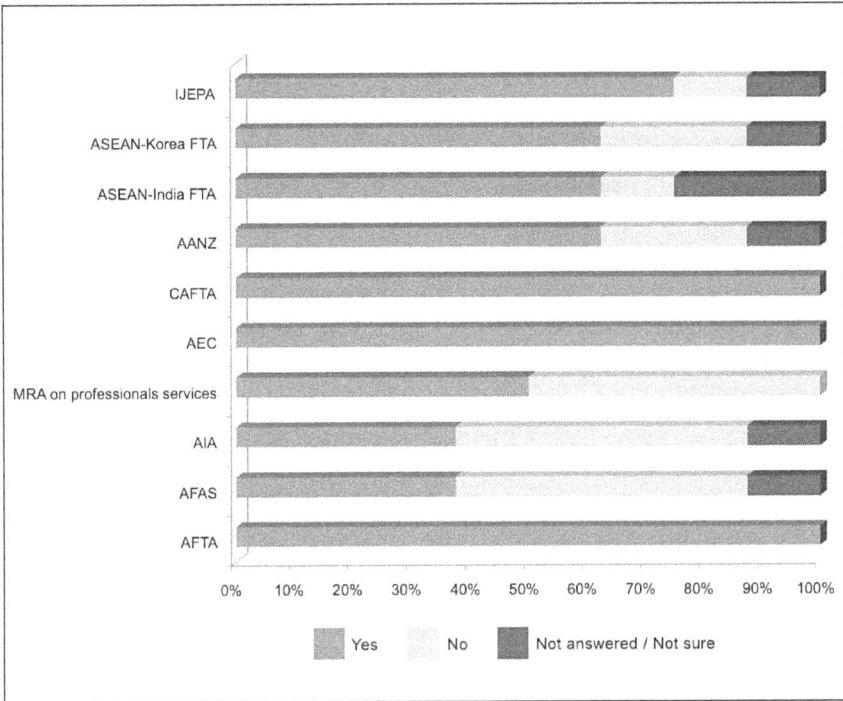

global levels. Most of the respondents get their information from industry associations and media publications. Nevertheless, their knowledge about the existing FTAs is quite different. They tend to focus only on issues that are directly related to their line of business. For instance, services companies tend to know more about AFAS and services-related MRAs, and less about everything else, while manufacturing companies tend to have a lot of information about CEPT. It is likely that we would have got a different result had the survey and interviews been conducted outside Jakarta or comprised small and medium enterprises rather than larger ones.

As a Kadin's official asserted, major players already have a good and comprehensive understanding about the AEC. The major players are large companies whose activities are related to export-import, foreign companies, and foreign affiliates or local companies that are involved in international production networks (mostly automotive and electronics companies). Companies that are located in Jakarta and its surroundings also tend to have a good knowledge about the AEC. However, the number of major players is very small and accounts for less than one per cent of the total number of business establishments in Indonesia. In addition, in general, information concerning the AEC fails to reach most members of the business community largely due to the fact that both government and the ASEAN Secretariat do not have a systematic mechanism to disseminate information. Respondent 7 concured, adding that there is a lack of coordination among the government's relevant agencies, particularly in providing information concerning all ASEAN-related regulations and agreements. In addition, the implementation of those regulations should be transparent and well coordinated among the relevant agencies.

Of the ten FTAs/EPAs mentioned in the questionnaire, the most familiar ones are CAFTA, AFTA, and the AEC, perhaps because they receive more media coverage than the other ones. CAFTA was only recently implemented (at the beginning of 2010). Most of the respondents consider Indonesia's competitiveness vis-à-vis China weak, pointing to the fact that many Chinese products are far cheaper than Indonesian products. The common perception is that Chinese producers are more efficient than Indonesian producers. They argue that there is an urgent need to improve Indonesia's competitiveness as that would not only enable Indonesia's companies to compete abroad, but would also enable them to compete in the domestic market. Indonesia's domestic market is big and, therefore, highly attractive to foreign companies. To improve the country's competitiveness the government needs to, among other things, improve the state of the country's infrastructure.

With regard to private sector engagement, major business associations in Indonesia have a special section that is devoted to tracking the developments of FTAs signed by the government. But most of them never took an active role in trade negotiations. They only gave inputs to ongoing trade negotiations in meetings held by the Ministry of Trade and/or the Ministry of Industry. The business sector is often reluctant to get involved in trade negotiations. This is for reasons such as there only being a few credible business associations and they have limited ability to assess the implications of FTAs, especially for the business sector.

## The Impact of the AEC

Opinions about the impact of the AEC vary, depending on the sector. Four respondents (out of seven) argued that the AEC does not have any impact on their businesses (Table 13.8). One such respondent (Respondent 3) is a provider of maritime services. Indonesia has ratified the International Maritime Organization's regulations. As a result, all regulations in this sector are already in line with international regulations. So are all FTA agreements, including the ones pertaining to maritime services. Hence the FTAs do not affect its business. The respondent also confirmed that cabotage restrictions still exist, that is, shipping services between domestic ports are reserved for domestic shipping companies.

Respondent 6, whose activity is in poultry, also agreed that those agreements do not have any impact on that business, but for a different reason. International trade in poultry is relatively low. For importers, the major restrictions are non-tariff barriers (NTBs) such as, the halal certificate and the requirement that the poultry be free from viral infections. On the other hand, the business faces difficulty in exporting its products since other countries also place high trade barriers against imported poultry and, therefore, this forces the firm to concentrate on the domestic market. Meanwhile, Respondent 7, an official of a pharmaceutical industry association, asserted that the AEC had no impact because all tariff lines in the pharmaceutical sector are already zero. Nevertheless, restrictions on free trade still exist. For instance, one of the import requirements is that an importer of pharmaceutical products should be a holder of manufacturing authority in Indonesia.

Respondent 2 also had the same opinion. The industry in this case pertains to unique and handmade products. Indonesia has a competitive advantage in these products and the country's abundance of natural resources is also favourable for this sector. Furthermore, Respondent 2 also argued that the Indonesia-Japan bilateral agreement is more important than the other agreements since Indonesia's major trading partner for this sector is Japan.

Meanwhile, Respondent 1 confirmed that the widespread relocation of production base for sport shoes to ASEAN, including Indonesia, was not because of AFTA but because the region has an abundant supply of labour and raw materials which promises firms with high value addition and competitive advantages.

Respondent 8 argued that even without FTAs, the openness of Indonesia's trade and investment in the automotive sector has been

**TABLE 13.8**

**The Impact of Selected Economic Partnership Agreements on Company/Association Business**

| No | Agreement/ Firm (Association) | Company/Association | | | | | | | |
|---|---|---|---|---|---|---|---|---|---|
| | | 1 | 2 | 3 | 4 | 5 | 6 | 7 | 8 |
| 1 | AFTA | no impact | no impact | no impact | Low (positive) | High (positive) | High (positive) | | Positive impact for big companies; negative for small companies |
| 2 | AFAS | no impact | | | | | | no impact | |
| 3 | AIA | no impact | | | | | High and positive | | |
| 4 | MRA on few selected professionals | no impact | | | | | | | Not sure |
| 5 | AEC 2015 | no impact | no impact | no impact | | High (positive) | High and positive | no impact | Not sure |
| 6 | CAFTA | no impact | High (positive) | | High (positive) | High (negative) | High and positive | no impact | Negative for sensitive list (auto-parts) |

| | | | | | |
|---|---|---|---|---|---|
| 7 | AANZ | no impact | no impact | Low (positive) | Not sure (still at consultation stage) | Positive impact for big companies; negative for small companies |
| 8 | ASEAN-India FTA | no impact | High and positive | High (positive) | Not sure | |
| 9 | ASEAN-Korea FTA | no impact | no impact | Low (positive) | Not sure | |
| 10 | IJEPA | no impact | High (positive) | Low (positive) | Not sure (still at consultation stage) | High and positive |

secured through the country's participation in the international production networks, particularly with Japanese automotive manufacturers. Nevertheless Pasha and Setiati (2008) argue that though it is widely perceived that the development of international production networks predates the proliferation of FTAs, it is conceivable that the existence of FTAs would enhance the existing international production networks. Moreover, the AEC can boost local industry given that the government in question can provide clear policies and a favourable environment for it to grow.

Some respondents argued that FTAs provide both opportunities and threats at the same time. Respondent 4 pointed out that CAFTA will benefit Indonesia and particularly his company. The Chinese market is larger than the Indonesian market and at least 400 million people in China have high purchasing power. But Indonesia should know also its strengths, weaknesses, and the needs of the Chinese well. Collaborative study on this issue, involving government institutions, universities, and the business sector, is highly desirable. The aim is to improve the competitiveness of the country's companies. In terms of human resource development, the alignment between the education sector and business sector is absolutely necessary; education curricula should suit the business sectors' needs so that the abundant supply of labour in Indonesia could be optimally utilized.

Thus, the respondents' overall opinion is contrary to the opinion of many, and is that FTAs, especially CAFTA, will generate a huge problem for Indonesian producers. They argued that Indonesia's producers cannot compete with Chinese producers and may lead to higher unemployment and industry decline, which in turn may jeopardize Indonesia's national interests.

Respondent 8 pointed out that there are two different impacts of the AEC and other initiatives on the parts and components industry in Indonesia. On the one hand, this allows MNCs and big companies to utilize the existing arrangements optimally by taking advantage of their economies of scale. On the other hand, domestic and small companies will likely suffer losses due to their internal weaknesses, such as the lack of access to working capital, inadequate human resources, and the lack of access to raw material etc.

Under AFTA, import tariffs on many products, including from the automotives sector, were cut to between 0 and 5 per cent in 2003. The import duty of 5 per cent was removed in 2010 for ASEAN Five countries, and by 2015 for the remaining countries. In fact, the Government of Indonesia had actually abolished the import duty on spare parts and components of cars for the export market (through Ministry of Finance Decree No. 79/PMK.010/2006). Due to domestic producers' objections, the government issued another regulation, No. 34/PMK.011/2007, to reduce import duty on basic materials of automotive components to zero, effective for only twelve months. The government also planned to extend the regulation to allow zero import duty on raw and supporting materials for automotive components in anticipation of the recent global downturn. The Government of Indonesia argued that the extension was required due to weakening competitiveness of the automotive sectors. Besides that, automotive products should meet a minimum of 40 per cent local content in any of the ASEAN member countries.

## Utilization of FTAs

Regarding AFTA/FTA utilization, some respondents claimed to have used AFTA/FTA privileges. The rest, however, said that they had not been able to exploit those privileges optimally. The major obstacles are the lack of knowledge or inadequate information and high NTBs noted earlier. According to Pushpanathan (2010c), there are several reasons for the low level of utilization of FTA privileges: lack of knowledge as to how to utilize those privileges; cumbersome process and procedures imposed by implementing agencies; and lack of capacity of some ASEAN countries to implement the provisions in the FTAs fully.

Nevertheless, the Deputy Trade Minister of Indonesia, Mahendra Siregar, was quoted by a local newspaper as saying that the demand for certificates of origin by exporters has been increasing. Between 1 January and 30 April 2010, the government issued 7,849 certificates under the ACFTA for US$83 billion worth of non-oil and gas exports, indicating a 45.5 per cent increase compared with the same period in 2009. During the same period, the number of certificates for exports to Japan reached 17,522, with a total value of US$936.4 million.

Regarding foreign investment, all respondents agreed with the importance of eliminating legal uncertainties, improving policy coordination among the various government agencies, improving infrastructure, and offering more tax incentives, as priority actions in attracting more investment. As for rules of origin (ROO), most respondents agreed that ROO is important in a FTA since it determines the products that are eligible for preferential treatment. A simplification of ROO would allow exporters to utilize the benefits of FTAs optimally.

The survey also asked respondents about the National Single Window (NSW) since one of the FTA principles is the free flow of goods and services and trade facilitation. Furthermore, at the heart of trade facilitation initiatives in ASEAN is the implementation of the NSWs and the ASEAN Single Window (ASW), together with related initiatives on customs modernization. Most of the respondents agreed that NSW is a good concept; it makes all procedures simpler and faster. Yet in the implementation, there are some obstacles such as coordination problems between government agencies, public dissemination, and support from stakeholders.

## Strategies towards the AEC

In general, producers could optimally utilize the AEC and the other agreements by focusing on the targeted market. Product selections depend on the countries' potential demand and government policies in each sector. Take Indonesia and Thailand as an example. For the automotive sector, Indonesian buyers prefer multipurpose vehicles or light commercial vehicles, while Thai producers make mainly pickup trucks and sedans. As Indonesia's potential market is large, Thai manufacturers need to adjust their output to suit Indonesia's market.

In addition, every respondent had his/her own strategy towards the ASEAN Economic Community. For example, Respondent 1 focused on customer satisfaction: as long as customers are happy with the products, they will, as loyal customers, always buy the products, even if the products' prices are higher than those of others. Respondent 2, on the other hand, relies on trade shows and promotions. In addition, most of the producers in the handicraft sector cooperate with big companies as the "parent" companies that provide them with capital and technical assistance to develop their businesses.

To improve the pharmaceutical sector, Respondent 7 argued that the government should demand that pharmaceutical companies improve the quality of their manufacturing processes to enable Indonesia to participate in the Pharmaceutical Inspection Convention and Pharmaceutical Inspection Co-operation Scheme (jointly referred to as PIC/S). PIC/S refer to two international instruments between countries and pharmaceutical inspection authorities, which provide active and constructive cooperation in the field of good manufacturing practices.

Kadin's official added that Indonesia should utilize its role as ASEAN chair in 2011 properly because ASEAN's achievement in 2011 will influence Indonesia's role in ASEAN in the future. In addition, Respondent 8 stated that in the case of the automotive industry, Indonesia needs to increase its research and development capabilities (R&D), as well as design capabilities because such capabilities will benefit local companies most.

Finally, most of the respondents agreed that the Government of Indonesia and the ASEAN Secretariat should have a comprehensive and systematic system of information sharing. Business associations, Kadin, and electronic and printed media should be utilized to help disseminate information.

## Conclusion and Policy Recommendations

Based on the AEC Scorecard I, for the period of 1 January 2008 to 30 September 2009, Indonesia has attained more than 80 per cent of the total measures. From the government's perspective, business communities should provide greater support to the AEC goals through intensive engagement in the implementation process. Their involvement should cover the whole range, from the formulation and design of ASEAN economic policies up to the implementation of those measures. But from the point of view of the business sector, their involvement in the process has been hindered by the lack of information regarding the process itself. Moreover, according to the survey, the level of awareness pertaining to the AEC depends on the size and line of business of the company in question; bigger companies or major players are better informed about the AEC and have utilized the AEC and, hence, are more optimistic about it. But their numbers are quite small — less than one per cent of the total business community.

With regard to the potential impact of the AEC, opinions vary depending on the business sector. MNCs and the bigger companies with significant economies of scale tended to have a positive view, whereas smaller companies tended to be more pessimistic about them. To assist the latter group, the government has prepared some measures such as local contents policy, credit facilities, and national product standards.

Intensive coordination and participation of all key stakeholders, including public and private sectors, civil society, as well as a systematic information dissemination system are key factors in solving the lack of awareness problem. Moreover, improvement in the level of competitiveness of the local companies in general, infrastructure development, legal certainty, and simplification procedures are key factors for achieving an AEC by 2015.

From the discussion above, there are some implications for policy-makers:

- Eliminate business uncertainty, implement appropriate regulations, and enforce regional agreements. This includes addressing issues such as non-tariff barriers and other behind-the-border problems. One aspect of eliminating business uncertainty includes improving the country's labour regulations. The existing labour regulations are deemed to be biased towards labour and relatively inflexible. Indonesia, for instance, has high severance pay — among the highest in the world. This and other restrictions, such as the prohibition of hiring long-term contract workers, tend to increase the country's effective labour costs. The role of monitoring agencies at the national and ASEAN levels is also vital to the enforcement of the various AEC agreements. In terms of investment, tax holidays or other forms of tax incentives may be necessary to attract more investment inflows.

- Enhance competitiveness of product and human resources. The improvement may be achieved by increasing R&D activities at the company as well as national level. Furthermore, extra funds and programmes for capacity building from the Ministry of Labour, Ministry of Industry, MNCs, private sector, and other related institutions may be necessary to support these activities. It is also important to build cooperation between the government, the private sector, and universities to conduct research and prepare human resources based on the needs of the business sector.

- Foster infrastructure development. The lack of infrastructure has become a classic problem in Indonesia, and examples are the inadequacy of road networks and the worsening of traffic congestions. They have become a major problem for Indonesian producers to transport their products. The problems associated with the availability of road networks and other infrastructure will undoubtedly have an adverse effect on the country's competitiveness.

- Strengthen coordination and the information dissemination mechanism at the national and ASEAN levels. At the ASEAN level, strengthening the ASEAN Secretariat's capacity is vital for achieving the AEC by 2015 since the ASEAN Secretariat is the main engine for coordinating, preparing, monitoring, and reviewing all the activities during the implementation process. This can be achieved in two ways. First, by expanding the secretariat staff to match the institution's workload. Second, by expanding its authority to allow it to warn any member state that fails to meet its obligations under the AEC.
- At the national level, there is the need to increase the dissemination of AEC-related information to all stakeholders. This requires greater coordination among all the relevant government institutions to provide information concerning AEC-privileges, as well as FTAs and how to utilize them, so as to allow the private sector to make informed decisions. It is also important to involve the private sector in preparing all the AEC-related measures to ensure their interests are taken into consideration. At the regional level, it is also necessary to ensure that there is policy coherence and coordination among all the member states. This will allow companies from one member country to do business in other member countries without having to worry about the kind of regulations they will encounter in those countries.
- It should be noted that ASEAN itself has prepared several mechanisms to allow business community participation in policymaking. For example, there have been regular sector-specific dialogues with the business community, as well as technical meetings with relevant member states' institutions. Yet, according to the survey, the participation of the private sector is still limited; smaller business associations and companies have not involved themselves in those processes. It is therefore necessary to set up an outreach programme to ensure the participation of all stakeholders. And finally, more efforts are necessary from the region's civil societies, strategic think tanks, and other institutions to tap their expertise and knowledge; they can give useful inputs on the implementation and monitoring of the AEC process.

As Pushanathan (2010*c*) argued, there are three areas that ASEAN will have to address to achieve the AEC by 2015. First, it must implement the remaining 20 per cent of the measures in its first AEC Scorecard (2008–09); transportation services, customs, and standards are priority improvement areas. Second, ASEAN needs to improve the region's competitiveness so as to allow companies from the region to compete with economic players from other regions and emerging economies. This might be achieved through administrative reforms. And third, addressing the low utilization of its preferential treatments must be given priority so that the full benefit of the AEC can be realized. He also stated that the ASEAN private sector is the "driver" of economic integration and the ASEAN Secretariat is the "lubricant" of this integration. A strengthened secretariat can contribute more to regional economic surveillance, compliance monitoring, economic dispute settlement, and implementing major economic integration programmes funded by ASEAN's dialogue partners. ASEAN must explore the tremendous potential of developing the ASEAN Secretariat and the Committee of Permanent Representatives of ASEAN to become progressive institutions for regional community building.

## NOTES

1. The List of Interviewees is as follows:

   Indonesian Footwear Association, ASEAN Handicraft Promotion and Development Association, Samudera Indonesia (sea transportation), PT. Birotika Semesta (DHL)/(expedition services), Kadin (Chamber of Commerce and Industry) Indonesia, Sierad Product (poultry sector), IPMG (pharmacy sector), Indonesia Automotive Parts and Components Industries Association.

## REFERENCES

ASC. "Is the ASEAN Economic Community Possible by 2015? Perspectives from the Business Community" <www.iseas.edu.sg/aseanstudiescentre/Is%20the %20AEC%20possible%20by%202015.pdf>.

ASEAN Statistics. <http://www.aseansec.org/22122.htm>.

ASEAN Economic Community Blueprint. <ditjenkpi.depdag.go.id/website_kpi/ Umum/Blueprint.pdf>.

Austria, Myrna S. "The Pattern of Intra-ASEAN Trade in the Priority Goods Sectors". REPSF Project No. 03/006e, 2004 <www.ausaid.gov.au/publications/ pdf/priority_goods_sector.pdf>.

Intal Jr., Ponciano, Dionisius Narjoko and Mercy Simorangkir, "ERIA Study for Further Improvement of the AEC Scorecard: Interim Report". Presentation at ERIA workshop, 4–5 Sept 2010.

Fiscal Policy Office — Ministry of Trade, Republic of Indonesia. "Penyusunan Instrumen Analisis Investasi dan Perdagangan". Study Report, 2007.

JETRO. "FY 2009 Survey on the International Operations of Japanese Firms" 2010 <http://www.jetro.go.jp/en/news/releases/20100318389-news>.

Ministry of Trade, Republic of Indonesia. "Menuju ASEAN Economic Community 2015" <http://ditjenkpi.depdag.go.id/Umum/Setditjen/Buku%20Menuju%20ASEAN%20ECONOMIC%20COMMUNITY%202015.pdf>.

Pasha, Mochamad and Ira Setiati. "A Case in International Production Network and Trade Liberalization: Indonesia's Automotive Industry" <www.unescap.org/tid/projects/tiri_csis.pdf>.

Pushpanathan, S. "ASEAN's Readiness in Achieving the ASEAN Economic Community 2015: Prospects and Challenges". Keynote address at the ASEAN Roundtable 2010 <http://www.aseansec.org/24656.htm>.

―――. "No Place for Passive Regionalism in ASEAN". *Jakarta Post*, 4 July 2010*b*.

―――. "The Importance of Private Sector". *Jakarta Post*, 2 September 2010*c*.

Tambunan, Tulus. "Is ASEAN still Relevant in the Era of the ASEAN-China FTA?" <www.apeaweb.org/confer/sea06/papers/tambunan.pdf>.

WITS UNCOMTRADE. World Integrated Trade Solution.

World Bank. *Doing Business 2011* <http://www.doingbusiness.org/reports>.

# 14

## Achieving the AEC 2015: Challenges for the Malaysian Private Sector

Mahani Zainal Abidin, Loh Geok Mooi, and Nor Izzatina Abdul Aziz

In January 2007, heads of ASEAN governments declared their strong commitment to accelerating the establishment of the ASEAN Economic Community (AEC) to 2015 as envisioned in the ASEAN Vision 2020. The ASEAN Economic Community Blueprint which comprises four thrusts was adopted. Out of the four thrusts in the AEC Blueprint, more progress has been made in the first, third, and fourth thrusts which aim at fostering (1) a single market and production base, (3) a region of equitable economic development, and (4) a region fully integrated into the global economy, compared with the second thrust (2) on making ASEAN a highly competitive economic region. Ministers have been tasked to implement the AEC Blueprint and report to the Council of the ASEAN Economic Community on the progress of its implementation.

Since then significant progress has been made on the free flow of goods under the first thrust via the removal of tariffs through the

ASEAN Free Trade Area (AFTA). Except for Sensitive and Highly Sensitive Unprocessed Agricultural Products, ASEAN Six, which includes Brunei Darussalam, Indonesia, Malaysia, the Philippines, Singapore, and Thailand, have eliminated the import duties on 99.65 per cent of traded tariff lines since 1 January 2010, while Cambodia, the Lao PDR, Myanmar, and Vietnam (CLMV) have 98.86 per cent of their traded tariff lines reduced to 0–5 per cent.

While AFTA has fostered intra-ASEAN trade since 1992 when it was first established, recent numbers since 2007 show little improvement in trade. This could be due to the unavoidable contraction in trade as a result of the global financial and economic crisis, especially since a significant portion of ASEAN's trade comes from supplying to the advanced economies that were affected by the global crisis. Intra-ASEAN trade rose by 13.6 per cent to US$458 billion and comprised 26.8 per cent of total ASEAN trade in 2008. However, in 2009 the momentum slowed as intra-ASEAN trade fell back to US$376 billion (US$403 billion in 2007), comprising 25.8 per cent of total trade, which was similar to the level in 2007 (25 per cent).

Apart from promoting the free flow of goods, ASEAN member nations are also committed to promoting free flow of services through the ASEAN Framework Agreement on Services (AFAS), which deals with the liberalization of services through successive rounds of negotiations with the aim of submitting increasingly higher levels of commitments for priority areas, as well as mutual recognition agreements on professional services. Priority areas for liberalization include air transport, e-ASEAN, health care, and tourism by 2010, and professions for mutual recognition agreement include architecture, accountancy, surveying, medicine, and dentistry.

As for the free flow of investment, ASEAN investment cooperation is being implemented through the ASEAN Comprehensive Investment Agreement (ACIA) whereby investment liberalization will be implemented with a view towards achieving a free and open investment environment in the region. Investment liberalization will be progressive and have clear timelines. With limited exceptions, national treatment and most-favoured nation treatment will be extended to ASEAN investors during the pre- and post-establishment stages of any investment.

Investment flows into ASEAN had been trending upwards before the global economic crisis and they peaked at US$74 billion in 2007. However, with the onslaught of the global crisis, ASEAN was not spared and foreign direct investment (FDI) into ASEAN fell by 36 per cent in 2008, and 21 per cent in 2009. The fall in FDI inflows into ASEAN was not as severe as that experienced by developed nations, which fell between 30 per cent and 44 per cent. Growth in intra-ASEAN investment flows was buoyant, increasing by 8.1 per cent to US$10.5 billion in 2008, but this level was not sustained as it collapsed by 57.7 per cent to US$4.4 billion in 2009.

While ASEAN governments remain committed and have abided by the declaration in the blueprint, it is important that the private sector also responds strongly to the AEC. Of late, investment and trade figures have not been very encouraging due to the global economic slowdown, but it is essential that intraregional economic activities be expanded. Indeed the success of the AEC will be determined by the participation from the private sectors which are the main beneficiaries of the AEC.

The objective of this report is to determine the responses of the Malaysian private sector to the initiatives by the Malaysian Government to promote the AEC, by gauging their level of awareness, the level of cross-border activities, as well as other positive or negative responses to government initiatives on the AEC. A survey was carried out in August 2010 for this purpose and the result is expected to represent the views of the private sector on the challenges they face in realizing the AEC.

## Malaysian Intra-ASEAN Trade and Investment under the ASEAN Economic Community

The ASEAN Economic Community (AEC) serves as platform for growth and prosperity in the Southeast Asian region. Even before the introduction of the AEC in 2007, Malaysia has been engaging with its neighbours as a trade partner and an investor.

Malaysian exports to ASEAN amounted to US$41.9 billion in 2006 and that number grew to US$42.9 billion in 2009. However, the share of Malaysian exports to ASEAN remained consistent over the two periods at 26 per cent in comparison to Malaysia's total export to the world. The biggest export market in ASEAN for Malaysia is Singapore, with 59.1 per cent of Malaysian exports to ASEAN going to Singapore in 2006. While the proportion of Malaysian exports to Singapore remained high at 57.3 per cent in 2009, a minor increase in Malaysia's exports to Indonesia, Thailand, and Vietnam was seen. Malaysian exports to the Lao PDR was the lowest for the period observed. Table 14.1 shows Malaysian exports and imports to other ASEAN members.

In value terms, Malaysia's total imports from ASEAN nations have increased from 24.5 per cent in 2006 to 32.7 per cent in 2009. Among ASEAN countries, Singapore commands the lion's share of imports to Malaysia. In the observed period, the share of Malaysian imports from Singapore had increased at the expense of both Thailand and Indonesia. In recent years, Malaysia's trade with ASEAN has been producing surpluses (exports in excess of imports) with the exception of 2009. It is interesting to know whether this will be a trend or just an anomaly, given the rise of other ASEAN members as manufacturing powerhouses.

Malaysia has established itself as an attractive investment destination worldwide while, at the same time, investing in other countries. The amount of investment outflows from Malaysia to the world has nearly tripled from US$39 billion in 2006 to US$113.2 billion in 2009. However, the share of Malaysian investment outflows to ASEAN in comparison to its investment worldwide fluctuated over the observed period. The

**TABLE 14.1**
**Malaysian Exports to and Imports from ASEAN**
(US$ millions)

| US$ million (per cent) | 2006 | | 2009 | |
|---|---|---|---|---|
| | Export | Import | Export | Import |
| Brunei | 346 (0.8) | 76 (0.2) | 421 (1.0) | 72 (0.2) |
| Cambodia | 108 (0.3) | 20 (0.06) | 152 (0.4) | 13 (0.03) |
| Indonesia | 4,074 (9.7) | 4,952 (15.5) | 5,140 (12.0) | 5,213 (11.9) |
| Lao PDR | 6 (0.01) | 49 (0.2) | 9 (0.02) | 0 (0) |
| Myanmar | 165 (0.4) | 125 (0.4) | 221 (0.5) | 132 (0.3) |
| Philippines | 2,173 (5.2) | 2,901 (9.1) | 2,270 (5.3) | 1,140 (2.6) |
| Singapore | 24,744 (59.1) | 15,329 (47.9) | 24,572 (57.3) | 26,943 (61.7) |
| Thailand | 8,502 (20.3) | 7,167 (22.4) | 8,099 (18.9) | 8,225 (18.8) |
| Vietnam | 1,758 (4.2) | 1,415 (4.4) | 1,990 (4.6) | 1,952 (4.5) |
| Total ASEAN[1] | 41,876 (26.0) | 32,034 (24.5) | 42,874 (26.1) | 43,690 (32.7) |

*Note:* Total ASEAN parentheses refer to Malaysian exports and imports share to ASEAN in comparison to its total exports to the world. The parentheses for each country refer to share of Malaysian exports and imports to each country in comparison to its total trade in ASEAN.

*Source:* IMF's Direction of Trade Statistics.

peak was in 2007, when 17 per cent of Malaysian investment abroad went to ASEAN members.

Malaysian investment in ASEAN has been growing at a steady pace and went to all ASEAN countries. In 2006 Malaysia invested US$1.8 billion in ASEAN, with Singapore taking the biggest share. By 2009 Singapore was still attracting most of Malaysia's investment, with total Malaysian investment in ASEAN having grown by 70 per cent compared with 2006. Prior to 2006 there was no investment made in the Lao PDR by Malaysians, but between 2006 and 2009, Malaysian firms made cumulative investments worth US$12 million in the country. Table 14.2 shows investment outflows from Malaysia to ASEAN and inflows from ASEAN members to Malaysia. The investment flows consist of both equity investment (foreign direct investment) and portfolio investment.

For the period 2006–9, outflows of investments from Malaysia to other ASEAN members were more than double the inflows of investments from other ASEAN members to Malaysia. Much of Malaysian investment abroad was concentrated in Singapore and Indonesia. Malaysian investments in Singapore could, to a large extent, be portfolio investments as Singapore's more advanced and liquid capital market serves as an outlet for Malaysian investors with a shorter term profit horizon. However, with countries such as Cambodia, the Lao PDR, Myanmar, and Vietnam, which have less-developed capital markets, there is high probability that the investments made in these countries are in productive business operations. Malaysian investment abroad also highly gravitated to its closest neighbours (with the exception of Brunei): Indonesia, Singapore, and Thailand. Investment in Vietnam, on the other hand, is mainly due to its rapid growth to establish itself as a middle-income economy.

It is expected that Malaysian firms will continue to pay attention to ASEAN as their investment destination. Malaysia's financial services sectors have been expanding in ASEAN. A notable case of a Malaysian firm investing in ASEAN is the CIMB Group that undertook the merger of PT Bank Niaga Tbk with PT Bank Lippo Tbk in 2008 to create the sixth-largest bank in Indonesia. Currently there are six Malaysian financial institutions that have investments in ASEAN (Ambank Group, CIMB Group, Maybank Group, Hong Leong Bank, Public Bank, and RHB Bank). However, the performance of other sectors, especially those with a high proportion of small and medium enterprises (SMEs), remains to be seen, particularly after the full implementation of the AEC.

**TABLE 14.2**
**Malaysian Investment Relationship with ASEAN**
(US$ millions)

| | 2006 | | 2009 | | 2006–2009 | |
|---|---|---|---|---|---|---|
| | To ASEAN | To Malaysia | To ASEAN | To Malaysia | To ASEAN | To Malaysia |
| Brunei | 7 | 4 | 10 | 5 | 46 | 19 |
| Cambodia | 2 | 2 | 45 | 2 | 149 | 11 |
| Indonesia | 274 | 23 | 613 | 102 | 4,650 | 264 |
| Lao PDR | 0 | 0 | 0 | 1 | 11 | 2 |
| Myanmar | 13 | 0 | 87 | 1 | 205 | 2 |
| Philippines | 34 | 2 | 29 | 15 | 110 | 36 |
| Singapore | 1,261 | 822 | 1,663 | 1,024 | 9,209 | 5,823 |
| Thailand | 122 | 47 | 368 | 369 | 815 | 844 |
| Vietnam | 68 | 109 | 228 | 177 | 992 | 619 |
| Total ASEAN | 1,781 | 1,011 | 3,043 | 1,696 | 16,187 | 7,620 |

*Source:* Bank Negara Malaysia.

## Status/Progress of Scorecard by Malaysia in the ASEAN Economic Community

The ASEAN Economic Community Scorecard is an official mechanism developed to track progress towards the ASEAN Economic Community (AEC) by 2015. The first scorecard was published in March 2010 and contained the progress that had taken place from January 2008 to December 2009. The second scorecard's measures are being implemented between January 2010 and December 2011.

Under the first scorecard (Scorecard I), 110 measures had been identified for implementation by ASEAN and its members. From the 110 measures, 68 were under Thrust I, 34 under Thrust II, 3 under Thrust III, and 5 under Thrust IV.

- Thrust I deals with measures to liberalize and facilitate the free flow of goods, services, investment, skilled labour, and capital.
- Thrust II focuses on laying the foundation for competition policy, consumer protection, intellectual property rights, and ratifying transport agreements.
- Thrust III focuses on studies and development of SMEs and the initiative for ASEAN Integration Work Plan 2.
- Thrust IV deals with the coming into force of the free trade agreements between ASEAN and other partners.

Scorecard I for the period 2008–09 shows that on average 73.6 per cent of targeted measures were implemented by every ASEAN member. Perfect implementation (100 per cent) can be found in the Thrust III and Thrust IV initiatives, while the lowest implementation rate experienced was under Thrust II (competitive economic region), that recorded on average a 50 per cent implementation rate. For Thrust III and IV, their implementation achievement of 100 per cent was due to their low number of targets (three and five measures implemented). Thrust I recorded a 82 per cent implementation rate on average. Overall implementation rate for Thrust I to Thrust IV was 73.6 per cent of measures targeted at the end of December 2009.

Malaysia has managed to implement 86 out of the 110 measures targeted, bringing its rate to 78.2 per cent, above the ASEAN average. The Malaysian Government considers the implementation of the measures as important as it reduces or eliminates the barriers for investment and trade and aligns national regulations to regional commitments through effective regulatory and structural reform. At the same time, implementation of the measures signifies the importance of ASEAN's efforts in improving the economic well-being of its members.

In the area of trade of goods (or free flow of goods), Malaysia ratified the ASEAN Trade in Goods Agreement (ATIGA) on 17 June 2009. Along with this, the tariff liberalization process has been taking place since 1 January 2010 which has resulted in the following:

- 12,169 tariff lines (98.69 per cent) have zero import duties
- 56 tariff lines (0.45 per cent) of selected tropical fruits and tobacco were reduced to 5 per cent
- 10 tariff lines (0.08 per cent) on rice were reduced from 40 per cent to 20 per cent
- 96 tariff lines (0.78 per cent) on alcoholic beverages and weapons are excluded from tariff reduction and elimination

Included under the effort to increase the flow of goods in ASEAN is the implementation of the National Single Window (NSW) to facilitate the creation of an ASEAN Single Window (ASW), where ASEAN member countries will operate and integrate to expedite cargo release and clearance. On Malaysia's part, the implementation of its NSW took place on 1 January 2009 and is supported by five core services, which have been in full operation since 19 November 2009 and consist of (1) e-Declare, (2) e-Permit, (3) e-Payment, (4) e-Preferential Certificate of Origin (e-PCO), and (5) e-Manifest. The services offered under the Malaysian NSW incorporate the usage of information and communi-cation technology to facilitate trade and improve the efficiency of the government delivery system that benefits the trading community. As an example, the approval of a preferential certificate of origin can now be done within a working day.

Another area under trade in goods that requires action under the AEC Scorecard is standards and conformance. Here Malaysia adopted Annex 3 of the World Trade Organization's (WTO) Technical Barriers to Trade (TBT) Agreements as the basis for standards development, based on international practices, beginning 31 December 2008. The adoption of WTO's TBT Agreement signifies the fourth thrust in the AEC, which is promoting the full integration of the region into the global economy. Conformance in cosmetic products took place in ASEAN where individual members adopted the ASEAN Cosmetic Directive (ACD) into their national legislation. Malaysia has incorporated the ACD into its

Guidelines for Control of Cosmetic Products starting 1 December 2007, while the harmonization of cosmetic regulation procedures has been in place since 1 January 2008. With this, companies are now required only to notify/declare their compliance to the ACD instead of registering with the National Pharmaceutical Control Bureau.

The free flow of services under the AEC is made possible under the ASEAN Framework Agreement on Services (AFAS), which adopted the framework under WTO's General Agreement on Trade in Services (GATS) by offering a positive list of services sectors that have been liberalized. Currently, under the seventh round, Malaysia has made changes in its services sectors not only to comply with the AEC timeframe, but also to increase its competitiveness. Between 1 January 2008 and 31 December 2009, the following steps have been made by the Malaysian Government:

- Schedule 10 new services subsectors under the Seventh Package;
- Schedule "none" for Modes 1 and 2 market access and national treatment, with exceptions to bona fide regulatory reasons subject to agreement by member states;
- Schedule at least 49 per cent of foreign equity on logistics services and other sectors;
- Schedule a maximum of three types of non-equity market access limitation for twelve sub-sectors of other sectors.

On investment, Malaysia has kept to the given timetable and ratified the ASEAN Comprehensive Investment Agreement (ACIA) on 16 August 2009. Despite the existence of the ASEAN Investment Agreement (AIA), the ACIA is a more comprehensive agreement that covers four pillars of investment such as liberalization, protection, facilitation, and promotion. An implementation of the ACIA under the AEC includes the selection of a reservation list (negative-list approach on reserved sectors) which was decided by Malaysia in October 2009.

In an effort to build ASEAN into a competitive economic region, the Malaysian Government has made major strides in improving its transportation infrastructure. The first is the ASEAN Framework Agreement on the Facilitation of Goods in Transit, parts of which have been ratified by Malaysia. Much headway has been made in the ASEAN Multilateral Agreement on the Full Liberalization of Air Freight Services (ratified on 15 December 2009) and the ASEAN Multilateral Agreement on Air Services (ratified on 15 December 2009).

There are only eight measures to be implemented under Thrust III and IV (equitable economic development and integration with the global economy) and Malaysia has managed to fulfil its implementation target.

Under the second AEC scorecard (Scorecard II), 146 measures have been targeted for implementation between 2010 and 2011. Out of the 146, 105 measures were scheduled to be implemented in 2010, while the remaining forty-one were scheduled for implementation in 2011. As of 30 June 2010, Malaysia has complied with 32 out of 142 measures targeted for the period 2010–11. The breakdown of the 32 is as follows; 16 measures under Thrust I, 12 under Thrust II, and 4 under Thrust IV. It is expected that the Scorecard II will require more attention and efforts from regulators as measures to be implemented are deeper and more comprehensive compared with those of Scorecard I.

## Malaysian Private Sector

In order to identify responses and challenges faced by the private sector (business community), a survey was conducted to obtain primary data resources. The survey took place from August to September 2010.

### Questionnaire

The aim of the questionnaire was to gauge private sector responses to the AEC. As the AEC is in its early implementation stage, the questionnaire was designed to measure businesses' awareness and their responses to measures that have been implemented and challenges faced. Since the majority of the measures that have been implemented come from Thrust I, the questionnaire was designed to cater to Thrust I initiatives. Thrust I initiatives are also the main concerns of businesses as they affect their businesses directly.

The questionnaire consists of two parts. The first is on the awareness of the private sector of the AEC and its components and transmission channels. The second part deals with the implementation (domestically or by ASEAN counterparts), private sector responses, and expectations of the measures taken under Thrust I. Questions were asked on mechanisms such as the ASEAN Free Trade Area (AFTA) and the Common Effective Preferential Tariffs (CEPT), the ASEAN Framework Agreement on Services (AFAS), the ASEAN Investment Agreement (AIA), the

ASEAN Comprehensive Investment Agreement (ACIA), and the Mutual Recognition Agreements (MRAs).

### Data and Survey Samples

The survey questionnaire was sent to sixty-six companies, out of which only sixteen responded. The breakdown of the sixty-six companies is as follows:

- Six questionnaires were sent to six professional associations (for nurses, dental and medical practitioners, accountants, surveyors, and lawyers);
- Five questionnaires were distributed to each of the following sectors: agriculture, plastics manufacturers, rubber products, pharmaceuticals, textile and apparels, car manufacturers and assemblers, business services, travel services, chemical production, logistics providers, private education institutions, and legal services.

However, a number of companies requested that their respective trade associations answer the questionnaires because they felt that these associations know more about the AEC than they themselves. Several questionnaires were then distributed through trade associations for private hospitals, airfreight forwarders, plastic manufacturers, textile and apparels, automotive, and travel services.

Admittedly, the response rate to the questionnaire of 20 per cent is poor. From the sixteen responses, seven respondents spent 40 to 50 minutes for a face-to-face interview while eight respondents replied through e-mail or fax. A phone interview was conducted with one respondent.

The response rates are equal between services-based and manu-facturing sectors (eight respondents each). Half of the total number of respondents were from professional or industrial associations, mostly from the services sector. Meanwhile, the bulk of respondents from the manufacturing sector comprised manufacturing firms (see Table 14.3).

Although the response rate is low, responses from professional or industrial associations can be treated as a collective sector response and more weight should be accorded to their opinions. The poor response rate can be attributed to the limited time available to conduct a comprehensive survey fully and the reluctance of businesses to answer individually. More information on the respondents and their cross-border activities are tabulated in Appendix 14.1.

**TABLE 14.3**
**Breakdown on the Nature of Respondents**

| Sector | Association or firms | Number of respondents |
|--------|---------------------|----------------------|
| Manufacturing | Associations | 2 |
| | Firms | 6 |
| Services | Associations | 6 |
| | Firms | 2 |

# Findings

### General Awareness of AEC

Responses from the surveyed companies indicate that 37.5 per cent (six respondents) of the respondents were fully aware and knowledgeable about the AEC and its contents, while 18.8 per cent (three respondents) had limited knowledge on the AEC. Awareness about other AEC initiatives such as the AFTA and AFAS was also low. Surveyed companies have poor awareness on investment-related and global integration initiatives (namely the ASEAN Investment Agreement and ASEAN Comprehensive Investment Agreement).

Understandably, manufacturers (eight respondents) were more aware of the AEC and AFTA, while service providers were more aware of the AFAS, as the appropriate agreements are relevant to their businesses. While most respondents indicate in the later part of the survey that they were eager to invest or increase their operation in other ASEAN countries, the awareness level on the AIA or ACIA was the lowest compared with other AEC initiatives. In addition, there were cases where respondents interviewed have never heard of terms such as ASEAN Investment Agreement or ASEAN Comprehensive Investment Agreement.

The awareness level of firms to AEC initiatives also correlates to their business operations and orientation. In general, manufacturing associations that were more knowledgeable and aware of the AEC were the ones that reported that most of their members' revenues came from ASEAN countries. In contrast, services-based respondents have smaller revenues generated from ASEAN countries, with the exception of private hospitals and tertiary education institutes. The services sectors are

**FIGURE 14.1**
**Awareness of the AEC and its Initiatives**
(1 = not aware, 5 = fully aware)

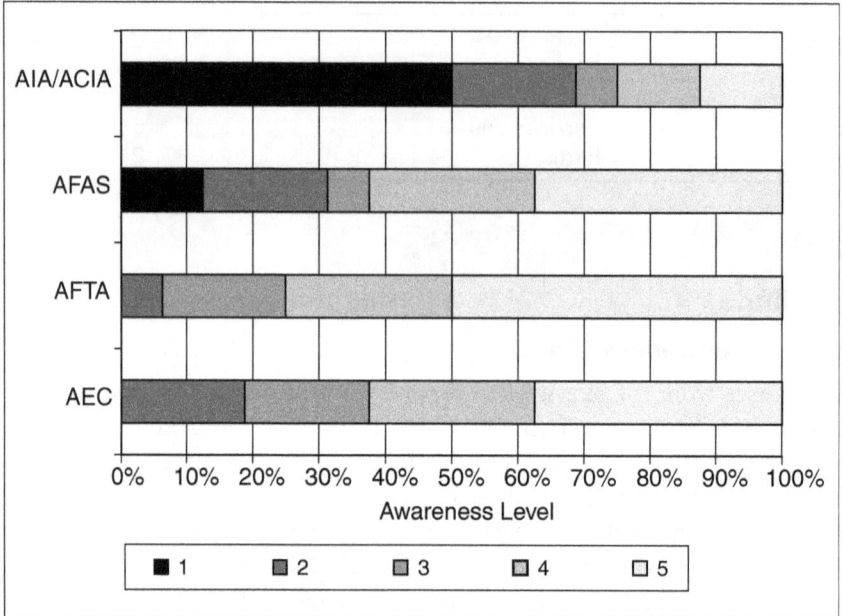

domestically oriented in their business outlook, and this might explain their lack of awareness and understanding of the AEC.

Despite the considerable lack of awareness of the AEC, all respondents were not prevented from:

1. exporting or importing goods
2. providing cross-border services
3. hiring foreign professionals from ASEAN
4. serving ASEAN customers in Malaysia
5. taking part in a regional production network across ASEAN

This finding questions the fundamental idea behind the AEC, which is to drive economic integration. Even without the AEC, transborder economic activities in ASEAN are bound to happen as firms look beyond their borders to expand, or, at least, source materials from other ASEAN countries. On the other hand, the lack of awareness also signifies ignorance on the part of some respondents with respect to AEC goals and how these will affect the respondents.

The media (newspaper and television) and government/ASEAN websites were identified by respondents as the main sources of information on the AEC and its initiatives. While the media might not be able to give a comprehensive picture of the AEC, websites have filled this gap and enabled firms to search for targeted information. Thirteen respondents indicated that government/ASEAN websites were an important source of information on the AEC. At the same time, four respondents reported dialogues/meetings held by ministries and government agencies as useful for getting in-depth information on the AEC. Two respondents indicated that the information provided by the channels above was not useful and cited the briefings given by the government/ministries as, at times, too theoretical.

Associations that responded to the questionnaire also stated that they have put in effort to inform and educate their respective members on the issues their industries will face under the AEC or other policy changes such as the Trans-Pacific Partnerships. Information gathering cost is a factor to be considered, especially for small firms, therefore the task of gathering information falls on associations, which have also acted as a bridge communicating their members' interests to the government and vice versa. Trade facilitation efforts have also been supported by associations, for example, the Malaysian Textile Manufacturers Association has been authorized by the Ministry of International Trade and Industry to issue and endorse certificates of origin for its exporters. Given the complexities and overlapping policy efforts by the Malaysian Government to enhance transborder economic activities under bilateral and multilateral engagements, we can expect the role played by associations to increase.

### Responses on Trade of Goods

AFTA is the main initiative under the AEC that reduces or eliminates tariffs on intra-ASEAN trade for goods. The Common Effective Preferential Tariff (CEPT) was the mechanism for reducing or eliminating tariffs in AFTA, but after 17 May 2010, CEPT was replaced by the ASEAN Trade in Goods Agreement (ATIGA).

From the total number of respondents, only eight are manufacturers; each acts as an exporter and/or importer of goods. They are in plastics, textiles and apparels, construction materials, medical equipment industries, chemicals and automotive sectors. The manufacturers reported that exports to ASEAN have consistently contributed to their yearly share of revenues/profits.

Of the eight respondents (associations and firms), seven managed to utilize the CEPT scheme fully in trading their goods in ASEAN. The percentage of exports traded by respondents using the CEPT scheme ranged from 11 per cent to 75 per cent.

Respondents that engage in intraregional trade in ASEAN, particularly in textile and apparel, are of the view that CEPT has been beneficial to their operations. However, a respondent representing a company engaged in the production of construction materials reported that the company's share of ASEAN trade has been stagnant and it has not been using or able to benefit from the CEPT scheme. Of the eight respondents, six said the elimination of tariffs under AFTA has had the biggest impact on their business activities, while a firm reported that the simple, harmonized, and standardized trade facilitation practice by custom offices in ASEAN and the uniformity on rules of origin (ROO) have been significant in improving its business operations. With regard to the regional supply chain, three respondents indicated that AFTA has influenced their decisions to locate their production networks in ASEAN. Another respondent indicated that despite ASEAN's role in creating a free trade regime in the region, the main consideration for having a production network in the region was due to low labour costs.

Despite the overall positive comments on the AFTA, seven respondents also pointed out several accompanying problems when utilizing the lower tariffs. The problems cited seem to be mainly in trade facilitation. This is a major obstacle that needs to be resolved as it can discourage more exporters from taking advantage of opportunities offered by the AFTA. The respondents have experienced difficulties in clearing their goods at other ASEAN country borders, particularly at customs, in terms of delays or the requirement of exporters to complete irregular forms. Two respondents explained that the product classifications of their goods have been suffering from unsynchronized product classifications originating from differences between the ASEAN Harmonized Tariff Nomenclature (8 digits) and the international tariff codes (HS 9), therefore causing the application of inconsistent tariffs. Two respondents have also reported that their goods at some point had been subjected to some sort of non-tariff barriers by officials from other ASEAN countries such as Indonesia and Vietnam. Inefficiency in the delivery system as a result of the lack of coordination between countries was encountered by a respondent who experienced physical arrival of products at the destination prior to the receipt of the e-PCO (Preferential Certificate of Origin). A respondent that utilized CEPT to establish its production network also experienced barriers in terms of delay in the application process involving its vendors.

Only one respondent surveyed admitted they have yet to utilize AFTA initiatives fully in their business operation. The main reasons given was the lack of understanding of the AFTA initiatives, while the most-favoured nation tariff rates differentials are miniscule for their traded products.

### Responses on Trade in Services

To find the effects of the AEC on trade in services done by the Malaysian private sector, a specific section of the questionnaire was designed to gauge the responses of services providers in Malaysia to the trade in services components in the AEC.

In total, there were eight responses from various services sectors, including accountancy, the medical profession, private education, and surveyors. The main trade in services activities undertaken by respondents are (1) catering to the needs of foreign clients or consumers in Malaysia (six respondents) and (2) hiring and using foreign professionals to support their core business activities (two respondents).

Although they were mostly aware of the existence of AFAS, six out of eight respondents reported that the implementation of AFAS has not improved their business operations, while the rest indicated an improvement in their services trade to ASEAN since the introduction of AFAS. On the question as to whether AFAS has benefited their business activities, three respondents concluded they have yet to benefit from AFAS. The rest managed to benefit in terms of increased demand from ASEAN clients, collaboration with other ASEAN counterparts, and enjoying a bigger talent pool for recruitment. Benefits could also be traced to the ease of hiring employees and bringing consumers from ASEAN to their facilities in Malaysia.

The inability of the majority of respondents to benefit from AFAS can be taken as a sign that they are still unable to position themselves well with the greater liberalization that will take place under AFAS. However, seven of the eight respondents said they were confident they would be able to compete with services providers from other ASEAN countries. In fact five respondents had reportedly taken steps to strengthen and improve their business operations to face stiffer competition from greater liberalization. Two firms from medical services had yet to take any steps to improve their business operations in view of the changes from AFAS. The main steps taken by firms to strengthen their business operation were by increasing their business size through merger and acquisition, capacity building, and the improvement of services offered (three responses), and applying pressure on the local chapter of professional associations to be more engaging and proactive in designing guidelines and higher standards in ASEAN (three responses).

Given the domestic orientation of services, the negative responses by services-based respondents on the liberalization process were expected. Reasons such as government regulations (three respondents), lack of scale/capital/funds (two respondents), lack of knowledge of targeted market (two respondents), and lack of business/clients networks (one respondent), were cited as obstacles hindering service firms from starting operations in ASEAN. While some barriers to expand might be due to the business nature of the respondents (that is, private clinics), regulatory burdens posed huge barriers for services firms to expand either domestically or abroad.

A few respondents considered government domestic policies or regulations as obstacles for them to expand their services abroad or even locally. A respondent in private tertiary education pointed out that the restrictions placed on the size of student intakes by the Malaysian Ministry of Health is preventing them from offering their services despite enquiries from interested individuals residing in ASEAN. The main reason behind this restriction is to prevent the overproduction of medical and health related professionals in Malaysia who are currently having difficulties fulfilling their required residencies at government hospitals due to limited spaces.

Medical and dental practitioners operate under restrictive rules and guidelines. For example, dental premises must be owned by a licensed dental practitioner who must have referrals from two other dental practitioners. Dental practitioners also have to comply to fee structures and operating hours set by the regulating body. The dental practice in Malaysia also prohibits employment of foreign dentists on private dental premises. Malaysia also exercises stringent guidelines on advertisements and this ruling has only been relaxed recently. Related government authorities are believed to be inhibiting the supply of foreign medical specialists needed for the growing medical services sector in Malaysia. Some of the reasons are linked to professional requirements to meet international standards. Regulations with regard to dental and private medical practices have over the years kept high standards in Malaysia compared with many other ASEAN countries, but some of these rules and regulations have also hampered growth in the local establishments and even in offering sufficient capacity to serve domestic consumers.

The effort to expand services trade through Mode 1, for example, is difficult with the lack of Internet connectivity in newer ASEAN member countries, making any outsourcing efforts harder (with the exception of Singapore). Under Mode 2, a respondent reportedly found that efforts to market their services in other ASEAN members were met with multiple layers of bureaucracy that led to instances where some Malaysian doctors were deemed to be breaking provincial law just by promoting and marketing Malaysian private hospitals services abroad.

The implementation of greater liberalization can be expected under trade in services in the AEC Scorecard II. The establishment of the ASEAN Core Competencies on Nursing Services and the eighth round of AFAS will be expected to include more services sectors. No doubt a huge transformation process is bound to take place in Malaysia's services sectors, and firms will have to reorientate their business strategies to meet the incoming challenges. From the responses gathered, the process would be made easier if domestic policies are accommodating for service providers in Malaysia to expand their services.

### Response on Investment

Of the sixteen respondents, eight admitted that they have investments in ASEAN in the form of a regional production network or an extension of domestic services offered in other ASEAN countries. Vietnam is the main destination for investment from Malaysia (four responses), followed by Indonesia and Cambodia (three responses each) and the Lao PDR (one response). Out of the eight respondents, four indicated that less than 10 per cent of their total investments are in ASEAN (ex-Malaysia), two respondents reported that between 11 and 25 per cent of their total investment are in ASEAN, and a respondent indicated that between 26 to 50 per cent of their investment are in ASEAN. There was no response from the eighth respondent.

Only three respondents gave positive responses when asked about their awareness of the main investment initiatives under the AEC. When told that the objective of the AIA/ACIA is to enable the creation of a level playing field in the region, nine respondents expressed doubts that it would benefit them, with a respondent citing an example that Malaysian companies are now susceptible to takeovers from other firms in ASEAN.

At the sectoral level, only four respondents gave a positive answer that the AIA/ACIA is beneficial for the growth of their respective sectors. Three respondents remained neutral on that issue while four viewed it as being capable of having negative effects on their sector. One of them did not respond to this question.

The surveyed respondents might not be fully aware of the AIA/ACIA, but they showed strong interest in increasing their investment in ASEAN. Nine respondents indicated that they were willing to look closer at AIA/ACIA and utilize it in their future investment in ASEAN. Apart from the lack of awareness in the AEC investment initiatives, challenges such as limited local knowledge (two respondents) and the lack of scale/funds/capital to expand (two respondents) are cited as hampering respondents from investing in ASEAN.

Face-to-face interview sessions conducted gave more information on the challenges of investing in ASEAN. A respondent reported that their factory in Vietnam was facing persistent labour strikes, made worse after the incidences of strikes in China early this year. Another respondent also made a remark that the high inflation rate in Vietnam was detrimental to its operations there. The respondents from manufacturing industries who were interested in investing abroad looked for places which were cost effective, had low wages, and required low skills. On the other hand, respondents from the services sector who invested abroad made their decisions based on market potential, such as market size and the growing middle income class in countries such as Cambodia, Indonesia, and Vietnam.

### Responses on Freer Labour Movement

The AEC Blueprint also covers the aspiration of freer professional and skilled labour movement across ASEAN. The main instruments are the sectoral schedule of Mode 4 under AFAS and the Mutual Recognition Agreements (MRAs) on a few selected professionals.

There were more respondents who viewed AFAS as not helpful in recruiting the skilled workforce needed in Malaysia. Rather, six respondents (five from the services sectors) felt that AFAS has encouraged highly skilled and experienced Malaysian workers to work abroad, citing Singapore as the main magnet in the region. The positive responses (five) on AFAS came from respondents who had experience in hiring professionals from ASEAN in sectors such as tertiary education and private hospitals.

Since the MRAs are limited to six professions, only three respondents in recent years were able to hire using standards outlined in the MRAs. The same respondents also reported that the procedures in hiring and getting a work permit for ASEAN foreign professionals under the MRAs is easier and timely, with the exception of dental practitioners. Of late, respondents have experienced smoother procedures even for professionals not covered by MRAs, such as lecturers.

Most respondents (eight) felt that increasing the number of professions covered by MRAs is a positive development that they look forward to. A firm suggested that MRAs be made on IT and design services. Two respondents were neutral on this issue while one respondent felt that expanding MRAs could erode the premiums received by domestic service providers.

While respondents seemed eager for the scope of MRAs to be enlarged, the majority of them (ten respondents) felt that professional associations' roles are important in order to maintain the standards of professionalism in the region and to ensure a level playing field. Respondents who had experience in hiring foreign professionals pointed out problems related to the domestic immigration office's inefficiency and reluctance to issue work permits.

Professionals, even those covered by the MRAs, reported that requirements, such as citizenship and language, are making it impossible for Malaysian services providers to work in other ASEAN countries. Other domestic regulations, such as the Dental Act 1971, prevent the hiring of foreign dental practitioners unless it is by the government. The same situation is also faced by medical professionals (doctors). A few respondents (three) were reluctant to hire professionals from abroad because the services provided may be of a different quality compared with that of domestic professionals.

## Policy Recommendations

### *Awareness about the AEC*

Awareness of the positive benefits of the AEC has to be raised. Lack of awareness and negative perception of the AEC can be a major hurdle in the successful implementation of the AEC. Industry associations play a very important role in raising the level of awareness and promoting ASEAN as a trade and investment area. Private sector participants generally had little knowledge about regional services and investment liberalization agreements among ASEAN member countries even though most of them were aware of AFTA.

Based on the scorecards, much has been done by the Malaysian Government. Knowledge of this has to be transmitted to the private sector. Industry associations are important channels for relaying the progress of the implementation of the AEC and also for obtaining private sector feedback as to whether the scorecard meets their expectations. Some industry players fear liberalization because it may disadvantage them. Thus, the implementation of the initiatives under the AEC in ASEAN must be explained clearly to dispel this misgiving. Dialogues and discussions between industry associations and government agencies will foster more effective implementation.

Currently, there are many rules and regulations that govern business practices within the services sector. Some of these may be restrictive and prevent the private sector from expanding their services into other ASEAN nations. Hence, the private sector, through their respective industry associations, also needs to engage with the Malaysian Government to provide a more conducive environment for the services sector which is on par with that of ASEAN neighbours. Meanwhile a balance must be found to promote the AEC as a way for firms in Malaysia to unleash their competitiveness while at the same time prepare them to compete with other ASEAN players that can do better as a result of subsidies or less regulation.

While the study has been targeted at the private sector, the survey also found that the public sector's level of awareness was also relatively weak, especially when it came to facilitating cross-border trades. Malaysian firms that attempt to take advantage of the agreements still encounter many obstacles. Even though regional governments may have already made agreements on tariff reduction, liberalization of priority service sectors, investments through mechanisms such as CEPT, AFAS, and AIA, the private sector encounters situations where some of the terms of the agreements have not been implemented at all levels. In some cases, customs or municipalities may insist on their own rules or terms that override the regional agreements. In more extreme circumstances, local service providers fearing liberalization may also act in concert with local municipalities to drive away ASEAN investors. Because of this, local municipalities, states, customs, and other related government bodies should be briefed by central government authorities to give priority to cooperation with ASEAN nations on trade and investments.

### Promote the Potential of ASEAN as a Platform of Production Network

Individually, many of the ASEAN nations have relatively small domestic markets and low per capita income to attract significant FDIs inflows, but collectively these nations can be a viable production network if costs of transportation can be reduced and goods and services can flow across borders seamlessly.

To encourage more trade and cross-border investments, there should be more clarity, industry standardization, and transparency in the activities of each sector, subsector, or profession. An outreach programme where more detailed cooperative mechanisms by sector and subsectors for both manufacturing and services is required if ASEAN is to become a platform for a regional production network.

### Expedite Trade Facilitation

To encourage more trade within ASEAN, the expeditious implementation of trade facilitation should be given a priority. Malaysian exporters encounter obstacles in trade facilitation and this may negate the advantages of reduced tariffs as agreed in CEPT. Focus should be given to smoother customs and logistics integration that will enable a smooth and speedy passage for the export and import of goods. Harmonized and standardized trade and customs processes and procedures with the establishment of an ASEAN e-Customs will reduce transaction costs, enhance export competitiveness, and facilitate the integration of ASEAN into a single market and single production base.

### Adopt Wider Investment Liberalization

Of the AEC components, investment has shown significant progress over a four-year period in terms of intra-ASEAN investment flows despite the lack of awareness on regional investment agreements under the AEC. More recently in 2009, however, intra-ASEAN investments collapsed by 57.7 per cent to US$4.4 billion in the aftermath of the global financial crisis. To arrest this decline in intra-ASEAN investments, more efforts can be made to increase the level of awareness on the official agreements (AIA and ACIA) in the business community.

In addition, partnerships that involve ASEAN with non-ASEAN investors should also be encouraged in order to increase levels of innovation among ASEAN member nations. It may, therefore, be more effective for ASEAN countries to opt for general investment liberalization that can make ASEAN countries a very attractive investment location and this will likely see a significant boost in investments, particularly in higher value added and technologically advanced companies.

### Assistance for SMEs

SMEs face more difficulties than larger companies in expanding abroad. The larger manufacturing firms and service providers are more positive about the AEC since they have already invested or have intentions to invest in ASEAN countries. On the other hand, the main focus of SMEs is the domestic market and they are generally less in favour of liberalization and expanding abroad as these firms fear erosion of market share by new players. The SMEs lack financial and technical capacity and they need financial support, knowledge of networks, and knowledge of the market to encourage them to venture into ASEAN countries. Government agencies can increase their assistance in providing them with the useful links and information needed.

### Facilitate the Movement of Skilled Workers

The free movement of skilled workers is still a challenging issue and there is a need to increase the number of MRAs. Currently language proficiency and professional standards vary widely across ASEAN countries. Even basic tertiary education qualifications differ across ASEAN countries and it may be necessary for ASEAN countries to recognize mutually a certain standard as the entry qualification for tertiary education.

Respondents from the services sector were more negative towards the AEC as they face more obstacles in exporting their services than those from the manufacturing sector. A more specialized and focused effort, possibly based on services subsectors or specialized activities, can be established to assist these services providers to build capacity and minimize the export obstacles. This measure will facilitate the harmonization of domestic regulations which involve many ministries or agencies and cross-industry technical requirements.

### APPENDIX 14.1
### Profile of Respondents and Their Cross-Border Activities

| Sectors | Respondents | A | B | C | D | E | F |
|---|---|---|---|---|---|---|---|
| Manufacturing | Textile and Apparels 1 | • | | | | • | • |
| | Textile and Apparels 2 | • | | | | • | |
| | Plastics | • | | • | • | • | • |
| | Constructions Materials | | • | • | | • | • |
| | Medical equipment | | | • | • | • | • |
| | Automotive 1 | • | | | | | |
| | Automotive 2 | • | | | | | |
| | Chemicals | • | | | • | | • |
| Services | Medical 1 | | | • | • | | |
| | Medical 2 | | | | • | | |
| | Medical 3 | | | • | • | • | |
| | Medical 4 | | | | • | | |
| | Education 1 | | | • | • | | |
| | Education 2 | | | • | • | | |
| | Accountancy | | • | | • | | • |
| | Surveyors | | • | | • | • | |

*Notes:*
A – export or/and import goods to/from ASEAN
B – provide cross-border services in ASEAN
C – hire professionals from ASEAN
D – serve ASEAN customers in Malaysia (Mode 2 of services trade)
E – invest in ASEAN
F – form part of a regional production network

REFERENCES

ASEAN. "ASEAN Economic Community Blueprint". Jakarta: ASEAN Secretariat, January 2008.

————. "ASEAN Economic Community Scorecard: Charting Progress towards Regional Economic Integration". Jakarta: ASEAN Secretariat, March 2010.

Bank Negara. "Monthly Statistical Bulletin July 2010" <http://www.bnm.gov.my/index.php?ch=116&pg=352&ac=4&eId=box1> (accessed 15 September 2010).

Dharmender Singh. "Rules on Healthcare Ads Relaxed, Say Liow". *The Star*, 24 September 2010 <http://thestar.com.my/news/story.asp?file=/2010/9/24/nation/7093952&sec=nation> (accessed 15 October 2010).

IMF. "Direction of Trade Statistics 2009". Washington, DC: International Monetary Fund, 2009.

# 15

## Role of the Private Sector in Regional Economic Integration: A View from The Philippines

Maureen Ane D. Rosellon and Josef T. Yap*

### Overview of the Philippine Situation

Sustainable economic development continues to be elusive for the Philippines. A wide spectrum of economic policies has been implemented during the past five decades. Yet the boom-bust cycle has remained a constant feature of the economy, along with a relatively high poverty incidence. The overview underscores one of the dilemmas that currently face policymakers in the Philippines: a dominant private sector in the Philippines, but one that not has not lived up to its potential.

Compared with other economies in Southeast Asia, the Philippines' economic growth record has been disappointing. While the region's middle- and high-income economies experienced at least 2 per cent average growth of real per capita gross domestic product (GDP) during the past fifty years, the Philippines recorded only a 1.9 per cent average (Table 15.1). As a result, the Philippines was not even described as a

**TABLE 15.1**
**Annual Average Growth Rate of Real Per Capita GDP, 1950–2006**
(%)

| Period | Hong kong, China | Indonesia | Korea | Malaysia | The Philippines | Singapore | Taipei, China | Thailand |
|---|---|---|---|---|---|---|---|---|
| 1951–60 | 9.2 | 4.0 | 5.1 | 3.6 | 3.3 | 5.4 | 7.6 | 5.7 |
| 1961–70 | 7.1 | 2.0 | 5.8 | 3.4 | 1.8 | 7.4 | 9.6 | 4.8 |
| 1971–80 | 6.8 | 5.3 | 5.4 | 5.3 | 3.1 | 7.1 | 9.3 | 4.3 |
| 1981–90 | 5.4 | 4.3 | 7.7 | 3.2 | –0.6 | 5 | 8.2 | 6.3 |
| 1991–2000 | 3.0 | 2.9 | 5.2 | 4.6 | 0.9 | 4.7 | 5.5 | 2.4 |
| 2001–06 | 4.0 | 3.3 | 4.2 | 2.7 | 2.7 | 3.2 | 3.4 | 4.0 |
| Average growth rate for 56 years | 5.9 | 3.6 | 5.6 | 3.8 | 1.9 | 5.5 | 7.3 | 4.6 |

*Source:* Asian Development Bank (2007).

"high-performing economy" by the World Bank in its 1993 study of the East Asian Miracle, while Thailand, Malaysia, and Indonesia were included in this select group.

Mainstream economists attribute this situation largely to economic protectionism and the import substitution policies that were followed after World War II up to the 1970s. The protection of selected sectors led to the misallocation of the country's resources, that is, the sectors in which the Philippines did not have a comparative advantage benefited from this policy stance. Moreover, the lack of competition removed the incentive of protected firms to become innovative and adopt modern technology. This resulted in monopolistic firms producing poor quality goods and services at relatively high costs, the burden of which was passed on to the Filipino consumer.

In response to this analysis, the Philippines — like many other developing countries — adopted the "openness model". This reform package began modestly in the early 1970s and was interrupted by the debt crisis in 1983–85. The reform programme, however, was accelerated in the late 1980s and has been the government mantra since. The general thrust of the reforms was closer global economic integration underpinned by liberalization, deregulation, and privatization. At the same time — similar again to other developing countries — the Philippines adopted measures to strengthen the supply capacity of its economy with a view to building competitive industries which would be the main beneficiaries of increased access to world markets. More attention was given to macroeconomic stability and exchange rate movements; appropriate sequencing of the liberalization of trade, financial, and capital-account regimes, supported by prudential regulation and financial sector reform; the strengthening of domestic institutional capacity; and attracting foreign direct investment (UNCTAD 2004).

The ASEAN Economic Community is a direct offshoot of the "openness model". The AEC is a realization of economic integration which aims to establish ASEAN as a single market and production base by 2015, and make it a region of high competitiveness, equitable economic development, fully integrated into the global economy (ASEAN 2008). These elements are incorporated in a blueprint — signed at the 13th ASEAN Summit in 2007 — that ensures consistency and coherence of actions, and implementation and proper coordination among stakeholders.

Unfortunately, the "openness model" did not generate the desired results and the Philippines has continued to lag behind its neighbours.

As seen from Table 15.1, the per capita GDP growth in 2001–06 was still below the peak reached in 1951–60 and was also lower than that of other East Asian economies. Moreover, the "openness model" did not generate the structural transformation that it was supposed to. Data in Table 15.2 show that the GDP share of value added from the manufacturing sector declined between 1980 and 2008. This stands in contrast to the experience of Thailand, Malaysia, and Indonesia.

The Philippines is therefore in a relatively unique position wherein a whole range of policies were implemented without much success. A critical factor is the nature of the private sector in the Philippines, which is characterized as an oligarchy (De Dios and Hutchcroft 2003). Hence, even if wide-ranging reforms have been implemented, the response from the private sector has been mixed. This is reflected primarily in an investment-GDP ratio that is lower than that of other countries in the region and has fallen consistently from 2000 to 2009 (Table 15.3). More recent analysis points to the role of the oligarchy in compromising institutions (De Dios 2008; Philippine Human Development Network 2009). Weak institutions have also constrained economic growth (De Dios 2008).

This chapter seeks to explain the reasons for the relatively weak private sector response to the opportunities provided by greater openness. Some factors are structural, pertaining largely to supply-side constraints such as poor infrastructure. Some of these factors, as mentioned earlier, are historical; and some are related to information availability and

**TABLE 15.2**
**Share of Manufacturing in GDP**
(%)

|             | 1980 | 1985 | 1990 | 1995 | 2000 | 2006 | 2007 | 2008 |
|-------------|------|------|------|------|------|------|------|------|
| China       | 43.9 | 37.0 | 35.5 | 40.6 | 40.7 | 43.1 | 43.0 | 42.8 |
| Indonesia   | 13.5 | 18.1 | 23.0 | 26.6 | 27.7 | 27.5 | 27.0 | 27.3 |
| Malaysia    | 21.6 | 19.3 | 22.8 | 24.7 | 29.9 | 29.0 | 27.4 | 25.8 |
| Philippines | 25.7 | 25.2 | 24.8 | 23.0 | 22.2 | 22.9 | 22.0 | 22.6 |
| Thailand    | 21.5 | 21.9 | 24.9 | 28.7 | 33.6 | 35.1 | 35.6 | 37.6 |
| Vietnam     | 16.1 | 16.4 | 12.3 | 15.0 | 18.6 | 21.2 | 21.3 | 21.1 |

Source: UN Statistics Division <http://unstats.un.org/unsd/snaama/dnltransfer.asp?fID=16; accessed, 23 Nov 2009>.

**TABLE 15.3**
**Gross Domestic Investment**
(% of GDP)

|      | Indonesia | Korea | Malaysia | Philippines | Thailand |
|------|-----------|-------|----------|-------------|----------|
| 1994 | 31.1 | 37.0 | 41.2 | 24.1 | 40.3 |
| 1995 | 31.9 | 37.7 | 43.6 | 22.5 | 42.1 |
| 1996 | 30.7 | 38.9 | 41.5 | 24.0 | 41.8 |
| 1997 | 31.8 | 36.0 | 43.0 | 24.8 | 33.7 |
| 1998 | 16.8 | 25.0 | 26.7 | 20.3 | 20.4 |
| 1999 | 11.4 | 29.1 | 22.4 | 18.8 | 20.5 |
| 2000 | 22.2 | 31.0 | 26.9 | 21.2 | 22.8 |
| 2001 | 22.0 | 29.3 | 24.4 | 19.0 | 24.1 |
| 2002 | 21.4 | 29.1 | 24.8 | 17.7 | 23.8 |
| 2003 | 25.6 | 30.0 | 22.8 | 16.8 | 24.9 |
| 2004 | 24.1 | 30.4 | 23.0 | 16.7 | 26.8 |
| 2005 | 25.1 | 29.7 | 20.0 | 14.6 | 31.4 |
| 2006 | 25.4 | 29.9 | 20.5 | 14.5 | 28.3 |
| 2007 | 24.9 | 29.4 | 21.7 | 15.4 | 26.4 |
| 2008 | 27.8 | 31.2 | 19.1 | 15.2 | 28.9 |
| 2009 | 31.0 | 25.9 | 14.0 | 14.0 | 21.9 |

Source: ADB, *Asian Development Outlook.*

technical capacity. A critical issue is whether the AEC will be able to help address some of the problems that have constrained private sector response to the opportunities provided by greater openness.

## Private Sector Involvement in the ASEAN Economic Community

The private sector is the driver of economic growth in most ASEAN member countries. The ASEAN business community, primarily through its investments, promotes economic growth, thereby supplying revenue to the economy, creating jobs, and bringing in technology and innovation. The government's main role is to provide a conducive business environment to encourage investment.

The same roles are played out in the process of global and regional economic integration. Member states implement measures to provide a good investment climate, which includes the elimination of behind-the-border, at-the-border, and across-the-border constraints to business; and to ensuring a more liberalized regional market. The progress of the integration process initially comes from the cooperation between governments and, to a lesser extent, the private sector. Later on, the business community should provide recommendations and direction for policymaking. Collaboration with the government also involves helping develop infrastructure, where private sector support is much needed. This would indicate an increasingly significant role for the private sector in the process of economic integration. For ASEAN economic integration to progress, public and private sector consultations should continue and the operation of businesses should incorporate the private sector's commitment to support economic integration in the ASEAN region.

### Commitments Under the AEC

One of the areas of cooperation is enhancing private sector involvement in the building of the AEC. In the AEC Blueprint, the participation of the private sector is identified in certain elements of the AEC:

- Under free flow of goods: Harmonization of standards, technical regulations, and conformity assessment procedures will be implemented through the ASEAN Policy Guideline on Standards and Conformance, where ASEAN calls for active participation (in terms of feedback) from the private sector.
- Under free flow of investment: The ASEAN Comprehensive Investment Agreement is a development of the Framework Agreement on the ASEAN Investment Area, which implemented investment cooperation; and the ASEAN Investment Guarantee Agreement, which implemented investment promotion and protection. In one of its pillars — facilitation and cooperation — one of the actions is consultation with ASEAN private sectors to facilitate investment.
- Under the priority integration sectors: The priority sectors are expected to be the catalyst for ASEAN economic integration and where resources will be initially focused. The task involves the identification of sector-specific projects or initiatives, which would result from regular dialogue or consultation with stakeholders, the private sector, in particular.

- Under food, agriculture, and forestry: To enhance intra- and extra-ASEAN trade and long-term competitiveness in these products, ASEAN encourages cooperation, joint approaches, collaborative research, and technology transfer among ASEAN member countries, organizations, and the private sector. Specifically, the recommendation is to use strategic alliances and joint approaches with the private sector to promote food safety, investment, and joint ventures, as well as promote agricultural products and market access.

- Under infrastructure development: The private sector is one resource to tap in energy and mining cooperation. One plan of action is to increasingly involve the private sector in the ASEAN Power Grid and the Trans-ASEAN Gas Pipeline projects, which aim at optimizing and securing the region's energy sources. The private sector will find investment opportunities in these projects in terms of financing and technology transfer. Likewise in mining, the private sector is encouraged to participate in mineral development. As greater investment is needed in developing regional infrastructure, ASEAN encourages the private sector, as well as international organizations, to increase its involvement in financing regional infrastructure projects, such as the ASEAN Power Grid, Trans-ASEAN Gas Pipeline, and ASEAN Highway Network.

- On implementation: Successful implementation of the programmes and measures in the integration process include partnership arrangements with the private sector, that is, the business community and industry associations, at both national and regional levels and, effectively, the participation of all stakeholders.

### Organized Private Sector Support in ASEAN

Economic leaders have acknowledged the important role of the business sector in formulating policies and actions in the process of integration. They get the views and recommendations of the private sector through business advisory councils. The ASEAN business community is a part of two business advisory councils: the APEC Business Advisory Council (ABAC) and the ASEAN Business Advisory Council (ASEAN-BAC).

ABAC is the private sector arm of Asia-Pacific Economic Cooperation (APEC), wherein ASEAN is a member. It is composed of top business and industry leaders convened by the APEC leaders. ABAC advises APEC leaders, through its reports and dialogue with both government and the private sector, on ways to improve the business and investment environment and to make sure the whole region reaps the benefits of globalization.

ABAC reports contain sentiments and proposals of the business community with respect to measures to liberalize trade and eliminate investment barriers. From discussions with the business community, ABAC has put together in its reports, recommendations to APEC leaders in different areas such as investment promotion; the facilitation of the movement of goods, labour, and investment; deepening and strengthening capital markets; the facilitation of trade agreements through the harmonization of standards; security in energy; the protection of intellectual property rights; the development of information communication technology; fighting corruption; post-crisis recovery measures; impact of climate change; the promotion of corporate social responsibility (ABAC 2007; 2008; 2009).

Evident is ABAC's support for liberalization in international markets as it has been constantly supporting WTO negotiations. But with the business community's frustration with the stalled Doha Development Agenda negotiations, ABAC initiated the examination of the possibility of an FTAAP (Free Trade Area of the Asia Pacific) as a regional alternative.

ABAC has also acknowledged the significant contribution of small and medium enterprises (SMEs), especially in job creation. For that reason, ABAC has continuously been in full support of and advocacy for enhancing SME and micro-enterprise development in APEC.

Furthermore, in the APEC annual meeting in 2010, ABAC recommended a new vision for economic integration in APEC (ABAC 2010b). That is, the flow of goods, services, investment, technology, and people will be liberalized consistently, with the evolving nature of regional supply chains and value chains in the Asia Pacific region. In this new vision, ABAC highlighted that the business community be closely involved and the links between ABAC and APEC senior officials be more defined and integrated. The business community's expertise can help policymakers in devising prudent initiatives and feasible solutions. A step towards this is the recent launching of a web-based gateway to information on tariffs and rules of origin, after a consultation with the business community found a lack of customs transparency in APEC (ABAC 2010a). With such readily available information, businesses can then take full advantage of special arrangements in the various free trade agreements.

In 2003 ASEAN heads of state and government established an assembly of top business and industry leaders — the ASEAN-BAC — whose primary mission is to promote public-private partnership in the process of integration and in the steps towards an ASEAN Economic Community (AEC). The main objectives of the ASEAN-BAC are (1) to provide private sector feedback and guidance to boost ASEAN's efforts towards economic integration and (2) to identify priority areas for consideration by ASEAN leaders. Accordingly, its activities are to (1) review/identify issues to facilitate and promote economic cooperation and integration, (2) submit annual recommendations for the consideration of the ASEAN heads of state and government, and (3) organize the annual ASEAN Business and Investment Summit (ASEAN-BIS) to coincide with the annual ASEAN Summits.

ASEAN-BIS is held annually to gather government and private sector organization and industry representatives in an interactive venue to come up with initiatives and action plans to boost productivity and competitiveness and enhance cooperation and integration in the region. This shows that the business community is a significant partner of ASEAN in meeting its objectives. ASEAN-BIS has been host to dialogues and discussions on the ASEAN business climate, growth areas, and integration efforts; opportunities in ASEAN regional partnerships; industry-specific integration in ASEAN; developing ASEAN's global competitive advantage; and enhancing cooperation with the international community. In 2009 ASEAN-BIS focused on the first-year implementation of the AEC Blueprint as well as tackled concerns and responses of the private sector with regard to the global financial and economic crisis. In the ASEAN-BIS dialogues, emphasis is likewise given to encouraging the international business community to appreciate ASEAN business and investment opportunities and to develop joint ventures and bring investments into the region.

One major achievement of the ASEAN-BAC is its contribution to the realization of an AEC Blueprint, which has benefited from the recommendations of the Task Force on Economic Integration, one of the various committees set up by the business council in fulfilling its mandate.

The cooperation between officials and business advisory councils (ABAC and ASEAN-BAC) has produced initiatives and actions towards deeper regional integration. Therefore, continuous close interaction between governments and the business community is important in strengthening regional economic integration. In essence, the private sector and the government are involved in a symbiotic relationship. The business community (represented by business advisory councils, sectoral, and working groups) provides guidance and direction to the government (represented by the country leaders, ministers, senior officials, committee on trade and investment, and others); and conversely, the government acts on the recommendations and implements them for a better environment and more liberalized market for business. With improved conditions for business, the private sector can be expected to invest, compete, and innovate; and thereby contribute to efficiency and, subsequently, growth in the community.

## The European Union Experience[1]

The European Union is one example of economic integration that demonstrates a single market that has established a borderless community with goods, services, people, and capital being able to move freely and has brought marked increases in intratrade in goods and services. The European Union progressed from a common market to a single market to a monetary union. It has twenty-seven member states, seventeen of which use the euro as currency.

The European Union's move towards a single market was warmly welcomed and strongly supported by the business community. This is considered one factor that induced both economic and political integration in the European Union. Jorgensen (1999) explained some rationale following this support from the European business community:

> Firstly, it was in the interest of the businessmen of the member states to move toward a common market first, a single market later and finally to an economic and monetary union. Secondly, it is part of the entrepreneur's ideals (let's say of the Schumpeterian entrepreneur) to avoid economic sclerosis and always move forward, towards new and more advanced equilibria, not only in the economic and technological field, but also in the institutional field.

Critics had suspected that the European Union's move towards a single market would build a Fortress Europe. In principle, this was possible. The European business community can appeal for protection from competition, and trade unions may opt to guard insiders at the expense of outsiders. Such a state of affairs could have encouraged strategic capitalism and national champions in the European Union.

As it turns out, the European business community did not seek protection from the state (union). The European market is big in itself, but eventually a closed and protected system for Europe would have resulted in missed opportunities in a bigger and dynamic global market. Moreover, a Fortress Europe would have meant lower growth and higher unemployment in the long run.

It was not without consequence to business when the integration of the European market proceeded. For instance, when national standards and the classification system that previously protected inefficient industries were harmonized, inefficient firms were wiped out by competition from foreign firms. But with an enlarged market of opportunities, the firms that survived and new firms that entered overshadowed the losses from the structural reforms.

The private sector bore the brunt of restructuring, but it recognized the necessity and has in fact become a part of the decision-making process. There were close consultations between European institutions and the business community that brought in initiatives and innovations in the process of European integration. In the discussions, each party was given autonomy and "no bargaining" or conditional agreements took place (for example, approve more liberalized markets in exchange for a relaxed competition policy). The roles are quite clear, the business sector used its efforts and participation in the decision-making process to focus on how to increase market liberalization while the European Commission took in ideas from the business community to use in formulating action plans. Several consultative committees were set up to tackle various issues as well as to ensure that information flows smoothly and stakeholders decide on issues with much deliberation.

In dialogues, the business or industry associations played an intermediary role between individual businesses and the government. On the one hand, business associations represented the interest of their members through which businesses could collectively influence the government. On the other hand, they could also be agents through which the government could influence business, for instance, in terms of disseminating information or building partnerships pertinent to business. With European integration, business associations and government information exchange developed at the national level and carried on up to the European level (Bennett 1997).

After forty years of European integration, a new and growing role for the European business community has developed. The European institutions are increasingly dependent on private sector initiatives with regard to market liberalization and safeguarding stakeholders (e.g., consumers). Businesses and trade unions are given more participation in social legislation, and NGOs are also increasingly involved in decisions related to development projects in developing/less-developed countries. For its part, the European and national institutions are playing a supervisory role, making sure that decisions are carried out while keeping the concerned sectors and entities functioning in order, with a view to integration, and not to the detriment of outsiders.

## Private Sector in ASEAN and the Philippines

The role of the private sector in ASEAN economic integration is clear-cut. The European Union experience provides a useful template. Some existing processes — ABAC and ASEAN-BAC — emulate the European Union example. This section discusses the extent to which the private sector has lived up to its role. Usage of FTAs gives a snapshot from the ASEAN perspective. A comprehensive study conducted by the Asian Development Bank (ADB) assessed the capacity of the private sector in the Philippines. Another ADB study looked into the critical development constraints that limit private investment and entrepreneurship. The next section attempts to explain these outcomes.

### Private Sector Usage of FTAs

Free trade agreements (FTAs) appear as a fundamental step towards regional integration. Arrangements in free trade agreements, such as the elimination of tariffs and other barriers, are intended for the benefit of businesses to trade within the region with more ease and less risks or costs. By using these arrangements, the private sector demonstrates its involvement and commitment to the process of economic integration.

Data show relatively low usage of AFTA (ASEAN Free Trade Area) preferences in 1998–99 (Figure 15.1). Overall, less than 3 per cent of intra-ASEAN trade used the AFTA preferential rates. It was found that most traders were inclined to pay the MFN (most favoured nation) applied rate, which meant avoiding the administrative costs and delays in availing CEPT (Common Effective Preferential Tariff) rates, or taking advantage

**FIGURE 15.1**
**AFTA Utilization Rates**
(per cent of Intra-ASEAN imports)

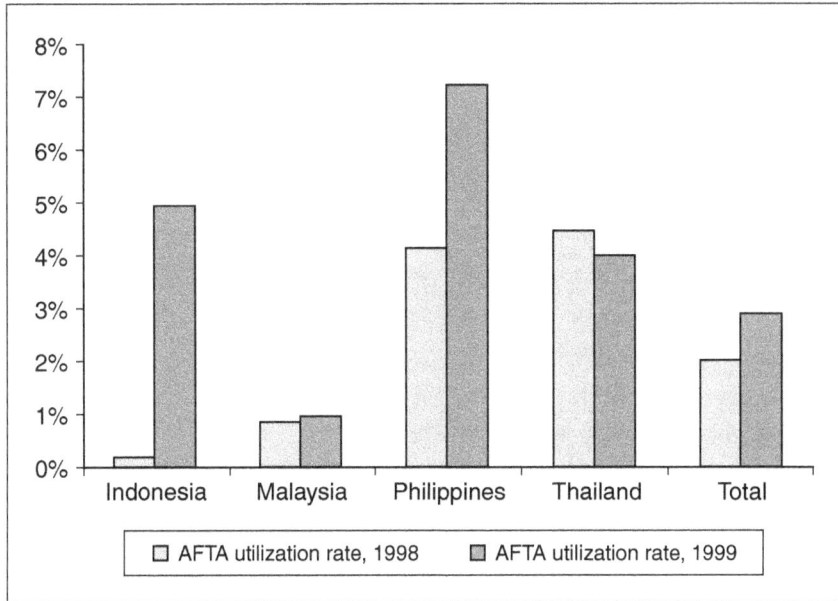

*Source:* Baldwin (2007).

of duty drawback or duty-free programmes in export processing zones and other investment incentive schemes.

Using a different measure, a JETRO (Japan External Trade Organization) (2004) report claimed that the share of CEPT exports to total ASEAN exports more than doubled from 10.8 per cent in 2002 to 22.5 per cent in 2003. This indicated an increase in the utilization of CEPT rates in the early 2000s.

Specifically for the Philippines, usage of AFTA ranges from 15 to 17 per cent, depending on the measure applied. Avila and Manzano (2007, as cited by Wignaraja et al. 2010), using computations based on the amount indicated in certificates of origin over value of trade, reported an overall utilization rate of 15 per cent for Philippine exporters, with users mostly in the transport sector. Meanwhile, based on certificates of origin issued and used by Philippine exporters, data in 2007 revealed

**TABLE 15.4**
**Use of Certificates of Origin in the Port of Manila, 2007**

| Certificates of Origin | Entries | % of Total |
|---|---|---|
| GSP Form A | 21,443 | 28.4 |
| **CEPT Form D** | **12,828** | **17.0** |
| General CO (White) | 40,659 | 53.9 |
| ACFTA | 507 | 0.7 |
| Total | 75,437 | 100.0 |

*Source:* Table 6, Medalla and Balboa (2009), based on data from Export Division, Port of Manila, Bureau of Customs.

a 17 per cent usage of the certificate of origin for CEPT out of the total certificates of origin (Table 15.4).

In a survey of Japanese-affiliated firms operating in ASEAN, Hiratsuka et al. (2009) found that the level of usage of FTA in the Philippines, measured as the percentage of firms in the country using FTAs, is relatively low (Table 15.4). In terms of exporting firms, usage remained at around 15 per cent in 2006–07, and declined to 11.8 per cent in 2008, but this was hypothesized to be part of the business cycle (Medalla and Balboa 2009). The table shows that, together with Vietnam, the Philippines posted low utilization rates compared with the rest of ASEAN, in terms of both export and import operations.

Overall AFTA utilization rates for ASEAN's export operations in 2006–08 are 19.7 per cent, 19.3 per cent, and 23.0 per cent, respectively (Table 15.5); but this is considered low compared with that in NAFTA (North American Free Trade Agreement), considering that the rules of origin criterion in ASEAN is less restrictive than in NAFTA. These findings suggest that the administrative costs for using AFTA are high as a result of complex and inefficient administrative procedures, which could particularly explain the low AFTA utilization rate in the Philippines.

A more recent study by Wignaraja et al. (2010) assessed the impact of FTAs on Philippine businesses by looking at the usage of AFTA by firms in the Philippine transport, electronics, and food sectors. A survey of 155 firms from the three sectors indicated that 20 per cent of these firms used AFTA, and 41 per cent plan to use FTAs. The survey also revealed that Philippine firms view FTAs as a means of increasing market access

**TABLE 15.5**
**Utilization of FTA\* by Japanese-Affiliated Companies**

|  | Exporting companies | | | Importing companies | | |
|---|---|---|---|---|---|---|
|  | 2006 | 2007 | 2008 | 2006 | 2007 | 2008 |
| ASEAN (total) | 19.7 | 19.3 | 23.0 | 16.0 | 16.7 | 19.7 |
| Indonesia | 18.5 | 14.7 | 35.9 | 20.8 | 17.7 | 28.7 |
| Singapore | 32.5 | 27.3 | 43.2 | ... | ... | ... |
| Thailand | 18.2 | 18.8 | 22.5 | 17.7 | 14.9 | 25.3 |
| **Philippines** | **15.2** | **15.7** | **11.8** | **10.8** | **11.4** | **8.0** |
| Vietnam | 6.6 | 14.3 | 9.4 | 9.5 | 24.0 | 12.5 |
| Malaysia | 26.8 | 23.0 | 23.8 | 15.7 | 19.3 | 20.0 |

*Note:* \* ASEAN as FTA partner.
*Source:* Hiratsuka et al. (2009).

and hence have shown interest in ASEAN's FTAs with China (especially for the food sector), Japan, Korea, and the European Union.

Findings further revealed high AFTA utilization rates in the transport sector, in the domestic firms, and in the large firms. Across sectors, users of AFTA were mostly from the transport sector (38.9 per cent of firms), followed by food (18.6 per cent), and electronics (11.8 per cent). The high margin of preference (5–43 per cent) in transport products and the successful implementation of the ASEAN Industrial Cooperation (AICO) are believed to explain the high AFTA utilization in the transport sector. In the AICO scheme,[2] firms can receive special preferential rates of 0–5 per cent. The transport firms claimed that AFTA's preferential rates allowed them to import cheaper raw materials and components, hence reducing production costs.

Domestic firms were also found to have higher AFTA utilization than foreign firms, as it is presumed that the latter export to countries such as the European Union and the United States where the Philippines has no outstanding FTA. Large firms were found to use AFTA preferential rates more than the smaller firms since the former gain more relatively because they export more, have export departments that handle documentation requirements for FTA compliance, or are required to do so, for example, for their production networks, or as subsidiaries or suppliers of multinational corporations (MNCs).

In addition, firms which use, have used, or plan to use AFTA reported that FTAs have influenced or motivated them to change their business plans and strategies to adapt to FTAs. Firms consider increased market access a major benefit of using FTAs. They have also attuned their business plans to the FTA market. Findings revealed that AFTA users and those who plan to use it — particularly for SMEs covered in the survey — have changed or plan to change their business plans in response to FTAs. As the SMEs have low AFTA utilization rates, the high rate of business response may reflect the SMEs' means to survive through new product development or intensified marketing.

Major reasons for low utilization or non-usage of AFTA are related to costs and delays associated with rules of origin compliance and AFTA's low margin of preference, which falls below 5 per cent for most of ASEAN, and the overall margin of preference far off the 5 per cent threshold (Medalla and Balboa 2009). However, some analysts also cite low awareness of the tariff scheme, which is now streamlined under the ASEAN Trade in Goods Agreement, as the primary reason for the low usage rate.[3]

AFTA's margins of preference on high-trade-volume goods (e.g., computer/machinery and electrical equipment) are found to be too small (about 0–1.5 per cent) to compensate for the administrative costs and delays of availing preferential tariffs (Baldwin 2007). MFN tariffs on high-trade-volume goods in ASEAN are very low (less than 2 per cent). In the European Union and NAFTA, if the MFN rate is low, exporting firms are inclined to pay the MFN rate even if administrative procedures or delays in complying with the rules of origin are of little cost to them.

In the Philippine study by Wignaraja et al. (2010), the low use of AFTA in the food sector was likewise attributed to small margins of preference, while in the electronics sector, low or zero MFN tariff rates and investment schemes available in export processing zones (e.g., duty-free importation and tax and non-tax incentives) or outside processing zones (e.g., tax holidays for customs manufacturing bonded warehouses) give little motivation to use AFTA preferential rates.

Moreover, the textile industry seemed to use FTA more, unlike the electronics and precision machinery industries where general tariffs are already low (Hiratsuka et al. 2009). This again illustrates that the margin between the MFN tariffs and the FTA preferential tariffs gives incentive to firms to utilize FTAs. A substantial reduction in FTA preferential tariffs may encourage non-participating firms or industries to start using FTAs in their business operations.

## Assessment of Philippine Private Sector

A study conducted by the Asian Development Bank (2005) determined that the private sector dominates the Philippine economy, generating on average 95 per cent of the nations GDP and employing 92 per cent of the registered workforce. The study cited the benefits of the openness model in terms of encouraging private sector participation in the power sector, telecommunications, and water supply. However, as mentioned in the introductory part, the openness model did not generate the economic transformation experienced by many other economies in the region. This is highlighted by the consistent fall in the investment rate from 2000 to 2009.

The ADB attributes this to the deteriorating investment climate in the Philippines. This is characterized by growing fiscal deficits, vested interests that appear to increasingly influence both legislative and judicial proceedings, and the weakness of the public sector in creating and enforcing freely competitive and/or regulated markets.

The private sector assessment was followed by another ADB study which revealed the following critical constraints to private investment and entrepreneurship:

- Tight fiscal situation;
- Inadequate infrastructure, particularly in electricity and transportation;
- Weak investor confidence due to governance concerns, in particular, corruption and political instability; and
- Inability to address market failures, leading to a small and narrow industrial base (ADB 2007, pp. 49–50).

## Impact of the AEC

This section looks into the impact of the AEC in terms of addressing some of these fundamental constraints. For the most part, these factors will prevent the private sector from participating actively in the AEC and will limit the benefits to the Philippines. Hence, policy measures that will increase utilization of ASEAN agreements and other FTAs flow directly from the above list of critical constraints (e.g., measures to expand fiscal space and improve physical infrastructure).

The most promising development related to the AEC is the establishment of the National Single Window (NSW) in the Philippines, which is related to trade facilitation. Planning and implementation of the project was overseen by a steering committee led by the Department of Finance and composed of agencies linked to the Bureau of Customs. The National Single Window project is expected to substantially speed up customs processing for importers and exporters, and enhance transparency and efficiency in transactions with the Bureau of Customs.

The mandate for a national single window emanates from ASEAN agreements including the Agreement to Establish and Implement the ASEAN Single Window (ASW), signed by ASEAN trade ministers in December 2005, the Protocol to Establish and Implement ASW, signed by finance ministers in December 2006, and the ASEAN Economic Community Blueprint signed by President Gloria Macapagal Arroyo in November 2007. Among the obligations of the contracting parties in these agreements is to ensure that line ministries and agencies cooperate with and provide information to lead agencies and make use of ICT in their national single windows to further expedite customs procedures within ASEAN.

In March 2010 there was a soft launch of the NSW system for ten agencies. The activities accomplished thus far include network connection work for Metro Manila agencies, executive briefings to department and agency heads, agency and importer system training, and on-site system support for agency users. Some agencies started to go live as early as May 2010 and thirty-one agencies were targeted to go live by July 2010.

## Understanding the Private Sector in the Philippines

### Response of Philippine Private Sector to AEC

The view of the Philippine private sector about the AEC can be discerned from the following statement of the Philippine Chamber of Commerce and Industry about the full implementation of AFTA-CEPT by 2010:[4]

> Given this, while supportive of efforts to deepen integration and further the liberalization of the country vis-à-vis the ASEAN region, the Philippine Chamber of Commerce and Industry, the recognized voice of Philippine business, recommends the deferment of the Philippines' accession to the full implementation of the AFTA-CEPT in 2010. We agree with the 5-year deferment proposed by Secretary Arthur Yap of the Department

of Agriculture. We call for the retention of status quo for ALL sectors to give time to domestic manufacturing and agricultural industries to enhance their efficiency and competitiveness.

For the commodities which remain in the sensitive list but are to be lowered to the 0–5 per cent tariff level by 2010 namely swine, poultry corn, sugar and rice, the last two considered most sensitive products, we agree with the position of the Fair Trade Alliance (FTA) and strongly recommend the highest trade flexibility to ensure food and livelihood security.

We strongly recommend the adoption of safeguard measures such as trade remedies, non-tariff barriers and effective anti-smuggling mechanisms to accompany liberalization efforts and to provide protection to domestic industries against the influx of imports and smuggling. This should be done on top of the implementation of a status quo for the reduction or total elimination of tariffs under the CEPT regime.

Underlying the industries' problem is the cost of doing business in the country; the cost of production in countries such as Thailand, Indonesia, Malaysia and Vietnam, is substantially lower than in the Philippines, hence the difficulty of competing with the prices of other major producers from the region.

The statement reflects the ambivalence of the private sector with regard to the openness model of development. While it is true that inadequate infrastructure is a major constraint, many sectors were also given time to adjust to greater competition. Thus, while part of the analysis makes it appear that the constraints are extraneous to the private sector, and all that is required is for government to provide good governance and address supply side constraints, it would be useful to look into the "deeper" constraints to economic growth.

### The Private Sector as Part of the Problem

An interesting issue would be whether institutional factors can partly explain the low investment rate (Table 15.3). This was recently attempted by Bocchi (2008) when he analysed why investment in the Philippines did not respond to higher economic growth in 2005–07. One major reason is the dominance of corporate conglomerates in strategic sectors such as agriculture, maritime and air transport, power, cement, and banking. These corporate conglomerates do not have an incentive to invest and expand their operations since their main source of profitability is a captured market. In turn, the resulting higher costs in these sectors discourage investment in sectors that have strong backward and forward linkages with them, particularly in manufacturing.

The analysis of Bocchi dovetails with the finding of Felipe and Lanzona (2006) that even at the height of trade liberalization, the degree of monopolization of the economy was increasing. As evidence they point to an increasing trend in the price-markup ratio between 1980 and 2003. These results corroborate what is well known about the Philippines, that is, the country is characterized by a lack of a "culture of competition". Monopolies and cartels are accepted as a part of doing business, an attitude that can be readily explained by institutional factors.

A case in point is the Philippine aviation industry. While the adoption of the open sky policy may be well on track, new entrants have to contend with the uneven playing field in the Philippine aviation market, which is largely dominated by Philippine Airlines (PAL), which still receives fiscal incentives and other unconditional guarantees it once enjoyed as a government corporation (Aldaba 2008). Furthermore, terminal space and landing slots are dominated by PAL, which managed to secure sole ownership of an airport terminal originally intended to serve as the country's domestic terminal. The allegation of institutional weakness and regulatory capture is also observed in the failure of the Civil Aeronautics Board (CAB) to collect from PAL the mandated regulatory fees. CAB, a government regulatory agency charged with the supervision and regulation of air carriers, has likewise been accused of interfering in favour of PAL in bilateral air rights negotiations (Rimando 2008).

By allegedly controlling the country's "gateways" through CAB (and its "zero sum" policy), PAL has not only ignored the needs of millions of overseas Filipino workers for frequent, cheaper, and shorter flights, but has shunned inconceivable economic opportunities and benefits for the Philippines from potential tourists, and trade and business linkages (Rimando 2008).

Another example of institutional weakness is in the Philippine power sector. Despite the moves to deregulate the country's energy sector through the passage of the Electric Power Industry Reform Act of 2001, there remains a cap on foreign ownership and cross-ownership, and the congressional franchise requirement on energy transmission and distribution. This casts doubt not only on the effectiveness of the act, but also on the capability of the Energy Regulatory Board to regulate the market and apprehend erring agents. Already a large private electricity distributor has been accused of favouring allied companies, essentially subsidizing costly and inefficient firms, with consumers ending up paying higher energy prices (SEPO 2009).

The Philippines may have made significant strides in deregulating the telecommunications industry, but cases of abuse of power by a dominant player are well documented. The Philippine Long Distance Company owns the backbone facility and has the most number of fixed-line subscribers. The company has been accused by other carriers of exploiting its market power by allegedly delaying interconnection, granting unequal access, and predatory pricing.

In addition to these, the latest government pronouncements such as the passage of Executive Order Nos. 261 and 264, grant protection and safeguard measure on an ad hoc basis to selected manufacturing industries, particularly cement, ceramic tiles, clear float glass, and related sectors where charges of cartel-like practices abound. The apparent reversal to traditional protectionist practices can effectively turn off investors, as this not only implies an unfair and uneven playing field, but also reflects the unreliability and unpredictability of government statutes and institutional weakness in enforcing rules and regulations (Aldaba 2008).

### The Role of Institutions and Culture

Taking advantage of the opportunities provided by the openness model of development requires effective institutions, which are defined as a "system of rules, beliefs, norms, and organizations that together generate a regularity of social behavior".[5] Stable and credible institutions are important for the development of the rule of law, the enforcement of contracts, and the protection of property rights. The latter are important preconditions for the support of anonymous exchange and long-term contracting, especially for credit, venture capital, and technological innovation. Economic development, therefore, is virtually impossible without the appropriate institutional support. The contents of policies themselves assume second-order importance since whether or not policies are taken, and the degree to which they are implemented, become matters that are endogenous to prevailing institutions and political economy (De Dios 2008).

The Philippines is an example of a country where "the exogenous introduction via colonial experience of political and economic institutions amid great and persistent social inequities and a parallel network of informal, personal, and kin-based institutions, clearly placed such institutions beyond the reach of the larger part of the population"

(De Dios 2008, p. 27). As a result, the formal institutions have not been given the proper respect and became largely ineffective. Instead, what became dominant almost by default were primordial institutions, such as the clan or family, or religious and ethnic affiliations, with their workings being superimposed upon the formal political process (De Dios 2008).

Consequently, what evolved in the Philippines was a semi-feudal economy dominated by elite factions. Instead of encouraging competitive behaviour, a culture of "rent-seeking" was engendered. The political and economic elite used state institutions as instruments of wealth accumulation. It was deemed that more money could be made by redistributing wealth through the political process than by actually creating wealth.

This is the context in which the absence of a "culture of competition" can be explained. What has dominated is a national oligarchy (De Dios and Hutchcroft 2003). In this system "there emerged a substantial homogeneity of interests on major issues of economic policy (including, of course, a commitment to prevent genuine land reform) beyond which it was far more advantageous for families to use their influence to gain particularistic favors than to seek generalized policy change favoring the interests of any given sector" (De Dios and Hutchcroft 2003, p. 48).[6]

Weak institutions and an oligarchic private sector are therefore two sides of the same coin. Admittedly the openness model of development has yielded favourable outcomes in terms of less monopolistic power, more diversified economic activities, and a healthier policy debate. However, unless there are major political and social reforms, economic transformation will not be possible.

Future analysis of economic development constraints should consider a multidisciplinary approach that can put more emphasis on the "deep parameters" affecting economic performance. For example, related to the institutional dimension, culture and values can partly explain the lack of social cohesion, spotty entrepreneurship, and the general inability to establish a credible and selfless political leadership in the Philippines. A Weberian framework would certainly cite the inconsistency between religion and capitalist development in the Philippines. Meanwhile, values such as *ningas cogon*[7] have definitely adversely affected economic growth. However, even if this analysis was accurate, effective policy prescriptions would still be elusive.[8] At best, the analysis would yield guidelines that will make policymakers aware of the limitations of economic reforms and enable them to contextualize these reforms.

NOTES

\* The authors acknowledge the assistance provided by Fatima Lourdes E. Del Prado, research specialist at PIDS. The usual disclaimer applies.

1. Largely based on Jorgensen (1999).

2. The AICO scheme is an industrial cooperation programme in ASEAN that aims to promote joint activities between ASEAN-based manufacturing firms. A major incentive from this scheme is that AICO products can enjoy preferential tariff rates of 0–5 per cent. Honda Cars Philippines, Toyota Motor Philippines, Philippine Auto Components, Inc., and Ford Motor Company have received special preferential rates of 0–5 per cent from AICO arrangements (Wignaraja et al. 2010).

3. As reported in *Business World*, 25 August 2010 in an article entitled, "Despite Missed Chances, ASEAN Still Good for RP". The author, Jessica Anne D. Hermosa, quotes Dr Ganeshan Wignaraja about the causes of the low usage rate of AFTA.

4. Philippine Chamber of Commerce and Industry, "Position Paper on the Full Implementation of the AFTA-CEPT by 2010 <http://www.philippinechamber. com/index.php?option=com_content&view=article&id=625:pcci-position-on-full-implementation-of-afta-cept-by-2010&catid=34:asean&Itemid=199>.

5. De Dios (2008) citing the definition of A. Greif, *Institutions and Paths to and the Road to the Modern Economy: Lessons from Medieval Trade* (Cambridge University Press, 2005).

6. This was a description of the situation in the Philippines in the mid-1950s, but is applicable to the present day.

7. "Ningas Cogon" is an old Filipino expression which literally means "grass flash-fire". It refers to cogon dry grass which blazes furiously when set alight, but only for a few minutes before turning to cold ashes. When applied to society, it refers to people who are enthusiastic about something, but then lose interest quickly. It applies particularly to personal efforts and business ventures. Some sociologists have cited this as a general weakness of Philippine society, which is inconsistent with successful entrepreneurship.

8. For example, a policy of "changing religions" is not feasible and is actually foolhardy.

REFERENCES

Aldaba, R.M. "Assessing Competition in Philippine Markets". PIDS discussion paper no. 2008–23. Makati City: Philippine Institute for Development Studies, 2008.

APEC Business Advisory Council (ABAC). *2007 APEC Business Advisory Council Report to APEC Leaders*. ABAC, 2007.

————. *2008 APEC Business Advisory Council Report to APEC Leaders*. ABAC, 2008.

————. *2009 APEC Business Advisory Council Report to APEC Leaders*. ABAC, 2009.

————. "APEC Helps Business Take Advantage of FTAs". ABAC news release, 6 June 2010*a* <http://www.abaconline.org>.

————. "Businesses have 5 Recommendations for APEC Trade Ministers". ABAC news release, 1 June 2010*b* <http://www.abaconline.org>.

ASEAN. *ASEAN Economic Community Blueprint*. Jakarta: ASEAN Secretariat, 2008.

————. "The Private Sector in ASEAN's Integration and Competitiveness Initiative: The ASEAN Business Advisory Council". Jakarta: ASEAN Secretariat, 2003 <http://www.aseansec.org/14818.htm>.

Asian Development Bank. *Private Sector Assessment: the Philippines*. Mandaluyong City: Asian Development Bank, 2005.

————. *Philippines: Critical Development Constraints*. Mandaluyong City: Economics and Research Department, Asian Development Bank, December 2007.

Baldwin, R. "Managing the Noodle Bowl: The Fragility of East Asian Regionalism". ADB working paper on Regional Economic Integration 7. Manila: Asian Development Bank, 2007.

Bennett, R. "The Impact of European Economic Integration on Business Associations: The UK Case". West European Politics. Online article. 1997.

Bocchi, A.M. "Rising Growth, Declining Investment: The Puzzle of the Philippines". Policy research working paper 4472. Washington, DC: World Bank, 2008.

De Dios, E.S. "Institutional Constraints on Philippine Growth". UP School of Economics discussion paper 0806. July 2008.

De Dios, E.S. and P.D. Hutchcroft. "Political Economy", in *The Philippine Economy: Development, Policies and Challenges*, edited by A.M. Balisacan and H. Hill. Quezon City: Ateneo de Manila University Press, 2003.

Felipe, J. and L. Lanzona. "Unemployment, Labor Laws, and Economic Policies in the Philippines", in *Labor Markets in Asia: Issues and Perspectives*, edited by J. Felipe and R. Hasan. London: Palgrave Macmillan for the Asian Development Bank, 2006.

Hiratsuka, D., K. Hayakawa, K. Shiino, and S. Sukegawa. "Maximizing Benefits from FTAs in ASEAN" 2009 <http://www.eria.org/pdf/research/y2008/no1/DEI-Ch11.pdf>.

Human Development Network. *Philippine Human Development Report 2008/2009: Institutions, Politics and Human Development*. Manila: Human Development Network, 2009.

Japan External Trade Organization (JETRO). "ASEAN's FTAs and Rules of Origin". Tokyo: JETRO, 2004.

Jorgensen, O. "The Role of Business in European Integration". Speech delivered at the 20th Annual Conference of the European Union Studies Association, 1999 <http://www.deljpn.ec.europa.eu/home/speech_en_Speech%2015/99.php>.

Medalla, E. and J. Balboa. "ASEAN Rules of Origin: Lessons and Recommendations for Best Practice". ERIA discussion paper 2009–17. Jakarta: ERIA, 2009.

Rimando, L. "PAL Controls Gateways Through CAB, Say Experts". ABS-CBN News, 2 March 2008 <http://www.abs-cbnnews.com/03/02/08/pal-controls-gateways-through-cab-say-experts> (accessed 10 April 2010).

Senate Economic Planning Office (SEPO). "Regulating Competition". Policy brief PB 09–04. Manila: Senate Economic Planning Office, 2009 <http://www.senate.gov.ph/publications/PB%202009-04%20-%20Regulating%20competition.pdf>.

UNCTAD. *Trade Development Report: Policy Coherence, Development Strategies and Integration into the World Economy*. Geneva: UNCTAD, 2004.

Wignaraja, G., D. Lazaro, and G. De Guzman. "FTAs and the Philippine Business: Evidence from Transport, Food, and Electronics Firms". ADB working paper 185. Tokyo: Asian Development Bank Institute, 2010.

# 16

# Role of the Singapore Private Sector in ASEAN Economic Integration

Juliana Giam

With the ASEAN governments increasingly calling on the region's private sector to play its part in regional economic integration, the weightage of the role of the business community has become intrinsic to ASEAN's economic aspirations. As a result, the ASEAN private sector is made more conscious of its place in the process of regional economic integration. However, a certain tension arises from the divergence between ASEAN's economic aspirations and the private sector's experience of those aspirations. At the local level, public-private sector partnership in the respective ASEAN countries varies in its degree of intensity.

A perspective on the role of the Singapore private sector in ASEAN economic integration serves to provide an indication of its involvement. In this context, consideration is given to the effectiveness of ASEAN economic agreements as perceived by the business community, their impact on trade and investment decisions, and prospects for achieving the ASEAN Economic Community (AEC) by 2015.

## The Singapore Business Federation

The scope of the topic is to be defined to set the framework of discussion. For the purpose of the perspective being delineated, the Singapore private sector will be taken to mean the private sector which is institutionalized at the apex level across domestic ethnic lines, across foreign business groups, and across industry sectors. Such a definition is realized in the Singapore Business Federation (SBF), the apex business chamber in Singapore.

The vision of the SBF, established in 2002, is to be the voice of the Singapore business community locally and to the world, creating business value for its members. Its mission is to act as the bridge between the government and business in Singapore to create and enhance a conducive business environment. SBF represents the business community in bilateral, regional, and multilateral forums for the purpose of promoting trade expansion and business networking. It represents more than 18,000 companies, as well as the local and foreign business chambers, the key national and industry associations from business sectors that contribute significantly to the Singapore economy.

By extension, the involvement of the Singapore private sector at the apex level in ASEAN economic integration would be through the SBF's constituted position in the high-level ASEAN private sector organizations that are institutionalized across generic industry lines. These regional business organizations, in turn, contribute to ASEAN economic integration by their access to the ASEAN governments. As a subtext, it should be recognized that there exist various industry-specific associations and certain foreign business chambers in Singapore that contribute to ASEAN economic integration through membership of their respective regional business associations which provide input to the ASEAN governments.

At the level of the SBF, ASEAN business organizations in which it is engaged comprise (1) the ASEAN Business Advisory Council (ASEAN-BAC) and (2) ASEAN Chambers of Commerce and Industry (ASEAN-CCI). These regional private sector organizations include in their ambit the range of business interests at the apex regional level.

The ASEAN Business Advisory Council, the highest-level ASEAN private sector organization, is the business advisory group mandated by ASEAN governments. It aims to provide private sector feedback on the implementation of ASEAN economic integration and identify priority areas for the consideration of ASEAN leaders. Established in 2003, ASEAN-BAC comprises three high-level CEOs of companies from each ASEAN member country appointed by the respective member country. ASEAN-BAC submits its recommendations during a dialogue with ASEAN leaders at the ASEAN Summit on an annual basis. It also has an annual consultation with the ASEAN Economic Ministers.

On its part, the ASEAN Chambers of Commerce and Industry is the regional chamber of commerce and industry formed by the apex business chambers of ASEAN in 1972. Its objectives are to accelerate economic growth and progress in the region through joint approaches, endeavours, and actions to strengthen the foundation and coordination for the enhancement of the communities of ASEAN; foster closer relations and cooperation between and among constituent members; provide mutual assistance in matters of common interest in the solution of economic problems in the area; and maintain closer relations and cooperation with regional and international organizations having similar aims and objectives.

With regard to dialogue with the ASEAN governments, ASEAN-CCI is invited to submit its recommendations to ASEAN governments at the level of the ASEAN Economic Ministers at their annual meeting.

Prior to the SBF, the apex business chamber was the Singapore Federation of Chambers of Commerce and Industry (SFCCI), established in 1978. Its primary role culminated in representing Singapore's private sector at the ASEAN level as ASEAN-CCI was then becoming active. The contribution of SFCCI to ASEAN economic integration may be considered on another occasion.

It is clear that in terms of their present roles, ASEAN-BAC has eclipsed ASEAN-CCI. This is particularly as ASEAN-BAC has been established by ASEAN governments and granted access to ASEAN leaders at their regular dialogues. One could also argue that as ASEAN-CCI has recorded a patchy performance with a decline in effectiveness over the years, the establishment of ASEAN-BAC by the ASEAN governments was a predictable outcome.

## SBF's Involvement in ASEAN Economic Integration

SBF's involvement in ASEAN economic integration through ASEAN-BAC and ASEAN-CCI is to be reviewed. In the context of ASEAN-BAC, key highlights of SBF's contribution would include championing the ASEAN

Green Lane project under ASEAN-BAC's initiative of the ASEAN Pioneer Project Scheme (APPS); establishing the ASEAN Business Awards; and initiating an ASEAN-BAC survey on ASEAN competitiveness for submission of findings to ASEAN Leaders.

The APPS aims to nurture the growth of SMEs in the region and offers businesses an avenue for fast-track approval and speedy facilitation across ASEAN. It will cover any business project involving two or more ASEAN countries. ASEAN governments will expedite project approvals and facilitate speedy implementation.

Since the idea of the ASEAN Green Lane project was mooted in 2003, SBF has been leading efforts to promote a seamless flow of goods across ASEAN to achieve an integrated manufacturing value chain and single ASEAN market. The project, complementing the public sector's ASEAN Single Window, aims to provide a paperless flow of goods, including e-security, e-payment, e-declaration, e-clearance, and e-Window. It envisages bringing about optimized efficiency and visibility through the integration of regional customs systems and innovative RFID (radio frequency identification) technology. Such efforts are to provide the competitive edge to ASEAN manufacturers, with smoother cross-border flow of products as against competitors from mainly China and India that can overflow the ASEAN market. The Green Lane initiative enhances the speed-to-market factor that is already supported by the geographical proximity of ASEAN member countries.

As a first step, the Green Lane project was to start as a pilot project between Singapore and Malaysia. Should the outcome yield positive results, it would move on to between Singapore and the Indonesian island of Batam, and between Malaysia and Thailand.

However, to date, the ASEAN Green Lane project has yet to take off. This is despite the ostensibly strong support of ASEAN leaders for the project. Delays have arisen due to vested interests — on the ground and at higher levels. This has drawn a frank comment by an ASEAN leader that even with agreement of the leaders, some decisions are not carried out. It shows up the challenges encountered in private sector initiatives for integration.

As for the ASEAN Business Awards, SBF, during its chairmanship of ASEAN-BAC in 2007, proposed the awards to recognize ASEAN companies that have contributed to the growth of the ASEAN economy, as well as to showcase promising ASEAN SMEs that could be global players. The awards are for the categories of Growth, Employment,

Innovation, and Corporate Social Responsibility. To promote the development of SMEs, a special section has since been created to profile SMEs as distinct from larger-size companies. Although not immediately linked to economic integration, such softer features as the ASEAN Business Awards foster a sense of regionalization as companies are selected based on having operational presence in two or more ASEAN countries. It is telling that the awards continue to attract prominent players in the region.

For direct feedback on how, in the post-crisis scenario, the ASEAN business community views ASEAN competitiveness and economic integration, SBF initiated, and ASEAN-BAC adopted, an ASEAN-BAC survey in May 2010 to obtain such input. The survey was initiated to gauge how businesses in the region view the climate for trade and investment in ASEAN, appraise the effectiveness of ASEAN policy initiatives, identity priority policy measures ASEAN leaders should address, and compare business views across the region. The findings were presented to the ASEAN leaders in October 2010 at the 17th ASEAN Summit in Hanoi, Vietnam.

As for SBF's contribution through ASEAN-CCI, the key indicator would be Singapore's term of ASEAN-CCI presidency from 2004 to 2006. Highlights of its achievements include the presentation of ASEAN-CCI's views to the Eminent Persons Group, formed to advise ASEAN leaders on the ASEAN Charter; the re-establishment of ASEAN-CCI Consultation with ASEAN governments back to the level of the ASEAN Economic Ministers after a palpable hiatus of some years; the re-establishment of linkages, weakened over the years, with the ASEAN-CCI Regional Industry Clubs (RICs) such as the ASEAN Federation of Textile Industries (as offshoots of ASEAN-CCI, RICs have traditionally channelled their input to ASEAN governments through ASEAN-CCI); strengthening relations with ASEAN dialogue partners such as China and Japan. In all, Singapore was credited with the "revitalization" of ASEAN-CCI by the then ASEAN Secretary-General.

Turning to the local level, the Singapore private sector's role in regional integration can also be construed from its involvement in the various ASEAN economic agreements, for example, the utilization of the economic agreements, and the impact of such agreements on business decisions. To this effect, since the signing of the AEC Blueprint in November 2007 in Singapore at the 13th ASEAN Summit, SBF has organized AEC seminars on an annual basis. The aim is to familiarize the business community in Singapore with the objectives of AEC 2015, its impact on business, and how businesses can benefit from the AEC target of transforming ASEAN into a single market and production base by 2015.

In addition, in June-July 2009, SBF supported a survey on ASEAN competitiveness. It covered three key areas related to investment strategies in ASEAN and the rest of the world since the global economic crisis in late 2008: the assessment on the pace of ASEAN economic integration; its importance to investment decisions; and prioritization of policy measures that ASEAN can undertake to improve the region's competitiveness for business investment. The findings of the survey are given in "2009 Business Perceptions on the ASEAN Investment Climate", Working Paper, by Marn-Heong Wong and Ng Kwan Kee, for the Lee Kuan Yew School of Public Policy: Asia Competitiveness Institute, National University of Singapore, in September 2009 (this SBF-supported survey in 2009 led to the ASEAN-BAC survey in 2010).

## Views of the Singapore Business Community

From the various AEC-related activities of SBF and the SBF-supported survey, a profile can be drawn of the views of the Singapore business community on the effectiveness of ASEAN economic agreements in general and the AEC Blueprint in particular, their impact on business decisions, and the prospects of achieving AEC by 2015.

Discussions at the respective AEC activities organized by SBF, reveal that whilst there is a sense of encouragement and wishfulness that ASEAN agreements and AEC 2015 beckon with the advantages of closer integration, such sentiments are at the same time peppered by sheer caution and scepticism. The more optimistic view lies generally in an expanded ASEAN market with the lowering of tariff barriers under the ASEAN Free Trade Area (AFTA), greater liberalization of investment regimes with schemes such as ASEAN Comprehensive Investment Agreement (ACIA), the free flow of services under the ASEAN Framework Agreement of Services (AFAS), the free flow of skilled labour with Mutual Recognition Arrangements (MRAs) for major professional services, and freer flow of capital.

The size of companies seems to affect their views. It is significant that SMEs tend to be in the more optimistic category in relation to regional integration. SME leaders in Singapore have urged fellow companies to expand within the region and to seriously consider investing in ASEAN neighbours for the many benefits that an integrated ASEAN economic community can bring. Their attention has been brought to the combined market size of 600 million, increased business opportunities, and lower business transaction costs.

The advantages that SMEs see include the speed-to-market factor due to geographical proximity, translating to faster delivery times and optimal cost efficiencies among regional production centres and networks in ASEAN. SMEs can in turn outsource less critical work to other SMEs in the lower cost centres. In terms of linkages with larger companies that would increasingly look towards ASEAN's integration, SMEs stand to benefit from positive spin-off effects in the form of more integrated linkages along both the horizontal and vertical supply chain.

The larger players, being more experienced, point out that whilst the ASEAN agreements are being held up as the way forward, delays or non-implementation of signed agreements are too common occurrences. Such phenomena can only adversely affect business confidence in the commitment of ASEAN governments. A popularly cited case in point lies with the ASEAN-China Free Trade Agreement which, on coming into force on 1 January 2010, just as quickly saw Indonesia, the Philippines, and Thailand (at least, some sections of their governments) baulking due to domestic lobby.

A more basic reaction from businesses is tied to the process itself of drawing up the ASEAN economic agreements. An underlying concern is that the agreements are concluded without the involvement of or consultation with the private sector. The governments have been said to prefer to "do their own thing", without taking due cognizance of the needs of the private sector which the agreements are meant to serve. Consequently, there is lack of familiarity or limited knowledge of the workings and details of the agreements and their impact on business.

More detailed views of the Singapore private sector on ASEAN competitiveness are gleaned from the aforementioned working paper. It is from the working paper, hereby gratefully acknowledged as a vital source of data, that significant points of the survey are captured below (with some figures rounded off in this chapter).

In the survey of SBF members (totalling seventy-one companies), the profile of respondents is as follows: about 70 per cent are head-quartered in Singapore, with the rest in developed countries. About 41 per cent, 29 per cent, and 30 per cent were small, medium, and large enterprises respectively, mainly involved in the export of, and investment in, finished goods or services. As background, in relation to choosing which country offers the best prospect for business investment after the crisis, the survey showed that a majority of the medium and large enterprises identified China as the top ranking country. In contrast, about 74 per cent of the small enterprises selected an ASEAN country as the best prospect.

As for the ASEAN region's attractiveness as a market after the crisis, the majority of respondents agreed that the region has become more important as a market for final goods and services, with reduced or slower growth in final demand from markets in developed countries. In terms of company size, more than half of the small firms and less than half of medium and large firms said that the ASEAN region has become more important in comparison with China as a marketplace.

With regard to the region's attractiveness as a production location after the crisis, the majority of respondents (especially the medium and large enterprises) found that the ASEAN region has become less attractive as a production location, with reduced or slower growth in final demand from markets in developed countries. The small enterprises found the region more attractive in this regard. When compared with China, a majority (especially the large enterprises) found that the ASEAN region has become less attractive as a production location. The small enterprises were less likely to agree.

On the issue of how important the implementation of the AEC Blueprint is to companies' decisions to expand investments in the ASEAN region, the views indicated moderate importance placed on the blueprint (on a scale of 1 to 5, with 1 being "not important" and 5 being "very important", the mean importance rating was 3.15). Interestingly enough, the SMEs (nearly 54 per cent) rated the AEC Blueprint as "quite important/very important" in their decisions to expand investment in the ASEAN region, compared with less than one-third of the medium and large enterprises. Thus the views from SMEs which surfaced at the SBF's AEC activities are borne out by the survey findings.

As for the overall assessment of ASEAN's progress in implementing measures to create an AEC, about half of the SBF respondents (the majority from large enterprises) felt that AEC implementation is either "very far behind schedule" or "behind schedule". Respondents felt that the slow pace of AEC implementation is not confined to a minority of ASEAN economies. About 75 per cent indicated that five or more ASEAN economies need to step up their pace of implementation urgently.

On whether ASEAN is likely to create an AEC by 2015, respondents expressed some confidence — with only 18 per cent saying that this is not likely. On average, the response for the prospect of ASEAN achieving the AEC by 2015 lies between "somewhat likely" and "moderately likely" (the mean likelihood rating compiled from responses of 1 to 5 is 2.71 — the mean likelihood rating by size of the enterprise concerned is 2.83, 3.31, and 2.1 for small, medium, and large enterprises respectively).

With regard to priority areas in the implementation of the AEC Blueprint that need to be accelerated, most respondents (nearly 60 per cent) identified "elimination of tariffs and non-tariff barriers to facilitate the free flow of goods" as the most important area for accelerated implementation. The reasons include cost reduction, trade enhancement to increase ASEAN competitiveness as an attractive market and investment destination, and the move towards ASEAN integration.

Other areas such as "elimination of restrictions to trade in services in the priority integration sectors of air transport, e-ASEAN, health care, tourism and logistics services"; "facilitation and cooperation to promote investments, including identifying and working towards areas of complementation ASEAN-wide"; "reform and enhancement of the rules of origin to facilitate the free flow of goods", were chosen as the most important for accelerated implementation in descending order.

In ranking areas in which ASEAN needs to improve to enhance its competitiveness as an attractive location for doing business, respondents identified governance factors as the most important. These areas include political and socio-economic stability, regulatory certainty, a corruption-free environment, and a high level of transparency. Institutional factors, such as tax and legal systems; business environment factors, such as market potential, quality of the environment for innovation and R&D,

were ranked by between 15 and 30 per cent of the respondents as most important. The areas regarded by relatively fewer respondents as most important were manpower; labour factors, such as labour regulations; and physical infrastructure factors, such as land, utilities, transport, and communications.

Overall the survey noted that, in general, there is confidence in ASEAN's attractiveness as a market after the global crisis. However, business views are divided on the importance of the AEC Blueprint in investment decisions in ASEAN and in the assessment of ASEAN's progress in creating AEC 2015. A significant finding is that responses to certain scenarios differ by company size.

## Concluding Comments

In considering the views of the Singapore business community on ASEAN economic integration, certain policy recommendations are put forward as follows:

1. In the context of public-private sector partnership, sustained consultation and involvement of the business community would expedite the process of ASEAN economic integration, especially as the economic agreements impact business. In concrete terms, regular dialogue between the respective Singapore government agencies and business organizations should be scheduled in conjunction with the major ASEAN government meetings, such as the ASEAN Summit, ASEAN Economic Ministers (AEM) Meeting, and ASEAN Senior Economic Officials Meeting. Such interactive engagement could be held before or after these meetings (depending on the issues at hand) to update the business community on the latest ASEAN economic developments and the implications for the private sector. At the same time, input from businesses should surface through such regular dialogue.

2. On the AEC Blueprint in particular, information on the specific gains from the AEC is not known widely among members of the private sector in Singapore. To better inform the private sector and assist enterprises in tackling the challenges of an impending AEC 2015, the government and business organizations could collaborate on programmes to deal with specific integration issues

on a systematic basis. In addition to industry-wide interaction, one approach would be the sectoral approach, that is, addressing concerns of the various industry sectors in line with the ASEAN priority integration sectors of Singapore. Practically, industry sessions could be organized to engage the various sectoral groups on the implications of the AEC and to obtain their feedback.

3. As SMEs form the backbone of the Singapore economy, it is imperative that they grow in tandem with the economic integration of the region. To this end, SME capacity-building programmes and assistance schemes by the government and private sector should be jointly aimed to address the effects of the AEC Blueprint on Singapore SMEs precisely. Such schemes are to be reviewed by all stakeholders on a continuous basis for SMEs to thrive in a more liberal regional environment. In the context of ease of doing business, SMEs would benefit from supply chain integration within the framework of ASEAN connectivity. Such an enabling environment would improve the capability of SMEs to harness the advantages of integration. Appropriate financial assistance for the respective SME programmes would be required.

4. For overall national coordination, due consideration should be given to the setting up of a national AEC unit under the purview of the Ministry of Trade and Industry. Such a national unit would bring together the various government ministries and agencies to monitor the progress of the specific targets of the AEC Blueprint. It would also track the respective deliverables as they affect corporate Singapore. Pointedly, the unit should be easily accessible to the private sector as a one-stop shop/ depository for timely and updated information on the AEC. Whilst different areas of expertise would naturally rest with different government agencies, a national focal point would at least serve as the initial point of contact from which further references could be sourced.

5. With respect to timelines, the AEC Scorecard needs to be transparent, detailed, and readily available for private sector use. There is untoward loss of business and public confidence resulting from lack of ASEAN credibility as reflected in a scorecard that has been sanitized for public consumption (refer to the first AEC Scorecard published by the ASEAN Secretariat in March 2010). By the same token, the business community is encouraged

that the AEC Scorecard mechanism will be further enhanced by regular consultations with the private sector. It is in the perennial interest of public-private sector partnership to advocate an AEC Scorecard that is pro-business, drawing out publicly not as much the display but more the demands of political commitment.

## NOTE

The opinions expressed are those of the author, and do not represent the opinion of the SBF.

# 17

# Thailand's Perspective on the Role of the Private Sector in the Process of Regional Integration

Eggaluck Suwannakarn and Pisesporn Wasawong

The ASEAN Free Trade Area (AFTA) was one of the first ASEAN attempts towards integration of its member nations. Moving towards a zero-tariff zone between its members is one result many regard as a success to date. Some argued initially that ASEAN nations produced similar products and were prone to compete more than cooperate, but this has proved to be wrong. In fact AFTA has been successful in expanding intraregional trade. For example, in the case of Thailand, the total trade (exports plus imports) with ASEAN nations increased from 17 per cent of her total trade in 1995 to 20 per cent in 2007, and ASEAN became the largest trade partner of Thailand. Thailand's FDI, as well as that of other ASEAN members, increased substantially and in the last five years ASEAN experienced a surge in capital inflows.

With the rise of China and India and in an increasingly globalized world, to remain competitive, ASEAN needs to move further along the integration path. The ASEAN Economic Community (AEC) therefore represents a reaction to global competition and a means of maintaining a balance of trade and investment with China and India. In 2007 ASEAN agreed with the AEC Blueprint, which included plans to continue the integration process towards "a single market" by 2015. Given that the ASEAN Blueprint has been put in place for more than three years, it is timely to examine its progress, including the role of the private sector in the process of ASEAN integration.

This chapter will focus on how Thai private businesses have responded to the single market initiative. The remainder of the chapter is structured as follows. The first section illustrates the level of Thai private business usage of the AFTA. The second section summarizes the private sector's opinions on AFTA usage, using the results of in-depth interviews. Results from questionnaires distributed at a focus group with members of the Thai Chamber of Commerce are provided in the third section. The final section provides recommendations for further implementation and a conclusion.

## Usage of the AFTA by the Thai Private Sector

It is worth noting that while ASEAN has become the largest trading partner of Thai businesses in various sectors (Figure 17.1), some rarely used AFTA privileges. As can be seen in Figure 17.2, many sectors have an AFTA utilization rate[1] of less than 50 per cent during the 2001–09 period. Note also that the companies, in practice, were under no obligation to use the AFTA privileges they received from the Bureau of Trade Preferences. As a result, their officially reported export values can be less than the values they applied for. This means the utilization rates reported in Figure 17.2 can be overestimated.

Table 17.1 shows the sectors that have the highest and lowest AFTA utilization rates between the years 2001–09. Specifically, manufacturers of plaiting material, basketwork, etc. (HS 46) is the sector that on average has the highest AFTA utilization rate, with more than hundred per cent, while some sectors, including manufacturers of pearls, precious stones, metals, coins, etc. and organic chemicals, have average utilization rates as low as 1.6 per cent. At the industry level (Figure 17.3), only nine of thirty-one industries had AFTA utilization rates greater than 50 per cent in 2009. Specifically, the nine industries are vegetable and fruit; paper pulp; wood; air-conditioning and refrigerator; motor vehicles; furniture; garments, silk and animal hair; and printing materials.

**FIGURE 17.1**
**The Importance of the ASEAN Market to Thai Entrepreneurs by Sector**

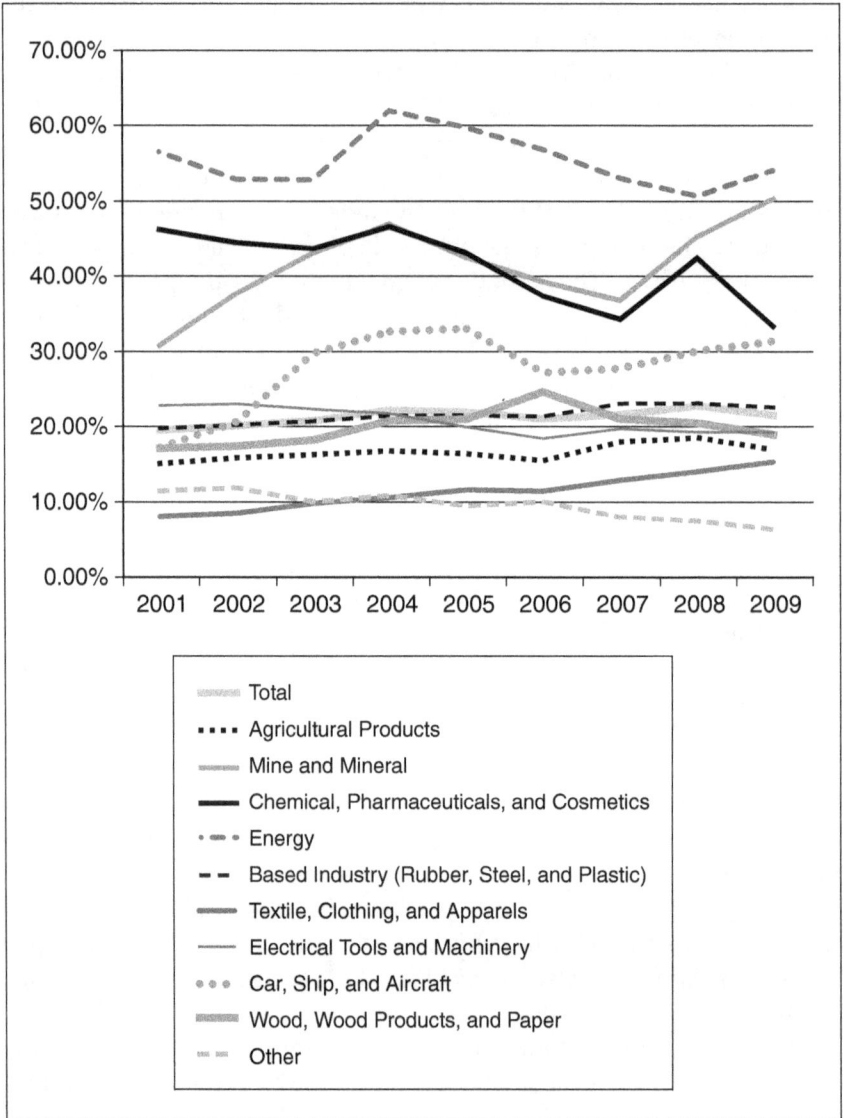

*Note:* Y-axis: The ASEAN share of Thailand's exports.
*Source:* Trade Map, UNCTAD.

FIGURE 17.2
AFTA Utilization Rate by 2-digit HS (2001–09)[2]

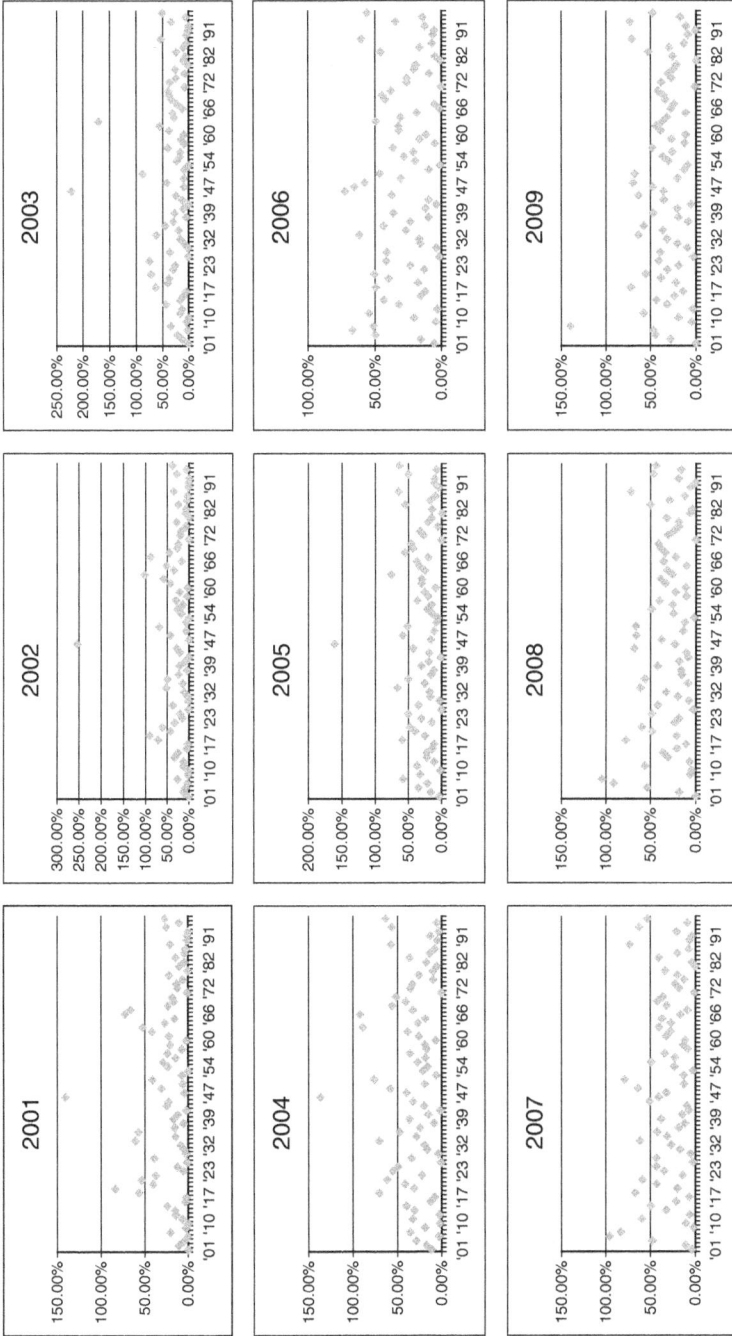

TABLE 17.1
Highest and Lowest AFTA Utilization Rates Classified by Product Groups (2001–09)

Unit: Per Cent

| HS | Description | 2001 | 2002 | 2003 | 2004 | 2005 | 2006 | 2007 | 2008 | 2009 | AVERAGE |
|---|---|---|---|---|---|---|---|---|---|---|---|
| | *Top Highest* | | | | | | | | | | |
| 46 | Manufacturers of plaiting material, basketwork, etc. | 140.7 | 255.2 | 222.7 | 137.0 | 161.2 | 72.6 | 41.0 | 23.1 | 35.9 | 121.0 |
| 63 | Other handmade textile articles, sets, clothing etc. | — | 102.6 | 171.0 | 89.3 | 76.3 | 49.5 | 40.8 | 26.3 | 37.4 | 74.1 |
| 24 | Tobacco and manufactured tobacco substitutes | — | 87.2 | 89.0 | 81.6 | 57.9 | 66.3 | 59.2 | 67.4 | 72.5 | 72.6 |
| 18 | Cocoa and cocoa preparations | 57.0 | 71.0 | 63.9 | 70.6 | 59.9 | 49.3 | 66.8 | 77.7 | 72.4 | 65.4 |
| 50 | Silk | 41.1 | 68.8 | 88.1 | 76.2 | 51.9 | 46.5 | 78.7 | 66.4 | 67.6 | 65.0 |
| 33 | Essential oils, perfumes, cosmetics, toiletries | 61.5 | 53.0 | 62.7 | 70.7 | 67.1 | 61.8 | 61.4 | 61.6 | 63.7 | 62.6 |
| 21 | Miscellaneous edible preparations | 54.0 | 61.6 | 72.6 | 61.9 | 48.3 | 50.3 | 58.5 | 59.9 | 55.6 | 58.1 |
| 87 | Vehicles other than railway, tramway | 20.9 | 35.0 | 54.0 | 57.6 | 65.2 | 60.4 | 73.4 | 72.1 | 71.2 | 56.7 |
| 48 | Paper & paperboard, articles of pulp, paper, and board | 30.9 | 43.1 | 42.0 | 58.4 | 59.2 | 57.8 | 63.6 | 66.1 | 69.9 | 54.5 |
| 35 | Albuminoids, modified starches, glues, enzymes | 57.8 | 50.0 | 44.9 | 47.7 | 50.8 | 43.5 | 42.5 | 56.3 | 57.7 | 50.1 |
| | *Top Lowest* | | | | | | | | | | |
| 29 | Organic chemicals | 2.5 | 1.8 | 1.9 | 3.8 | 3.3 | 4.0 | 5.6 | 7.9 | 10.0 | 4.5 |
| 91 | Clocks and watches and parts thereof | 1.1 | 0.8 | 1.3 | 13.1 | 11.4 | 5.5 | 4.7 | 0.8 | 1.0 | 4.4 |
| 5 | Products of animal origin, nes | — | — | 14.5 | 0.0 | 0.3 | 0.8 | 4.8 | 1.6 | 8.6 | 4.4 |

| 41 | Raw hides and skins (other than furs) and leather | 2.0 | 0.4 | 0.2 | 1.8 | 1.9 | 4.0 | 7.5 | 8.8 | 6.1 | 3.6 |
|----|----|----|----|----|----|----|----|----|----|----|----|
| 36 | Explosives, pyrotechnics, matches, pyrophorics, etc. | 0.7 | 19.5 | 1.3 | 0.6 | 0.2 | 1.7 | 0.4 | — | 1.1 | 3.2 |
| 1 | Live animals | 0.0 | 0.4 | 1.3 | 11.5 | 4.0 | 5.7 | 4.2 | 0.3 | 0.3 | 3.1 |
| 97 | Works of art, collectors' pieces, and antiques | 0.3 | — | 1.7 | 0.2 | 1.1 | 2.2 | 1.2 | 6.6 | 3.0 | 2.0 |
| 93 | Arms and ammunition, parts, and accessories thereof | 1.9 | 6.9 | 2.9 | 0.1 | 0.1 | — | — | 0.4 | 0.9 | 1.9 |
| 27 | Mineral fuels, oils, distillation products, etc. | 1.1 | 1.6 | 1.4 | 0.7 | 0.3 | 1.7 | 2.9 | 3.1 | 3.6 | 1.8 |
| 71 | Pearls, precious stones, metals, coins | 1.1 | 0.6 | 7.8 | 0.4 | 0.4 | 0.5 | 1.6 | 0.5 | 1.3 | 1.6 |

*Notes*: If the rate is 100 per cent, it implies that the values granted AFTA status equal total export values.
If the rate is less than 100 per cent, it implies that the values granted AFTA status are less than total export values.
If the rate is more than 100 per cent, it implies that the values granted AFTA status are greater than total export values.

*Source*: Authors' calculations based on data from Bureau of Trade Preferences, Department of Foreign Trade, Thailand.

FIGURE 17.3

AFTA Utilization Rate in 2009 Classified by Sector

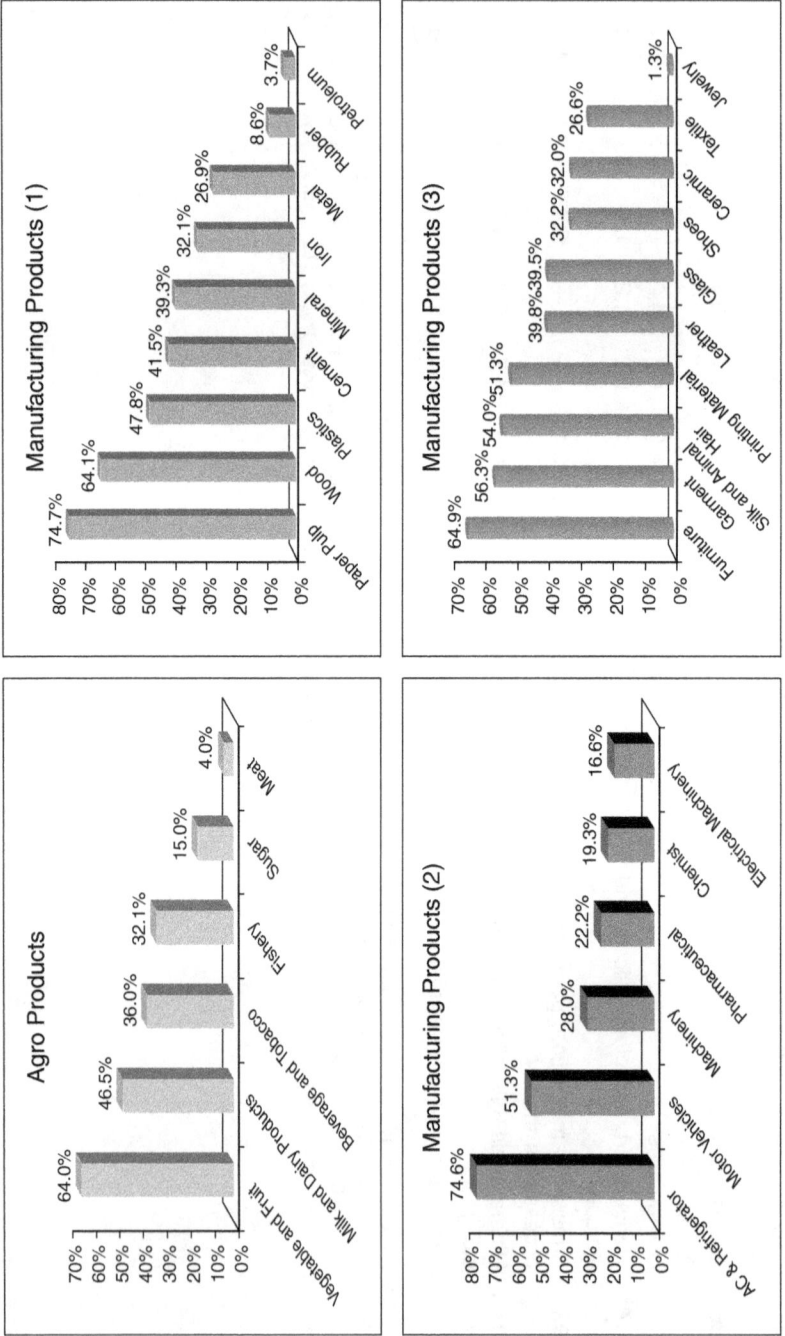

*Source:* Authors' calculations based on data from Bureau of Trade Preferences, Department of Foreign Trade, Thailand.

## Why They Have Not Used the Privilege? Interview Evidence of AFTA Impact

To gain an understanding of the effect of AFTA on Thai private businesses, interviews were conducted with key Thai conglomerates from various sectors in May–June 2010. Interview questions were directed to attitudes towards the usage of ASEAN economic agreements, in particular, AFTA and the AEC's Single Market Initiative. The most common answers to the question "why have you not used the AFTA privileges" are (1) poor knowledge about regional trade agreements in ASEAN, (2) presence of non-tariff barriers (NTBs) in the region, (3) presence of "non-harmonized" rules of origin (ROO) in ASEAN, and (4) confusion caused by the "Spaghetti Bowl Effect".

### Lack of ASEAN Knowledge

"The Thai private sectors especially those categorized as the SMEs have very little knowledge about ASEAN." The accuracy of this statement has been confirmed by two empirical studies.

In 2009 the University of the Thai Chamber of Commerce conducted a survey on "Thai Chamber of Commerce Members and their AEC Awareness". Not surprisingly to academia (but perhaps the opposite to policymakers), the survey found that only 11.1 per cent of the members cited that they understand what the AEC is about, while the rest (88.9 per cent) responded that they do not understand the initiative.

This finding is similar to what we found in this study. To ascertain Thai businesses' level of understanding of ASEAN, we surveyed a sample of 134 members of the Thai Chamber of Commerce.[3] The survey results are shown in Table 17.2.

From Table 17.2, it is not an exaggeration to say that the Thai private sector knows very little about ASEAN. In other words, little interest has been shown in ASEAN developments by Thai businesses, even within so-called large enterprises.[4] However, the survey found that there is "asymmetric knowledge" about ASEAN among Thai businesses as the average level of knowledge of ASEAN by large firms was 4.4 (out of 10), whereas medium and small enterprises scored averages of 2.8 and 2.3 respectively.

Aware of this problem, business institutions, together with government departments in Thailand, have been trying to promote awareness of ASEAN developments, in particular, the AEC, among Thai businesses

**TABLE 17.2**
**Thai Entrepreneurs: ASEAN Knowledge Score by Categories**

| Categories | Score (0-10) |
|---|---|
| **By Industry** | |
| Food and Agricultural Products | 3.000 |
| Fashion | 2.231 |
| Motor Vehicles and Spare Parts | 3.000 |
| Steel Electronic and Machinery | 3.417 |
| Petroleum Chemical Rubber and Plastic | 3.053 |
| Other and Services | 3.259 |
| **By Size of Businesses** | |
| Small Enterprise | 2.250 |
| Medium Enterprise | 2.844 |
| Large Enterprise | 4.359 |
| **By Level of Education** | |
| Below bachelor degree | 1.406 |
| Bachelor degree | 3.116 |
| Higher than bachelor degree | 5.667 |
| **By Province** | |
| Bangkok | 3.174 |
| Samutprakarn | 2.087 |
| Samutsakorn | 3.500 |
| Nakornprathom | 2.333 |
| Nonthaburi | 2.667 |
| Pathumthani | 3.389 |
| Other Provinces | 3.100 |
| **By Age** | |
| Under 31 | 2.433 |
| 31–40 | 3.250 |
| Over 40 | 3.861 |
| **By Gender** | |
| Male | 4.286 |
| Female | 2.650 |
| **Average** | **3.097** |

and the public in general. According to a senior official at the Board of Trade of Thailand, one of the core activities of the Thai Chamber of Commerce since 2009 has been to provide more knowledge about the ASEAN market, with initiatives such as the AEC Prompt Web Access. The Department of Foreign Trade and the Department of Trade Negotiations, the main public agencies in Thailand responsible for international trade, have also conducted many activities that are aimed at building knowledge of the ASEAN market among Thai businesses and the public, including organizing public seminars. To facilitate these movements, the Royal Thai Government has significantly increased its budget on activities aiming to build "market access knowledge" at international levels for Thai businesses (Figure 17.4).

**FIGURE 17.4**
**Annual DTN Budget on Knowledge Building Activities and Its Share of the DTN's Total Annual Budget**

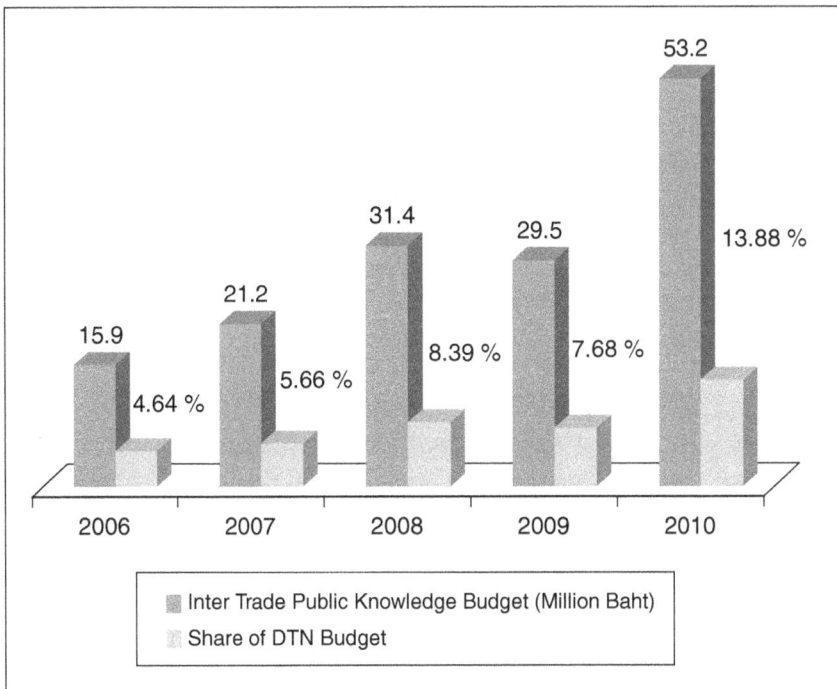

*Note:* DTN = Department of Trade Negotiations.
*Source:* The Department of Trade Negotiations, Ministry of Commerce, Thailand.

## The Presence of Non-Tariff Barriers (NTBs)

Results from the survey also show a worrying sign for ASEAN policy-makers as many respondents cited the presence of non-tariff barriers (NTBs) as one of the main threats towards regional integration in ASEAN. For many years ASEAN businesses have called for the removal of NTBs, and responses from ASEAN leaders show that this issue has been recognized. Nevertheless, the problem still exists and it seems that the resolution of this issue is rated the most important by Thai entrepreneurs.[5]

Some empirical studies provide a good explanation of the concern about NTBs. In 2009 Mitsuyo Ando and Ayako Obashi studied the presence of non-tariff barriers in ASEAN member countries. Based on data published on the ASEAN Secretariat webpage, the study measured the level of non-tariff measures (NTM) usage of all ASEAN members and calculated a NTM "Frequency Ratio".[6] Table 17.3 presents comparative levels of NTM usage in the ASEAN region. Overall, the data show that Thailand has the second-lowest level of NTMs usage, while Indonesia, Myanmar, and the Philippines have very high levels of NTM usage.

It is not an exaggeration to say that impacts of NTBs are much felt when tariffs are reduced. And this is a major concern among many Thai exporters. There is also a lot of ambiguity regarding the progress in eliminating NTBs in ASEAN. However, as addressed in the April ASEAN Round Table 2010,[7] many work programmes, including a Trade Facilitation Framework as well as a plan to establish an ASEAN Trade Repository by 2015, have been under way to reduce or eliminate NTBs in ASEAN. Lack of information on the latest developments in ASEAN's NTB treatment perhaps leads to dissatisfaction in the Thai business community.

## The Presence of "Non-harmonized" Rules of Origin (ROO)

In principle, rules of origin (ROO) could be a form of hidden protection since they are a requirement for using parts and components from, or the production within, member countries. Nonetheless, complying with ROO is not without cost.

First, "non-harmonized" ROO exist in certain sectors. This is not irregular given that ROO are usually negotiated on an industry-by-industry basis, and each country is likely to design its own ROO. Due to this complex nature, so far there is no consensus on internationally

TABLE 17.3
**ASEAN Frequency Ratio for NTMs**
(all industries by country, per cent)

| | Cambodia | Thailand | Laos | Singapore | Vietnam | Malaysia | Brunei | Indonesia | Myanmar | Philippines |
|---|---|---|---|---|---|---|---|---|---|---|
| Overall NTMs | 6 | 11 | 20 | 27 | 34 | 43 | 46 | 100 | 100 | 100 |

*Source:* Mitsuyo Ando and Ayako Obashi 2009.

accepted ROO.[8] Nonetheless, they create disparity in advantages for member countries in some sectors, and this can prove to be another obstacle for businesses to participate in ASEAN integration.

In the agricultural sector, most of the survey respondents from Thailand's key agro-based conglomerates agree that the integration regime in ASEAN would in general benefit trade expansion, both within and outside the region. Given that some of the Thai agro-based regional producers have already invested within the region, especially in the form of contract farming, an ability to devise suitable ROO plays a key role in reducing their cost of production, but, according to the interviewees, only when harmonized. Otherwise, the "non-harmonized" ROO will create disadvantages rather than benefits.

For example, one representative from the Thai Feed Mill Association pointed out an impediment caused by member countries applying different ROO. Specifically, to be declared an ASEAN originated product, Thai feed mill producers are allowed to use all kinds of imported raw materials except fish meal and soybean meal, or they can exercise the 40 per cent Regional Value of Content rule. On the other hand, feed mill producers from other ASEAN members are allowed to use all kinds of imported raw materials to apply for the ASEAN origin status.

The differences between ROO used in the ASEAN feed mill industry seem minimal. However, it turns out that those small details create distortion in feed mill production in the region, according to an executive from the Thai Feed Mill Association. In particular, he complains that such ROO where other ASEAN members can enjoy the importation of any kind of feed mill materials to get the AFTA privilege reduce the competitiveness of Thai feed mill producers, who can source such materials, including soybean meal, locally in Thailand. In other words, the ROO imposed on the ASEAN feed mill industry not only reduces costs of producing feed mill in ASEAN as a whole, but also reduces Thailand's cost competitive edge in the industry.

Another problem of non-harmonized ASEAN ROO for the Thai private sector is that ASEAN member countries have different industry structures. To be specific, a representative of a Thai vegetable oil producer voiced her concerns on the different ROO applied to Vietnamese and Thai producers. For the former country, refined vegetable oil from imported raw materials is able to get the ASEAN ROO, while Thailand does not accept such processes. The reason is simple, Thai producers do not import vegetable oil raw materials as they generally control the whole supply chain of vegetable oil production, and search locally for raw materials through contract farming.

Note that private sector opinions towards the ASEAN ROO vary among certain sectors. While Thailand's agricultural producers seem to undervalue the ROO used in the region, key car assemblers in Thailand think differently. Because of the industry's particular structure, the assemblers have positive attitudes towards ASEAN regional integration. The current type of ROO that has been applied so far within the region does not significantly generate any distortion effect in the car production industry. Selected to be a regional hub of many leading car multinational enterprises, Thailand has had a situation where locally assembled vehicles are heavily reliant on locally manufactured parts to minimize logistics costs in procuring numerous parts. It was therefore unlikely to be affected by regional-content or changing-in-tariff heading types of ROO.

### The "Spaghetti Bowl Effect"

The World Bank, in its 2009 *World Development Report*, claims that countries are becoming more similar in their economic structures since intra-industry trade has risen for primary, intermediate, and final goods, and the largest rise is for intermediate inputs (World Bank 2009). Nonetheless, this is not the case for all ASEAN members. Among the ASEAN countries, the proportion of intermediate inputs in total output from external sources increased for Thailand and Singapore, declined for Indonesia, and moved sideways for Malaysia and the Philippines (Kalra 2010). Given the argument by the World Bank that "intermediate goods trade has increased fastest in parts of the world that have reduced trade and transport costs the most", it can be argued that Thai private sectors have gained benefits from the reduced costs of international trade and transport, and these costs will be crucial to the successful integration of regional blocks, including ASEAN.

However, during the interviews, there were also criticisms from many interviewees, not surprisingly, about the increased complication of "technically-focused" ROO from the many trade agreements involved. Referred to as the "Spaghetti Bowl Effect" by many, it is what businesses cited as the crucial barrier to ASEAN integration,[9] as the situation has increased rather than decreased the costs of international trade and transport. The situation is getting worse as ASEAN members have independently engaged in their own trade agreements with non-ASEAN economies, and ASEAN "unity" has deteriorated.

In AFTA, ROO require at least 40 per cent of gross output value to use ASEAN member inputs. The only exemption is for textile and clothing, which require 55 per cent of regional content and the substantial transformation criterion. In the Thailand-Australia FTA (TAFTA) for example, the ROO which is applied for most products is the change-in-tariff-heading type. With these two FTAs, details are different in each item so that there are more than a thousand rules applied to each individual item. Also, many of them are subject to change in tariff heading at four-digit HS system whereas some are at six-digit HS. In addition, each set of ROO is often quite expensive to document and significant costs are incurred in the application for privileges under different free trade agreements.

## Why Have They Not Used the Privilege? Evidence from a Focus Group

Interview evidence suggests four reasons private businesses in Thailand have not used the AFTA privilege. To reassess if there are other factors that could hinder the integration process in ASEAN and find out what should be a policy response, we convened a focus group with members of the Thai Chamber of Commerce and government officials. For thirty-one out of the total thirty-eight participants representing industrial associations (see Appendix 1 for the attendance list), we presented what we found in the first two sections of this study, distributed copies of a self-report questionnaire, and expected a large number of responses in return.

Unfortunately the response rate was exceptionally low, with only four copies of the questionnaire filled and submitted.[10] Given the fact that AFTA has been in place since 1993, while ASEAN has actively engaged in trade agreements with non-ASEAN economies only over the last few years, such evidence of the lack of interest in ASEAN integration in the Thai business realm could be expected. Nevertheless, the information received from the questionnaires is useful.

First, the knowledge disparity among Thai private businesses of regional trade agreements in ASEAN is again evident. As can be seen from Table 17.4 below, none of the questionnaire respondents stated that they understand the AEC initiative, while at least half of them know about the other agreements. As such, three out of four respondents

**TABLE 17.4**
**Thai Entrepreneurs: Knowledge of ASEAN Trade Agreements**
(% of Respondents)

| AEC / FTA / Economic Partnership Agreements | Know Agreements | | Business Impact Evaluation | | | | | |
|---|---|---|---|---|---|---|---|---|
| | No | Yes | High | | Low | | Should have no impact | Not sure |
| | | | + | – | + | – | | |
| 1 AFTA | – | 100 | 25 | 25 | 25 | | 25 | |
| *2 AEC* | *100* | – | | | | | | *100* |
| 3 ASEAN-China FTA | 25 | 75 | 25 | | 25 | | 25 | 25 |
| 4 ASEAN-Australia-New Zealand FTA | – | 100 | 25 | 25 | 25 | | 25 | |
| 5 ASEAN-India FTA | 25 | 75 | | | 50 | | 25 | 25 |
| 6 ASEAN-Korea FTA | 50 | 50 | | | 25 | | 25 | 50 |
| 7 ASEAN-Japan FTA | – | 100 | | | 75 | | 25 | |

claimed their firms have no strategy or adjustment plans for the AEC, while the rest claimed their response has consisted solely of collecting information related to the AEC.

Second, information collected from the questionnaires presents a list of factors that have obstructed private businesses' use of AFTA privileges. Expectedly, factors that were analysed in the previous section are also found here. Specifically, when asked to rank the three most important factors that hinder their participation in ASEAN integration, the most common answers were lack of ASEAN knowledge, NTB costs, and ROO costs. Policy recommendations received from this focus group are therefore more ASEAN knowledge-building activities, NTB reduction negotiations, and ROO negotiations for more appropriate rules that suit the industrial production structure.

## Conclusion and Policy Inferences

Since the inception of AFTA in 1993, work towards ASEAN integration has continually progressed; we have never lacked efforts from regional leaders, policymakers, and academics in improving policies, institutions and public relations campaigns that support the "single" ASEAN initiative.

To its credit, ASEAN has become the largest trading partner of Thai businesses in various sectors, and is evidently developing to be their prime investment destination also.

Nonetheless, those who argue that working towards ASEAN integration by 2015 is indeed a steep hill to climb have a point. While the top-down liberalization approach mentioned above has so far been effective, realizing an AEC by 2015 also requires a bottom-up style that involves interest and action from businesses. Unfortunately, this has not been the case for Thai private businesses.

With data collected at the firm/industry level through interviews, questionnaires, and a focus group, this study provides evidence that a key foundation for ASEAN regionalism, the private sector's participation, is still weak in Thailand. Factors holding back their interest include limited knowledge of ASEAN, the presence of NTBs, the presence of non-harmonized ROO, and confusion caused by the "spaghetti bowl effect".

The clock is ticking away with about four years left to improve things. But in our view, work to strengthen the foundation is advisable and indeed achievable. Regional collaboration to increase awareness and knowledge of ASEAN among businesses and the public in general has to be strengthened. Mass communication is much needed to compensate for the failure of communication through public seminars or closed-door academic meetings that have limited participation from businesses on a larger scale.

This relates to the second recommendation. We know many work programmes have been under way to reduce or eliminate NTBs in ASEAN. Still, the fact that we found that resolution of this issue is rated most important by Thai entrepreneurs implies a need for urgent action from business institutions, government departments, and academic institutions to provide information on the latest developments in ASEAN's NTB treatment. It is therefore timely to review the progress and effectiveness of ASEAN's central NTB database system and its implementation.

This is built on by the third recommendation. The review of the progress and effectiveness of ASEAN's central database must go beyond tax and non-tax barriers. It must include information of, or a handbook for, ROO under different FTAs, HS systems (i.e., HS2002, HS2007, and HS2012), products, and member countries. Together with negotiations for "harmonized" ROO that suit member countries' production structures,

ROO information sharing is very important and demands a lot of effort, and hence, budget allocations.

Our last recommendation focuses on ways and means to reduce costs for businesses in applying for privileges under different free trade agreements in which ASEAN is involved. First, capacity of, and/or budget for, human resources in the national foreign trade department have to be enhanced since they have to deal with documents, technical issues, and business queries. This could be through either providing extra funds for capacity-building programmes or by transferring duties to private entities/experts.

Second, minor administrative details related to ROO certificate applications have to be kept as unobtrusive as possible. For example, it is appropriate now to review how long businesses are required to keep their certificate application documents for assessment in the future. For example, confusion, and hence costs incurred, have increased since different FTAs have different time period requests (for instance, three years for AFTA and AJCEP [ASEAN-Japan Comprehensive Economic Partnership] and five years for TAFTA and JTEPA [Japan-Thailand Economic Partnership Agreement]).

Third, it appears that some businesses misunderstand that revealing their production cost structure as part of the ROO certificate application could result in increased corporate tax payments. It is therefore advisable that they are properly and correctly informed, or are legally protected if they do not intentionally commit tax fraud.

Our honest assessment is that economic integration in ASEAN will only work bottom-up if private participation in the process is realized. Even though many top-down work/assistance programmes have been implemented domestically and regionally to remove integration impediments, further action and implementation from businesses are much needed. In the case of Thailand, it is realistic to expect less involvement in the process of ASEAN integration from the private sector unless their key impediments are addressed and removed at pace. That is where the top powers (that is, regional leaders, policymakers, and academics) have vital roles to play.

## APPENDIX 17.1
## Focus Group Attendance List

| Organization | Number of Participant |
|---|:---:|
| Thai Gem and Jewelry Traders Association | 1 |
| Pharmaceutical Research and Manufacturer Association | 1 |
| Thai Plastic Industries Association | 1 |
| Thai Shrimp Association | 2 |
| Thai Retailers Association | 1 |
| The Thai Rubber Association | 1 |
| Thai International Freight Forwarders Association | 1 |
| Thai Contractors Association | 2 |
| Thai Textile Manufacturing Association | 1 |
| Thai Broiler Processing Exporters Association | 1 |
| Thai Fishmeal Producers Association | 1 |
| Thai Autoparts Manufacturers Association | 2 |
| Thai Manufacturers of Writing Instruments for Export Association | 1 |
| Thai Soybean and Rice Bran Oil Association | 2 |
| Thai Leathergoods Association | 1 |
| Thai Rice Exporters Association | 1 |
| Thai Food Processors' Association | 2 |
| Thai Cosmetic Manufacturers Association | 1 |
| KangZen-KenKo International Co., Ltd | 2 |
| Philip Morris (Thailand) Limited | 1 |
| Denso International Asia | 1 |
| C.P. Intertrade Company Limited | 4 |
| National Bureau of Agricultural Commodity and Food Standards | 2 |
| Department of Export Promotion | 2 |
| Office of Small and Medium Enterprises Promotion | 1 |
| Department of Foreign Trade | 1 |
| Department of Business Development | 1 |
| Office of Agricultural Economics | 1 |
| Thai Customs Department | 1 |

## NOTES

1. AFTA utilization rate is the percentage of values which exporters applied for privileges under AFTA and *declared to have* originated in ASEAN by the Bureau of Trade Preferences, over total export values into the ASEAN market. If the rate is 100 per cent, it implies that the values granted the AFTA status equal total export values. If the rate is less than 100 per cent, it implies that the values granted the AFTA status is less than total export values. If the rate is more than 100 per cent, it implies that the values granted the AFTA status is greater than total export values.

2. X-axes indicate two-digit HS codes for goods that Thailand export *only over a nine-year period*. The codes are '01 '03 '04 '07 '08 '09 '10 '11 '12 '13 '15 '16 '17 '18 '19 '20 '21 '22 '23 '25 '27 '28 '29 '30 '32 '33 '34 '35 '37 '38 '39 '40 '41 '42 '44 '46 '47 '48 '49 '50 '52 '53 '54 '55 '56 '57 '58 '59 '60 '61 '62 '63 '64 '65 '66 '67 '68 '69 '70 '71 '72 '73 '74 '76 '79 '80 '82 '83 '84 '85 '87 '90 '91 '92 '94 '95 and '96.

3. Questions asked in the survey were simple. Examples are "What is ASEAN?" "Who are the members of ASEAN?" and "What are the pros and cons of ASEAN?"

4. We also surveyed a number of large enterprises, including the Siam Cement Group and the CP group, all of which could be categorized as regional or multinational companies.

5. Some even argue that "with the NTBs, it is easier to move goods outside ASEAN than within ASEAN".

6. Can be calculated with the formula

$$F_{ji} = T_{ji} / T_i \times 100$$

Where $F_{ji}$ = Frequency Ratio for NTMs type j of industry i

$T_{ji}$ = numbers of product that have NTMs type j

$T_i$ = numbers of product in industry i

7. The ASEAN Round Table is a flagship event organized by the ASEAN Studies Centre at the Institute of Southeast Asian Studies, Singapore.

8. See Imagawa and Vermulst (2005), Baldwin (2006), and James (2006).

9. Baldwin (2006) shows that in the ASEAN-China FTAs, it is likly there are ten sub-agreements between China and each ASEAN country. Each FTA has its own liberalization speed and consequences, as well as its own ROO.

10. It is worthwhile to note that the Thai Rice Exporters Association has responded with their official letter saying "they could not identify any factors hampering rice trade development in ASEAN, other than the fact that rice has always been placed in a sensitive or a highly sensitive product group in ASEAN trade agreements and that holds back the integration process". The four submitted questionnaires were from three members of the Thai Food Processors' Association and one member of the Thai Fishmeal Producers Association.

## REFERENCES

Ando, Mitsuyo and Ayako Obashi. "The Pervasiveness of Non-tariff Measures in ASEAN: Evidences from the Inventory Approach". Asia-Pacific Trade Economists' Conference, UNESCAP, 2009.

Baldwin, R. "Managing the Noodle Bowl: The Fragility of East Asian Regionalism". CEPR Discussion Paper, No. 5561, Centre of Economic Policy Research, Oxford, 2006.

Bureau of Trade Preferences, Department of Foreign Trade, Thailand.

Department of Trade Negotiations, Ministry of Commerce, Thailand <www.thaifta.com>.

Imagawa, Hiroshi and Edwin Vermulst "The Agreement on Rules of Origin", in *The World Trade Organization: Legal, Economics and Political Perspectives Vol. 2*, edited by P.F.J. Macrory, A.E. Appleton, and M.G. Plummer. New York: Springer.

James, W. "Rules of Origin in Emerging Asia-Pacific Preferential Trade Agreements: Will PTAs Promote Trade and Development". Asia-Pacific Research and Training Network on Trade, Working Paper Series, No. 19, 2005.

Kalra, Sanjay. "ASEAN: A Chronicle of Shifting Trade Exposure and Regional Integration". IMF Working Paper (WP/10/119), 2010.

University of the Thai Chamber of Commerce. "Thai Chamber of Commerce Members and their AEC Awareness". 2009.

World Bank. "The 2009 World Development Report: Reshaping Economic Geography". 2009.

# 18

## The Private Sector's Participation in Regional Integration: A Perspective from Vietnam[1]

Vo Tri Thanh and Nguyen Anh Duong

After her national unification, Vietnam undertook continuous economic reforms under pressure from severe economic problems. During the period 1980–87, some micro-reform attempts were made with a bottom-up approach, reflecting the enhancement of incentives at the micro level. These micro-reforms enhanced voluntary and decentralized interactions between individual agents and induced producers to increase outputs during the period 1982–85 (Vo and Nguyen 2006*a*). However, the micro-reforms in this period led to no fundamental changes in resource misallocation, trade restrictions, or macroeconomic management.

Since the start of *doi moi* (renovation) in 1986, Vietnam has strived to transform herself from a centrally planned economy into a socialist-oriented market economy. Such a transformation relies to a large extent on its establishing and strengthening market institutions, developing the private sector, and undertaking proactive international economic integration. More importantly, these measures were combined, rather than undertaken separately.[2] Specifically, the development of the private sector came in line with the facilitation of its participation in the international economic integration process.

As a key direction for more fundamental economic changes, Vietnam has improved its microeconomic foundations to support private sector development. Since 1979 two main steps have been implemented along the following lines: (1) the formal recognition of private ownership and right of doing business, and the promulgation and implementation of various legal frameworks on business/company types; and (2) the gradual relaxation of market entry.[3]

In another aspect, Vietnam, recognizing the inefficiency of SOEs, attempted to "restructure and/or equitize state-owned enterprises (SOEs)" rather than "privatize" them. Whilst substantially reducing subsidies and "cheap" credit to these enterprises, it gave them greater autonomy. In recent years, SOE reforms in Vietnam included the listing of these enterprises in the stock market, equitizing large SOEs and some general corporations, transforming big SOEs and some general corporations into holding-subsidiary companies, and establishing business groups.

The acceleration of international economic integration, including the gradual liberalization of the trade regime, has played a key role in enhancing efficiency and promoting economic growth. Vietnam has had trade relations with almost all countries and territories to date and became a member of the Association of Southeast Asian Nations (ASEAN) and the World Trade Organization (WTO) in 1995 and 2007 respectively. Additionally, within the ASEAN framework, Vietnam has signed and implemented various multilateral free trade agreements (FTAs). These moves have created huge market access for Vietnamese enterprises and played a key role in boosting exports, which in turn drove economic growth in the country.

The economic integration process still continues to accelerate in East Asia. ASEAN member countries have fully implemented their commitments in trade in goods and are gradually liberalizing services trade. ASEAN has also negotiated and implemented ASEAN Plus One FTAs with other major partners in East Asia, including China, South Korea, and Japan. It is ASEAN that has proved to be the core of wider East Asian integration, of which East Asian enterprises are both the drivers and beneficiaries.

Thanks to numerous bold measures, Vietnam has achieved major socio-economic successes in a range of areas. Economic growth has accelerated, despite slowing down in 2008 and 2009 due to the global financial crisis. Income to people has improved, causing the poverty rate to drop sharply. In particular, the periods with these successes are also those with rapid economic integration and effective private sector development. The huge socio-economic achievements over the past two decades also strengthened the confidence of the government, the business community, and the people to make further joint efforts towards market- and integration-based economic development.

This chapter attempts to present the private sector's perspective of ASEAN economic integration in Vietnam. In doing so, it looks into the country's experience in developing the private sector in relation to the country's integration process. More specifically, the chapter analyses the country's ability to increase value added in regional trade activities. Aditionally, the chapter lists some problems for Vietnam's private sector as the country continues to deepen her regional economic integration.

Apart from this introduction, the remainder of the chapter is structured as follow: The next section briefly describes the current position of Vietnam's private sector, via indicators such as new business establishments and employment structure by ownership. The following section then analyses integration of Vietnam's private sector, from the perspective of participation in regional production networks and ability to reap value added. In the final section, the authors make policy recommendations to facilitate the deeper participation of Vietnam's private sector in the implementation of ASEAN agreements.

## Current Status of the Private Sector in Vietnam

The continuous improvement in the business and investment environment since *doi moi* has induced the development of the private sector. The economic role of the (domestic) private sector has increased significantly.

Table 18.1 presents the GDP structure by ownership from 1997 to 2009 and shows that the domestic, non-state sector's share of the country's GDP was the highest. However, this share fell continuously until 2006 before climbing up again to above 46.5 per cent in 2009. Besides, the contribution of the non-state sector is significantly higher than that of

**TABLE 18.1**
**GDP by Ownership, at Current Prices**
(%)

|  | 1997 | 1999 | 2000 | 2003 | 2006 | 2007 | 2008 | 2009 |
|---|---|---|---|---|---|---|---|---|
| **Total** | 100.00 | 100.00 | 100.00 | 100.00 | 100.00 | 100.00 | 100.00 | 100.00 |
| State | 40.48 | 38.74 | 38.52 | 39.08 | 37.39 | 35.93 | 34.35 | 35.14 |
| Non-State | 50.45 | 49.03 | 48.20 | 46.45 | 45.63 | 46.11 | 46.97 | 46.53 |
| Collectives | 8.91 | 8.84 | 8.58 | 7.49 | 6.53 | 6.21 | 6.02 | 5.22 |
| Private | 7.22 | 7.26 | 7.31 | 8.23 | 9.41 | 10.18 | 10.81 | 11.54 |
| Individuals | 34.32 | 32.93 | 32.31 | 30.73 | 29.69 | 29.72 | 30.14 | 30.78 |
| Foreign-invested sector | 9.07 | 12.24 | 13.28 | 14.47 | 16.98 | 17.96 | 18.68 | 19.30 |

Source: General Statistics Office (GSO).

the foreign-invested sector, even though the gap has been continuously narrowed.

In another aspect, the number of newly registered enterprises increased rapidly (Table 18.2). The number of newly registered enterprises rose by more than 4.5 times, from over 14,000 in 2000 to over 65,000 in 2008. Even in early 2009, despite the negative impact of the global financial crisis and economic recession, the number of newly registered enterprises was relatively large, almost equivalent to that in 2008. The total capital of newly registered enterprises went up even faster. This figure was only around VND 14 trillion in 2000, but skyrocketed to almost VND 148 trillion in 2006, more than VND 494 trillion in 2007, and nearly VND 570 trillion in 2008.

**TABLE 18.2**
**Number and Registered Capital of Newly Registered Enterprises**

|  | 2000 | 2003 | 2006 | 2007 | 2008 | 2009 |
|---|---|---|---|---|---|---|
| Number of enterprises | 14,441 | 27,678 | 46,663 | 58,908 | 65,318 | 83,000 |
| Registered capital (trillion VND) | 13.83 | 57.75 | 148.07 | 494.09 | 569.53 | 148.29* |
| Average capital (billion VND) | 0.96 | 2.09 | 3.17 | 8.39 | 8.72 | 4.30* |

Note: * For the first six months of 2009.
Source: (Former) SME Development Agency and (current) Enterprise Development Agency of the Ministry of Planning and Investment.

Despite the large number, however, the newly registered enterprises are mostly small or medium in size. The average registered capital of these enterprises went up from less than VND 1 billion in 2000 to nearly VND 3.2 billion in 2006, and over VND 8.7 billion in 2008. Interestingly, while the impact of the global financial crisis and economic recession did not stall the number and total capital of newly registered enterprises, their average capital actually fell sharply to only VND 4.3 billion for the first half of 2009. More importantly, despite their high registration rate, as of 2009 the proportion of enterprises that remained economically active was just around one-half (Le and Dau 2010).

Recent years also witnessed a stable high ratio of investment to GDP of around 40 per cent. This could be largely attributed to the rapid rise in both domestic private and foreign investment (Table 18.3). In fact, growth in private investment has accelerated from 9 per cent in 1996 to 11.3 per cent in 2001, before jumping to 31.4 per cent in 2002 and almost 48 per cent in 2004. Since 2005, however, private investment growth has been rather stable. Nevertheless, the impact of the country's accession

**TABLE 18.3**
**Investment growth and structure by ownership**

Unit: Per cent

| | Investment growth | | | | Investment structure | | |
|---|---|---|---|---|---|---|---|
| | Total | State | Private | Foreign | State | Private | Foreign |
| 1996 | 20.6 | 40.9 | 9.0 | 3.2 | 49.1 | 24.9 | 20.0 |
| 1997 | 24.0 | 24.9 | 12.4 | 33.5 | 49.4 | 22.6 | 28.0 |
| 1998 | 8.1 | 21.4 | 13.5 | −19.8 | 55.5 | 23.7 | 20.8 |
| 1999 | 12.0 | 18.3 | 13.5 | −6.7 | 58.7 | 24.0 | 17.3 |
| 2000 | 15.3 | 16.2 | 9.7 | 19.9 | 59.1 | 22.9 | 18.0 |
| 2001 | 12.8 | 14.0 | 11.3 | 10.4 | 59.8 | 22.6 | 17.6 |
| 2002 | 17.4 | 12.5 | 31.4 | 15.9 | 57.3 | 25.3 | 17.4 |
| 2003 | 19.5 | 10.3 | 47.0 | 10.1 | 52.9 | 31.1 | 16.0 |
| 2004 | 21.6 | 10.5 | 47.5 | 7.9 | 48.1 | 37.7 | 14.2 |
| 2005 | 17.9 | 15.6 | 18.8 | 23.6 | 47.1 | 38.0 | 14.9 |
| 2006 | 17.9 | 14.5 | 18.1 | 28.4 | 35.5 | 38.1 | 16.4 |
| 2007 | 28.9 | 12.4 | 19.7 | 97.1 | 39.9 | 35.3 | 24.8 |
| 2008 | 22.2 | 5.9 | 26.0 | 42.9 | 34.6 | 36.4 | 29.0 |
| 2009 | 15.3 | 40.5 | 13.9 | −5.8 | 40.6 | 33.9 | 25.5 |

*Source:* GSO and the Task Force on Implementation of Enterprise Law and Investment Law (2008).

to the WTO and the global financial crisis caused a dramatic fall in the share of the private and foreign-invested sectors in total investment to 13.9 per cent and –5.8 per cent respectively, in 2009.

The investment structure, however, generally shifts towards a higher share of foreign investment and smaller share of state investment (Table 18.3). From 1996 to 2001, the share of state investment went up from 49.1 per cent to 59.8 per cent, while that of the private sector decreased from almost 25 per cent to 22.6 per cent. Since 2002, however, the contribution of private investment has risen considerably and peaked at 38.1 per cent in 2006, before going down to over 36.4 per cent in 2008. Meanwhile, the share of state investment fell almost continuously (except in 2007) to 34.6 per cent in 2008. That of foreign investment fluctuated before jumping from just under 15 per cent in 2005 to 29 per cent in 2008, when private investment made up the largest share in total investment.

The private sector has also been the largest source of employment (Table 18.4). The number of employed persons in this sector rose from around 33.7 million in 2000 to around 39.2 million in 2008. Such a rise

### TABLE 18.4
### Employment by Ownership

|  | 2000 | 2001 | 2002 | 2003 | 2004 | 2005 | 2006 | 2007 | 2008 |
|---|---|---|---|---|---|---|---|---|---|
| **Total** | **37,610** | **38,563** | **39,508** | **40,574** | **41,586** | **42,527** | **43,339** | **44,174** | **44,916** |
| State | 3,501 | 3,604 | 3,751 | 4,035 | 4,108 | 4,039 | 3,949 | 3,985 | 4,073 |
| Non-State | 33,735 | 34,511 | 35,167 | 35,763 | 36,526 | 37,355 | 38,057 | 38,628 | 39,168 |
| Foreign-invested sector | 374 | 449 | 590 | 776 | 953 | 1,133 | 1,333 | 1,561 | 1,674 |
| **Share** | **100.00** | **100.00** | **100.00** | **100.00** | **100.00** | **100.00** | **100.00** | **100.00** | **100.00** |
| State | 9.31 | 9.34 | 9.49 | 9.95 | 9.88 | 9.50 | 9.11 | 9.02 | 9.07 |
| Non-state | 89.70 | 89.49 | 89.01 | 88.14 | 87.83 | 87.84 | 87.81 | 87.44 | 87.20 |
| Foreign-invested sector | 0.99 | 1.16 | 1.49 | 1.91 | 2.29 | 2.66 | 3.08 | 3.53 | 3.73 |

*Source:* GSO and authors' calculations.

accounted for almost all the increase in total employment (that is, over 7.3 million) over the same period. In relative terms, however, the private sector became slightly less important. The share of the non-state sector in total employment went down from 89.7 per cent in 2000 to 87.2 per cent in 2008. The employment structure by ownership, thus, indicates that the private sector will play the dominant role for many more years to come.

## Integration of Vietnam's Private Sector into Regional Production Networks

Notwithstanding the well-acknowledged positive impacts of the economic integration process on improving of the business and investment environment, as well as the development of Vietnam's private sector, the firms have generally found themselves far from being deeply and effectively integrated into the regional production networks. This can be illustrated by the study by Tran et al. (2010) on electrical and electronics automotive component manufacturing and the textiles and garment industries in Vietnam.

In fact, Tran et al. (2010) focus on two types of production networks. In the first type (type I), the member supplies its products or by-products to final assemblers[4] and/or manufactures parts and components and supplies them to first-tier and second-tier buyers in the production networks. In the second type (type II), meanwhile, the member supplies its products or by-products to final assemblers (usually large machinery and equipment manufacturers, business groups, multinational companies) and/or manufactures parts, components and supplies them to first-tier, second-tier, and third-tier buyers in the production chain, and/or exports its products or by-products, and/or imports raw materials or intermediate inputs.

The questionnaire survey by Tran et al. (2010) shows that about 25 per cent of the surveyed enterprises (39 enterprises) participated in a type I production network, while 56 per cent (93 enterprises) are in a type II production network. The survey results indicate that about two-thirds of SMEs acquired raw materials from counterparts in the same region or from other domestic suppliers. Besides, among Vietnam's enterprises engaging in import activities, 91 per cent had imported from East Asian economies, and only 19 per cent had imported from those in other regions. As an inference, East Asian economies are becoming the main suppliers of materials to Vietnam's SMEs, thanks to their geographical proximity as well as the enhanced trade relationships between East Asia and Vietnam. To this extent, the trade agreements within the ASEAN and ASEAN Plus One framework are important to Vietnam's enterprises in that they provide better access to cheaper sources of imports and/or that they make some import activities previously impossible become economically viable.

Tran et al. (2010) also looked into partners of Vietnam's SMEs in production networks by analyzing the proportion of export-oriented SMEs in terms of their exporting regions within or outside East Asia. The enterprises exporting solely to East Asian economies made up 45 per cent of the sample, while those exporting to other economies (for example, the European Union, the United States, and Australia) accounted for over 31 per cent, with the rest being those exporting to both areas. That is, up to 69 per cent of the surveyed SMEs sold their products to East Asia. The figure is rather high, but could be even higher if the enterprises supplying indirectly — via selling to other exporters — to East Asian partners are counted. Apparently, Vietnam's SMEs are found to possess strong linkages with East Asian production networks.

Such strong linkages help explain the dramatic rise in bilateral trade between Vietnam and East Asian economies in general, and between Vietnam and ASEAN in particular. Bilateral trade between Vietnam and China rose rather fast, from around US$7 billion in 2004 to over US$20 billion in 2008. During the same period, Japan and South Korea also saw their trade with Vietnam more than double, to reach more than US$17 billion and more than US$9 billion, respectively.

ASEAN remains the largest trade partner of Vietnam, with total bilateral trade jumping from approximately US$4.8 billion in 1996 to almost US$29.8 billion in 2008, before decreasing to around US$25.9 billion in 2009 (Table 18.5). Following its access to ASEAN in 1995, Vietnam's export to the latter went up considerably, from just under US$1.8 billion in 1996 to over US$2.6 billion in 2000, and to roughly US$10.2 billion in 2008. However, Vietnam's imports from other ASEAN member countries rose even faster, from nearly US$3 billion in 1996, to approximately US$19.6 billion in 2008. Due to the global financial crisis and economic recession, Vietnam's exports to and imports from ASEAN went down in 2009.

**TABLE 18.5**
**Vietnam's Bilateral Trade with ASEAN**

|  | 1996 | | 2000 | | 2008 | | 2009 | |
|---|---|---|---|---|---|---|---|---|
|  | Value (US$ b.) | Share of total | Value (US$ b.) | Share of total | Value (US$ b.) | Share of total | Value (US$ b.) | Share of total |
| Exports to ASEAN | 1,778 | 23.8 | 2,619 | 18.1 | 10,195 | 16.3 | 8,913 | 16.0 |
| Imports from ASEAN | 2,992 | 26.5 | 4,449 | 28.5 | 19,571 | 24.2 | 16,953 | 20.0 |
| Trade with ASEAN | 4,770 | 25.4 | 7,068 | 23.5 | 29,766 | 20.8 | 25,866 | 18.4 |

*Source:* Authors' calculations from IMF Direction of Trade database.

It should be mentioned that the importance of ASEAN as a trade partner of Vietnam has been declining in relative terms (Table 18.5). The share of ASEAN in Vietnam's exports fell from 23.8 per cent in 1996 to 16.3 per cent in 2008 and 16 per cent in 2009. The contribution of ASEAN to Vietnam's imports rose from 26.5 per cent in 1996 to 28.5 per cent in 2000, before dropping sharply to almost 20 per cent in 2009. This declining importance of ASEAN, however, has been solely attributed to the more significant rise in Vietnam's trade with other partners — such as the United States, the European Union, and Japan — rather than to the "trade diversion" effect away from ASEAN. This necessitates a revisit of the trade-creation effect of AFTA/CEPT agreements on Vietnam's trade in recent years.

According to a report by the Ministry of Industry and Trade, the proportion of Vietnam's firms using Form-D certificate of origin for AFTA/CEPT treatment was below 20 per cent in 2009, although it was an improvement over those in previous years (for example, the figure in 2007 was 8 per cent). This casts some doubt over the competitiveness of Vietnam's enterprises, particularly in penetrating the ASEAN market. The rather low utilization of AFTA/CEPT treatment could be attributed to several reasons. First, information about preferential treatment under

AFTA in particular, and under FTAs in general, has not been disseminated widely. Due to the lack of information access, enterprises are unaware of the preferential treatment they can enjoy. In this regard, the role of business associations might have been ineffective, as the costs of documentation should be relatively modest.

Second, many products of Vietnam fail to meet the eligibility criteria for AFTA/CEPT treatment. Specifically, to get such treatment, Vietnam's exports must contain at least 40 per cent of local content. However, except for some agricultural, forestry, and aquacultural products, many export products of Vietnam rely significantly on imported inputs. Again, this partly results from the firms' lack of awareness of preferential treatment available under CEPT/AFTA and associated conditions.

Third, for many products, the most-favoured-nations tariff rates do not differ significantly from those under the CEPT/AFTA framework. Accordingly, the additional benefits to firms from incurring compliance costs (to meet the eligibility criteria) to get preferential treatment under CEPT/AFTA remains less than attractive. Again, it should be further noted that the elasticities of exports to the ASEAN market are insufficient to induce firms to apply for the slightly smaller tariff under the CEPT/AFTA scheme.

Finally, the product structures of ASEAN member countries, including Vietnam, are relatively similar. Consequently, ASEAN member countries find little interest in importing products of Vietnam's firms, once they know these products are already available locally. According to the recent report by the Multilateral Trade Assistance Project (2010), the complementarity of Vietnam's exports to the import needs of ASEAN has been rather limited, and only better than that to China's import demand. In fact, the faster growth of Vietnam's export to China recently (by 44 per cent in the first half of 2010) reflected better trade complementarity between the two, thereby reducing the application for preferential treatment under CEPT/AFTA of the former's enterprises. Besides, Vietnam's export products complement better the import needs of Korea and Japan (Table 18.6).

In another aspect, Vietnam's export structure has been remarkably close to that of ASEAN, and the extent of similarity has been increasing continuously (Table 18.7). With other partners, Vietnam's export structure has been less similar. Thus, Vietnam's exports are merely competing with those of other ASEAN member countries, rather than filling the domestic demand of the latter countries.

**TABLE 18.6**
**Trade Complementarity of Vietnam's Exports with Some FTA Partners**

|            | 2004   | 2005   | 2006   | 2007   | 2008   |
|------------|--------|--------|--------|--------|--------|
| with ASEAN | 36.507 | 39.507 | 42.342 | 44.170 | 46.824 |
| with China | 29.642 | 30.891 | 34.178 | 35.589 | 41.536 |
| with Korea | 43.659 | 46.464 | 47.939 | 46.562 | 47.407 |
| with Japan | 51.260 | 54.103 | 56.639 | 55.599 | 56.683 |

*Source:* MUTRAP (2010).

**TABLE 18.7**
**Export Similarity of Vietnam with Several FTA Partners**

|            | 2004   | 2005   | 2006   | 2007   | 2008   |
|------------|--------|--------|--------|--------|--------|
| with ASEAN | 39.323 | 40.597 | 43.662 | 45.391 | 50.003 |
| with China | 41.783 | 41.508 | 42.093 | 43.495 | 44.595 |
| with Korea | 25.296 | 25.526 | 28.404 | 30.488 | 34.641 |
| with Japan | 19.910 | 20.625 | 23.023 | 25.154 | 27.807 |

*Source:* MUTRAP (2010).

In the reverse direction, imports from ASEAN partners account for an even greater share in their trade with Vietnam. This also indicates that Vietnam is suffering from a sizeable trade deficit with them. More importantly, the trade deficit seems to have widened over time. That is, notwithstanding the better economic opportunities for enterprises from trading with East Asian economies, Vietnam as a whole has failed to acquire a better balance in trade. This actually led to higher pressures on the exchange rate, as well as the availability of foreign currencies to finance trade, and ends up hurting the enterprises themselves.

In another aspect, the rise in total trade and the better access to regional production networks are yet to be accompanied by higher value added content for Vietnam's enterprises. These enterprises are generally recognized as weak in both support activities and primary activities. Therefore, they tend to become marginalized at the lower/ lowest end of the production chain, regardless of whether the chain is producer-driven or buyer-driven.

In producer-driven chains, the multinational corporations have market power in capital and technology-intensive sectors, such as automotive and motorbike industries. They therefore control the whole production system, based around a set of backward and forward linkages. Like many developing countries, Vietnam has frequently used tax incentives as rewards/penalties to push localization. Yet the actual effects of those measures in promoting development of supporting industries were often disappointing. The recent notable failures in promoting the localization of the automotive industry may reignite the need to reconsider the strategy, particularly as the final date for full tariff phase-out[5] is coming closer.

In buyer-driven chains in, say, labour-intensive sectors such as garments, footwear, etc., the large international retailers, branded marketers, and trading companies set up a series of assembled production networks, typically in low-wage locations. Vietnam has been facing two problems. Firstly, as alternative low-wage locations can be found, international production with buyer-driven chains becomes increasingly competitive and this puts continual downward pressure on wages. Secondly, the efficient and continual upgrading of export composition, with higher value added, proves to be challenging for Vietnam, due to its inadequate attention to the role of services in the value chains.[6]

## Major Impediments to Further Participation of Vietnam's Private Sector in Regional Economic Integration

Despite remarkable achievements in socio-economic development, Vietnam is currently facing great challenges. Growth imbalances have emerged, from both supply and demand sides, as well as across different ownership types.[7] In addition, weaknesses and vulnerabilities are present in several areas, such as in the SOE sector, the financial system, public investment, and the education and training systems. The unfavourable impact of the global financial crisis and economic recession also gives rise to the need for changing Vietnam's growth model. Yet the direction of such change remains unidentified, thereby imposing uncertainty on the development context for private enterprises.

To mitigate the risks from the broader development context, private enterprises need to be better informed and involved in events taking place around them, among other things. Participating proactively in

FTA negotiation processes is among the key movements in this line. However, Vietnam's enterprises still play only a limited role in the negotiation and implementation of international commitments, including FTAs. This problem results from inadequate attention of both enterprises and the government agencies concerned. The Law on Signing and Implementing International Treaties in 2005 makes no provision for the role of the public, especially the business community, in supplying agencies responsible for FTA negotiations with information on their competitiveness, ability to increase market share, direct and indirect risks, benefits, and other concerns on FTA implementation (Center for International Trade Policy Consultation 2010). In fact, some of this information can be gathered, but only on a infrequent basis and without credibility and representativeness.

In early 2010, the Vietnam Chamber of Commerce and Industry conducted a survey on trade policy and the regulatory capacity of business associations. During Vietnam's negotiations for WTO accession, about 70 per cent of the surveyed business associations were not consulted, while the cases without consultation of business associations but with consultation of enterprises accounted for over 13 per cent. The situation was even worse during the negotiation of non-WTO agreements, with the corresponding figures being over 81 per cent and 0 per cent. Even in cases where consultation of business associations took place, almost 30 per cent of cases supplied information collected from the mass media, which embodies little credibility. As such, around 89 per cent of the surveyed associations do not know or hardly understand the issues under discussion in the WTO framework, and approximately 81 per cent do not know or hardly understand the non-WTO commitments related to their areas. In addition, almost 15 per cent of the surveyed associations do not know, and around 50 per cent hardly know, WTO-rules-violating measures of overseas governments, which can cause damage to their enterprises.

Besides, further participation of Vietnam's private sector in regional economic integration may be constrained by the inherent issues of the country. The improvements so far in the microeconomic foundations of a market economy were, in addition, insufficient. There remain other major obstacles for private firms to develop, including difficulty in accessing resources such as land, credit, and skilled labour,[8] and state monopoly in some key sectors. This stems largely from the underdeveloped market for production factors, which in turn could be attributed to the lack of an enforceable framework for developing these markets. Infrastructure and public services in Vietnam are still underdeveloped. Besides, after Vietnam became a WTO member and participated in more FTAs, impediments to further private sector development arose not only from administrative agencies, but also from unfair competition practices in the market, particularly from large enterprises. Finally, the constant revisions and amendment of the legal system present another constraint on private sector development, as the associated costs may be well beyond the financing capacity of private firms.[9]

## Policy Recommendations for Further Participation of Vietnam's Private Sector in Regional Economic Integration

On her way to industrialization and further socio-economic development, Vietnam should continue implementing simultaneous measures for institutional reforms, private sector development, and more effective international economic integration. In doing so, the country should rely more heavily on the private sector. The development of such a sector, therefore, is of fundamental importance, and not just to the market-oriented transition that the country is pursuing. Accordingly, Vietnam needs to change its way of thinking further, particularly with respect to undertaking horizontal policies to avoid distorted resource allocation. The change in ideology that marks an important starting point has already taken place, but fails to suffice in the new context of regional economic integration. As one of its policy directions, Vietnam should undertake effective measures to improve her private sector's effective participation in regional economic integration.

First, to allow for better international competitiveness of the private sector, the FTA negotiation process should be relevant to the private sector itself. This necessitates the greater role of dialogue with the private sector before Vietnam attempts to engage in any FTA negotiation. As it is impossible for such dialogue to embody the participation of all enterprises, care should be taken with regard to the representativeness of the ones selected for participation. Business associations may undertake such a role as representatives of firms. At a broader level, also, the government must be able to balance the benefits to enterprises and other stakeholders from FTA negotiation and implementation. Within their activities, the government should allow for the private sector's participation in trade promotions and market research in foreign markets, so that they can enjoy greater benefits from trade liberalization.

Second, measures should be undertaken to improve firms' utilization of preferential treatment under ASEAN agreements. To do so, the firms must be properly and frequently informed about the preferential treatment made available under those agreements. This way, the choices available to firms are enhanced. Given their limited size, private firms in Vietnam cannot collect and filter such information on their own; instead, this should be the responsibility of business associations and government agencies concerned. These organizations should go even further by facilitating discussions between firms, particularly between those experienced in export activities, and potential entrants into regional trade.

As discussed above, for many products, the tariff rates under MFN schedules and ASEAN agreements do not differ significantly. In the longer term, therefore, higher utilization of regional trade agreements is possible only if Vietnam's private sector can benefit even from a small tariff reduction. Technically, this requires flatter average cost curves of the firms. Intuitively, a necessary condition is that the firms must be able to enhance their production capacity without incurring significant rises in costs. From the firms' perspective, an improvement in technology and cost effectiveness of production is vital. At a broader level, policy measures to reduce the cost of compliance to rules of origin under CEPT/AFTA and other ASEAN agreements and to encourage more efficient production by private firms prove critical.

Finally, to complement the above policies, Vietnam should also continue to facilitate the development of the private sector, to ensure its viability even in the context of accelerating regional economic integration. To do so, the country should strive to improve her business and investment environment further. Administrative reforms should be continued, if not accelerated. Government Project No. 30 on simplifying administrative procedures has led to a significant decrease in the burden for private enterprises in completing required administrative procedures. However, the threat remains against further effectiveness of the project, since it fails to resolve fundamentally the root causes of burdensome administrative reforms, specifically, risk aversion in relaxing procedures and/or the incentives for civil servants to facilitate business activities. Besides, as suggested by Nguyen and Luu (2010), Vietnam should facilitate the participation of the private sector in dialogues with government agencies, thereby allowing for pressing issues to be addressed in a timely manner.

In addition, Vietnam also needs policies that are supportive to both private sector development and enhancement to their competitiveness. These supporting policies should be horizontal, rather than sector-specific. That is, the policymaking process should consider the net potential impacts of policy at the aggregate level, rather than merely following a winner-picking approach. On the one hand, Vietnam should better enforce a competition policy, to make way for more equal treatment of SOEs and private counterparts. On the other hand, of particular importance are measures to make the markets for production factors more enabling to private enterprises. Their access to credit should be improved, not only through efforts of their own, but also with the joint support of the government and business associations. The quality of labour should also be improved, via more effective and fundamental reforms of the education-training system.

More importantly, the above policies should follow no fixed doctrine. Instead, they should be combined with full accountability and appropriate consideration of the development context. The lack of good policy coordination may actually increase compliance costs for firms, rather than creating incentives for their viable participation in regional economic integration. Accountability is also necessary to justify policy changes, if needed. Eventually the policy should serve to broaden the choices available for firms, rather than place too much concern on any harm that the regional economic integration process may do them.

## NOTES

1. Paper prepared for the Institute of Southeast Asian Studies.
2. For further discussion see Vo (2009) and Dinh et al. (2009).
3. More details can be found in Vo and Nguyen (2006a).
4. Usually large machinery and equipment manufacturers, business groups, multinational companies.
5. By 2018, according to the CEPT/AFTA agreement.
6. For further reference, see Vo and Nguyen (2006b).
7. For further discussions, see Central Institute for Economic Management (2010).
8. The proportion of workers with tertiary/college or higher qualifications only increased slightly, from 5.7 per cent in 2006, to 6.8 per cent in 2009 (Ministry of Planning and Investment 2010).

9. A recent study by the Task Force on Implementation of Enterprise Law and Investment Law (2008) also found that administrative procedures in construction, particularly in land-using projects, are complicated, confusing, and costly.

## REFERENCES

Central Institute for Economic Management. "Restructuring Vietnam's Economy in 2011–2020 in line with Improvement of Productivity, Efficiency and Competitiveness" [Đề án tiếp tục đổi mới và đẩy nhanh chuyển dịch cơ cấu kinh tế giai đoạn 2011–2020 theo hướng nâng cao năng suất, hiệu quả và năng lực cạnh tranh của nền kinh tế], Report to the Government of Vietnam (in Vietnamese), 2010.

Centre for International Trade Policy Consultation. "Enterprises and International Trade Policy" [Doanh nghiệp và chính sách thương mại quốc tế] (in Vietnamese), 2010.

Dinh, H.M., Q.L. Trinh, and A.D. Nguyen. "Trade, Growth, Employment, and Wages in Vietnam". Study no. 1, research project on "Globalization, Adjustment and the Challenge of Inclusive Growth: Furthering Inclusive Growth and Industrial Upgrading in Indonesia, the Philippines and Vietnam", 2009.

General Statistics Office <http://www.gso.gov.vn>.

Le, D.B., and A.T. Dau. "A Quick Assessment of Quality of Vietnam's Private Enterprises after 10 Years of Implementation of the Enterprise Law" ['Đánh giá nhanh chất lượng của khu vực kinh tế tư nhân Việt Nam qua mười năm thực hiện Luật Doanh nghiệp'] (in Vietnamese), 2010.

Ministry of Planning and Investment. "Assessing the Impacts of International Economic Integration on Vietnam's Macroeconomic Situation" ['Đánh giá tác động của hội nhập đối với ổn định kinh tế vĩ mô ở Việt Nam sau 3 năm gia nhập WTO]. Report to the Government (in Vietnamese), 2010.

MUTRAP (Multilateral Trade Assistance Project). "Impact Asessment of FTAs on Vietnam's Economy". Mimeographed. Hanoi, August 2010.

Nguyen, T.T.A, and M.D. Luu. "Efficiency and Competitiveness of the Private Sector in Vietnam". Paper prepared for the Central Institute for Economic Management (CIEM) and Department for International Development (DFID). Draft as of June 2010.

The Task Force on Implementation of Enterprise Law and Investment Law. Assessment Report on 2-Year Implementation of the 2005 Enterprise Law and Investment Law, 2008.

Tran, T.C., V.D. Bui, T.T. Nguyen, and D.C. Trinh. "Integrating Small and Medium Enterprises (SMEs) into the More Integrated East Asia Region: The Case of Vietnam" (2010). In *Integrating Small and Medium Enterprises (SMEs) into the More Integrated East Asia*, edited by T.T. Vo, D. Narjoko, and S. Oum. Forthcoming.

Vo, T.T. "Economic Reforms in Vietnam: What Lessons Can Be Learnt?" In *Market and Socialism in the Light of the Experiences of China and Vietnam*, edited by Janos Kornai and Yingyi Qian. Palgrave Macmillan, 2009.

Vo, T.T., and T.A. Nguyen. "Institutional Changes for Private Sector Development in Vietnam: Experiences and Lessons". Paper for presentation at the conference, "Advancing East Asian Economic Integration: Microeconomic Foundation of Economic Performance in East Asia", Manila, 23–24 November 2006*a*.

Vo, T.T., and A.D. Nguyen. "Vietnam in the Regional Production Network". Paper presented at the International Conference on Comparative Study on Industrial Competitiveness between China and Vietnam in the Context of East Asian Trade Liberalization, and the Experiences of Japan. Danang, February 2006*b*.

# PART III

# Conclusion and Recommendations

# 19

# Conclusion and Recommendations for an Effective AEC

## Sanchita Basu Das

ASEAN has made commendable progress on the road to an ASEAN Economic Community (AEC). It has worked in integrating the regional economy, notably, by eliminating tariffs on intra-ASEAN trade and laying the foundations for economic integration through measures pertaining to investments, customs, harmonized tariff nomenclatures, product standards, services, and infrastructure.

In 2010 the ASEAN Six countries applied zero tariffs on 99 per cent of the goods traded within the region. The ASEAN Trade in Goods Agreement (ATIGA)[1] came into effect on 17 May 2010. This is a significant achievement as it provides more coherence and transparency for businesses in ASEAN (Parsons 2010). It also addresses the issue of the complex linkages needed for doing business in an integrated market. Again, ASEAN leaders adopted the Master Plan on ASEAN Connectivity in October 2010 so as to speed up the ASEAN connectivity process both within and outside the region.

The year 2010 also saw positive developments in the interactions between ASEAN members and East Asian countries in general. On

1 January 2010, ASEAN witnessed the realization of the ASEAN-China Free Trade Area (FTA) and ASEAN-Korea Free Trade Agreement, and the enforcement of the ASEAN-Australia-New Zealand FTA and the ASEAN-India Trade in Goods Agreement. The ten ASEAN members, in addition to their role in promoting cooperation and dialogue in the region, also became "bridge builders" among countries in the greater scope of Asia.

Despite this progress, the implementation and utilization of initiatives under AEC has to date remained far from impressive. Indeed, a large percentage of intra-ASEAN trade is eligible for low or zero tariffs, but only a very small percentage of intra-ASEAN trade utilizes the lower AFTA preferential rates. This is because the region faces a number of other obstacles, the most important of which are the non-tariff barriers (NTBs) to trade. While some such barriers are necessary — for example, to protect the environment or the health of humans, animals, and plants — others unnecessarily distort trade flows and restrict competition. Surveys of business firms operating in the region reveal that a problem common to several, but not all, ASEAN countries is corruption in the form of bribery to facilitate import clearances, licence applications and renewals, testing, customs inspections, and work permits (ASC Report No. 4 2009). Other factors, such as lack of private sector awareness, lack of clarity in the application of the rules of origin (ROO), problems with customs procedures, and lack of dispute settlement mechanisms, are equally important. In the case of investments, national policies against the entry of foreign investments in certain sectors of the economy are the biggest deterrents. The result is the uncertainty about, and lack of interest in, the region among investors.

Thus, it is difficult to identify 2015 as the target date for creating an ASEAN Economic Community. On the other hand this can be seen as an ongoing process for which the "core" elements have to be set by 2015. ASEAN member states have to realize that time is not on their side. Hence, they must focus on the "core" elements of integration and implement them earnestly in the shortest possible time. This could possibly be in the following areas of the AEC Blueprint:

- Free flow of goods
- Free flow of investment
- Free flow of selected services
- Infrastructure connectivity

- Enhancement of external economic relations
- Institutional mechanism

These core elements of the AEC Blueprint can be seen as the seeds of integration that can make the region a single market and production base. They should be achieved efficiently by 2015.

## Policy Recommendations for ASEAN Economies

Achieving the milestones set in the AEC Blueprint is a humongous task. It requires cooperation and coordination among the different sectors of the economy. Each member country has to act in harmony, both at national and regional levels, to ensure that it does not lag far behind the others. For example, under the Mutual Recognition Arrangements (MRAs), several priority sectors have been identified for the development of sectoral MRAs. This requires the active participation of all member countries, including the accreditation of national conformity assessment bodies. To implement these measures, critical attention should be given to: (1) coordination with other relevant agencies such as customs, (2) improvement of technical infrastructure, (3) changes in legislation, and (4) post-marketing surveillance (Soesastro 2005).

Currently, with countries having varying considerations towards complete liberalization (particularly in the services sector), protectionism still persists in some sectors. Eliminating protectionism and integrating sectors require the establishment of sectoral groups, which will function as working groups with meaningful agendas. Their activities should be based on sectoral strategies and policy papers that could be implemented at the provincial, national, and regional levels. Efforts by these sectoral groups can be directed towards identifying and eliminating NTBs.

ASEAN has to work squarely towards bridging the development gaps among its member states. While the new ASEAN members are addressing the gaps in infrastructure and the lack of human resources and adequate institutions, much more needs to be done. In fact, it is not necessary for the CLMV countries to catch up with the ASEAN Six, but they should reach a level of development that will allow them to participate effectively in the AEC process.

Thus, even though the governments of the ten countries are taking small but definite steps in their regionalization drive, the creation of a single production base and a single market should be pursued with a sense of focus and urgency. Given that ASEAN members, with the exception of Singapore, Brunei, and, to a lesser extent, Malaysia, have limited capacity to provide financial support, the governments have to identify windows of assistance among donors and dialogue partners so as to comply with the ASEAN commitments by 2015 and beyond.

## Policy Recommendation for ASEAN Businesses

Besides the ASEAN governments, it is the ASEAN-based businesses that will ultimately make regional economic integration operational. However, the ASEAN business sector is not sufficiently involved in the building of the AEC. It has not been kept sufficiently informed of developments and is not effectively consulted in policymaking. ASEAN firms often think nationally and defensively about competition from the region or elsewhere. Their views about economic integration also differ according to their sizes. The needs of SMEs, with respect to regional integration, are not sufficiently taken into account.

Given the above, at this juncture, private-sector involvement should be a key mission of the economic integration strategy. For this to happen, the following points have to be kept in mind:

- The most important task is to raise awareness of the benefits of the AEC to business people. Importance must be given to public-private sector partnerships and regular consultations. Written material on ASEAN and the AEC should be readily available to businesses in English and local languages. Industry associations have to play a significant role in this regard and have to arrange workshops and involve mass media in disseminating information about ASEAN and the AEC. They have to serve as intermediaries between the market players and government agencies for the effective implementation of the AEC. To accommodate a more active role for them in the economic integration process, the secretariats of business groups needs to be strengthened and a business centre in the ASEAN Secretariat could be established.
- Even though agreements such as ATIGA and ACIA[2] are adopted and seen as important developments in ASEAN, the agreements contain immense information of policy significance to businesses, which is not easy for businessmen to grasp and assess the new opportunities that can emerge. It is vital that ASEAN bodies

— governments, the secretariat, and the business associations
— address this information gap quickly.

- The AEC Scorecard should be made transparent, detailed, and readily available for private sector use. Businesses have lost confidence in the scorecard, as much of the explanation is not clear enough for public understanding. It deals only with paper measures and regional agreements and does not tell the public how these measures/agreements are actually implemented. Hence, the contents of the scorecard must be fed efficiently to the private sector. It is recommended that the AEC Scorecard be supported by regular consultations with the private sector.

- To achieve the AEC 2015, measures for trade facilitation should be given priority. Focus should be trained on smoother customs and logistics integration. It is also advisable to review the progress and effectiveness of ASEAN's central NTBs database system and its implementation. Another way is to create and maintain a database on NTBs to trade on the basis of surveys of relevant firms. If some NTBs are necessary, ASEAN must (1) develop regional standards and subject the NTBs to them, (2) streamline and regionally harmonize licensing and customs procedures, and (3) develop common approaches to testing methods and conformity assessments. Moreover, the issue of corruption needs to be addressed.

- The movement of skilled workers is still challenging in ASEAN. Currently, language proficiency and professional standards vary widely across ASEAN countries. Even basic tertiary education qualifications differs across ASEAN countries. It may be necessary for ASEAN countries to recognize a certain standard mutually as the entry qualification for tertiary education.

- ASEAN should unlock the potential of SMEs as they account for 40–70 per cent of most of the economies. They are also more vulnerable to economic integration than the larger firms. The SMEs lack financial and technical know-how and thus need support and knowledge of markets to venture into ASEAN countries. Government agencies need to increase their assistance in providing the support and information needed. It should educate and energize the sector so that SMEs are aware of how to take advantage of regional economic integration. They should know whom to talk to when undertaking cross-border business in ASEAN.

There should also be proper investment and trade development networks that can provide assistance in setting up an office, simplifying the forms, or providing some guarantees that improve investor confidence.

- ASEAN leaders should also look into building capacity for less-developed countries. This would help their national bodies and sectoral associations participate more actively in ASEAN and AEC processes. Due consideration should be given to aligning the subregional programmes into the overall objectives of the AEC.
- Changes need to be made in the domestic regulations, and the changes must be implemented at all levels (such as customs, municipalities) of the country. Members of the private sector, through their respective industry associations, need to engage with the government to provide a more conducive environment for the sectors which have to compete with ASEAN neighbours. Countries should continue to facilitate the development of the private sector in their respective economies before venturing abroad. Administrative reforms should be continued and institutions developed.

So far the top-down approach to establishing a single market and production base has been carried out. But realizing an AEC also requires a bottom-up style that involves the interests, requirements, opinions, and actions of the business sector, taking into account the market forces in operation. Participation of the sector is needed in the qualitative, as well as quantitative monitoring and assessment of the implementation of integration measures. The linkage between domestic and foreign businesses needs to be developed and the flow of information to the business sector needs to be deepened. As the private sector's participation is still weak in ASEAN economies, leaders and policymakers have vital roles to play in engaging private businesses in ASEAN matters.

## Conclusion

Despite all the hiccups and challenges faced by the member countries, ASEAN economic integration efforts will not be derailed easily. Member countries are taking steps to incorporate commitments to the AEC into their countries' national agendas. For example, on the trade facilitation front, Singapore, Malaysia, and the Philippines have established the

National Single Window and are moving towards creating an ASEAN Single Window. According to the first AEC Scorecard, ASEAN has a 75.5 per cent achievement rate for the period 2008–09.

In the next few years, the private sector should become the principal actor in shaping the AEC. It is "the time" for the business community to be involved in future policy actions and be able to develop knowledge and capacity to act on market signals inherent in the initiatives. From now on, ASEAN's integration agenda also needs to focus on the essentials so that it is not engaged in several directions. Trade and investment liberalization should be undertaken first since they are the main drivers for a single market and production base. In parallel, measures to enhance connectivity, transparency, and predictability should be implemented as they are key determinants in making the region more attractive to investors. In the end, what is needed is the political will and the exercise of top leadership, to achieve at least a partial economic structure by 2015. The rest of the process, as envisaged in the AEC Blueprint, can follow beyond 2015.

## NOTES

1. ATIGA consolidates and streamlines all existing instruments and provisions on trade in goods and incorporates ministerial decisions to provide them with legal standing.
2. ACIA (ASEAN Comprehensive Investment Agreement) incorporates both the 1998 Framework Agreement on the ASEAN Investment Area (AIA) and the 1987 ASEAN Agreement for the Promotion and Protection of Investments.

## REFERENCES

ASEAN Studies Centre. "ASEAN Economic Community Blueprint". Report No. 4. Singapore: Institute of Southeast Asian Studies, 2009.
Hadi Soesastro. "Accelerating ASEAN Economic Integration: Moving Beyond AFTA". CSIS Working Paper series, WPE 091, March 2005.
Parsons, David. "Challenges to Achieving the ASEAN Economic Community". In *Life after the Charter*, edited by S. Tiwari. Singapore: Institute of Southeast Asian Studies, 2010.

# Index

www.ingramcontent.com/pod-product-compliance
Lightning Source LLC
Chambersburg PA
CBHW021846020426
42334CB00013B/212